AF541988

NOBILITY UNDER THE MUGHALS
(1628–1658)

SOUTH ASIA INSTITUTE, NEW DELHI BRANCH
HEIDELBERG UNIVERSITY
SOUTH ASIAN STUDIES NO. XXXV

Nobility Under the Mughals

(1628–1658)

FIRDOS ANWAR

MANOHAR
2026

First published 2001
Reprinted 2021, 2022, 2023, 2025, 2026

ISBN 978-81-7304-316-1

Published by
Ajay Kumar Jain *for*
Manohar Publishers & Distributors
4753/23 Ansari Road, Daryaganj
New Delhi 110 002

Printed at
Replika Press Pvt. Ltd.

To
The memory of my parents
SYED AHMAD HUSAIN SAHEB
and
BEGUM IMAM BANDI

Contents

Acknowledgements 9
List of Abbreviations 11
1. Introduction 13
2. Numerical Strength of the Nobility and its Composition 18
3. The Crown and the Nobility 43
4. The Mansab System and the Nobility 76
5. Administration and the Nobility 116
6. Conclusion 190
Appendices 195
Bibliography 291
Index 297

Acknowledgements

This book is the revised version of a Ph.D. thesis submitted with the same title to the University of Delhi in 1990. It is being published in the series of the South Asia Institute of Heidelberg University, Germany.

Among those whose valued help I have to acknowledge, I must mention Dr D. Rothermund, formerly Director, South Asia Institute Heidelberg, whose unfailing courtesy and expert advice greatly eased this task.

I must express my profuse thanks to Dr Monica Boehm Tettle Bach, Director, South Asia Institute, Heidelberg, for her valuable suggestions and abounding human affection. Grateful thanks are also due to Dr J.K. Boutze of the South Asia Institute for his helpful comments.

I must express my deep sense of gratitude to the late Dr Nurul Hasan under whose active guidance I completed this work. His personal attention will always remain a pleasant memory.

I am greatly indebted to Dr Satish Chandra for his utmost generosity in sparing time for me to discuss some complex aspects of this study.

Special thanks are also due to my teacher the late Dr M. Athar Ali, who had helped me in many ways. Dr Irfan Habib has always been kind and generous to me. I have benefited a lot from his brilliant ideas. Dr H.C. Verma's courtesy has been valuable to me.

I must also thank all my teachers and colleagues for advice and suggestions. For many acts of kindness at various stages of the work, I must render thanks to my friend Dr T.A.P. Singh.

I am indebted to the authorities and staff of the South Asia Institute of Heidelberg University; the Research Library of the Centre of Advanced Study, Department of History, Aligarh Muslim University; Andhra Pradesh Archives, Hyderabad; the Indian Council for Historical Research; and the Delhi University libraries for extending all possible help in consulting the material relevant to this book.

Finally, I express my sense of obligation to my wife Shamima Qaisar, my elder brother Shakil Ahmad, and my two children Hasan Bakhtawar and Iram Anwar for their cooperation and moral support in the preparation of this work.

FIRDOS ANWAR

Abbreviations

H.D.	*Hyderabad Documents*
I.H.C.	*Proceedings of the Indian History Congress*
I.H.R.	*Indian Historical Review*
J.D.	*Jaipur Documents*
J.R.A.S.	*Journal of the Royal Asiatic Society*
Lahori	*Badshah Nama*
M.U.	*Maasir-ul-Umara*
Mirat	*Mirat-i-Ahmadi*
S.D.S.	*Selected Documents of Shahjahan's Reign*
Salih (B)	*Amal-i-Salih* (Calcutta edn.)
Salih (L)	*Amal-i-Salih* (Lahore edn.)
T.S.	*Tarikh-i-Shahjahani*
Z.Kh.	*Zakhirat-ul-Khawanin*
Manucci	Storia Do Mogor, 1653–1708

CHAPTER 1

Introduction

Shahjahan's reign occupies an important place in Indian history. It may be regarded as an important link between the centralization of Akbar and the gradual but evid dismemberment of the empire under Aurangzeb. One may trace the development of two diametrically opposed trends during this period—political, economic and administrative attainments of a high order on one hand and a creeping crisis in the fundamental structure on the other. Modifications in the mansab system and re-scheduling of jagirs underline the precautionary efforts made to fight such alarming developments. Over and above these, during this period the Mughal emperor lost power and glory due to the combined efforts of his three younger sons and the nobility. Thus, any study of this period will not be devoid of interest.

Although B.P. Saxena's *History of Shahjahan of Delhi* is a valuable monograph covering this whole period, it concentrates on the person of the emperor rather than taking an overall review of the governing class. An authentic account of the ruling class in its totality was made by M. Athar Ali. His *The Mughal Nobility under Aurangzeb* opened new horizons for investigation and research. It is, therefore, worthwhile to examine Shahjahan's period in the light of statistical formulations as done by M. Athar Ali. No extant work on this period specifically related to the ruling class is known to exist, though some interesting attempts[1] have been made to study the various components of this large group. In the absence of any comprehensive work, the present book, I hope, will offer some interesting and useful insights into the period of Shahjahan.

In order to avoid any confusion regarding the term 'nobility', it may be stated at the very outset that this has not been used in the sense of an offshoot of European feudalism. Convenience of communication is the main facilitating factor in adopting the term 'nobility' which, in the words of M. Athar Ali, '. . . generally denotes the class of persons who were officers of the king and at the same time formed the superior class in the political order. . . .'[2] Besides this, as pointed out by the same writer, this is a conventional equivalent to the Arabic-Persian term 'umara', which was applied to all the officials holding the mansab of 1000 and above during the seventeenth century. It may also be added that this study does not pretend to cover all the mansabdars and all the aspects of their political or personal lives. The first thing that deserves consideration in this regard is the paucity of sufficient evidence for the mansabdars below 1000. The lists of the contemporaries, no doubt, mention their names but do not give enough details necessary to reconstruct their account on the lines of the 'umara'. The biographical dictionaries too do not extend the required support in such cases. However, to tap the huge documentary evidence, which gives such details as their mansab, placement, jagirs, etc., is beyond the ambit of a single book. Therefore, with these limitations, this account is confined to only those mansabdars holding 1000 zat and above, as they were those termed 'umara'.

An attempt has been made to determine, tentatively, the size and composition of this nobility. Besides the long lists given by Lahori, Waris and Salih, this attempt is necessary because these contemporaries have divided this whole period into three decades (1628–38, 1638–48, 1648–58) and have prepared their lists pertaining to each of these decades. The first two decades are covered by Lahori, and the last one by Waris. However, Salih gives the list covering Shahjahan's complete reign. This division seems to be rather arbitrary as it fails to correlate the fluctuation in the number of mansabdars with the mainstream of the contemporary political and economic changes which were bound to affect the establishment as a whole, of which the nobility was an essential part. This also fails to highlight other significant aspects like the influx of the Deccanis, its impact upon other groups, and the major reforms in mansab in 1642 which had far-reaching consequences. Therefore, it is necessary to look for some such tentative dates which suggest a process of change in the overall existing conditions subsequently affecting the policies and attitudes. With the help of these dates, the description of the strength of the nobility will prove to be more useful in explaining issues like the number of nobles at various times; why and when the number increased or decreased and at what rate; how it affected the resources of the state; and the internal cohesion of the nobility. Internal cohesion may be analysed with reference to various religious and ethnic groups within the Mughal nobility. Questions like the fluctuating number of various groups and its possible reasons; the proportion of foreigners and Indians; and the position of Hindus in this group, deserve close attention and need careful evaluation. An attempt has also been made to elucidate these divisions and determine their effect on internal cohesion and to examine whether these groups merely acted as political factions.

Next is an attempt to analyse the nature of the mutual relationship that existed between the crown and the nobility. Years ago, S. Nurul Hasan highlighted the fundamental contradiction as well as interdependence between the rulers and their nobility, referring specially to the periods of Humayun and Akbar.[3] Therefore, it may be useful to analyse the implications of interdependence and the issues of contradiction between Shahjahan and his nobility. This study unfolds the reasons for almost total support of the nobility to the crown through various crises, and highlights the grounds of the limited role of racial or religious sentiments in the political life of the ruling class.

A detailed study like this may help in locating possible reasons for big or small rebellions, and in understanding the harsh or mild attitude of the crown in tackling them. It will also be interesting to trace the impact of changing political and economic conditions upon the fortunes of this group, and its reaction to it. How far the emperor's attitude towards the nobility was coloured by religious sentiment or racial bias, or whether he was guided mainly by the demands of the changing conditions, is another question to be answered. The crown's attitude towards the nobility with regard to the affairs of the Deccan, Central Asian and Qandhar expeditions also needs elucidation, as it had a direct bearing upon their positions and prospects. The nature of the clause of escheat, the extent of its implementation and its impact upon the nobility, present yet another aspect related to the crown–nobility relationship.

Third, one may raise some issues related to the mansab—the sole mechanism to organize the Mughal nobility. From Moreland and Abdul Aziz to Irfan Habib and Athar Ali, innumerable efforts have been made by different writers to analyse various aspects of this system. These studies present a microscopic analysis of some minute technical complexities of this institution. The reforms introduced in mansab during this period have also been dealt with by Noman Ahmad Siddiqi and others. However, Athar Ali in his recent writings,[4] has shown some new and interesting directions of research and enquiry. Pursuing a similar line of investigation, such issues as the importance and relevance of the mansab in regulating the mutual relations between the crown and the nobility, particularly with reference to the significance of sawar mansab, have been taken up. Were the fluctuations in mansab figures due to the individual will of the emperor, or did they reflect the changing political and economic conditions? How did this fluctuation affect the fortunes of the different religious, ethnic and family groups within the nobility? It is to be examined whether any definite proportion was maintained between zat and sawar ranks. The bulk of the Mughal nobility had no permanent base in land, but depended on its military assignments, determined by the sawar rank. The mode of reaction of the nobility to these fluctuations reflects the success or failure of Shahjahan's policy towards the mansab. Promotion in mansab is another interesting aspect of this study which has not been thoroughly analysed so far. Issues like the peak period of promotion; the possible reasons for it; the link between the changing conditions and the imperial attitude towards promotion, etc., need closer attention. A rough calculation of these figures and their comparison will be helpful in locating some major grounds for promotion. With reference to the details of the political careers and family lineage of the nobles, it may be studied whether promotion could be obtained by mere flattery and manipulation, on racial, religious or family grounds, or whether it was a meaningful device to reward the nobles for their services, keep them satisfied, and also confirm the crown's hold over them.

Last, it may be interesting to know about the participation of the nobility in administration. The celebrated works of P. Saran and Ibn-e-Hasan only disclose the nature of various offices, jurisdiction of the officials, imperial hold over them, etc. Athar Ali, on the other hand, has suggested new grounds of enquiry by studying the governors of Shahjahan's reign.[5] There is enough scope to also examine important offices at both central and provincial levels with reference to such interesting questions as the possibilities of some link between the mansab and the post, tenure of office, or racial and religious composition of various offices. The motivating force behind these appointments (with special reference to the role of racial and religious factors) also needs careful and impartial analysis. With the help of the career-details of the nobles, one can pinpoint the specific disciplines from which the officials were picked up for particular posts, as well as those to which they were sent after the end of the former assignment.

To answer such questions even tentatively, the statistical method of analysis has been followed. In spite of its various drawbacks, this method helps to exercise a check upon the generalizations made by contemporaries then, and even by modern historians. Various hypothetical and sentimental statements related to racial or religious matters may easily be tested and a more balance picture, based upon actual figures, be projected with the help of this method. However, its basic requirement is accuracy of the data. The conclusions arrived at through this method should in no way be regarded as the last word, simply as tentative suggestions.

Shahjahan's period is rich in sources. There is a vast amount of material consisting of the official and non-official histories, biographical dictionaries, administrative manuals, official records, other documents, letters and foreigners' accounts. Only a few of the Persian sources were published: the bulk is available only in manuscript form. The details of political developments, military expeditions, economic changes and other social and cultural aspects of life are available in the official and non-official histories like the three *Badshah Namas*, *Tareekh-i-Shahjahani* by Sadiq Khan, *Khulasat-ut-Tawareekh* by Sujan Rai, *Chahar-Chaman* by Chandra Bhan, etc. *Zakhirat-ul-Khawanin* and *Maasir-ul-Umara* extend valuable help in constructing the biographical details of various leading nobles, and throw light on the political, economic and social conditions of this period. Archival material, specially the huge collection of Shahjahani documents in the Andhra Pradesh Archives and the large number of documents in the Rajasthan Archives offer very useful information regarding the details of administration. This helps in getting a grip on the complexities of the mansab and the jagirs; understanding the nature of local problems; the attitude of the ruling class as well as the details of the agrarian system. There is no dearth of European travellers' accounts related to this period. Besides the variety of information supplied by these works, their real contribution lies in providing those details which are ignored by native writers. Yet their generalization, bias against Indians and lack of understanding of the existing system form drawbacks against which one should always be on guard.

With little time available and also because of the inaccessibility of some works, the vast source material could not be utilized fully. Lack of incorporation of such material is regretted. For the sake of conciseness, notes are given only wherever absolutely necessary.

With a view to clarifying and substantiating various statements and conclusions arrived at in this work, it has been considered desirable to add a few appendices and tables which, it is hoped, would be found useful (in spite of their limitations).

NOTES

1. For example, Manohar Singh Ranawat's *Shahjahan Ke Hindu Mansabdar* (Jodhpur, 1973). The work contains lists of Hindu mansabdar drawn from the detailed lists of Lahori, Waris and Salih and a few appendices. Rendering of a selected list of Hindu mansabdar based on contemporary sources is a useful endeavour on Ramawats' part, but a cursory glance at the appendices suggests that the author has confined his search exclusively to the lists of the above-mentioned authorities and has not consulted the texts in full! That is why he has wrongly placed some mansabdar in Appendix 1 (pp. 58–60) as 'omissions'. If one goes through these works carefully, it is easy to trace all these so-called 'omitted' mansabdar: for example, Jadun Rai Deccani (see Lahori, I, pp. 182 and 308); Kheluji Bhonsle (Lahori, I, pp. 227 and 507–8); Shahuji Bhonsle (Lahori, I, pp. 327–8 and 442); Minaji Bhonsle (Lahori, I, p. 328); Samaji Bhonsle (Lahori, I, p. 328); Tanaji Deccani (Lahori, I (b), p. 121); Rawal Kalliyan Jaisalmeri (Lahori, I, p. 183); Baswant Rao Kartalab Khan (Lahori, I, pp. 183 and 307; Lahori, I (b), p. 299; Salih, III (B), p. 454); Bhojbal (Lahori, I (b), p. 148).

   For more details, see the list of Shahjahan's mansabdars pertaining to the three phases of his reign in Appendices A, B and C at the end of the book.
2. M. Athar Ali, *The Mughal Nobility under Aurangzeb*, Bombay, 1968, p. 2.
3. S. Nurul Hasan, 'New Light on the Relations of the early Mughal Rulers with their Nobility', I.H.C., Madras, 1944.
4. M. Athar Ali, 'Mansab and the imperial policy under Shahjahan', I.H.C., Aligarh, 1975.
5. M. Athar Ali, 'Provincial Governors under Shahjahan, I.H.C., Jabalpur, 1970.

CHAPTER 2

Numerical Strength of the Nobility and its Composition

The mansabdars formed an integral part of the Mughal ruling class. Politics, administration, society and economy were directly or indirectly affected by this group. Being an essential organ of the Mughal government, its size and number is important for us. The relevance of probing into this matter increases when we try to assess the share of this group in the economic resources of the empire. This would also help in making a rough estimate of the total military strength of the Mughal empire. The fluctuations in the number of the nobles may be correlated with the political and economic developments of this period. This may reflect the primacy of political and economic changes over the individual will of the ruler in raising or curtailing their number. Since the nobility was composed of various ethnic groups, an assessment of their number and the proportion they bore to the total number is necessary to begin with a rough estimate of the total strength of the nobility.[1] This estimate covers the mansabdars of 1000 zat and above, as only they were entitled to be called 'umara' in the seventeenth century.[2]

Fortunately, contemporary accounts provide rich evidence in this connection. Lahori, Waris and Salih not only mention the day-to-day awards and promotions, but also give detailed lists of the mansabdars. *Badshah Nama* of Lahori preserves two such lists, each relating to the early two decades of Shahjahan's period. Waris give the third list pertaining to the last decade. Salih, however, covers the entire regime of almost 30 years. Besides this, we have *Zakhirat-ul-Khawanin* of Farid Bhakkari and *Maasir-ul-Umara* of Shah Nawaz Khan. These works not only give biographical details of the mansabdars, but also help in clarifying some complications relating specially to the dates of promotions and awards and the real number added to the zat or sawar rank, which are sometimes either left out by Lahori, or presented in an incomprehensible manner.

It seems that no attempt has been made to workout the number of Shahjahan's nobility with reference to the changing political and economic conditions. Abdul Aziz has simply converted Lahori and Salih's information into figures, accepting the decadewise division suggested by these contemporaries.[3] The latest attempt in this regard has been made by M. Athar Ali.[4] Unlike Lahori, he has arranged this evidence regnal-year-wise. Being so useful, this exhaustive list, however, does not help much in establishing a link between the number of the nobles and the changing political and economic conditions of this period.

Thus, the contemporary as well as modern writings are not directly helpful in our formulations, and we will have to toil afresh with the contemporary evidence available to us.

Lahori's first list pertaining to the first ten years gives the names, mansabs as well as the dates of death of the nobles. It covers a long range of mansabs, starting from the highest, i.e. 9000 zat and coming down to 500 zat. The second list, dealing with the next decade, follows the same pattern. Salih also follows Lahori's style with regard to the names and both parts of the mansab (i.e. zat and sawar) but he fails to be cautious like his predecessor, as only in a few cases does he mention the date of death, which leads to confusion. Besides this, he has mixed dead and living nobles.

If we look into the above-mentioned lists, the total number of mansabdars of 1000 zat and above in the first list of Lahori is 293. There are 306 mansabdars in his second list, while Salih's list contains 427 mansabdars of this category. The number of various mansabdars in these three lists is given in Table 2.1.

The totals of Lahori's first list and Salih's list seem to be incorrect due to repetitions.[5] After removing these, they come to 292 and 424 respectively. Lahori's statement that in the twentieth regnal year there were 8000 mansabdars and 7000 ahadis and barq-andaz sawars is not of much help.[6] First, we have no list of those mansabdars below 500 zat. Second, no such statement is made by Salih for the closing years. Besides this, we cannot form any idea of the strength of different grades of nobles from this figure of 8000.

From Table 2.1, it emerges that the number of mansabdars was increasing constantly: from 293 it rose to 306, and swelled to 427 in the closing years. Apparently, it seems that by the twentieth regnal year there was an addition of 13, and of 134 by the thirtieth regnal year, over the first total of Lahori (viz., 293).This may lead to the conclusion that there was a nominal rise in the strength of mansabdars in the first 20 years (i.e. 13), and a comparatively greater rise in the last 10 years (an addition of 121 over 306). This way, the overall rise would be of 134 over the total number of the first list of Lahori (viz., 293).

Too many repetitions in Lahori's two lists lead to a misleading conclusion. By 'repetitions', this author means repetition of the mansab and not the

TABLE 2.1: TOTAL NUMBER OF MANSABDARS IN THE LISTS OF LAHORI AND SALIH

Mansab	*Lahori*		*Salih*
	First decade	*Second decade*	*30 solar years of Shahjahan's reign*
5000 zat and above	33	32	49
3000 to 4500 zat	68	63	88
1000 to 2700 zat	192	211	290
TOTAL	293	306	427

names of the mansabdars. Some new names also emerge in the second list of Lahori and in the final list of Salih; since we have to account for the mansabdars, close attention has to be given to promotions from the lower grades and to the new awardees. If we keep an eye on these promotions and new entries, our findings will be 'different.

Close scrutiny of these two lists of Lahori reveals that in all, 155 additions were made to the total number of the first list. Initially, the second list contains 306 mansabdars. Out of this, 151 are common to both lists, so the net increase in different grades is of 155 mansabdars by the twentieth regnal year.

Now, we examine Salih's final list. Its total comes to 424 (excluding repetitions within the list). If we compare it with the second list of Lahori (removing the repetitions of his first list), we will get an addition of 147 mansabdars of different grades over and above the addition of 155 of Lahori's second list. For convenience, these additions of Lahori (in the second list) and of Salih (in the final list) are shown in Table 2.2.

Table 2.2 suggests large additions to various grades of mansabdars in the three decades of Shahjahan's reign. These additions are mainly because of promotions from lower ranks to the higher grades. Since all the common mansabdars are excluded from the second list of Lahori and the final list of Salih, it may be presumed that by the twentieth regnal year, 155 mansabdars were added to the total number of 292 by way of promotions or new awards, and by the thirtieth regnal year, 147 more mansabdars were added to various grades over and above the initial strength (292). Thus, the total number of mansabdars of 1000 zat and above during the 30 years of Shahjahan's reign comes to 594.

However, I feel that this method of reaching the total strength of mansabdars in a prolonged period of 30 years, completely disregarding deaths, withdrawals, retirements and disassociation due to rebellion or other causes at different stages, is not entirely reasonable.

This long period of 30 years is undoubtedly important for social, political as well as economic developments. These developments were bound to affect the whole establishment, and the nobility being an important organ to the governing authority could not escape these influences. These changes should

TABLE 2.2: TOTAL ADDITIONS IN THE NUMBER OF MANSABDARS OVER THE THREE DECADES

Mansab	*Lahori's first decade*	*Lahori's additions in the second list over the first list*	*Salih's additions to the second consolidated list of Lahori*
5000 zat and above	33	13	8
3000 to 4500 zat	68	27	28
1000 to 2700 zat	191	115	111
TOTAL	292	155	147

have affected their political, economic and social status as well. This gives some scope to make an estimate of the strength of this group on the basis of some important developments which should have coloured the attitude of the crown and would have affected the strength of the nobility favourably or unfavourably. Lahori and Salih, disregarding the fate of the nobles, divided the reign of Shahjahan into three phases quite arbitrarily, for which there seems to be no apparent justification.

After a careful examination of the whole reign, I find two important landmarks in this period of 30 years, 1636 and 1642. The period up to 1636 marks the consolidation of power in Shahjahan's reign and its triumph over the rebellions of Jujhar Singh Bundela and Khan-e-Jahan Lodhi and the conquest of the Deccan, resulting in the absorption of the kingdom of Ahmadnagar. The treaty of 1636 brought a period of comparative peace in the Deccan, but it also marks the absorption of the Deccan nobility, on one hand, and the settlement of new provinces on the other.

The need to pacify the older nobility, to reward the old supporters and to integrate the Deccan nobility, resulted in far-reaching reforms in 1642 in the system of mansabdari, and in its relationship with that of jagir. This affected the positions, fortunes and financial resources of the nobles, and also affected the condition of the army.

In the light of these developments and the consequent changes that emerged at different times, the whole reign of Shahjahan may be divided into three phases: 1628–36, 1637–41 and 1642–58. The strength and fluctuations in the strength of the nobility may be more reasonably analysed with reference to these three phases.

The lists of Lahori and Salih are no doubt helpful, but not sufficient to reconstruct the numerical strength of the nobility pertaining to these three phases. The first list of Lahori is more helpful, because in many cases it gives the mansabs of our first and second phases. Salih is obviously useful for the last phase (1642–58).

According to these phases, three lists of nobles have been prepared.[7] The number emerging from these is shown in Table 2.3.

A cursory comparison of the figures of the first phase with Lahori's first list would show an increase in each grade. This is precisely because of Lahori's omissions. Many nobles whose mansabs are given at the appropriate places are not mentioned in the list—for what reasons, it is difficult to

TABLE 2.3: STRENGTH OF MANSABDARS DURING THE SUGGESTED PHASES

Mansab	*1628–36*	*1637–41*	*1642–58*
5000 zat and above	38	27	38
3000 to 4500 zat	79	54	81
1000 to 2700 zat	225	174	329
TOTAL	342	255	448

explain. Differences are there in the figures of the third phase and the final list of Salih too, but they are not very prominent.

Before accepting the veracity of Table 2.3 entirely, it will not be irrelevant to mention a marked difference in the trends suggested by Table 2.3 and Table 2.1. The latter suggests a constant rise in the number of the mansabdars, while Table 2.3 suggests (in three different phases) a notable decline in the number of the nobility in the second phase from a much higher figure of 342 to 255. This decline suggests Shahjahan's awareness of the hazards of free expansion of the mansab, which was bound to result in the insufficiency of revenue from land. To check this crisis, the decline of the second phase may, therefore, be regarded as a precautionary measure. The conditions of this phase, fortunately, were favourable for him, and the emperor made full use of the opportunity.

For a better understanding of Table 2.3, it is necessary to make a rough estimate of the number of mansabdars of various grades at the beginning of Shahjahan's reign. It seems that there were about 28 mansabdars of 5000 zat and above, 70 of 3000 to 4500 zat and 176 of 1000 to 2700 zat.[8] If these figures are to be compared with the figures of the first phase in Table 2.3, we will note an addition of 10 mansabdars to the first category (of 5000 zat and above), of 9 to the second (of 3000 to 4500 zat) and of 49 to the third (of 1000 to 2700 zat). It is interesting that the additions to the first category (of 5000 zat and above) are proportionately higher than the two lower categories (of 3000 to 4500, and 1000 to 2700 zat). These increases in all grades of mansabdars were perhaps due to promotions and new awards which were necessary to keep the confidence of the nobles in the midst of such a grave political situation. The inclusion of a fairly good number of Deccani nobles in higher grades, as a demand of political requirements and military strategy, also contributed to this enhancement in the number of mansabdars, specially of the first class (5000 and above).

The next period (1637–41) suggests a marked decline. The strength of mansabdars of 5000 and above falls from 38 to 27. For the second and third grades (3000 to 4500, and 1000 to 2700) too, a decline from 79 to 54 and from 225 to 174 respectively is notable. The decline in the number of mansabdars of the first two categories is more defined than in the third.

What mechanism would have been adopted to curtail the number of nobles from a higher figure of 342 (first phase: 1628–36) to a lower figure of 255 in the second phase (1637–41), is an interesting question to be looked into. If we go through the tables of mansabdars in Appendices A, B and C, the foremost development which catches our attention is the large number of vacancies caused due to death, flight, withdrawal, retirement and promotion to higher mansabs in each catagory of nobles till the end of the first phase. Almost 158 mansabdars belonging to various catagories (5000 zat and above; 3000 to 4500 zat; 1000 to 2500 zat) cease to exist on the rolls for the foregoing reasons.[9] This brings down the number of nobles to a much lower figure of 184 as compared to the strength in the first phase. However, our second phase gives a total of 255 nobles. This means that during the second phase, a total addition of only 71 mansabdars was made against the existing 158 vacancies. This figurative representation, thus, suggests a cautious policy of Shahjahan to keep the number of his nobility within controllable limits to compensate the earlier generous expansion demanded by the political and military exigenecies of the first phase. Moreover, most of the nobles engaged with the Deccan War had already been rewarded for their services by way of promotions till the year 1636. During this phase, therefore, there was not much scope for extensive promotion in mansabs or for unusual new awards too.

As Table 2.3 shows, in the third phase (1642–58), the number of mansabdars increases again. The grade of 5000 and above swells from 27 to 38. In the two others groups (i.e. 3000 to 4500, and 1000 to 2700) also, the number rises from 54 to 81 and from 174 to 329 respectively. It is to be noted here that the increase in the third category is more striking as compared to the first two. If this rise of 1642–58 is to be compared with the rise of 1628–36, we will find that there is no addition to the number of the first class of mansabdars (5000 and above). The strength of mansabdars of 3000 to 4500 remains almost the same (with a marginal rise of only 2). But the third category (1000 to 2700) gets a tremendous rise in its number. The decline of the second phase (1637–41) also affected this group lightly in comparison to the first two classes (5000 and above, and 3000 to 4500).

This rise in the number of mansabdars in 1642–58 can be safely explained in the light of the important political developments and extensive military activities of the Mughal empire. The Balkh-Badakhshan and then the Qandhar expeditions dominated the scene. The full cooperation of the bulk of the nobility was required to meet the situation, and this would have led not only to promotions from the lower classes, but also to absorption of new elements, which, however, did not form any sizeable number. It appears that promotions were mostly given to mansabdars of below 1000. But they were promoted mostly to add to the number of our third class of mansabdars (1000 to 2700).

In the light of what has been said above, it may tentatively be suggested that the rise or decline in the number of the nobility was closely associated with the prevailing conditions and the increasing or decreasing utility of this group. After Shahjahan's involvement in the Deccan, more active support was required from this class, hence more promotions and new additions to the mansab. Political expediency also required the association of Deccanis in the Mughal nobility. They were rewarded with high mansabs for their betrayal to their earlier masters. Old nobles too were rewarded for their services. All this led to a rise (from 274 to 342) in the number of the nobility in the first phase. In the second and less eventful period (1637–41), also due to the death of many nobles, a sharp decline may be seen in their total strength. The number again rises in the last phase, specially in the case of mansabdars of 1000 to 2700. This raised the total number of the nobles from 255 to 448, and exposed the futility of Shahjahan's efforts in the second phase to control the size of the nobility.

COMPOSITION OF THE NOBILITY

Shahjahan inherited a heterogeneous nobility. Akbar made valuable contributions in this regard. But this heterogeneous character of the Mughal nobility should not be interpreted in terms of universal generosity or open-hearted welcome to all meritorious candidates to this class. It was 'a closed aristocracy and entrance into this class was not easily available to ordinary subjects, whatever their merits'.[10]

Khanazads[11] (the descendants and relatives of mansabdars) were usually accommodated in the nobility. Unusual favours were extended to this group.[12] This speciality of the Khanazads is evident from the number of mansabs they held. In 1628–36, out of a total of 342 mansabdars holding the rank of 1000 and above, their number was 161. In the second phase (1637–41), when the total number fell to 255, they held a number which was more than half the total, i.e. 129. Their number increased in the last phase (1642–58): 251 out of 448. The details are given in Table 2.4.

The figures given in Table 2.4 suggest a constant rise in the number of khanazads. In the first phase, they were slightly less than half. In the second and third phases, they were more than half the total number of mansabdars. But their proportion in the highest category (5000 and above) falls in the third phase. From a number of 19 out of 27 (in the second phase), they fall to 25 out of 38 in this phase. But in the lower two grades (i.e. 3000 to 4500, and 1000 to 2700) their rise is constant but gradual. In

TABLE 2.4: PROPORTION OF KHANAZADS AMONG THE MANSABDARS OF SHAHJAHAN

Mansab	*Total*	*Khanazads*
1628–36		
5000 zatand above	38	23
3000 to 4500 zat	79	45
1000 to 2700 zat	225	93
GRAND TOTAL	342	161
1637–41		
5000 zat and above	27	19
3000 to 4500 zat	54	32
1000 to 2700 zat	174	78
GRAND TOTAL	255	129
1642–58		
5000 zat and above	38	25
3000 to 4500 zat	81	51
1000 to 2700 zat	329	175
GRAND TOTAL	448	251

the period 1628–36, they numbered 45 out of 79, and 93 out of 225 in the above two grades respectively. Their number rises in the second phase (1637–41) in these two grades. Out of 54 mansabdars of the second category, they numbered 32, and out of 174 of the third category, they were 78. A similar tendency may be noted in the last phase. Out of totals of 81 and 329 of the two lower categories in succession, their numbers are 51 and 175 respectively.

From these figures, it emerges that from the beginning till the end of Shahjahan's reign, heredity was given due weight and khanazads were the recipients of special favours from the Mughal crown. The importance of khanazads is more than evident from the Jaipur documents. It was perhaps due to this tradition that during Aurangzeb's period when non-khanazads (specially Deccanis) were given extra favour, a hue and cry was raised.[13]

ZAMINDARS

No doubt a big portion of the Mughal ruling class consisted of the descendants and relatives of the mansabdars, yet there was a sizeable number of such nobles whose elders and relatives had not been in Mughal service. The zamindars, who had both power and prestige even before joining Mughal service, fall in this category. They played a vital role in the political, economic and cultural life of the Mughal period. Because of their privileged position, Humayan had extended favours to them.[14] Akbar came out with a well-defined policy and included them in his nobility in large numbers.[15] They were given high mansabs, rich jagirs, important military and administrative positions. Their 'watans' were left untouched, thus granting them almost autonomous status in their ancestral domains. This policy was likewise favoured by Akbar's successors.

In the first phase of Shahjahan's reign (1628–36), there were not less than 75 zamindars out of a total of 342 mansabdars. About 27 of these were new entrants. During the years 1637–41, in spite of a sharp decline in the total, they maintained their position and numbered 54 out of 255. Out of these, about 19 were those whose predecessors did not hold mansabs. In the last phase (1642–58), however, their number declines. Out of 448 mansabdars, only 80 were zamindars, and out of them only 18 were new entrants. These facts are evident from Table 2.5.

The figures given in Table 2.5 suggest a gradual decline in their proportion. The decline is more marked in the cases of those zamindars whos relatives did not hold mansabs. From 19 out of the total of 54 (of the second phase), these zamindars fell to 18 out of the total of 80 (in the third phase). The proportion of those whose predecessors held mansabs earlier was stable througout. This confirms the favourable attitude towards the khanazads, of whichever category.

RACIAL AND RELIGIOUS GROUPS

Even before Shahjahan, the Mughal nobility had taken composite shape. It included Turanis, Iranis, Afghans, sheikhzadas Rajputs, etc. The Deccanis were accommodated in the seventeenth century with the advancement of

TABLE 2.5: PROPORTION OF ZAMINDARS AMONG THE MANSABDARS OF SHAHJAHAN

Mansab	*Total mansabdars*	*Zamindars whose blood relatives were already mansabdars*	*Other zamindars*	*Total*
1628–36				
5000 zat and above	38	8	4	12
3000 to 4500 zat	79	19	1	20
1000 to 2700 zat	225	21	22	43
GRAND TOTAL	342	48	27	75
1637–41				
5000 zat and above	27	5	–	5
3000 to 4500 zat	54	12	1	13
1000 to 2700 zat	174	18	18	36
GRAND TOTAL	255	35	19	54
1642–58				
5000 zat and above	38	7	–	7
3000 to 4500 zat	81	18	2	20
1000 to 2700 zat	329	37	16	53
GRAND TOTAL	448	62	18	80

Mughal power in that region. 'These various elemnts were incorporated into the Mughal service largely as a result of historical circumstances, but partly (specially the Rajputs) as a result of planned imperial policy.'[16]

In spite of this clear-cut division, there was a sense of unity among the nobility. In critical hours, this ethnically divided nobility stood united, almost completely disregarding racial and religious bonds and ties. During the rebellion of Jujhar Singh Bundela in its first phase, the Rajputs formed the bulk of the forces appointed to crush him.[17] A similar but more alarming situation came up when, in the opening years, Khan-i-Jahan Lodhi raised the standard of rebellion. The leading Afghan nobles like Bahadur Khan Rohila, Ahmad Khan-Niyazi, Ahdad-Khan Mahmand, Jahan Khan Kakar, Pir Khan Miyana, Habib Khan Sur, etc., unitedly opposed him.[18] More interesting is the fact that Bahadur Khan Rohila (son of Darya Khan) was in the imperial camp while his father was a close companion of Khan-i-Jahan.[19] Many more other such examples of cohesion may also be produced.

So it is felt that racial or religious considerations may not be over-emphasized. The main concern of both the Mughal crown and the nobility was the stability of the empire with which their mutual interests were bound. There is hardly any example where this common interest was sacrificed by either of the two for racial or religious causes.

Our authorities like Lahori, Waris, Salih, Farid Bhakkari and Shah Nawaz Khan have made passing references to the ethnic backgrounds of the nobles. Because they were not ethnographers, their aim was mainly to record the developments pertaining to politics, society, economy, etc. It is, therefore, unwise to claim definite identification of the ethnology of each and every mansabdar. Intercaste marriages pose another problem in racial identification. Afghans and sheikhzadas, Irasnis and Turanis—all entered into matrimonial relations without giving any thought to the 'purity' of their race. Karimdad Afghan, for example, had his daughter married to Sadullah Khan, a sheikhzada.[20] Likewise, Aitmaduddaulah's daughter was married to Hakim Beg, a Mughal,[21] and so on. So it is difficult to be quite certain of the purity of the race of a large number of the nobility.

Besides this, racial or religious factors do not seem to have played very substantial role in shaping the attitudes of the crown or of the nobility. The grant of mansabs, promotions and appointments to higher administrative and military positions were usually based on political exigencies, the benefit to the government, and the performance and services of the mansabdars.

The submission, therefore, is that perhaps ethnic and religious factors did not play primary role in uniting or disbanding the Mughal nobility during this period, nor did the crown promote or hurt any group only because of these reasons. Thus, the rebellion of Khan-i-Jahan Lodhi may not be regarded as an 'Afghan' uprising. Similarly, the suppression of Jujhar Singh Bundela may not be interpreted in terms of Shahjahan's 'anti-Rajput' or 'anti-Hindu' policy. As the cooperation or opposition of the nobility was not initially rooted in racial or religious factors, the favourable or unfavourable attitude of the crown too was not based entirely upon these considerations. This was perhaps due to Akbar's efforts to identify the interests of the nobility with the welfare of the crown and the stability of the empire. He trained them to rise over and above their racial and religious bonds and affiliations to serve the Mughal crown.

Yet, the existence of these racial and religious groups cannot be denied. That race and religion were exploited by the crown and the nobles, is also evident. So it is relevant to explain the position and strength of these groups during Shahjahan's reign.

IMMIGRANT NOBILITY

The leading components of this category were Iranis and Turanis. As is evident from Iqtidar Alam Khan's study, these two elements were the chief components of the nobility inherited by Akbar, and they also formed the bulk of the nobility in spite of various fluctuations in the fortunes of the Turani faction.[22] They maintained this distinction in Shahjahan's period as well.

In the first phase, their number was 146 out of 342. In the coming years (i.e. 1637–41 and 1642–58), they improved their position further, as is evident from Table 2.6.

TABLE 2.6: PROPORTION OF IMMIGRANTS AMONG THE MANSABDARS OF SHAHJAHAN

	1628–36		*1637–41*		*1642–58*	
	Total	*Immigrant nobles*	*Total*	*Immigrant nobles*	*Total*	*Immigrant nobles*
5000 zat and above	38	20	27	19	38	25
3000 to 4500 zat	79	33	54	28	81	40
1000 to 2700 zat	225	93	174	78	329	163
GRAND TOTAL	342	146	255	125	448	228

These figures suggest that from slightly less than half (at the beginning of the reign) they rose to more than half of the total number of the nobility in the closing years. Thus, the nobility Shahjahan inherited contained a huge number of immigrant nobles. It was against established traditions to eliminate the khanazads in particular and others in general with a heavy hand. Hence the dominance of this group. They were favoured from the beginning till the end, more so due to their loyalty for the crown and their outstanding services to the empire. This was the only dominant faction which was least affected with fluctuations in the political currents, and which remained powerful and prestigious throughout Shahjahan's period.

Still, one cannot ignore the sizeable number of the Indian nobles.[23] Though not in the majority, they formed an effective group of the ruling class.

TURANIS AND IRANIS

Turanis

Turanis and Iranis were the two important factions of the Mughal nobility since the days of Akbar. It was during his days that a major transformation took place in the structure of the Mughal nobility.[24] The result was that the essentially Turani complexion gradually made room for a 'homogeneous nobility' drawn from various racial and religious stocks. Yet, they remained an important element of the Mughal governing class.

No doubt the ruling house belonged to Turani stock and Shahjahan showed more attachment to it by styling himself as 'Sahib Qiran-i-sani', but this did not have much effect upon the fortunes of this group. In the first phase (1628–36), they numbered 53 out of 342. They improved during 1637–41, as there were 50 Turanis out of the total of 255. With a slight addition, almost the same strength was there in the last phase (1642–58), i.e. 96 out of 448. More details in this regard are given in Table 2.7.

The figures in Table 2.7 suggest a firm rise of Turanis in the highest grade (5000 zat and above) from the very beginning of the regime. In the last phase, they made notable progress in the second (3000 to 4500 zat) and third (1000 to 2700) grades. Still, Turanis neither formed the majority nor

TABLE 2.7: PROPORTION OF TURANIS AMONG THE MANSABDARS OF SHAHJAHAN

Mansab	*Total*	*Turanis*
1628–36		
5000 zat and above	38	6
3000 to 4500 zat	79	12
1000 to 2700 zat	225	35
GRAND TOTAL	342	53
1637–41		
5000 zat and above	27	7
3000 to 4500 zat	54	10
1000 to 2700 zat	174	33
GRAND TOTAL	255	50
1642–58		
5000 zat and above	38	10
3000 to 4500 zat	81	17
1000 to 2700 zat	329	69
GRAND TOTAL	448	96

occupied any place of unique distinction in Shahjahan's period as they had claimed during Humayan's period or at the beginning of Akbar's reign.

Iranis

The Iranis emerged as a powerful faction even during the reign of Akbar due to their 'undivided support' to the Mughal crown.[25] The process continued during Jahangir's reign. Their excellent services, devotion and sincerity carved out a distinct place for them in the court of Jahangir.[26]

The Iranis maintained their improved and elevated position during Shahjahan's reigh. They emerged as the only dominant group of nobles. In spite of all fluctuations in the number of the nobility and in the political currents of this period, Iranis maintained their hold as the only major faction of Shahjahan's nobility.

The hypothesis can be established with the help of statistical evidence. In the first phase (1628–36), there were 93 Iranis in all out of 342 mansabdars. During 1637–41, when a considerable decline may be seen in the overall strength, they improved their position and numbered 75 out of 255. In the third phase (1642–58), out of 448 mansabdars, 132 were Iranis. The break-up is given in Table 2.8.

The first interesting fact that emerges from Table 2.8 is that the Iranis maintained their distinct position from the beginning till the end. As compared to the Turanis, they were always in an overwhelming majority. If we look

TABLE 2.8: PROPORTION OF IRANIS AMONG THE MANSABDARS OF SHAHJAHAN

Mansab	*Total*	*Iranis*
1628–36		
5000 zat and above	38	14
3000 to 4500 zat	79	21
1000 to 2700 zat	225	58
GRAND TOTAL	342	93
1637–41		
5000 zat and above	27	12
3000 to 4500 zat	54	18
1000 to 2700 zat	174	45
GRAND TOTAL	255	75
1642–58		
5000 zat and above	38	15
3000 to 4500 zat	81	23
1000 to 2700 zat	329	94
GRAND TOTAL	448	132

into the various grades of mansabdars, the Iranis were definitely well placed. Their number in the first category (5000 zat and above) exceeds all other ethnic groups in all phases. In the lower grades (i.e. 3000 to 4500 zat, and 1000 to 2700 zat) too, the Iranis maintained this lead over all other factions of the nobility. However, in the third phase a marked decline may be seen in their proportion in the first and second grades, when compared with the proportion of the preceding phase.

INDIAN MUSLIMS

Popularly known as 'sheikhzadas', Indian Muslims are described by Manucci as those 'who are descended from the family of Mohammad but very remote from the Sayyids. This race hold land and also remain in service at the courts, great and petty; they are very subtle, of great intelligence, very litigious and great lawyers. Others became recluses and holymen and by that false pretence gained a living'.[27] The Sayyids of Barha, etc., and converts to Islam are also included in this category. Regarding the Sayyids, Manucci remarks, '. . . These men are venerated among Mohamedans; . . . these hold themselves to be fine soldiers, learned men, virtuous and saintly. . . . They can collect twelve thousand cavalry and a large number of infantry'.[28]

From Iqtidar Alam Khan's study, it emerges that Indian Muslims came to the limelight between 1560 and 1575 when Akbar took to reorganizing

TABLE 2.9: PROPORTION OF INDIAN MUSLIMS AMONG THE MANSABDARS OF SHAHJAHAN

Mansab	*Total*	*Indian Muslims*
1628–36		
5000 zat and above	38	2
3000 to 4500 zat	79	6
1000 to 2700 zat	225	24
GRAND TOTAL	342	32
1637–41		
5000 zat and above	27	2
3000 to 4500 zat	54	5
1000 to 2700 zat	174	21
GRAND TOTAL	255	28
1642–58		
5000 zat and above	38	5
3000 to 4500 zat	81	5
1000 to 2700 zat	329	49
GRAND TOTAL	448	59

his nobility.[29] Thenceforth, they were treated with special favour and carved out a place of distinction in the Mughal nobility.

They enjoyed high mansabs and important military and administrative positions during Shahjahan's period too. In the first phase, their number was 32 out of 342. They improved their position in 1637–41, as their number was 28 out of 255 mansabdars. In the last phase (1642–58), they improved further, as they numbered 59 out of the total of 448. The details may be seen in Table 2.9.

It is evident from Table 2.9 that this group made constant progress during all the phases and adjusted remarkably well to changing conditions. They made notable progress, specially in the first grade (5000 zat and above). Their proportion rose from 5 per cent (first phase) to 7 per cent (second phase) and reached 13 per cent in the last phase. In the second cadre (3000 to 4500 zat), they suffered slightly during the last phase, but the loss was compensated for by an addition of 6 per cent to the first and 3 per cent to the last category. On the whole, it may be said that they made remarkable progress during this regime.

AFGHANS

The Afghans had a say in the political life of India since the days of the sultans of Delhi. Under Balban, the Khaljis and Tughlaqs, they were trusted for their bravery and were favoured by the rulers. However, they really came to the limelight during the Sayyid period, when the Lodhi Afghans ultimately acquired real authority.[30]

Right from the days of Babar down to Akbar, there had been an almost constant armed tussle between the Mughals and the Afghans. Akbar had no trust in them due to his bitter experience.[31] But they rose to eminence during Jahangir's period.[32] Khan-e-Jahan Lodhi came so close to the emperor that he had no rivals at the court.[33]

Shahjahan inaugurated his regime with a normal, favourable policy towards the Afghans. Of the Afghan nobles, out of the total number of promotees, i.e. 176, 21 were favoured between February 1628 and April 1628.[34] This number is slightly more than that of Indian Muslims, who were only 20. In 1628–36, they were 37 out of 342, but thereafter a gradual decline in their overall strength can be seen. In the second phase (1637–41), their number was 24 out of 255. Similarly, they suffered a decline in the last phase as they numbered only 38 out of 448 mansabdars. These facts are given in Table 2.10.

Constant but gradual decline in their number is borne out by the figures in Table 2.10. Their share in the total falls from 11 per cent to 9 per cent in the second phase, and then to 8 per cent in the last phase. A marginal improvement over the preceding phase, however, may be seen in the second category in the last phase. These figures highlight Shahjahan's distrust in this faction. But this does not mean that the Afghans were completely out of

TABLE 2.10: PROPORTION OF AFGHANS AMONG THE MANSABDARS OF SHAHJAHAN

Mansab	*Total*	*Afghans*
1628–36		
5000 zat and above	38	2
3000 to 4500 zat	79	9
1000 to 2700 zat	225	26
GRAND TOTAL	342	37
1637–41		
5000 zat and above	27	1
3000 to 4500 zat	54	2
1000 to 2700 zat	174	21
GRAND TOTAL	255	24
1642–58		
5000 zat and above	38	1
3000 to 4500 zat	81	8
1000 to 2700 zat	329	29
GRAND TOTAL	448	38

favour. They still occupied important positions among Indian nobles, after the Rajputs and sheikhzadas.

RAJPUTS

Farid Bhakkari has mentioned Humayun's advice to Akbar that the Rajputs should be treated with kindness and love because they were obedient and faithful: rebellion and disobedience were alien to them. Farid observes that that is why Akbar favoured the Rajputs so much that it became a subject of comment.[35] This favourable attitude helped Akbar in balancing his nobility and in building up a new faction, which generally remained loyal to him.

With Shahjahan's coronation, some notable changes from Akbar's attitude draw our attention. The chronograms composed to suit the occasion throw some light upon it.[36] These are as follows:

(*a*) 'Julus-i-Shahjahan Dadah Zeb-i-Millat-o-Din'
(i.e. 'Shahjahan's coronation glorified the faith and the creed').
(*b*) 'Zinate-Shara' (i.e. 'Glory of the Shara').

Besides this, measures like the abolition of sajdah,[37] replacement of zaminbos with chahar tasleem,[38] and almost total liquidation of salutation in the case of Muslim religious heads[39] confirm this change.

But this change seems to be quite superficial as this did not affect the basic nature of Mughal-Rajput relations, perhaps because the favourable attitude towards the Rajputs had gradually become a tradition which could

TABLE 2.11: PROPORTION OF RAJPUTS AMONG THE MANSABDARS OF SHAHJAHAN

Mansab	*Total*	*Rajputs*
1628–36		
5000 zat and above	38	6
3000 to 4500 zat	79	12
1000 to 2700 zat	225	35
GRAND TOTAL	342	53
1637–41		
5000 zat and above	27	4
3000 to 4500 zat	54	8
1000 to 2700 zat	174	29
GRAND TOTAL	255	41
1642–58		
5000 zat and above	38	6
3000 to 4500 zat	81	15
1000 to 2700 zat	329	53
GRAND TOTAL	448	74

not be easily shed in the face of their firm devotion and remarkable services to the throne.

It was because of this unbreakable bond of friendship that the superficial show of favouritism for orthodox Islam hardly affected Shahjahan's policy towards the Rajputs. They stood as the only leading group in the Mughal nobility after the Turanis and Iranis. In 1628–36, the Rajputs formed a strength of 53 out of 342. They progressed during the second phase (1637–41) and were 41 out of 255, In the last phase, their number reached 74 out of the total of 448. This is shown in Table 2.11.

It is clear that the overall strength of the Rajputs increased from the first phase till the last, though it was not a large jump. Thus the basic policy of favouring the Rajputs continued under Shahjahan without being affected much by his superficial show of favouritism for Muslim orthodoxy.

DECCANIS

The word 'Deccani' was generally applied to those nobles who had been in the service of the Deccani kingdoms before joining the Mughals.[40] However, in the case of Irani and Turani nobles, the reverse holds true. They were designated 'Irani' and 'Turani' mostly on the grounds of their native places rather than their service under the Uzbek Khans or the Shah of Persia. Darab Khan, son of Taklu Khan,[41] for example, was in the service of Shah Tahmasp Safavi, but he is called a 'Turani'. An Afghan noble called Sher Khan Tarin remains an Afghan, although he was serving the Safavids.[42] Therefore, 'Deccani' was not a racial group as such. It was fabricated on political grounds only. In this category, therefore, mansabdars of various racial and ethnic groups can be included—Turanis, Iranis, Afghans, Marathas, etc. The approximate strength of the Deccanis drawn from different racial and religious groups in given in Table 2.12.

It is clear from Lahori's account that a large number of Deccanis were absorbed in Mughal service during the first phase, simply because of the need of the time, which was mainly occupied with the Deccan campaigns. The influx of the Deccanis becomes more evident if we make an estimate of their strength in the nobility before the outbreak of the Deccan wars. Till

TABLE 2.12: PROPORTION OF DECCANIS AMONG THE MANSABDARS OF SHAHJAHAN

Mansab	*1628–36*		*1637–41*		*1642–58*	
	Total	*Deccanis*	*Total*	*Deccanis*	*Total*	*Deccanis*
5000 zat and above	38	9	27	2	38	2
3000 to 4500 zat	79	12	54	7	81	9
1000 to 2700 zat	225	27	174	17	329	18
GRAND TOTAL	342	48	255	26	448	29

October 1629 (as it emerges from Lahori's annual record), there were not less than 4 Deccanis among the mansabdars of 5000 and above, 4 in the second category (3000 to 4500), and about 7 among the mansabdars of 1000 to 2700. The figures of the first phase thus suggest a notable rise in their number. As a reward for their betrayal of their previous masters, they were to be accommodated in higher categories of the mansab. That is why their number in the first class (5000 zat and above) exceeds the number of other established groups like the Rajputs, Indian Muslims and even Turanis.[43] There was a notable rise in their numbers in the two lower categories (3000 to 4500 zat, and 1000 to 2700 zat) also.

The situation, however, changed with the pacification of Deccan affairs. After 1636, there was a sharp decline in their number. From 15 per cent, they fell to 10 per cent in the aggregate. More striking is their decline among mansabdars of 5000 and above. During the second phase (1637–41), there was, no doubt, a decline in the overall strength of the nobility, yet groups other than the Afghans improved proportionwise.

The fall in the number of Deccanis reaches a low in the last phase. There is more than 50 per cent reduction of their strength in the last phase compared to their number in the first phase. This heavy reduction can be understood if one bears in mind such vital issues as the huge influx of Deccan nobles, large-scale expansion of the mansab resulting in the insufficiency of revenues available from land, and the tradition of rewarding old supporters and the need to pacify the older nobility. In the third phase, when still more expansion was made in mansabs, Shahjahan thought it wise to further reduce the number of Deccani nobles who were neither having a strong base in the nobility, nor were politically as relevant for the state in the changed conditions. It was perhaps because of this cautious policy of Shahjahan to exercise a check upon the strength of the Deccanis that even in the first phase of Aurangzeb's reign (1658–78) they 'did not form a very large proportion'.[44]

MARATHAS

It seems that the Marathas were included in Mughal service under political and military pressure. 'Ever since Malik Ambar', remarks Athar Ali, 'utilised the Maratha chiefs and their followers (Bargirs) on a larger scale, the Mughals had begun to realise the value of the Marathas in the Deccan Wars.'[45] Jahangir recruited and made good use of them.[46] During Shahjahan's period, it seems that state policy towards the Marathas was usually guided by fluctuations in the political and military conditions of the Deccan. As and when their utility in the Deccan ceased, they had to suffer. The point gets reinforced when we examine their number in Table 2.13.

The inclusion of Marathas in large number is evident from Lahori's account pertaining to our first phase. Since the Deccan was the main concern for Shahjahan during this period, the Marathas being an important element of Deccan politics had to be incorporated in Mughal service as a demand

TABLE 2.13: PROPORTION OF MARATHAS AMONG THE MANSABDARS OF SHAHJAHAN

Mansab	*1628–36*		*1637–41*		*1642–58*	
	Total	*Marathas*	*Total*	*Marathas*	*Total*	*Marathas*
5000 zat and above	38	6	27	1	38	1
3000 to 4500 zat	79	9	54	6	81	6
1000 to 2700 zat	225	17	174	12	329	9
GRAND TOTAL	342	32	255	19	448	16

of political expediency. They were mostly accommodated in the higher mansabs to keep them satisfied. That is why they emerged as the second powerful group among the Indian nobles after the Rajputs. After the settlement of the Deccan problem, however, they gradually declined in number as well as in position. In 1637–41, a notable fall in their number can be noticed in the first category of mansabdars as well as in their total strength. This decline becomes more pronounced in the last phase, as there were only 16 Marathas out of a total of 448. All the Deccanis shared almost the same fate during the second and third phase. It seems that Aurangzeb too adopted the same attitude towards the Marathas. In the words of Athar Ali, '. . . Aurangzeb by force of circumstances had to open the gates wide to admit the Marathas in his service with succeeding years'.[47] The Marathas, thus, were not favoured as the consequence of a deliberate policy as was consciously adopted in the case of the Rajputs. The growth and decline in their number basically depended upon the demand of political exigencies in the Deccan.

OTHER MUSLIMS

In the category of 'Other Muslims', all those Muslims were put whose ethnic groups could not be identified, or those who belonged to such races as the Arabs, the Abbasinians, etc. They formed a good number of the total strength of the nobility. Their number in different phases of Shahjahan's reign is shown in Table 2.14.

TABLE 2.14: PROPORTION OF OTHER MUSLIMS AMONG THE MANSABDARS OF SHAHJAHAN

Mansab	*1628–36*		*1637–41*		*1642–58*	
	Total	*Other Muslims*	*Total*	*Other Muslims*	*Total*	*Other Muslims*
5000 zat and above	38	2	27	–	38	–
3000 to 4500 zat	79	10	54	5	81	7
1000 to 2700 zat	225	27	174	11	329	19
GRAND TOTAL	342	39	255	16	448	26

Table 2.14 shows a good proportion of these mansabdars in the total of the first phase. Their position was more sound than that of Marathas among the Deccanis, Afghans and sheikhzadas, the other established groups. This was mainly because of the absorption of Deccani Muslims—many of them being Abbasinians—who were favoured as a matter of political expediency. The attitude adopted towards the Deccanis, therefore, was bound to affect this group as well. They had to suffer from the second phase onwards. In the second phase, they were reduced to 16 out of the total of 255. Proportionwise, they had to suffer equally in the last phase. Not a single mansabdar of this group could reach the mansab of 5000 zat during these two phases. Two of them, visible in this first category in the first phase, died earlier.[48] Both of them, namely Rahim Khan, son-in-law of Malik Amber, and Yaqut Khan Habshi, were Deccanis.

OTHER HINDUS

All those Hindu mansabdars falling outside the well-known racial groups like Rajputs or Marathas are covered under the head of 'Other Hindus'. The number of such mansabdars is not very large. But there are some renowned persons in this group who were known for their profound knowledge of Diwani affairs. Bihari Mal and Todar Mal, the two brothers, always distinguished themselves in the office of the Diwani.[49] Rai Kashi Das was made the Diwan of such important provinces as Bengal.[50] Diyanat Rai Gujrati and Rai Raghunath enjoyed the high-sounding title of 'Rai Rāyān' and held responsible positions of Diwan-i-Tan and Khalsa.[51] Therefore, their number in the total strength of mansabdars is a matter of concern to us. Table 2.15 gives their details.

Table 2.15 shows a gradual growth in the number of other Hindu nobles from the beginning till the end of Shahjahan's reign—no doubt this rise is confined mainly to the lowest category of our table (1000 to 2700 zat). Their rise is not based upon any hereditary claim or any distinction of higher descent, but it was simply their merit, capacity and devotion which brought them to this elevated level of the umara. Simultaneously this reflects that the emperor, eulogized with such fanatic chronograms on the eve of his rule,[52]

TABLE 2.15: PROPORTION OF OTHER HINDUS AMONG THE MANSABDARS OF SHAHJAHAN

Mansab	*1628–36*		*1637–41*		*1642–58*	
	Total	*Other Hindus*	*Total*	*Other Hindus*	*Total*	*Other Hindus*
5000 zat and above	38	–	27	–	38	–
3000 to 4500 zat	79	–	54	–	81	–
1000 to 2700 zat	225	3	174	2	329	7
GRAND TOTAL	342	3	255	2	448	7

did not allow the clergy to interfere with his political formulations, and people with merit were picked up quite freely to serve the state irrespective of their religious back grounds.

NOTES

1. See my article on this subject in *Archiv Orientalni 59*, Czechoslovakia, 1991, pp. 374–88.
2. For a detailed discussion on this point, see Abdul Aziz, *The Mansabdari System and the Mughal Army,* Delhi, Idarah-i-Adabiyat-i-Dilli, 1972, pp. 143–56; also see M. Athar Ali, *The Mughal Nobility under Aurangzeb*, Bombay, 1968, p. 2.
3. Abdul Aziz, op. cit., n. 2 above, pp. 125–9.
4. M. Athar Ali, *The Apparatus of Empire,* Delhi, 1985, pp. 95–345.
5. Lahori has repeated Shuja s/o Masum Kabuli: he is mentioned under 1500 zat and also under 1000 zat (Lahori, *Badshah Nama*, I, (b), Calcutta, 1867, pp. 304 and 308, hereafter 'Lahori'). It seems that his mansab before and after promotion has been stated separately under the two above-mentioned heads (Lahori, I, p. 451). So the total strength comes to 292.

   In Salih's list, more repetitions occur, namely, Shah Beg Khan 4000/3000 (Lahori, II, Calcutta, 1868, p. 721; Salih, *Amal-e-Salih*, Vol. III [B], Calcutta, 1930, p. 452—hereafter Salih), appears again on p. 454; Qabad Khan 4000/4000 (Salih, III [B], p. 452) can also be seen on p. 456 (B), and Yadgar Beg 1000/500 emerges twice on p. 467 (B). Removing such repetitions, we get a total figure of 424 instead of 427.
6. Lahori, II, p. 715.
7. The lists are given in Appendices: A, B and C at end of the book.
8. These figures refer to the first three years (1627–8 to 1630–1) and are based on promotions and appointments recorded by Lahori and Salih, but I have preferred the evidence of Lahori to that of Salih.
9. The figures may be checked with the evidence cited in Appendices: A, B and C at the end of book.
10. Athar Ali, op. cit., n. 2 above, p. 11.
11. Ibid.
12. After the death of Mirza Rustam Safavi, his widow raised objections to the actions of mutasaddis of Akbarabad (who tried to confiscate the property of the deceased mansabdar) on the grounds that they had been serving the Mughal dynasty for the previous 50 years. The claim was honoured by Shahjahan, and the property (except elephants) was conferred upon the descendants: *Z.Kh.*, I, Karachi, 1961, pp. 100–1; *M.U.*, III, p. 440. Many more examples of this favourable attitude towards khanazads are available in our sources.
13. Athar Ali, op. cit., n. 2 above, pp. 12, 28–9 and 93.
14. *Z.Kh.*, I, p. 104.
15. For the details of Akbar's policy towards the zamindars, see S. Nurul Hasan, 'Zamindars under the Mughals', I.H.C., 1964.
16. Athar Ali, op. cit., n. 2 above, p. 15.
17. Lahori, I, pp. 241–2; Salih, I, Calcutta, 1923, pp. 318–21. Also see Appendices 3.1 and 3.3.
18. Lahori, I, pp. 293–6. Also see Appendix 3.2.
19. Lahori, I, p. 294; *Z.Kh.*, III, pp. 48–9; *M.U.*, I, pp. 415–24.
20. *M.U.*, II, pp. 247–8.
21. *M.U.*, I, pp. 573–4.
22. Iqtidar Alam Khan, 'The Nobility under Akbar and the Development of His Religious Policy', *J.R.A.S.*, London, 1968.
23. See Table 2.16.
24. For further details, see Khan, op. cit., n. 22 above.

25. For details of the composition of the Mughal nobility under Akbar, see Khan, ibid.
26. For Jahangir's period, I have relied only upon *Zakhirat-ul-Khawanin; Maasir-ul-Umara* and the valuable table of Jahangiri nobles given by Athar Ali, op. cit., n. 4, pp. 41–90.
27. Manucci, II, p. 427.
28. Ibid., pp. 426–7.
29. Khan, op. cit., n. 22 above.
30. For further details regarding their role during the Sultan period, see Rita Joshi, *The Afghan Nobility and the Mughals*, Delhi, 1985, pp. 21–32.
31. Ibid., pp. 32–82.
32. Ibid., pp. 89–114.
33. For the intimacy between Jahangir and Khan-i-Jahan Lodhi, see *M.U.*, I, pp. 716–23, *Z.Kh.*, II, pp. 69–116.
34. Lahori, I, pp. 113, 117–23, 158–61, 176–7, 180–6, 195 and 202–3.
35. *Z.Kh.*, I, p. 104.
36. Salih, I (B), p. 229.
37. Lahori, I, pp. 110–11; Salih, I (B), p. 258.
38. Lahori, I, p. 112; I (b), pp. 236–7; Salih, I (B), p. 258.
39. Salih, I (B), p. 258; Lahori, I, pp. 111–12.
40. It is difficult to define the term in strong words because there is a good deal of fluctuation in the attitude of the contemporaries then. For example, Sadat Khan Bhakkari, though called 'Deccani', has been specifically excluded from this category (*Z.Kh.*, II, pp. 353–4); Shaikh Sufi Deccani, on the other hand, has been included in this group, although we have no details of his career (Salih, I (B), p. 382); Athar Ali, op. cit., n. 4, p. 110, S-489). So this term is used quite loosely here.
41. *M.U.*, II, p. 1.
42. Ibid., p. 654.
43. Compare Table 2.12 with the tables of other ethnic groups in this chapter.
44. Athar Ali, op. cit., n. 2 above, p. 27.
45. Ibid., p. 29.
46. This observation is entirely based upon *Zakhirat-ul-Khawanin; Maasir-ul-Umara* and Athar Ali, op. cit., n. 4, pp. 41–90.
47. Athar Ali, op. cit., n. 2 above. p. 29.
48. Rahim Khan died in 1631–2; Lahori, I (b), p. 295; Yaqut-Khan Habshi expired in 1633, Lahori, I, p. 523, I (b), p. 294.
49. *Z.Kh.* II, pp. 408–9; Lahori II, pp. 143, 279, 206 and 319; M.U., II, p. 286.
50. Lahori, II, pp. 285, 408 and 606.
51. Diyanat Rai got the title of 'Rai Rāyān' in January 1639 (Lahori, II, p. 134) and Rai Raghunath in April 1656 (Salih, III (L), p. 217). For further details, see *Z.Kh.*, III, pp. 81–2; *M.U.*, II, p. 282.
52. As cited on p. 33.

APPENDIX 2.1: INDIANS AND IMMIGRANT NOBLES

Mansab	*Indians*	*Immigrants*	*Group not known*	*Total*	*Remarks*
				1628–36	
5000 zat and above	16	20	2	38	The place of birth of the two whose group is unknown could not be traced. But both of them were Deccanis.
3000 to 4500 zat	36	33	10	79	The ten mansabdars whose group is not known were Deccanis. Their place of birth is not known.
1000 to 2700 zat	105	93	27	225	The places of birth of all the 27 whose group is not known are not mentioned.
GRAND TOTAL	157	146	39	342	
				1637–41	
5000 zat and above	8	19	–	27	–
3000 to 4500 zat	21	28	5	54	In case of all the five whose group is not known, the place of birth is also not known. But three out of them were Deccanis.
1000 to 2700 zat	85	78	11	174	Out of these 11 whose group is unknown, 5 were Deccanis, but their places of birth are not known.
GRAND TOTAL	114	125	16	255	
				1642–58	
5000 zat and above	13	25	–	38	–
3000 to 4500 zat	34	40	7	81	Out of these seven whose group is not known, four were Deccanis, but their places of birth are not known.
1000 to 2700 zat	147	163	19	329	Out of the 19 mansabdars whose group is not known, 7 were Deccanis, but their places of birth are not known.
GRAND TOTAL	194	228	26	448	

APPENDIX 2.2: RACIAL AND RELIGIOUS COMPOSITION OF SHAHJAHAN'S NOBILITY

Mansab	*Iranis*	*Turanis*	*Afghans*	*Indian Muslims*	*Other Muslims*	*Total Muslims*	*Rajputs*	*Marathas*	*Other Hindus*	*Total Hindus*	*Grand total*
					1628–36						
5000 zat and above	14	6	2	2	2	26	6	6	–	12	38
3000 to 4500 zat	21	12	9	6	10	58	12	9	–	21	79
1000 to 2700 zat	58	35	26	24	27	170	35	17	3	55	225
GRAND TOTAL	93	53	37	32	39	254	53	32	3	88	342
					1637–41						
5000 zat and above	12	7	1	2	–	22	4	1	–	5	27
3000 to 4500 zat	18	10	2	5	5	40	8	6	–	14	54
1000 to 2700 zat	45	33	21	21	11	131	29	12	2	43	174
GRAND TOTAL	75	50	24	28	16	193	41	19	2	62	255
					1642–58						
5000 zat and above	15	10	1	5	–	31	6	1	–	7	38
3000 to 4500 zat	23	17	8	5	7	60	15	6	–	21	81
1000 to 2700 zat	94	69	29	49	19	260	53	9	7	69	329
GRAND TOTAL	132	96	38	59	26	351	74	16	7	97	448

APPENDIX 2.3: KHANAZADS AND ZAMINDARS

Mansab	*Khanazads*	*Non-khanazads*	*Zamindars whose blood relatives were in service*	*Zamindars who entered service themselves*	*Total zamindars*	*Grand total*
			1628–36*			
5000 zat and above	15	11	8	4	12	38
3000 to 4500 zat	26	33	19	1	20	79
1000 to 2700 zat	72	110	21	22	43	225
GRAND TOTAL	113	154	48	27	75	342
			1637–41			
5000 zat and above	14	8	5	–	5	27
3000 to 4500 zat	20	21	12	1	13	54
1000 to 2700 zat	60	78	18	18	36	174
GRAND TOTAL	94	107	35	19	54	255
			1642–58			
5000 zat and above	18	13	7	–	7	38
3000 to 4500 zat	33	28	18	2	20	81
1000 to 2700 zat	138	138	37	16	53	329
GRAND TOTAL	189	179	62	18	80	448

CHAPTER 3

The Crown and the Nobility

In the system of government of the Mughals, the king was the real fountainhead of authority, at least theoretically. The nobility was the king's creation. Every ruler since the days of Humayun built up his own nobility along with the old lot of nobles he inherited. The aim was to tighten his grip over a sizeable number, for the purpose of the safety of his person and his empire. To this end, Akbar selected Indian Muslims and Rajputs, and by showing more favours to the Iranis vis-à-vis the Turanis, he tried to establish an equilibrium in his nobility.[1] The king could govern only through this class—his umara and his mansabdars. The nobility, thus was an indispensable organ of the state machinery. It was through this group that imperial policies could be implemented and imperial designs executed. This group had a definite say in matters of state and its opinion, could be based on personal or group interests.[2] The nobility was dependent upon the crown in more than one way. The mansab system and the rotation of jagirs played a vital role in making the nobility more and more dependent upon the crown. The financial resources of this group were mainly controlled by the crown. Thus, we find that in one way or another, the crown and the nobility were interdependent. In spite of this interdependence, there was a dichotomy between the crown and the nobility. Although both of them lived upon the exploitation of the agricultural surplus, still, there was a marked difference between the approaches of the two. The jagirs which were assigned to the mansabdars in lieu of their muqarrarahtalab were transferred regularly. A parallel set of imperial officials was left in the jagirs to run the administration. The presence of the imperial news reporters kept the emperor well informed about the activities of the jagirdars. Through such means, the emperor tried to keep his mansabdars under his control, and also shield the peasants from undue harassment at the hands of the jagirdars. There is no dearth of evidence to suggest that the king was anxious to see his subjects safe and satisfied. Action was taken against those nobles, officials or mansabdars who tried to do harm to the ri'āya in unlawful ways. In July 1632, for example, Baqar Khan Najme Sani was dismissed from the subedari of Orissa on these grounds.[3] When the people complained against the high-handedness of Tarbiyat Khan, the Hakim of Kashmir, he was dismissed from the post in 1641–42.[4] Similarly, when Ahmad, son of Pira, ruined his jagir due to mismanagement, the jagir was resumed in July 1644 and he was put on cash payment.[5] The mansab was also curtailed in some such cases. For example, in the case of Fath, son of

Zakaria Rohila, a mansabdar of 1000 zat and 1000 sawars, 100 sawars were reduced as a punishment for molesting the rai'yat (6 June 1655).[6]

In the documents relating to the grant of jagirs, we come across imperial instructions to jagirdars with regard to the well-being and prosperity of the rai'yat, to increase agrarian production, to increase the population and make their jagirs more densely inhabited.[7]

From these facts, it emerges that there was every possibility of jagirdar's high-handedness by his exploitative tendencies, thereby causing total ruin of the rai'yat, who were tillers of the soil and upon whose shoulders the whole economy rested. Total suppression of this section led to permanent loss of revenue, and obviously the emperor was not prepared to tolerate it. That is why the king always took precautionary measures to save the rai'yat from undue pressure of his mansabdars and officials by curbing their powers and by penalizing them for defying his order in this regard.

Another contradictory issue between the crown and the nobility was of the share in power.[8] The nobles obviously got power as a share from the crown. It could be enhanced at the expense of the other. As and when the king tried to centralize power, there was usually a reaction from the side of the nobles to check him. These pulls and pushes had drastic effects upon the fortunes of both during the days of Humayun. Akbar defined his relations with the nobility afresh and demanded total subjugation from them—of course, with some concessions such as forgiving wrongdoers after they had submitted themselves to his mercy, extending sympathy to the family of deceased mansabdar by giving mansabs, wazāif and khal'at and by usually distributing the property of the deceased mansabdar among his heirs, etc.[9] These traditions served as guidelines to determine the attitude of the crown towards the nobility, and these were followed by Akbar's successors too.

During Shahjahan's period, we come across innumerable such instances which suggest a sympathetic and pacifying attitude being adopted towards the nobility.

The first thing is that the descendants of mansabdars were usually favoured. After the death or during the lifetime of a mansabdar, his blood relatives were normally granted mansabs. This tradition continued throughout this reign with almost no effect of changing political or other conditions, as is shown in Chapter 2. This means that it was almost a matter of policy to extend favours, in mansabs and otherwise, to the relatives of mansabdars.

Shahjahan seems to have adopted a policy of compromise with his nobility. There is ample evidence to suggest that nobles were usually pardoned, and a dearth of evidence which would highlight a vengeful attitude of the crown.[10] Jujhar Singh Bundela for example, was pardoned and restored to his original mansab of 4000/4000 in February 1629.[11] Similarly, after having submitted Raja Jagat Singh was forgiven and restored to his old mansab (along with his son Raj Rup).[12] Penitent mansabdars who had left Mughal service and joined some other ruler were given a cordial welcome, on their return. Jadun Rai, who joined Mughal service under Jahangir, went over (along with his relative) to the side of Nizam Shah under Shahjahan. But he was killed there along with his two sons, Achla and Raghu, and also his grandson Baswant Rai. However, his brother Jagdev Rai (with his son Bahadurji), escaped from Daulatabad, prayed for forgiveness and was reinstated in Mughal service in August 1630. Jagdev got a mansab of 4000/3000; Tilang Rai, grandson of Jadun Rai, got 3000/1500; Bithuji, another grandson of Jadun Rai, got a mansab of 2000/1000.[13] The zamindari of the late Jadun Rai was restored to his family and a good jagir was also assigned to it in the deccan.[14] In April 1633, when Kheloji, a mansabdar of 5000/5000, left Shahjahan's service and joined the Nizam Shahi state, his brothers Maloji and Parsoji, who remained on the Mughal side, were never treated as suspects.[15] They were rewarded with Khal'at, horses and elephants.[16] Throughout their careers, they were the recipients of royal favours and reached the high mansabs of 5000/5000 and 3000/2000 respectively.[17] Similarly, Syed Mansur Khan Barha, son of Syed Khan-e-Jahan Barha, in spite of his constantly erroneous ways, was always forgiven by the emperor.[18] There are innumerable other such examples which confirm the tradition of forgiveness and compromise by Shahjahan towards almost all sections of the nobility. Sometimes this favour was given through the mediation of a prince or princess or some noble. In other cases, it was extended on some auspicious occasion or festivity.

The next thing that throws light upon Shahjahan's attitude towards the nobility is his deliberate attempt to be sociable in his dealings with the nobles. He visited some nobles at their havelis on different occasions. When Asaf Khan, because of his illness, could not visit the court for a few days, the emperor personally went to see him.[19] On Allami Afzal Khan's request, he visited his house.[20] When Allami Sadullah Khan was confined to bed due to illness, he had the honour of the emperor's visit to his house.[21] After the death of Saif Khan, son of Amanat Khan, Shahjahan went to Malika Banu, the widow of the khan.[22]

Besides this, after the retirement or death of a mansabdar, his sons or near relatives were usually shown imperial favour and sympathy. Relating to increments in mansab on such occasions, we have ample evidence, but it is difficult to recount it here. Some interesting examples may, however, be cited. After the assassination of Salabat Khan Roshan Zamir at the hands of Raja Amar Sing Rathor (in August 1644) his son Muhammad Murad was given a mansab of 500/100 at the age of 4.[23] Similarly, at the age of 11, Sadullah Khan's son Lutfullah got a mansab of 700/100.[24] Syed Munawwar and Syed Sher Zaman, in spite of their young ages, got a mansab of 1000/250 after the death of their father, Syed Khan-e-Jahan Barha.[25] Shah Nawaz Khan adds that to look after the matters of each of them, a mutasaddi was appointed by the court.[26] Thus, it is clear that Shahjahan took special care of the relatives of the mansabdars. This confirms the importance of khanazads vis-à-vis the crown. It also suggests that the king was willing to have cordial relations with his nobility but with a certain dignity.

The crown-nobility relationship may also be evaluated from a brief analysis of the king's attitude towards the property of a deceased mansabdar, and from the reaction of the nobles to it. I am aware of the brilliant discussion on the subject by M. Athar Ali , but it is mainly with reference to Aurangzeb's period.[27] Since this matter apparently involved 'financial benefit' of the crown and simultaneous 'loss' of the nobility, it requires due attention for the reign of Shahjahan too.

The practice of confiscating the property of a deceased mansabdar may be traced back to Akbar's days as pointed out by M. Athar Ali. From Manucci's account, its existence under Jahangir gets confirmed.[28] Regarding Shahjahan's period, we draw such information form Lahori, Salih and Farid Bhakkari, as well as Shah Nawaz Khan. Bernier also has a word to say in this connection.[29]

Let us first examine Lahori's evidence. About Yaminud Daulah Asaf Khan, he writes that the khan left behind Rs. 2 crore and 50 lakh in cash. Out of this, Rs. 20 lakh were distributed among his sons and daughters, and the haweli of Lahore was conferred upon Dara.[30] It is also stated that Asaf Khan had specified his assets himself and had requested the emperor to resume all this in full.[31] Another case is that of Khan-e-Dauran-Nusrat Jang, after whose death only Rs. 60 lakh were resumed.[32] Lahori does not mention his total wealth, but according to Farid Bhakkari, the khan left Rs. 1 crore in cash and other things worth Rs. 2 crore.[33] Perhaps these two are the only instances of escheat mentioned by Lahori.

However, Salih's work, which covers Shahjahan's entire reign, cites more examples of escheat. About Islam Khan Mashhadi, he writes that the hoarded wealth of the khan was conferred upon his heirs after his death.[34] Raja Bithaldas Gaur is another interesting case. He left Rs. 10 lakh, which were distributed by the emperor among his sons. Raja Anurodh got Rs. 6 lakh, Arjun Rs. 3 lakh, Rs. 60,000 went to Bhim and Rs. 40,000 to Harjis.[35] About Ali Mardan Khan, Salih writes that his total wealth—cash and kind—worth Rs. 1 crore was seized.[36] He also adds that Rs. 50 lakh were distributed among his sons (i.e. Rs. 30 lakh to Ibrahim Khan, Rs. 20 lakh to three other sons and daughters) and only Rs. 50 lakh were resumed against the state demand (*mutaliba*).[37]

Farid Bhakkari's account gives interesting information on this subject. He has mentioned six such cases. With regard to Khan-e-Dauran Nusrat Jang's wealth, Farid differs with Lahori, and refers to the total confiscation of his wealth.[38] But his statement cannot be preferred over the exact figures of Khan-e-Dauran's wealth given by the official historian mentioned above. However, in the case of Islam Khan Mashhadi, he has made an interesting addition. It is that the khan, during his lifetime, burnt all the original records in order to hide his actual assets and sent a fake list to the king. But Shahjahan, being well aware of all this, gave due consideration to the khan's sincere devotion and past services to the Mughal crown, and 'gave' away all his wealth to his heirs.[39] Shah Nawaz Khan repeats this story.[40] In the case of Ali Mardan Khan, unlike Salih, Farid does not say a word about the confiscation of his wealth.[41] However, he has made an important addition by referring to a reaction to an attempt of escheat in case of Mirza Rustam-

Safavi. When the mutasaddis of Agra tried to capture the wealth of the deceased khan, his widow prepared to check them, pleading that since their family had served the Mughals for 50 years, how, then, could their property be seized like that of others? When this matter was reported to Shahjahan, he was so overcome by this plea that he left all the property of the khan (except his elephants) with his heirs.[42] This incident is reproduced by Shah Nawaz Khan also.[43] Almost the same attitude of the crown is shown in Mahabat Khan's case. He had declared all his wealth quite candidly before his death, and had warned his wife too not to hide a single penny. Everything (except elephants) was restored to his heirs after his death.[44] This case is also repeated by Shah Nawaz Khan.[45] Perhaps the last case of escheat mentioned by Farid is that of Bahadur Khan, son of Darya Khan Rohila, whose belongings (except elephants) too were left to his heirs after his death.[46] Shah Nawaz confirms this.[47]

Last, a word about the evidence we get from Shah Nawaz Khan. As is evident from the foregoing account, he has simply reproduced what was said by our three other historians. Quite rarely has he added anything new. For example, in the case of Khan-e-Dauran, he adds that the khan had fixed the share of each of his sons in his wealth, but Shahjahan quite generously gave to his sons even more than the desire of their father.[48] About Wazir Khan Hakim Alim Uddin, a sheikhzada of Chinot, he says only this, that Wazir Khan prepared a complete list of his wealth and belongings and submitted it to the emperor.[49] So, in his case, nothing can be said about the application of the practice of escheat.

After this brief survey of evidence relating to escheat, one can make some general observations on this point. The foremost thing that strikes a reader is the rarity of cases where escheat is applied. From the voluminous contemporary and near-contemporary works mentioned above, one gets just seven or eight cases where this principle was applied. Is this because of the carelessness of these writers? Perhaps not, because all of them could not have been silent on such an important issue. More than one tentative explanation may be given for this limited evidence. First, escheat was not usually applied to all the nobles, hence there is no general record of such cases. This point gets added credibility when we look at the mansab and status of those nobles in whose case escheat was applied. All these nobles belonged to the first category of mansabdars (i.e. 5000 and above), hence they were very big people, socially, politically as well as financially. Since many of them enjoyed the favour of do-aspa sih-aspa, it is obvious that they commanded huge forces, which certainly increased the degree of the crown's dependence upon them. Perhaps, this means that escheat was forced upon such high nobles who were influential and commanded much respect due to their social and political status and their huge armies. It was simplay an attempt to assert the ultimate authority of the Mughal crown with regard to even confiscation of the personal property of such high dignitaries. In other words, escheat was meant to underline the fundamental principle that a noble, howsoever wealthy, powerful or influential he might be, was nothing more than a creation of the crown and that it was the emperor—the real fountainhead of authority—who bestowed dignity and wealth upon him and had the prerogative of resuming his wealth and property partly or in full.

That escheat was nothing more than the display of the practical application of an important royal prerogative is also evident from the fact that, usually, the entire assets of a deceased noble were not confiscated. In most cases, either the elephants were taken away or such an amount resumed which was equal to the state's demand (*mutaliba*) against a particular noble. This means that escheat was symbolic of the crown's supermacy, more than anything else.

Since escheat covered only a fraction of the total wealth left by a noble, it may be presumed that it did not do much financial harm to the nobility. So it was also not such a significant thing to merit greater attention of historians than it has, hence the casual references to escheat in their respective works.

Another interesting thing is that most of the nobles voluntarily submitted the details of their assets before their deaths. This shows that the need of reporting one's assets was not regarded as high-handedness of the crown against the nobility. The fact that, generally, the seizure of property, either partly or fully, was not opposed by the heirs of the mansabdars reveals that the nobles too were also aware of symbolic and superficial implications of escheat. As such, they did not oppose it as injustice or usurpation of their property, and accepted the share allocated by the emperor quite happily either according to the will of the deceased or at his own sweet will. This also shows that the dying noble, in general, was not much exercised by this practice, as it usually did not do much harm to the prospects of his descendants. Shahjahan's attitude towards the wealth of Islam Khan Mashhadi, who is recorded as having burnt all his records in order to hide his real assets, would have given the requisite satisfaction to the nobles, would have eliminated their misgivings totally, and would also have minimized instances of fabrication.

It may, therefore, tentatively be suggested that the ruin or devastation of the nobility was not the aim of escheat. Nor it was meant to enrich the royal exchequer as a temporary or permanent source of income. In was more likely calculated ploy to highlight the dependence of the nobility upon the Mughal crown. This display of supremacy was necessary to make the nobles realize that their personal wealth too could be appropriated by their heirs only with the consent of the king. This principle was also applied to the assets of Mumtaz-Uz-Zamani, which amounted to Rs. 1 crore. Shahjahan personally decided the share of the princes and princesses in this wealth.[50] This evidence further strengthens the argument that the system of escheat during Shahjahan's period was basically theoretical and legal in nature, and had only nominal financial significance. That is why it did not cause any breach between the crown and the nobility.

Since the Mughal nobility consisted of various heterogeneous groups, it is necessary to examine the attitude of the crown towards these ethnic groups and vice versa with reference to the proposed three phases.

FIRST PHASE: 1628–36

The first stage which highlights the attitude of the nobility is the brief succession tussle. The participation of the nobles on behalf of Shahjahan proved to be an important issue in deciding the crown's behaviour towards them, at least in the opening years.

As is evident from Lahori's account, the nobility played a vital role in putting Shahjahan on the throne. Nur Jahan was backing Shaharyar, but Asaf Khan nullified her designs by putting Bulaqi (son of Khusro) on the throne to avoid any risk of the throne being occupied by a powerful individual.[51] In the meantime, he sent Banarsi, his confident, to prince Shahjahan in the Deccan with word to reach the court as soon as possible.[52] Shaharyar, on the other hand, decided to fight for the throne; in fact, to lose it forever. About 26 nobles participated in this clash. Out of them, 8 were Iranis, 3 Turanis, 4 Indian Muslims and 1 Rajput.[53] It is thus clear that the Iranis were the overwhelming majority among the supporters of Shahjahan, and they became better claimants for greater favours in case of his success. In his farman to Asaf Khan, Shahjahan showed his gratitude to the khan for his sincere and matchless efforts in securing the throne for him.[54] That is why, immediately after the coronation, among the mansabdars who were given favours in mansab, the number of Iranis was about 62 out of a total of about 176 mansabdars of 1000 zat and above.[55]

The loyalty and devotion of the Iranis was tested off and on throughout the period of Shahjahan. At critical moments, they gave full cooperation to the crown and rendered remarkable service. In 1628–36, they stood by the side of the Mughal crown through thick and thin. Whether it was the rebellion of Jujhar Singh or the *coup d'ĕtat* of Khan-e-Jahan Lodhi, the Iranis proved themselves to be loyal and sincere servants of the state.[56]

With the arrival of Khan-e-Jahan Lodhi in the Deccan, this land became a hotbed of military activity. The Mughal forces ravaged the territory for not less than a period of about six years. The Iranis proved their mettle during these expeditions. Leading nobles like Yaminuddaulah Asaf Khan, Khwaja Abul Hasan, Mahabat Khan-Khan-e-Khanan, Shah Nawaz Khan, Sipahdar Khan, Ilahwardi Khan, Khalil Ullah Khan, Zafar Khan, Asalat Khan, Multafit Khan, Iltifat Khan, Mutamid Khan, etc., made valuable contributions as commanders as well as warriors and vigilant guards.[57] Mahabat Khan and his son Khan-e-Zaman died in the Deccan while discharging their duties.[58]

Apart from military efficiency, the administrative capability of the Iranis during this period (1628–36) also deserves mention. At the apex, the highest position of the Vakil was occupied by Yaminuddaulah Asaf Khan.[59] Azam Khan and Afazal Khan, both Iranis, held the distinguished positions of Diwan-i-Kul.[60] All the Mir Bakhshis during this period were Iranis.[61] Similarly, both persons holding the office of Mir-e-Saman during the first phase (1628–36) were Iranis.[62]

At the provincial level too, the Iranis seem to have served the crown with excellence during this period. They served as subedars of the three capital cities (Akbarabad, Delhi and Lahore); Islam Khan, Safdar Khan and Azam Khan in Agra,[63] Mahabat Khan, Lashkar Khan, Aitqad Khan, Baqar Khan and Asalat Khan in Delhi[64] and Asaf Khan (represented by Inayatullah Yazdi) in Lahore.[65] They held this position in other important provinces too. Other leading administrative positions were also held by the Iranis in different provinces.[66]

Thus, we find that the Iranis had proved their worth as efficient administrators and skilful commanders from the very beginning of Shahjahan's reign. The favourable attitude adopted towards them, thus, was the result of a great degree of trust reposed in them, and was also the reward for their good behaviour, loyalty and utmost devotion to the state. That is why they maintained a lead upon all other groups and came out as the only dominant faction in the Mughal nobility.[67] This confirms the unshaken faith Shahjahan had in them and indicates a greater degree of the crown's dependence upon the Iranis.

It seems that the Iranis were conscious of their privileged position. When, in the midst of the Deccan campaigns, Yaminuddaulah Asaf Khan was sent there as commander-in-chief (1631–2),[68] he organized a convivial party where Azam Khan, who was already serving in the Deccan, disclosed to him that the emperor was no more dependent upon them. Asaf Khan immediately reacted to the comment and said, 'Still, the state's business will not be complete without you and me.'[69] This loose talk was, however, reported to the emperor who felt disgusted and said that though Asaf Khan had obliged him, yet he should not be asked any more to help in the business of the state.[70]

It may, however, be said that Shahjahan continued the policy of Jahangir and showed utmost favour to the Iranis during this first phase.[71]

In spite of the fact that the ruling family belonged to Turanian stock, the Turanis could not rise up to the level of the Iranis. In the tussle for succession referred to earlier, out of a total of 26 nobles who took active part, the number of Turanis was less than that of Iranis. Their share in royal favours after coronation came down in the same proportion. Only 26 Turanis seem to have received favours out of a total of 176 mansabdars of 1000 zat and above. After his accession when Shahjahan took to the distribution of important administrative positions afresh, though the number of Turanis is negligible as compared to Iranis among the dismissed nobles, yet the interesting thing is that the unseated Iranis were well placed, while the 2 Turanis removed from old offices were given inferior positions.[72] Out of 6 Iranis removed from old administrative positions of different subas, Khwaja Abul Hasan was appointed as subedar of Kashmir, Qasim Khan as subedar of Bengal and Saif Khan as subedar of Bihar (and later on of Allahabad), while the 2 Turanis of this category, namely Fidai Khan Hidayat Ullah and Jahangir Quli Khan (son of Azam Khan) were not placed in such high positions. The former was made tiyuldar of Jaunpur and the latter nazim of Sarkar Surat.[73]

During the rebellions in the opening years, the participation of the Turanis in their suppression is certainly less than that of Iranis. For example, among the mansabdars sent against Jujhar Singh (in the first phase of his rebellion) they were 3 out of 29.[74] Their number declined further in the armies sent against Khan-e-Jahan Lodhi: we find only 4 Turanis out of a total of 78 mansabdars.[75]

In the Deccan campaigns too, the Turanis lagged behind the Iranis. In 1631–2, when Asaf Khan was given the supreme command of the Deccan war, only 3 Turanis seem to have served there in distinguished positions, namely, Abdullah Khan Feroze Jang, Khan-e-Dauran Nusrat Jang and Sardar Khan.[76] When Mahabat Khan was fighting against the Deccanis (in 1633), out of the whole lot of about 40 mansabdars, perhaps only 3 Turanis were serving there—Khan-e-Dauran Nusrat Jang, Nazar Beg Aurang and Yulam Bahadur.[77] In 1633, Prince Shuja was sent to the Deccan on Mahabat Khan's request. The total number of mansabdars who participated in this struggle up to 1634 was about 51; out of these the Turanis were about 7.[78] During the campaign against Sahu, etc. (in 1636), out of 77 mansabdars, 11 were Turanis.[79] In the same year, when Khan-e-Jahan Barha was deputed to crush Adil Shah of Bijupur, 45 mansabdars participated in the struggle, and out of these 7 were Turanis.[80]

Thus, we find that in 1628–36, in all types of military activities the participation of the Turanis was less in frequency as well as in quality. Except for Khan-e-Dauran Nusrat Jang and Abdullah Khan Feroze Jang, perhaps no other Turani was given command of forces in these campaigns.

In central administrative offices like that of the Diwan, Mir Bakhshi and Mir-e-Saman, no Turani seems to have held any position.[81] At provincial level, their representation was just nominal. Except for Safdar Khan who was appointed subedar of Agra (1631),[82] and Qulij Khan who held the subedari of Delhi in 1628–9,[83] no other Turani was assigned this post in these subas during this period (1628–36). In the Deccan, with the exception of Khan-e-Dauran Nusrat Jang (1634), all the subedars were Iranis.[84] In other provincial offices too, the number of Turanis was less than that of Iranis.[85]

Thus, we may say that whether in the battlefield or in administration, Turanis were not preferred over Iranis. This may be because of the king's assessment of their calibre, or due to the trend Shahjahan inherited from his father.[86]

Shahjahan seems to have adopted a favourable attitude towards the Afghans in the opening years of his reign. This again was in continuation of Jahangir's attitude, and also due to their active support he had received from this group as a prince. In his circle, he had such devoted Afghan nobles as Dilawar Khan Biranj, Bahadur Khan, Ali Khan Tarin, Muhammad Khan Mahmand, Rahim Khan Kakar, Ilahdad (son of Rahim Khan), etc., who served the prince even at the cost of their lives.[87] After his coronation, therefore, a large number of Afghans were favoured with mansabs and jagirs. Out of 176 mansabdars who received royal favours in 1628, 21 were Afghans.[88] They were accommodated in high administrative positions. In 1627–8, Sher Khan Nahar Khan replaced Saif Khan as subedar of Gujarat.[89] Khan-e-Jahan Lodhi took the charge of Suba-i-Malwa in place of Khan-e-Zaman (son of Mahabat Khan).[90] Bahadur Khan was appointed jagirdar of Kalpi.[91] Nazar Bahadur Kheshgi was made faujdar of Sarkar Sambhal in 1628–9.[92]

Khan-e-Jahan Lodhi's rebellion, however, seems to have affected the fortunes of the Afghans a bit unfavourably. The favours shown to him by the emperor were below his expectations. Mahabat Khan's appointment as sipahsalar, and other important changes in the beginning which indicated the rise of a new circle over and above the old Jahangiri nobles added to his suspicion, and ultimately he decided to run away from Agra (1629).[93] The details of his rebellion given by Banarsi Prasad are quite illuminating.[94]

There are some interesting features which emerge from close analysis of this clash. It seems that the rebellion was the reaction of a noble against Shahjahan's attempt at raising a new circle of his supporters by treating an old and eminent noble rather coldly.[95] The change in the court's atmosphere and the lack of that distinguished treatment which Khan-e-Jahan had enjoyed, gave way to his suspicion which went on multiplying with the passage of time.[96] Since he was holding 7000 sawars, do-aspa sih-aspa and had some supporters behind him, he decided to defend his position and privileges.[97] Shahjahan was determined to assert the supremacy of the Mughal crown while Khan-e-Jahan was trying to assert his position as his privilege. Perhaps Shahjahan was trying to make him realize that his status and position was a royal favour, and not his right. This rebellion, therefore, presents a glaring example of mutual distrust between the crown and the nobility. The settlement of this clash, depended entirely upon the strength of the nobility, which rested on their sawar rank. The defeat of Khan-e-Jahan and the success of the imperialists, on the other hand, establishes the interdependence of the king and the nobility and the internal cohesion within the nobility.

This rebellion should not be attributed to any reaction of a particular racial group. The evidence suggests that the Afghan nobles were divided and were present on both sides. Out of 78 mansabdars who were sent to crush Khan-e-Jahan, about 8 were Afghans.[98] In the opposition camp too, the number of Afghan mansabdars seems to be almost the same.[99] Evidence is available to show that while joining Khan-e-Jahan, the nobles were guided by personal interest rather than racial sentiments. It is borne out from the expectations of Bahlol Khan Miyana, who disclosed to the khan during the course of discussions that '. . . we had left our watan and imperial service in the hope of your Badshahi, where we would become dwazdah hazari (mansabdar of 12000) but now when you have no such plan [why] should we be killed with you?'[100] He and Sikandar Khan left Khan-e-Jahan in disgust and joined the imperial circle.[101] There was a difference of opinion even among his own sons. That is why Muzaffar left his father even before the battle of Sahinda.[102] After this battle, his remaining surviving sons joined royal service.[103]

Thus, it may be said that political considerations and personal interests were usually preferred over racial considerations. Khan-e-Jahan's Afghan supporters were mainly guided by personal interest. Similarly, the nobles in the imperial camp were also thinking in terms of their political, social and economic benefits which depended entirely upon their undivided support to the Mughal crown in critical hours. It was this strategy which persuaded Bahadur Khan Rohila[104] to join the imperial side against his father Darya Khan Rohila[105] who was in Khan-i-Jahan's camp.

The rebellion of Khan-e-Jahan did not affect the general attitude of the Afghan nobility. They served the Mughal crown quite faithfully in the Deccan campaigns. People like Shahbaz Khan, Mubarak Khan Niyazi, Abdul Rehman Rohila, Shamsuddin Kheshgi, Pir Khan Miyana, Rashid Khan, Mubariz Khan, Ahmad Khan-Niyazi, Nazar Bahadur Kheshgi, Sher Khan Tarin, Ahdad Mahmand and Bahadur Khan Rohila fought for the Mughal crown till the end of the Deccan campaigns.[106]

The fact remains that the rebellion of Khan-e-Jahan had some effect upon the position of Afghans in the Mughal nobility. In the second phase (1637–41), when large-scale curtailment was done in the number of the nobility, the Afghans were among these who suffered most.

In administrative positions, both at central and provincial levels, the representation of Afghans becomes almost nil. After Sher Khan and Khan-e-Jahan, no Afghan was appointed subedar of any province during this phase. However, two appointments, viz., Rashid Khan's appointment as faujdar of the Trans-Jamuna region in July 1632,[107] and the appointment of Dilawar Khan in the same capacity in Sarkar Mewat (February 1628)[108] are mentioned by Lahori and Salih.

But this does not mean that the Afghans were ignored altogether after the rebellion of Khan-e-Jahan Lodhi. Sher Khan,[109] Bahadur Khan,[110] Dilawar Khan,[111] Mubariz Khan,[112] and Rashid Khan[113] held high mansabs and distinguished positions. For their submissive attitude and devoted services, they were even promoted to higher ranks. Ahmad Khan Niyazi, for example, was promoted from 1500/1500 (in 1630) to 2500/2000 in 1636.[114] Bahadur Khan was elevated from 4000/2000 (in 1628) to 4000/4000 (in 1635).[115] Dilawar Khan Biranj's rank was enhanced by 1500 sawars in 1631.[116] Many more Afghans like Mubarak Khan Niyazi,[117] Mubariz Khan Rohila,[118] Nazar Bahadur Kheshgi,[119] Purdil Khan[120] and Rashid Khan[121] were promoted to higher ranks during the period 1628–36.

It may, therefore, be submitted that the rebellion of Khan-e-Jahan did not cause any drastic changes in the attitudes of the king or the Afghan nobility. This ethnic group, in critical hours, acted more as a political faction on both sides, and the king also did not withdraw his patronage and favours just for the sake of racial bias against them.

The Indian Muslims had sympathized with Asaf Khan during the succession tussle. Syed Hizbir Khan Barha, Daulat Khan Mai, Syed Jafar and Syed Alam Barha were the active supporters of Prince Shahjahan.[122] Therefore, they were rewarded immediately after the coronation. Out of 176 mansabdars who received royal favours, 20 were Indian Muslims.[123] Mansabdars like Syed Alawal Barha,[124] Murtaza Khan,[125] Jan Nisar Khan,[126] Ihtimam Khan,[127] Syed Shujat Khan,[128] Khan-e-Jahan Barha,[129] etc., served remarkably in the Deccan wars. During this period (1628–36), they held important administrative positions. Qazi Muhammad Said was appointed Diwan-i-Buyutat in October 1633 and Arz-i-Mukarrar in April 1635.[130] Mulla Abdul Latif Gujrati held the office of Diwan-i-Tan (November 1632 to March 1638).[131] They were assigned responsible posts at provincial level too. Wazir Khan and Daulat Khan Mai served as subedars of Punjab and Thatta respectively.[132] Syed Diler Khan Barha, Syed Abdul Wahab and Jan Nisar Khan acted as faujdars of Baroda, Hisar and Lakhi-Jangal[133] during this period (1628–36).

We thus find that Indian Muslims proved their worth on the battlefield as well as in administrative positions. Therefore, this phase marks the beginning of their rise in the coming period.

Rajputs formed the second-largest group of the Mughal nobility after Iranis. Their favourable attitude during the succession tussle earned high favours for them. In February and March 1628, 34 Rajputs were favoured out of the whole lot of about 176 recipients of imperial favour.[134] They rallied around the throne in critical hours in overwhelming majority. They supported the state, rising above racial and religious considerations. They formed the majority among the mansabdars who were sent against Jujhar Singh Bundela.[135] Out of 29 mansabdars sent under Mahabat Khan, Abdullah Khan and Khan-e-Jahan Lodhi, 11 were Rajputs.[136] Likewise, during the rebellion of Khan-e-Jahan Lodhi, they represented the imperialists in majority.[137] This army, which consisted of 78 mansabdars, had 31 Rajputs.[138] In the second phase of Jujhar Singh Bundela's revolt too, their representation was the highest, as they numbered 15 out of 43 mansabdars sent to crush him.[139]

They rendered remarkable services in the Deccan wars. In the Telingana expedition under Rao Ratan, there were 7 Rajputs out of a total of 19 mansabdars.[140] Mahabat Khan had 15 Rajputs out of a total of 40 mansabdars during the conquest of Daulatabad (1633).[141] When Prince Shuja was sent to the Deccan on Mahabat Khan's request (1633), their number amounted to 15 out of 51 mansabdars.[142] In February 1636, Khan-e-Dauran and Khan-e-Zaman were deputed against Sahu. They had 77 mansabdars with them, out of which 18 were Rajputs.[143] In the same expedition, a large number of Rajputs joined Khan-e-Jahan Barha.[144] Thus, throughout the Deccan expeditions, Rajputs served the Mughal crown with full devotion, and distinguished themselves.

As a reward for such exemplary service, they were promoted to higher ranks and emerged as the first leading group among the Indians, and as the second-largest group in the nobility as a whole.[145]

In order to make an assessment of Shahjahan's attitude towards the Hindu nobles during this first phase (1628–36), we will have to account for the Marathas and other Hindu mansabdars in addition to the Rajputs whose position has been explained above.

As mentioned in Chapter 2, the Marathas were welcomed into Mughal service because of political exigencies. Therefore, any consistency in the attitude of both the crown and the Marathas cannot be confirmed. Both parties changed their strategy according to their respective benefits. When Shahjahan was involved in the Deccan wars, they were given such favour that they had never enjoyed before. They were put at par with the leading groups like Turanis and Rajputs, at least in the first class of mansabdars (5000 and above).[146] They, however, were very aware of the personal benefits they could gain by joining Mughal service, or by leaving this side, depending upon the circumstances. This option, which perhaps was not normally available to all other established groups of Mughal mansabdars, was the strongest cause for their withdrawal from the Mughal camp. Jadun Rai, a mansabdar of 5000/5000, left the Mughals and joined Nizam Shah.[147] His brother Jagdev Rai who had left with him rejoined Mughal service in August 1630, got a mansab of 4000/3000, and left again in 1632–3.[148] Similarly, Kheloji, who joined in August 1628 and got the rank of 5000/5000, left in August 1633.[149] Sahu Bhonsle (5000/5000) not only left in 1632–3, but created serious problems for the Mughals in the Deccan in 1636.[150]

So it may be said that the mutual attitude of the crown and the Marathas from the very first phase was a sort of temporary alliance, unlike the permanent bond between the Mughals and the Rajputs.

From the foregoing account, it becomes clear that the other Hindus were given good opportunities to rise and were assigned important and responsible positions.

On the whole, Shahjahan seems to have adopted a liberal attitude towards the Hindu nobles. On one hand, it was due to their excellent services in the Deccan and elsewhere, on the other due to the established traditions of rewarding the old nobles and patronizing others for their calibre and services. In this phase, they were 88 out of 342 nobles.[151]

To conclude the discussion on the first phase, it may be submitted that this phase was mainly occupied with the Deccan wars, so a huge influx of Deccanis is noticeable. From almost 5.5 per cent in the opening years, they jumped to 14 per cent of the total towards the end of this phase.[152] This rise is unique for the rest of the nobility, not only during the first phase, but throughout the reign of Shahjahan.

Second, the Iranis seemed to be the most confidence worthy servants of the crown. They enjoyed not only the highest proportion in the total, but also the highest share in higher mansabs.

Last, the influx of the Deccanis raised the proportion of the Hindu mansabdars in the total number.[153]

SECOND PHASE: 1637–41

By the year 1636, '. . . the affairs of Deccan having been at last settled and the Mughal boundary clearly marked and publicly recognised by the local princes, Shahjahan returned to North India . . .'[154] writes Jadu Nath Sarkar. This phase, thus, brings a period of comparative peace in the Deccan. The terms of the treaties[155] made with Adil Shah and Qutub Shah, howsoever harsh they might be, saved the Deccan from constant arson, loot and much bloodshed. Though this settlement was temporary, yet for a long span of about 20 years there were no such depredations and hectic military expeditions in this region. Shahjahan was satisfied with the huge amount of wealth he could snatch away from the rulers of the Deccan and was proud of the recitation of his name in the Khutba in Golconda.[156]

Besides glory, splendour, wealth and territorial gains, the previous phase also passed on such problems as the expansion of the nobility on a larger scale due to the influx of Deccanis and the settlement of new provinces.

Another important development took place in this phase, and this was the voluntary surrender of the Persian commander of Qandhar, Ali Mardan Khan, to the Mughals.[157] The occupation of Qandhar added one more feather to Shahjahan's cap and elevated the prestige of the Mughal empire.

Inspired with constant success, growing wealth and political stability in India, Shahjahan planned a forward policy for the north-west frontier region. In 1639, the emperor moved up to Kabul;[158] Dara was sent with huge forces to Ghazni,[159] and Said Khan and Khan-e-Dauran were allotted huge forces to crush the Hazaras.[160] All these steps were meant simply to create fear in the minds of the Khans of Central Asia,[161] and thus the initial spadework was done for large-scale military expeditions to Central Asia.

These important developments may be of some help in explaining the mutual attitudes of the crown and the nobility during this phase.

The first notable thing of this phase is a sharp decline in the overall strength of the nobility. It falls from 342 to 255, as is shown in Chapter 2. This drastic cut in the strength may be justified in view of the large expansion due to the absorption of Deccanis in the previous phase. As the situation was comparatively peaceful, Shahjahan did not miss the opportunity of exercising a check upon the size of his nobility, which otherwise would have overburdened the establishment.

However, this decline did not disturb the proportion of different categories of mansabdars. The first category (5000 and above) bears a proportion of almost 11 per cent of the total, as was the case in the first phase.[162] Mansabdars of 3000 to 4500 also retain the same proportion, viz., about 20 per cent of the total.[163] In the last category (1000 to 2700) too, the proportion of almost 67 per cent of the total is maintained.[164] Thus, we find that, proportionwise, the structure of the nobility is not much affected by this notable decline in the number of mansabdars in this phase.

The change in the political atmosphere in this phase also affected the crown's attitude towards various racial and religious groups. There was hardly any change in the position of the Iranis. They maintained their lead over all other ethnic groups.[165]

This phase seemed to be quite favourable for the Turanis. It seems that they were deliberately raised to prominence. As compared to the Iranis, the Turanis made more swift progress in numbers in almost all categories of mansabdars.[166] More notable is their rise in the first class of mansabdars.

Their rise among mansabdars of 5000 zat and above is about 10 per cent over the figures of the first phase, while in the case of Iranis this increase comes to about 7 per cent.[167]

The rise of the Turanis might have some link with their performance against the Safavids during the occupation of Qandhar (1638). There is ample evidence which suggests their distinct role in this struggle. After the surrender of Qandhar by Ali Mardan Khan, in order to defend it from the Persians, the military expeditions that were sent included a large number of Turanis. The total number of mansabdars who participated in these expeditions was about 58: out of them, 19 were Turanis, and the Iranis were only 9.[168] On one hand, this proportion suggests growing confidence of the emperor in this group and on the other, it shows that the Iranis perhaps could not be possibly relied upon while facing the Persians. That is perhaps why Turani commanders like Said Khan Zafar Jang, Khan-e-Dauran Nusrat Jang, Qulij Khan, etc., were assigned leading positions and Persians like Jansipar Khan and Zulfiqar Khan Qaramanlu were placed in subordinate positions at that time.[169]

This change in favour of the Turanis is also evident from the important administrative positions held by them. In 1639, Safdar Khan (a Turani), was appointed subedar of Akbarabad for the second time;[170] thus far the post had mostly been held by Iranis. After the transfer of Qulij Khan in 1629, only Iranis held the post of subedar of Delhi, but then Ghairat Khan Khwaja Kamgar, a Turani, got this job in 1637.[171] Said Khan Zafar Jang, who got the subedari of Kabul in 1631, was allowed to continue there for a long period of about ten years, which is a rare example as far as tenure of office is concerned.[172] Above all, the subedari of Qandhar was conferred upon Qulij Khan (1638).[173] For the first time at the centre, a Turani, Tarbiyat Khan, was appointed Bakhshi-i-Doam in 1637.[174] Khalil Beg is the first Turani Mir-Tuzuk who got the post in 1640.[175] Thus far, this office had been held mostly by Iranis.[176]

Thus, we may say that in this phase, perhaps the Turanis were elevated in order to counterbalance the superiority of the Iranis, and were given better opportunities to improve their fortunes.

This phase may be regarded as the most difficult phase for the Afghans. Though there seems to be no marked difference in the imperial policy towards them in the foregoing period, perhaps due to the prolonged wars in the Deccan, yet after the settlement of Deccan affairs, a change in attitude towards the Afghans becomes apparent. Though their proportion in the overall strength was not reduced much, their real loss is evident from their decline in the two upper classes of mansabdars. In the category of 3000 to 4500 zat, their share seems to have been reduced to less than half the proportion they held in the first phase.[177] Yet the exceptions cannot be overlooked. Rashid Khan Ansari, a trusted noble, was holding the charge of Burhanpur during this period.[178] In addition to it, he also got the administration of Sarkar Bijagarh.[179] Thus, it appears that Rita Joshi seems to be in error when she writes that after Sher Khan, no other Afghan was appointed subedar of any province during Shahjahan's reign.[180] On the other hand, Indian Muslims seem to have improved both their position and strength in this phase. They were lagging behind the Afghans in the first phase, but later they gained not only in strength, but also in the degree of reliability and confidence. Their real gain lies in the proportion they held in the upper two classes of mansabdars. Among the mansabdars of 5000 zat and above, they rose from 5 per cent (in the first phase) to 7 per cent of the total.[181] They improved their position even among the mansabdars of the second category.[182]

This improvement in the position and power of Indian Muslims is probably due to their almost undivided support to the Mughal crown from the first phase itself. This may be regarded as a reward for their long-standing and continuous services to the state.

The representation of Indian Muslims increases in high administrative offices during this phase. Wazir Khan was appointed subedar of Akbarabad in 1640.[183] The subedari of Allahabad was conferred upon Syed Shujat Khan in 1637.[184] Jan Nisar Khan was holding the charge of Sivistan during this period.[185] Thatta remained under the charge of Daulat Khan Khawas Khan up to 1640.[186] Such evidence confirms the rise of Indian Muslims.

A word may be said about Shahjahan's attitude towards Rajputs in the changed political scenario. In the aggregate, they seem to have gained proportionwise.[187] This suggests that Jujhar Singh's rebellion in the first phase did not create any distrust against them, and also that they had left a better impression than the Afghans, who had to suffer in this phase. The attitude of the Rajputs in critical conditions had always been appreciable. During the occupation of Qandhar, for example, they figured in overwhelming numbers (14 out of 58) and formed the second-largest group after the Turanis among the nobles deputed on this expedition.[188]

The submission that the attitude of the crown was subject to the utility of the nobles or a group of nobles in changing political conditions seems to be more true in the case of the Marathas. After the end of the Deccan wars, they seem to have lost the position they had occupied during the first phase. Not only did they decline in number in this second phase,[189] more important is the fact that they lost a big share in the most prestigious category of mansabdars (viz. 5000 zat and above). In this class, they fell from 17 per cent (in the first phase) to 5 per cent.[190] Their decline in the third category is also notable.[191] Thus, it may be said that there was no such elaborate policy for this group as there was for the Rajputs. Their rise or decline depended entirely upon the changing political conditions and the extent of their requirement for the empire.

Almost the same trend may be seen in the cases of all the Deccani nobles. Since they were not as indispensable for the state after the settlement of Deccan affairs, their strength in the total number of the nobility begins to decline in this phase.[192] The imperial attitude becomes more clear from a drastic fall in their proportion in the prestigious category of mansabdars (5000 zat and above). It comes down from 20 per cent (in the first phase) to just 8 per cent of the total in this phase.[193] Perhaps not even a single

Deccani was either included in service or given any promotion during this phase.[194] Their position may also be assessed from the inconsequential administrative responsibilities assigned to them. In this phase only one Deccani, namely Atish Khan Habashi, was appointed as faujdar of Bhagalpur (1640).[195] It is interesting that he was not from that lot which joined service in the wake of the Deccan wars, but from those who came to the Mughal side during Jahangir's reign.[196]

As far as the position of the Hindus was concerned, it may be said that there was a decrease of about 2 per cent in their proportion in this phase as compared to their share in the first phase. This was mainly due to a drastic cut in the strength of the Marathas. So it may not be attributed to any religious bias. In this phase the Rajputs did improve their proportion, but it could not make up for the loss caused by the curtailment in the number of the Marathas.

In conclusion, it may be said that in this phase, which was politically almost peaceful and economically prosperous, Shahjahan tried to reduce the size of his nobility which was increased in the first phase due to military and political exigencies. This policy particularly affected the Afghans, Marathas, Deccanis and Hindus as a whole. The second interesting thing is that the Iranis maintained their lead over all other groups. The third notable fact is the rise of Turanis in this phase as a counterweight to the Iranis.

THIRD PHASE: 1642–58

After 1641, some important developments took place which made this period eventful. Important provinces like the Deccan, Gujrat, Bihar and Bengal were put under the four princes.[197] These administrative arrangements had far-reaching consequences which are well known and need not be repeated. Suffice it to say that this long stay of the three princes (who were dissatisfied with Dara) in such important and distant subas, should have contributed in deciding their future courses of action. It was from the Deccan, Gujrat and Bengal that a successful rebellion could be launched by the younger princes which ultimately sealed the fate of Shahjahan. It was during this period that Shahjahan launched his expensive Central Asian expeditions (1645–7) leading not to the gain of a single penny, but to the loss of a lot in men and money.[198] The disgust and ultimate withdrawal of Mughal forces from Balkh put an edge upon the designs of the shah of Persia, and he laid siege to Qandhar in 1648, which surrendered in 1649. Shahjahan made all possible attempts to beat the Persians back but in vain. These repeated failures exposed the hollowness of the Mughal empire. In order to regain lost prestige and compensate the monetary loss, Shahjahan ultimately turned towards the Deccan for a second time (1656) because this was his tried land, and his initial success and hoarded wealth were mainly due to the military exploits in this region in the first phase.

This increasing stress upon military activities led to a vast expansion in the number of the nobles, though Shahjahan had tried to neutralize the effect of the rise of the first phase during the second phase. This rise in the third phase led to the insufficiency of revenue available from land. The Hyderabad documents refer to complaints of less realization from jagirs.[199] This led to the introduction of the reforms of 1642 in the mansab system. These were intended to bridge the gap between jama figures and the actual hasil. The reduction in the contingents of mansabdars and introduction of the month scale in effect led to the reduction in the net emoluments of the jagirdars.

These developments in general suggest that this was a difficult period compared to the previous two phases. The younger princes and the ambitious nobles took full advantage of the situation. Shahjahan's illness was the most ripe opportunity for such elements to strike, which were either feeling restless under the existing regime, or which were hopeful of better opportunities in case of success in this struggle against the reigning monarch.

Thus, it appears that the last phase was full of significant developments which affected the fortunes of the nobility on one hand and coloured the attitude of the crown on the other.

The first thing that becomes clear during this period is the increasing utility of the nobility. In order to implement its designs, the crown was in need of full cooperation and sincere devotion of its officials and commanders. Incentives were to be given to assure their full support and rewards were to be given to the old supporters. This is confirmed by a notable rise in the total strength of the nobility. This rise was of almost 76 per cent over the number in the previous phase.[200]

But taking account of the whole reign, the rise of this phase was not more than 31 per cent over the figures of the first phase.[201] This shows that in spite of all pressures, Shahjahan adopted a cautious policy of expansion.

It seems that an attempt was made to exercise a check upon the number of the upper two categories of mansabdars. Irrespective of the overall rise, the number of mansabdars of 5000 zat and above remains the same as it was in the first phase (viz. 38).[202] As the number in this category did not rise, its proportion in the total strength of this phase came down accordingly. It was reduced to about 8 per cent of the total (i.e. 448)—a loss of about 3 per cent as compared to the proportion in the first and second phases. The same is the case with mansabdars of the second category (3000 to 4500 zat). From 23 per cent of the first phase, they fell to 18 per cent of the total strength in this phase.[203] The lowest category (1000 to 2700 zat) seems to be the only gainer. From 66 per cent in the first phase, this group reached a proportion of about 73 per cent of the total in this phase.[204] This is because of the new entries during the Central Asian campaigns, which are not as important as the swift promotions given to mansabdars of below 1000 zat.

The rise in the overall strength of the nobility and the corresponding decline in the number of mansabdars of the upper two categories had a definite impact upon the fortunes of different racial and religious groups of nobles. No doubt, numberwise the Iranis maintained their distinction among the whole lot, but statuswise they seem to have suffered a setback as their representation in the first category (5000 zat and above) declined considerably.[205] Equally important is the fact that their participation in leading military expeditions declined considerably during this phase. This is clearly borne out from their number among the participants of the Central Asian expeditions. Among the nobles who served under Murad and Aurangzeb in Balkh and Badakhshan, the number of Iranis was 22 out of 148, which was less than that of Turanis.[206] More important is the fact that when Qandhar was besieged by the Shah (1648–9), there was not a single Irani among the defending officials: there were only Turanis, Afghans, Indian Muslims and Rajputs.[207] This shows a kind of distrust in Iranis while facing the Shah of Persia. This is also confirmed from their poor representation in the imperial forces sent against the Persians. Out of 45 mansabdars who seem to have served under Prince Aurangzeb (1649), only 6 were Iranis.[208] The number of Turanis and Rajputs separately was more than double this number.[209] In the second Qandhar expedition (1652), a further decline may be seen in their number. Out of about 50 mansabdars who joined Aurangzeb this time, the number of Iranis was 3, while the Turanis were 16 and Rajputs 18.[210] In the last expedition (1653) too, there were only 7 Iranis out of 69 mansabdars who were given under Dara's command.[211] The number of Turanis was three times more than that of Iranis.[212]

Thus, a change may be noted in Shahjahan's policy towards the Iranis, which strengthwise, however was not adverse for them. Besides, it may be stated that they were not being ignored either. They held important administrative positions, and still had the largest number in the total strength of the nobility.

As compared to Iranis, more favour seems to have been shown to Turanis as they remained almost on the same footing among mansabdars of 5000 zat and above, but gained in the second and the third categories and also improved their proportion in the overall strength.[213] This was perhaps because of their enhanced military utility, which is evident from the figures given in Appendices 3.4 and 3.5 relating to the leading military campaigns.

It may thus be said that the favourable swing of the pendulum in the case of Turanis, which is notable in the second phase, continues in this (last) phase too. They were preferred over Iranis in significant campaigns, earned name and fame, and got promotions which added to their military strength and raised their status in the official hierarchy. But they never rose to supersede the Persians, who still maintained their lead over all other groups in the Mughal nobility.

In this phase too, the Afghans seem to have lost in the aggregate. Though there was an improvement in their total number, it could not keep pace with the tremendous rise in the total strength of the nobility.[214] However, they were given better opportunities to show their calibre and were assigned trusted jobs. They rendered good service during the Balkh-Badakhshan and Qandhar campaigns. The growing imperial faith in them is evident from their growing proportion in the contingents of mansabdars sent to serve in those regions.[215] Their representation increased during the Qandhar expeditions more than it did during the Balkh and Badakhshan campaigns.[216] Bahadur

Khan Rohila was promoted to the highest rank of 5000 zat/5000 sawar, (do-aspa sih-aspa) and was assigned the charge of Suba-i-Balkh with Asalat Khan in 1646.[217] Afghan nobles like Nazr Bahadur Kheshgi, Shamsher Khan-Tarin, Alawal Tarin and Jamal Khan Nohani served remarkably well in the Central Asian campaigns and were rewarded generously by Shahjahan.[218] From careful examination of Lahori, it emerges that during this phase, the rate of promotion increased appreciably in the case of the Afghan nobles.[219] This further confirms the growing trust of the Mughal crown in them.

This period proved to be most fertile for Indian Muslims. Not only did their number multiply during this phase, their proportion also increased among mansabdars of 5000 zat and above.[220] This seems to be the only group elevated so generously to this honoured category of mansabdars.[221] If we recall the decline of the Iranis and the stagnation of the Turanis in this class,[222] the rise of Indian Muslims becomes more significant. This favourable policy of the crown (which had already begun in the previous phase) now reached its peak. This position was, to a certain extent, earned by Indian Muslims by extending their undivided support to the Mughal crown at all critical times in as well as outside India. Among the Indian nobility, this was the only group which always stood united by the side of the emperor and never raised problems for the state. The Rajputs and Afghans stand nowhere compared to them, at least in this quality.[223]

The rise of Indian Muslims and the growing confidence in them is also evident from their representation in administrative offices. For the first time an Indian Muslim, Sadullah Khan, was appointed Mir-e-Saman in 1643.[224] Thus far, this office had been held exclusively by Iranis. The office of Sadri-kul seems to have become a privilege of this group. After Musvi Khan, an Irani, the sadrs were picked up only from this faction.[225] Sadullah Khan was the first Diwan belonging to this group. Appointed to this post in 1645, he continued till his death in 1656.[226] This long tenure of almost 11 years remains unsurpassed during the entire reign of Shahjahan. Their representation increased notably in prestigious provincial offices too.[227] They were posted in crucial areas in sensitive positions. All this confirms the growing faith of Shahjahan in the Indian Muslim nobles.

The rise in the overall strength of the nobility in this phase affected the proportion of the Rajputs favourably.[228] They seem to have improved in the upper two categories of mansabdars, which highlights the improvement in their status and strength on one hand, and the higher degree of confidence reposed in them on the other. This is confirmed further by their leading participation in the expedition sent against Raja Jagat Singh of Mau (1641–2). Not less than 14 Rajputs joined this expedition in which about 56 mansabdars seem to have participated.[229] It seems that there was no change in their attitude towards the crown. Their loyalty and identification of interest with the crown, which had been confirmed much earlier during the rebellion of Jujhar Singh Bundela, was proved repeatedly.[230] The presence of the Rajputs on the imperial side against Jagat Singh in large number also proves that it was not a 'Rajput rebellion' as such. The sincerity of the Rajputs and their remarkable services during the significant developments of this phase elevated their status vis-à-vis the crown. The point becomes more significant if we keep in mind the attachment of most of them with land, which was already a strong source of power for them.

The imperial attitude towards the Marathas (and vice versa) was guided mainly (as in the previous phases) with the increase of their requirement by the empire in political exigencies. As mentioned earlier, there was no such policy for them as there appears to have been in the case of the Rajputs. Similarly, the full strength of the Marathas was never available to the Mughal crown, there were regular withdrawals by them at critical junctures. Whether this purely diplomatic and timely contact was because of the attitude of the Mughal crown or of the Marathas towards the crown, cannot be explained with any degree of certainty. The fact, however, remains that after the settlement of 1636, there was a constant decline in the strength of the Marathas in proportion to the existing total number of the Mughal nobility.[231] In this phase, they were reduced to almost half the strength they had in the first phase, though there was considerable rise in the total number of nobles from the first to the last phases.[232]

The decline in the number of the Marathas further brought down the proportion of Hindus in the nobility. The improvement in the proportion of Rajputs and other Hindu mansabdars, however, suggests a favourable attitude of the state towards them.

From the foregoing account, we may conclude that Shahjahan did not expand or reduce the size of his nobility arbitrarily. The pressure of political developments and requirements was paramount. Just as he had to raise the number of nobles in the first phase (1628–36) due to political expediency,[233] after the settlement of the Deccan problem (during the second phase), Shahjahan tried to exercise a gradual check upon it, as a result of which the number fell drastically. The plan for the conquest of Central Asia, the defensive measures in Qandhar and the revival of hostilities in the Deccan, again built up pressure for military activities and gave a new turn to the political conditions. All this led to a large-scale expansion of the nobility in the third phase. Still, Shahjahan remained cautious in promoting mansabdars, with the result that the bulk of this rise was confined to the lowest category, and there was a notable decline in the proportion of the upper two grades.

Second, the rise or decline of any racial or religious group was based mostly upon its utility for the state, which was determined by its attitude and performance as well as political expediency. After 1636, the gradual decline of Iranian representation in leading military expeditions is worth nothing. They were mostly kept busy with administrative jobs either at the centre or in the provinces. Equally important is the fact that there was hardly any notable improvement in their proportion in the overall number from the beginning till the end of this reign. This suggests that perhaps the rise or eclipse of a particular group of nobles depended more upon its military utility than anything else. The involvement of the Turanis, on the other hand, seems to have increased considerably in military expeditions after 1636, (as shown above), with the result that their proportion rises appreciably during the second and third phases. Indian Muslims and Rajputs, similarly, made satisfactory progress in the second and third phases. Their performances were equally satisfactory in leading military expeditions. The policy of appeasement of Afghans during the third phase was perhaps the reward for their growing devotion to the state, which was also tested on the battlefield. This rise in their share among mansabdars of 3000 to 4500 confirms this attitude. Indian Muslims made notable progress in mansabs, administrative jobs as well as military assignments.

It seems that Shahjahan's cautious policy of maintaining an equilibrium was not readily acceptable to the bulk of his nobility. The resentment or dissatisfaction of the nobles is evident from the basic fact that most of those who participated in the 'war of succession' sided with the rebel princes. From M. Athar Ali's exhaustive table, it emerge that about 231 nobles in all participated in this struggle. Out of these, only 87 were on the imperial side and the bulk (i.e. 144) was with the younger princes.[234] More interesting is the fact that the old, established nobles such as Iranis or those who were sufferers (like the Afghans) were present in large numbers in the opposition camp. Out of 144 such nobles, the leading figure is that of the Iranis (i.e. 31).[235] In the case of Afghans, 27 joined hands with the princes and only 1 Afghan noble was on the imperial side.[236] The majority of Deccani Muslims and Marathas also seem to have sided with the rebel princes.[237] On the other hand, the nobles who could make remarkable progress during the 30-year-reign of Shahjahan, joined the opposition group, though in small number. For example, out of 28 Indian Muslims, only 10 sided with the younger princes, and out of 33 Rajputs who participated in this struggle, only 11 joined the opposition.[238]

As to what led to this refractory attitude of the nobility, it may be tentatively submitted that it had its roots in the built-in contradiction between the crown and the nobility. Shahjahan did try to maintain an equilibrium between this contradiction and interdependence by adopting a policy of compromise (while maintaining his prestige) with his nobles by granting pardon, restoring the assets of deceased mansabdars to their heirs, etc. Simultaneously, however, he tried to strengthen his grip over the nobility. Turanis were raised as a counterweight to the Iranis, and Indian Muslims were favoured at the cost of these two old and established groups. A cool attitude towards the Afghans, and an almost indifferent attitude towards the Marathas after 1636 cost him their support at a critical hour. The majority of the Iranis, Afghans, Marathas and Deccanis participating in this struggle sided with the younger princes; Indian Muslims, zamindars in general and Rajputs in particular, remained in the imperial camp in overwhelming majority.

The reforms of 1642 in the mansab system may also be regarded as a contributory factor in creating a disgust among the bulk of the nobles. The reduction of the contingents implied a cut in the power of the nobility, as the bulk of the nobility derived power from its military contingents and not from land. Similarly, the introduction of the month scale meant, in effect, reduction in the net emoluments of the mansabdars. Thus, both from the viewpoints of military strength as well as financial prospects, these reforms did not suit the interests of the bulk of the nobility.

Since khanazads enjoyed almost half the total strength of the nobility and were thus in a privileged position, Shahjahan's moderate policy in raising their mansabs in order to accommodate non-khanazads in jagirs may also be regarded as a contributory factor in developing this contradiction.

In the light of the above, it may be said that Shahjahan could not be fully successful in establishing an equilibrium between contradiction and interdependence of the crown and the nobility. Perhaps that is why his long confinement at Agra passed almost unnoticed, and no attempt was made for his release.

NOTES

1. For further details, see Iqtidar Alam Khan, *Nobility under Akbar and the Development of His Religious Policy*, *J.R.A.S.*, London, 1968.
2. After the Persian occupation of Qandhar (1648–9), according to the advice of the nobles, no immediate action was taken: Salih, III, p. 70(B). Likewise, on the eve of the battle of Samugarh, Shahjahan consulted Shaista Khan regarding his personal appearance on the battlefield, but the Khan's advice was contrary to the wish of the emperor, with the result that he did not move out of the fort: *M.U.*, II, p. 695.
3. Lahori, I, pp. 430–1.
4. *Tareekh-i-Shahjahani*, Rotograph, Department of History, Aligarh Muslim University, p. 98.
5. *S.D.S.*, p. 133.
6. Ibid., pp. 195–6.
7. Ibid., pp. 168, 171, 175–7, 186–7, etc.
8. For some detailed discussion on this point, see S. Nural Hasan's article 'New Light on the Relations of the Early Mughal Rulers with their Nobility', I.H.C., 1944.
9. See A.A. Rizvi, Religious and Intellectual History of the Muslims in Akbar's Reign, Delhi, 1975, Chapter 10; Iqtidar Alam Khan, op. cit., n. 1 above.
10. Perhaps there is one case when Shahjahan took revenge upon a noble for his past deed, and that is of Rustam Khan Shighali. He was a confidant of Prince Khurram, but when Mahabat Khan was chasing the rebel prince, Rustam Khan deceived him and joined hands with Mahabat Khan, thus causing serious damage to the prince. After his coronation, therefore, Shahjahan resumed his mansab and jagir and he died in a pitiable condition. It is worth quoting Shahnawaz Khan on this point. He says: 'It is said that Shahjahan did not take revenge upon any noble who had shown arrogance but Rustam Khan. Ultimately his condition became so worse [*sic*] that he had no horse for riding and no servant (to serve [him])'; *M.U.*, II, pp. 199–201.
11. Lahori, I, pp. 254–5; Salih, I, p. 330 (B); *M.U.*, II, p.216.
12. Lahori, II, pp. 269–70, 276–8, 285 and 291.
13. Lahori, I, pp. 308–10; *M.U.*, I, pp. 520–3.
14. Ibid.
15. Lahori, I, pp. 507–8.
16. Ibid.
17. Lahori, I (b), pp. 295 and 299; II, pp. 720 and 724; Salih, III, pp. 451 and 455 (B).
18. *M.U.*, II, pp. 449–52.
19. Lahori, I, p. 395.
20. Ibid., pp. 495–6.
21. *M.U.*, II, p. 448.
22. Ibid., p. 420.

23. Ibid., p. 733.
24. Salih, III, p. 217 (L); *M.U.*, II, p. 448.
25. Lahori, II, pp. 473–4; *M.U.*, II, pp. 465–8.
26. *M.U.*, II, pp. 465–6.
27. M. Athar Ali, *Mughal Nobility under Aurangzeb*, Bombay, 1968, pp. 63–8.
28. Manucci, I, Calcutta, 1965, p. 171.
29. He writes, '. . . the barbarous and ancient custom obtains in this country, of the king's constituting himself sole heir of the property of those who die in his service'. Travels in the Mughal Empire, Atlantic Publishers, Delhi, 1989, pp. 163–5.
30. Lahori, II, pp. 258–9; *Tareekh-i-Shahjahani*, p. 96.
31. Lahori, II, PP. 258–9.
32. Ibid., pp. 426–8.
33. *Z.Kh.*, III, p. 25.
34. Salih, III, p. 9 (B).
35. Ibid., pp. 131–2 (L).
36. Ibid., pp. 243–5. Salih has used the words, 'ba halqa-i-zabt dar-amad'.
37. Ibid.
38. *Z.Kh.*, III, p. 25.
39. Ibid., pp. 26–7.
40. *M.U.*, I, pp. 165–6.
41. *Z.Kh.*, III, pp. 27–9.
42. Ibid., I, pp. 100–1.
43. *M.U.*, III, p. 440.
44. *Z.Kh.*, II, pp. 163–5.
45. *M.U.*, III, pp. 407–8.
46. *Z.Kh.*, III, p. 49.
47. *M.U.*, I, pp. 423–4.
48. Ibid., p. 757.
49. Ibid., III, pp. 933–6.
50. Lahori, I, p. 393.
51. Ibid., p. 70.
52. Ibid., p. 71.
53. Ibid., pp. 72–3.
54. Ibid., pp. 114-15.
55. Ibid., pp. 113, 117–23, 158–61, 176–7, 180–6, 195 and 202–3.
56. See Appendices 3.1, 3.2 and 3.3
57. Lahori, I, pp. 319, 404–6, 300–1, 319–20, 428, 499–500, 294–6, 339–43, 305–6, 538, 423 and 411–12; Lahori, 1 (b), pp. 35, 140, 155 and 137.
58. Lahori, 1 (b), pp. 59–60 and 257.
59. Lahori, I, pp. 179–80.
60. Lahori, I, pp. 186 and 257. For the term 'Diwan' and its technical implications, see Ibn-e-Hasan, *Central Structure of the Mughal Empire*, Delhi, 1970, pp. 147–8 and Chapter 5.
61. Lahori, I, pp. 159, 186, 538–9 and 542; 1 (b), 83, 86 and 279. Also see Ibn-e-Hasan, ibid., Chapter 6.
62. Namely Afzal Khan (1628–9) and Mir Jumla (1629–35): Lahori, I, pp. 176–7 and 257–8; I (b), p. 86. Also see Ibn-e-Hasan, ibid., pp. 235–52.
63. Lahori, I, pp. 125, 255, 369, 440, 472; I (b), pp. 8, 87 and 105.
64. Ibid.
65. Ibid.
66. See Chapter 5 for further details.
67. The lead of the Iranis upon all other groups during this period is also evident from their highest share in total zat and sawar ranks, as will be shown in Chapter 4.
68. Lahori, I, pp. 404–5.
69. *M.U.*, I, p. 157.

70. Ibid.
71. See M. Athar Ali, The Apparatus of Empire, Oxford University Press, Delhi, 1985, pp. 41-90.
72. Lahori, I, pp. 125–6. Lahori has recorded eight such cases of removal of subedaras; out of these, Fidai Khan Hidayat Ullah and Jahangir Quli Khan (son of Azam Khan) were the two Turanis removed from the nizamat of Bengal and deputy subedari of Allahabad respectively. Also see Lahori, I, pp. 221, 226, 228, 418, 426 and 432.
73. Ibid.
74. See Appendix 3.1.
75. See Appendix 3.2.
76. Lahori, I, pp. 356–61, 404–6 and 411–17.
77. Ibid., pp. 496–9, 500–1, 508–21, 525, 528 and 532–3.
78. Ibid., pp. 537–8, 542; Lahori, I (b), pp. 35–40, 43–4, and 46. These Turani nobles were Khan-e-Dauran, Yakka Taz Khan, Baqi Beg Uzbek, Ghairat Khan Khwaja Kamgar, Nad Ali, Salih Beg and Karimdad Qaqshal.
79. Lahori, I (b), pp. 135–9 and 146–8.
80. Ibid., pp. 135, 137, 140–1, 143, 148–50, 154–60 and 217–21.
81. See the tables of the respective offices in Chapter 5.
82. Lahori, I, pp. 126 and 369.
83. Ibid.
84. Lahori, I (b), p. 63.
85. For details about the probable number of Turanis in different administrative offices, see the tables in Chapter 5.
86. During Jahangir's period, there were 60 Turanis out of the total of 271 mansabdars. This number is much below the level of Iranis (who were 82 out of 271): Athar Ali, op. cit., n. 71, pp. 41–90.
87. Lahori, I, pp. 122–5.
88. Ibid., pp. 113, 117–23, 158–61, 176–7, 180–6, 195 and 202–3.
89. Mirat, I, Baroda, 1928, p. 203; Lahori, I, p. 76.
90. Lahori, I, p. 199.
91. Lahori, I, p. 191.
92. Ibid., p. 255.
93. Ibid., pp. 275–6.
94. Banarsi Prasad Saxena, *History of Shahjahan of Dihli*, Allahabad, 1958, pp. 66–80.
95. *Z.Kh.*, II, pp. 69–116; M.U., I, pp. 716–31.
96. Ibid.
97. Ibid.
98. See Appendix 3.2.
99. From the details given in *Maasir-ul-Umara* and *Zakhirat-ul-Khawanin*, it emerges that there were about seven or eight Afghan mansabdars in Khan-e-Jahan's camp (*M.U.*, I, pp. 716–31; *Z.Kh.*, II, pp. 69–116). Out of these, two were his own sons, one was his son-in-law and the rest were his other relatives and friends. Rita Joshi, in her *The Afghan Nobility and the Mughals (1526–1707)*, Delhi, 1985, has mentioned the names of his Afghan supporters, but without giving any contemporary evidence (p. 121). Strangely enough, she has included the name of Bahadur Khan Rohila in this list, who is known for his loyalty for the Mughals (Lahori, I, pp. 322–3 and 327).
100. *Z.Kh.*, II, p. 109.
101. Ibid.
102. Ibid.
103. Among Khan-e-Jahan's sons, Alam Khan was sanctioned a daily allowance of Rs. 5 and Ahmad Khan was given a mansab of 400/100 (*Z.Kh.*, II, pp. 112–13).
104. Lahori, I, pp. 294 and 322–3; *Z.Kh.*, III, pp. 48–9; *M.U.*, I, pp. 415–24.
105. Lahori, I, pp. 300 and 338–9; *Z.Kh.*, III, pp. 48–9; *M.U.*, II, pp. 18–21.
106. Lahori, I, pp. 298, 300–1, 356–61, 496–9, 500–1, 508–11, 512–14, 515–19, 521, 525 and 537–8; I (b), pp. 35–40, 43, 44, 46, 135–6, 140, 177, 217–18, 220–1 and 225.

107. Lahori, I, p. 431.
108. Salih, I (b), p. 272.
109. Lahori, I, p. 78; I (b), p. 294.
110. Lahori, I (b), pp. 86–7.
111. Lahori, I, p. 398; I (b), p. 296.
112. Lahori, I (b), p. 63.
113. Ibid., p. 60.
114. Lahori, I, p. 296; I (b) p. 138.
115. Lahori, I, p. 117; I (b), pp. 86–7.
116. Lahori, I, pp. 117 and 398.
117. Lahori, I, p. 298; I (b), pp. 136 and 138.
118. Lahori, I, p. 182; I (b), p. 63.
119. Lahori, I, p. 184; I (b), p. 134.
120. Lahori, I, pp. 383–4; I (b), p. 14.
121. Lahori, I, p. 183; I (b), p. 60.
122. Lahori, I, pp. 72–3.
123. Ibid., pp. 113, 117–23, 158–61, 176–7, 180–6, 195 and 202–3.
124. Lahori, I, pp. 508–9.
125. Ibid., pp. 496–9.
126. Ibid., pp. 410–11.
127. Lahori, I (b), pp. 135–6.
128. Ibid.
129. Lahori, I, pp. 404–5 and 537–8; I (b), pp. 140–1.
130. Lahori, I, p. 543; I (b), p. 87.
131. Lahori, I, p. 446; I (b), p. 92.
132. Wazir Khan held the post from May 1632 to September 1639 (Lahori, I, p. 425; II, p. 158) and Daulat Khan acted in this capacity in 1635–40 (Lahori, I (b), p. 101; II, p. 198).
133. Diler Khan held the faujdari of Baroda till December 1632 (Lahori, I, p. 448). Syed Abdul Wahab was posted in Hisar in March 1628 (Lahori, I, p. 191) and Jan Nisar Khan's tenure in Lakhi Jangal started in November 1631 and ended in April 1633 (Lahori, I, pp. 399 and 476).
134. Lahori, I, pp. 113, 117–23, 158–61, 176–7, 180–6, 195 and 202–3.
135. See Appendix 3.1.
136. Ibid. Also Lahori, I, pp. 241–2.
137. See Appendix 3.2.
138. Ibid.
139. See Appendix 3.3. Lahori, I (b), pp. 96–7, 99–100, 109 and 114–15.
140. Lahori, I, p. 298.
141. Ibid., pp. 496–9, 500–1, 508–9, 510–13, 515–19, 520–1 and 525.
142. Ibid., pp. 537–8; I (b), pp. 35–40, 43–44 and 46.
143. Lahori, I (b), pp. 135–7.
144. Lahori, I (b), pp. 140.
145. See Table 2.11, and also Tables 2.16 to 2.18 above (Chapter 2).
146. See Table 2.13 (Chapter 2).
147. Lahori, I, pp. 182, 308–10; *M.U.*, I, pp. 520–3.
148. Lahori, I, pp. 308–10; I (b), p. 297; *M.U.*, I, p. 522.
149. Lahori, I, pp. 227 and 507–8.
150. Ibid., p. 442; I (b), pp. 35–6, etc.
151. If we compare these figures with the figures of Jahangir's period (51/271, Athar Ali, op. cit., n. 71, pp. 41–90), we will notice a net increase of about 7 per cent. Also see Table 2.17 (Chapter 2).
152. See Chapter 2, 'Deccanis'.
153. Sri Ram Sharma, however, regards this period as the most difficult time for the Hindus

as 'during the sixth to the tenth years of his reign he (Shahjahan) embarked upon the active career of a persecuting king': *The Religious Policy of the Mughal Emperors*, Munshiram Manoharlal, Delhi, 1988, p. 94. Strangely enough, it is during this phase only that Hindu mansabdars reached such a number which raised their proportion in the aggregate so much that they could never attain it in the succeeding two phases; see Table 2.17 (Chapter 2).

154. J.N. Sarkar, *Short History of Aurangzeb*, Calcutta, 1954, p. 12.
155. Lahori, I (b), pp. 167–74, 210–11. B.P. Saxena has very ably analysed these treaties in his *History of Shahjahan of Dihli*, pp. 166 and 176–8.
156. The total gains of these expeditions in cash and kind amounted to Rs. 200 lakh (Lahori, I (b), p. 265). These gains are mentioned, with much pride, in a letter addressed to Shah Safi of Iran. Also see Saxena, op. cit., n. 94, p. 176.
157. Lahori, II, p. 34.
158. Lahori, II, p. 139.
159. Ibid., p. 150.
160. Ibid., pp. 148–9.
161. Ibid., pp. 152–3. The preparations horrified Nazr Muhammad and he immediately sent Mansur Haji with presents worth Rs. 40,000.
162. See Table 2.3 (Chapter 2).
163. Ibid.
164. Ibid.
165. For all the figures, see Table 2.8 (Chapter 2).
166. See Table 2.7 (Chapter 2).
167. See Tables 2.7 and 2.8 (Chapter 2). This favourable attitude is further elaborated in Chapter 4, where this issue is examined in the light of a break-up of mansab figures.
168. Lahori, II, pp. 33–9, 42–6 and 53–64.
169. Lahori, II, pp. 33–7, 40–1 and 42–4.
170. Ibid., pp. 130 and 215. The Irani subedars were Islam Khan Mashhadi (Lahori, I, p. 369), Azam Khan (Lahori, I (b), p. 105) and Saif Khan (Lahori, II, p. 130).
171. Lahori, I (b), p. 280; II, p. 158.
172. Lahori, I, pp. 400–1; II, p. 222.
173. Lahori, II, pp. 35 and 223–4.
174. Lahori, I (b), p. 279; II, p. 135.
175. Lahori, II. p. 218.
176. The Irani Mir-Tuzuks were Khalilullah Khan (Lahori, I, p. 451), Murshid Quli Khan (Lahori, I, p. 451) and Mir Khan (Lahori, I (b), pp. 105–6).
177. See Table 2.10 (Chapter 2). The decline in their position is also shown with the help of the mansab figures in Chapter 4.
178. Lahori, II, pp. 98–9.
179. Ibid.
180. Rita Joshi, op. cit., n. 99, p. 142.
181. See Table 2.9 (Chapter 2). This improvement in their position is confirmed with the help of mansab figures as we shall see in Chapter 4.
182. Ibid.
183. Lahori, II, p. 215.
184. Ibid., p. 274.
185. Ibid., p. 128.
186. Ibid., p. 198.
187. See Table 2.11 (Chapter 2).
188. Lahori, II, pp. 33–9 and 42–4.
189. See Table 2.13 (Chapter 2).
190. Ibid.
191. Ibid.
192. See Table 2.12 (Chapter 2).

193. Ibid.
194. See Lahori's first and second lists of mansabdars (Lahori, I (b), pp. 293–312; II, pp. 717–37). With the exception of Sarwar Khan Habshi (whose increased mansab is given in the second list), there seems to be no change in the mansabs of the Deccanis. Also see the list of the mansabdars in Appendices A, B and C at the end of this work.
195. Lahori, II, p. 180.
196. *M.U.*, I, pp. 188–9.
197. Aurangzeb's first vice-royalty of the Deccan ended in 1644 and his second term began in 1652 (Salih, III, p. 148 (L); Dara got Bihar in 1657 (Salih, III, p. 267 (L); Shuja was assigned Bengal in 1648 (Salih, III, pp. 19–20 (L) and in 1654 Gujrat was given to Murad (Salih, III, p. 125 (L).
198. M. Athar Ali has very ably analysed these campaigns in his artcle 'The Objectives behind the Mughal Expedition to Balkh and Badakhshan', I.H.C., 1967, and has pointed out Shahjahan's wisdom in planning a forward policy in the north-west. Yet, the heavy loss which the state had to bear cannot be overlooked. Also see Saxena, op. cit., n. 94, Chapter 8.
199. H.D., Basta no. 10, Acc. nos. 4054, 4199, etc.
200. See Table 2.3 (Chapter 2).
201. Ibid.
202. Ibid.
203. Ibid.
204. Ibid.
205. See Table 2.8 (Chapter 2).
206. See Appendix 3.4.
207. Salih, III, pp. 73–92 (B).
208. See Appendix 3.5.
209. Ibid.
210. Ibid.
211. Ibid.
212. Ibid.
213. See Table 2.7 (Chapter 2).
214. See Table 2.10 (Chapter 2).
215. See Appendices 3.4 and 3.5.
216. Ibid.
217. Lahori, II, pp. 554 and 564.
218. In 1646, Nazr Bahadur Kheshgi was promoted to 3000/2500 (Lahori, II, pp. 479–80). As a reward for his services in Central Asia, Shamsher Khan Tarin was raised to 2000/1500 (Lahori, II, p. 594). Similarly, Alawal Tarin was given a promotion of 500 zat in 1646 for his performance in the battle against Nazr Mohd. (Lahori, II, p. 554).
219. With the help of mansab figures, this issue is further highlighted in Chapter 4.
220. See Tables 2.9 (Chapter 2).
221. Ibid.
222. See Tables 2.7 and 2.8 (Chapter 2).
223. Afghans had made their condition precarious after the rebellion of Khan-e-Jahan in the first phase. Though the rebellion of Jujhar Singh Bundela and Raja Jagat Singh did not affect the fortunes of the Rajput nobility, the fact remains that at least two prominent Rajputs, leaving aside the rebellions of petty zamindars, did raise the banner of rebellion. However, no such example may be given in the case of Indian Muslims throughout the period of Shahjahan.
224. Lahori, II, p. 347.
225. Ibid., pp. 315–16; Salih, III, pp. 2–3 (L).
226. Lahori, II, pp. 431 and 433; Salih, III, p. 216 (L); M.U., II, p. 448. For details relating to the office tenure of the diwans, see Chapter 5.
227. The role of the nobles in administration has been analysed in detail in Chapter 5.

228. See Table 2.11 (Chapter 2).
229. Lahori, II, pp. 237–41 and 261–78.
230. See Appendices 3.1 and 3.3.
231. See Table 2.13 (Chapter 2)
232. This somewhat indifferent attitude of the crown towards the Marathas is also evident from the fact that among the mansabdars of 5000 zat and above, they declined from 16 per cent in the first phase to just 3 per cent during this (last) phase. Except Afghans, no other group had to suffer as much Their decline becomes more significant if we bear in mind the vast difference of proportion between them and Afghans (during the first phase) in this superior category of mansabdars. This can be checked in Tables 2.10 and 2.13 (Chapter 2).
233. According to M. Athar Ali's list (*Apparatus of Empire*, pp. 41–90), the number of the nobility under Jahangir did not exceed a total of 271. This author finds almost the same number (i.e. 274) during the opening years of Shahjahan's reign, from Lahori's account. The number rises only during the Deccan wars. This again confirms the relevance of military requirements and political conditions with the rise or decline in the number of the nobility.
234. M. Athar Ali, op. cit., n. 27 above, pp. 112–35.
235. Ibid.
236. Ibid.
237. Ibid.
238. Ibid.

APPENDIX 3.1: RACIAL AND RELIGIOUS COMPOSITION OF MANSABDARS AGAINST JUJHAR SINGH BUNDELA FIRST PHASE: 1628–9

	Iranis	*Turanis*	*Afghans*	*Indian Muslims*	*Rajputs*	*Total Muslims*	*Total Hindus*	*Grand total*	*Source*
Mahabat Khan's army	2	1	3	2	2	8	2	10	Lahori, I, pp. 241–2.
Abdullah Khan's army	–	1	4	–	3	5	3	8	
Khan-e-Jahan Lodhi's army	2	1	2	–	6	5	6	11	
TOTAL	4	3	9	2	11	18	11	29	

APPENDIX 3.2: RACIAL AND RELIGIOUS COMPOSITION OF MANSABDARS SENT AGAINST KHAN-E-JAHAN LODHI: 1629–31

	Iranis	*Turanis*	*Afghans*	*Indian Muslims*	*Other Muslims*	*Rajputs*	*Marathas*	*Other Hindus*	*Grand total*	*Source*
Azam Khan's army	6	–	1	2	3	12	4	1	29	Lahori, I, pp. 293–6.
Raja Gaj Singh's army	3	3	6	1	2	11	2	–	28	
Shaista Khan's army	8	1	1	1	1	8	1	–	21	
TOTAL	17	4	8	4	6	31	7	1	78	

APPENDIX 3.3: RACIAL AND RELIGIOUS COMPOSITION OF MANSABDARS SENT AGAINST JUJHAR SINGH IN THE SECOND PHASE OF HIS REBELLION: 1635

	Iranis	*Turanis*	*Afghans*	*Indian Muslims*	*Other Muslims*	*Rajputs*	*Total Muslims*	*Total Hindus*	*Grand total*	*Source*
Khan-e-Jahan Barha's army	1	1	2	1	1	6	6	6	12	Lahori, I (b), pp. 96–7, 99–100, 109 and 114–15.
Abdullah Khan's army	2	1	1	–	–	3	4	3	7	
Khan-e-Dauran's army	2	2	5	–	–	2	9	2	11	
Aurangzeb, C.I.C.	2	1	1	5	–	4	9	4	13	
TOTAL	7	5	9	6	1	15	28	15	43	

APPENDIX 3.4: RACIAL AND RELIGIOUS COMPOSITION OF MANSABDARS WHO PARTICIPATED IN BALKH-BADAKHSHAN EXPEDITION

Iranis	*Turanis*	*Afghans*	*Indian Muslims*	*Other Muslims*	*Rajputs*	*Other Hindus*	*Total Muslims*	*Total Hindus*	*Grand total*	*Source*
Initial Attempt by Ali Mardan Khan										
3	3	2	–	–	4	–	8	4	12	Lahori, II, pp. 415–16, 424, 457–60, 461–3 and 466–7.
Murad's Campaign: 1646–7										
17	23	8	19	7	43	2	74	45	119	Lahori, II, pp. 483–8, 491, 503, 506, 520, 523–7, 537–40, 541–2, 545, 549–52, 566, 578, 617, 623–4 and 642–3.
Aurangzeb's Campaign: February–October 1647										
9	18	9	4	2	20	–	42	20	62	Lahori, II, pp. 632–4, 640–1, 643–9, 663–6, 653–6, 672–5, 686–7, 688–92; Salih, III, p. 14 (L).
Total Number of Mansabdars who Served in this Campaign (after removing repetitions)										
22	34	10	24	10	46	2	100	48	148	

APPENDIX 3.5: RACIAL AND RELIGIOUS COMPOSITION OF MANSABDARS WHO PARTICIPATED IN QANDHAR EXPEDITIONS

Iranis	*Turanis*	*Afghans*	*Indian Muslims*	*Other Muslims*	*Rajputs*	*Other Hindus*	*Total Muslims*	*Total Hindus*	*Grand total*	*Source*
					First Expedition under Aurangzeb: 1649					
6	15	4	5	–	15	–	30	15	45	Salih, III (L), pp. 70–2.
					Second Expedition under Aurangzeb: 1652					
3	16	5	6	2	18	–	32	18	50	Salih, III (L), pp. 135–9.
					Third Expedition under Dara: 1653					
7	22	8	8	5	17	2	50	19	69	Salih, III (L), pp. 53–7 and 162–8.

CHAPTER 4

The Mansab System and the Nobility

The only powerful mechanism available to the Mughals to organize the nobility was the mansab system. It was through this institution that the nobles entered the service and became mansabdars. The status, strength and resources of the nobility were determined by the mansab. Thus, the mansab had a pivotal role in regulating the fortunes of the nobility.

The mansab also had a big role in defining the relationship between the crown and the nobility. Since it was awarded by the king, it confirmed the supreme authority of the crown to create mansabdars. As this award implied political, economic as well as social benefits, it further consolidated the crown's hold upon the nobility. Promotion, reduction or cancellation of the mansab (even theoretically) was the sole privilege of the crown, which added to the dependence of the nobility upon the crown, and in the same proportion it added to the latter's capacity to control the former. Besides assuring the loyalty of the nobility, the mansab system also served as a standing safeguard of efficiency and discipline. 'The very insecurity of wealth and rank', rightly observes Abdul Aziz, 'acted as a powerful incentive for individual distinction.'[1]

Thus, the mansab system was important for mutual relations between the crown and the nobility and also for the military and administrative efficiency of the state. Since civil and military services were governed collectively through this mechanism, it also showed the crown's dependence upon the nobility, as the execution of imperial orders and policies was made by these mansabdars. This dependence is also implied in the award of the sawar mansab which determined the military obligations of its holder, because from the very beginning the bulk of the Mughal nobility was not attached to land. The jagir was not their personal property.[2] So 'Their position', observes S. Nurul Hasan rightly, 'did not depend on their being in control of a particular territory, but on their military capacity'.[3] This military capacity was determined by the sawar rank, so this rank becomes an important element in regulating the crown-nobility relationship: on one hand the military strength of the empire depended upon the contingents of the nobles, on the other this strength determined the power and position of the mansabdars. A greater share of a group in the total awarded sawar mansab, therefore, suggests greater faith and more dependence of the crown upon that group. Thus mansab implied elements of interdependence as well as contradiction between the crown and the nobility.

For these and many other reasons, scholars have given due attention to the mansab system. Moreland Abdul Aziz, Irfan Habib and Athar Ali are some of the respected scholars who have made valuable contributions in this connection. It is therefore considered unnecessary to speak about the minute technical complexities of this institution.

However, M. Athar Ali, in his recent writings, has shown some new and interesting directions of research and enquiry.[4] He has posed questions like: Why and when did the mansab increase under Shahjahan? Was there any reflection of political developments in the ebb and flow of mansab grants? What was the position of individual groups vis-à-vis the mansab?

With intensive research, Athar Ali has collected mansab figures from official chroniclers of Shahjahan's period relating to grant, promotion and reduction. With these, he has drawn three tables relating to the three decades of Shahjahan's reign, which give these details separately for each year. It is in the light of these figures that he has tried to answer a few of the above-mentioned questions. Trying to make out Shahjahan's policy towards mansabdari relating to the first decade, he puts forward a tentative hypothesis: 'Does it mean that Shahjahan was inclined to enhance the sawar mansab (requiring maintenance of large military contingents), while he was not willing to increase the zat mansab, which involved only an increase in the personal pay of the mansabdars?'[5] The justification for this view is found in the dwindling financial resources at the time of Shahjahan's coronation. The 'primacy of sawar enhancements over zat' is also extended by Athar Ali to the second decade as a keynote of the mansab policy. In the third decade, however, he observes a dramatic change from sawar rise to zat enhancement. The reason for this change, according to him, was perhaps that, 'mansabs were now being given not to increase or maintain military strength but to win over support for factional purposes (principally perhaps, for strengthening Dara Shikoh's position)'.[6]

Thus, Athar Ali has touched upon one major issue, viz., when and why increments were given in zat and sawar mansabs during the whole reign of Shahjahan. Other relevant questions posed by him at the beginning of his paper are yet to be looked into, and this gives me some ground to speak.

At the very outset, I must make it clear that I have not depended upon the suggested decades of the official historians which divide this whole period into three parts of almost ten years each, for the reasons explained earlier. The proposed three phases (viz. 1628–36, 1637–41 and 1642–58) can be more helpful in explaining political and other developments in understanding the impact of changing political and military situations upon the imperial attitude towards the nobility than the decades suggested by the contemporaries then. The consequent effect of these changes upon mansab grants and promotions can help in getting a rough idea of Shahjahan's policy towards mansabdari as such, and the question as to how these changes affected the imperial policy and the fortunes of various groups of mansabdars may also be answered more accurately with the help of these phases.

The second thing which explains the method applied here is that in order to find the figures of net rise or decline in zat or sawar, the difference between the grand total figures of the recorded awards during the proposed phases has been worked out. If the total award of one phase is less than the award of the subsequent phase, the difference of the two figures gives the net figure of rise in zat or sawar mansab in this subsequent period. But if the total awarded zat and sawar mansab of one phase exceeds the figures of its succeeding phase, then the difference of these two total awards gives the net decline in zat and sawar mansab in that subsequent period. The reason for not depending upon the total of those increments which are mentioned by the official chroniclers in their annual accounts is simply because of the fact that at more than one place the promotion figures have not been mentioned during these annual accounts by these contemporaries, resulting in differences of the total figures of the different phases.

Through this method, one can easily point out the fluctuations in the total figures of the mansab. These may be correlated to the changing political conditions and their reflections in the ebb and flow of the mansab.

However, in order to trace the possible trend of promotions, one will have to rely upon the accumulation of promotion figures mentioned in individual cases by Lahori and others, as we shall see later.

The first thing to engage our attention is to make a rough estimate of the total award of mansabs during these three above-mentioned phases. To reach safer conclusions, the information is arranged in tabular form. Table 4.1 has been prepared basically with the help of Lahori and Salih. It contains the total of the highest recorded mansabs of the nobles during the specific phases. This total is classified under various ethnic groups of nobles. Mansabs below 1000 zat have not been included, and awards of do-aspa sih-aspa have been counted as double.

The first notable thing here is the difference between the total mansab figures of the first phase and the total of Lahori's first list, which is too close to this proposed phase. This is mainly because of many omissions of appointments, promotions as well as reductions in the list of the official historian.[7]

Second, the decadewise list of the contemporary chronicler suggests a constant rise in mansab figures. In Lahori's first list, the total of the zat mansab (of 1000 zat and above) comes to 6,78,300, and it rises to 6,94,500 in his second list. Simultaneously, the sawar figures increase by a number of 7000 from the first to the second decade. Hence, these lists fail to convey the total impact of the changing political and military conditions on the mansab.

From Table 4.1, however, it emerges that in both zat and sawar mansabs, considerable reduction was made after the end of the hectic military expeditions in the Deccan.

In the third phase, the mansab figures move rapidly upwards, as one can see the revival of hectic military activities specially in the north-west during this period.

That there was a link between the changing political and military conditions and the fluctuations in the mansab figures during different phases, can be explained with the help of a brief survey of the developments of this period.

TABLE 4.1: TOTAL GRANT OF ZAT AND SAWAR MANSABS (FOR THREE PHASES)

	Iranis	*Turanis*	*Afghans*	*Indian Muslims*	*Other Muslims*	*Total Muslims*	*Rajputs*	*Marathas*	*Other Hindus*	*Total Hindus*	*Grand total*
						1628–36					
Zat	2,48,000	1,22,000	80,500	68,500	80,000	5,99,000	1,21,500	1,03,500	3000	2,28,000	8,27,000
Sawar	2,08,122	1,01,100	70,950	48,700	44,750	4,73,622	86,900	77,550	1050	1,65,500	6,39,122
						1637–41					
Zat	1,97,500	1,21,000	44,000	58,000	33,000	4,53,500	82,500	42,500	2000	1,27,000	5,80,500
Sawar	1,68,900	1,09,700	33,300	51,950	19,900	3,83,750	66,400	24,700	400	91,500	4,75,250
						1642–58					
Zat	3,00,500	2,19,000	75,000	1,14,000	51,500	7,60,000	1,53,500	36,500	6500	1,96,500	9,56,500
Sawar	2,32,550	1,76,100	69,000	92,450	32,400	6,02,500	1,31,500	20,400	3400	1,55,300	7,57,800

Shahjahan inaugurated his reign in the midst of some serious internal as well as external political problems. Nazr Mohammad's threat to Kabul[8] in 1628 and Jujhar Singh Bundela's rebellion[9] in the same year was followed by Khan-e-Jahan Lodhi's upheaval.[10] The last one took a serious turn with the entry of the rebel in the Deccan, and engaged Shahjahan's attention till 1636. The situation could be faced only with huge military contingents. That is why the mansab figures rise during this phase, as shown in Table 4.1.

The settlement of 1636 with the Deccani rulers brought peace in both camps.[11] For about 20 years thereafter, the Deccan remained almost free from Mughal raids. Thus, from 1637 we enter a comparatively more peaceful period. Except the brief problems created by Champat-Bundela,[12] Pratap Ujjainia[13] and the Afghan tribal uprising in Naghz under Karimdad,[14] there is hardly any other serious problem to engage our attention during this period. On other hand, it is during these years that Zafar Khan led a successful expedition against Tibbat. Culminating all this was the peaceful surrender of Qandhar by Ali Mardan Khan in 1638.[15] Therefore, it seems that this brief period was almost free from serious political problems, and may be marked as a blissful time for the enjoyment of the exploits of the Deccan and the notable benefit of Qandhar. So during this peaceful phase, there was hardly any urgency for increasing the mansabdars and multiplying the figures of the mansab. Hence, in this phase, one may notice a sharp decline in the overall mansab figurs, as is evident from Table 4.1

Finding his position almost completely secure internally, and taking advantage of the possession of Qandhar, Shahjahan started working on an advanced defensive policy in the north-west. Lahori has made a passing reference to such developments in 1639.[16] From 1642 onwards, therefore, one may see the reviving stress upon military activities. During this last phase, the Mughal armies marched up to Balkh and Badakhshan and made the Uzbeks realize their refined skill in winning pitched battles. But the Mughal's expedition to Central Asia apparently was a heavy loss in men and money. This reverse put an edge upon the designs of the Persians, and they besieged Qandhar, which the Mughals ultimately lost in spite of the three consecutive attempts made by Aurangzeb and Dara. The last of the major developments of this phase was the renewal of hostilities in the Deccan and the revival of military activities there. Political problems resurfaced so military prowess regained supremacy. That is why, perhaps, the mansab figures again rise swiftly during this phase. Thus, it may be said that the rise or decline in mansab figures was closely linked with the changing political conditions and increasing or decreasing military activities.

A rough estimate of the net rise or decline in mansab figures may be made according to the above-mentioned method of finding the difference between the total figures of the three phases. But the rise in the first phase cannot be estimated without determining, even tentatively, the initial mansab figure of this reign. No complete list of Jahangir's nobles is available in contemporary works. For the opening years of Shahjahan's period too, there is hardly any such list as we have for the first and second decades in Lahori.

Thus, in the absence of any direct evidence, the initial mansab figures cannot be determined decisively. The compilation of mansab figures, mentioned by Lahori in connection with the coronation festivities,[17] should not be regarded as the initial mansab figures because (*a*) they cover only a fraction of the nobility; (*b*) include large figures of promotions; and (*c*) because it becomes quite clear from Lahori's language that he was mentioning a few such cases only and not the total initial mansab. If this estimate is to be based upon the total of mansab figures reached up to 1630–31 (at the verge of the commencement of the Deccan expeditions), perhaps this will not be acceptable because in many individual cases Lahori has not mentioned any mansab till 1630–1. Thus, the only reasonable method of finding this initial figure is perhaps to pick up the total promotion figures of this phase (1628–36) and then deduct it from the total award of this period. From Lahori's annual account, one may get the total promotion figures of about 1,09,700 zat and 1,49,500 sawar during this period, while the total figure of mansab awards of this phase is about 8,27,000 zat and 6,39,122 sawar (as shown in Table 4.1). The difference of these two figures gives a rough estimate of the required initial mansab, viz., 7,17,300 zat and 4,89,622 sawar.

The rise or decline in the second and the third phases, however, may be worked out by simply finding the difference between the total mansab awards of these phases, as shown in Table 4.2.

These figures also give some strength to the hypothesis that the fluctuation in mansab figures had its root in the changing political conditions, which, sometimes, led to the intensification of military activities. Hence, the rise in mansab figures as well as mansab holders and vice versa.

Another important issue which may be raised with regard to mansabs is: What was Shahjahan aiming at? In order to make a tentative assessment of his policy towards the mansab, we will have to keep in mind the initial financial difficulties of his reign.

While giving a resumé of the economic condition of the Mughal empire from Akbar's days to Aurangzeb's period, Shah Nawaz Khan blames Jahangir for his carelessness,[18] which gave a free hand to the mutasaddiyan, who multiplied corruption. He adds that the financial condition became so bad that the expenditure exceeded the income of khalisa almost three times.[19] Immediately after the coronation, therefore, Shahjahan gave due attention to this alarming situation, and ordered the confiscation of the mahals, worth Rs. 1 crore and 50 lakh.[20]

In the light of such a deplorable financial condition, one can appreciate Shahjahan's policy towards the mansab from the opening years of his reign. Immediately after his coronation during 1628–9, Shahjahan seems to have adopted a very cautious policy in this regard. From Lahori's narrative, it emerges that during this period, a promotion of only 15,000 zat and 16,750 sawars was given to the mansabdars.[21]

This moderate policy of Shahjahan towards the mansab was, however, disturbed due to the political developments (mentioned earlier) which led to the intensification of military activities in the first and third phases, and his

TABLE 4.2: NET RISE/DECLINE IN ZAT AND SAWAR MANSABS

	Iranis	*Turanis*	*Afghans*	*Indian Muslims*	*Other Muslims*	*Total Muslims*	*Rajputs*	*Marathas*	*Other Hindus*	*Total Hindus*	*Grand total*
						1637–41					
Zat	(–) 50,500	(–) 1000	(–) 36,500	(–) 10,500	(–) 47,000	(–) 1,45,500	(–) 39,000	(–) 61,000	(–) 1000	(–) 1,01,000	(–) 2,46,500
Sawar	(–) 39,222	(+) 8600	(–) 37,650	(+) 3250	(–) 24,850	(–) 89,872	(–) 20,500	(–) 52,850	(–) 650	(–) 74,000	(–) 1,63,872
						1642–58					
Zat	(+) 1,03,000	(+) 98,000	(+) 31,000	(+) 56,000	(+) 18,500	(+) 3,06,500	(+) 71,000	(–) 6000	(+) 4500	(+) 69,500	(+) 3,76,000
Sawar	(+) 63,650	(+) 66,400	(+) 35,700	(+) 40,500	(+) 12,500	(+) 2,18,750	(+) 65,100	(–) 4300	(+) 3000	(+) 63,800	(+) 2,82,550

initial attempt to keep the mansab figures under control was foiled. During the second phase, taking advantage of the stabilized and peaceful conditions, Shahjahan tried to resume his policy of keeping a check upon wide expansion in the mansab, but the pressure for military activities was again built up in the last phase by the above-mentioned political developments, and again a much more wide expansion had to be made in the mansab figures.

The fact remains that Shahjahan proved his skill in giving promotions judiciously. He devised a method of granting more increments in sawar mansab than in zat. This feature is noted by M. Athar Ali in his article referred to earlier. This can be more fully appreciated with the help of Table 4.3.

The first thing that emerges from Table 4.3 is the predominance of sawar promotion over zat promotion. This indicates that perhaps Shahjahan was thinking in terms of exercising economy by adding less to the zat mansab, (as the salary against this was to be pocketed by the mansabdar) while a promotion in sawar was a direct addition to the military strength of the empire.

One may also note a sharp decline in promotion figures during the second phase, for obvious reasons. Yet the policy of giving more enhancement in sawar continues in this period too.

The tremendous rise in promotions during the last phase highlights the importance of the developments of this period. In the first phase, the problems were generally internal in nature, while this phase introduced developments of international importance. In a sense, the prestige of the Mughal empire was at stake before the external world. That is why, perhaps, the promotion figures almost doubled in the third phase.

Another significant aspect of Shahjahan's policy towards the mansab seems to be the maintenance of a certain proportion between zat and sawar mansab from the very beginning of his reign. As mentioned earlier, adopting a policy of moderation, the emperor was giving promotions in such a way that the major benefit should be shared by the state, without ignoring the zat mansab. As brought out earlier, the nobility had no permanent base in land. Its real strength lay in military contingents. Swift addition to the sawar mansab, therefore, would mean (*a*) maintaining huge contingents and thereby adding to the military strength of the empire, (*b*) adding to the institutional strength of the nobility, and contributing to the individual or group strength of the nobles, and (*c*) leading to a corresponding rise in the degree of the crown's dependence upon its nobility. Because of these implications, the sawar mansab had to be increased with caution. The famous rebellions of Shahjahan's reign confirm this doubt. Jujhar Singh Bundela and Raja Jagat Singh (who rose in rebellion) had the advantage of both land (being zamindars) and contingents (being mansabdars). Khan-e-Jahan Lodhi, on the other hand, is a specific case of higher sawar mansab. Enjoying the mansab of 7000/7000, 'hama do-aspa sih-aspa', he could easily think in terms of crossing swords with the imperial forces in case of dissatisfaction.

TABLE 4.3: TRENDS OF PROMOTIONS IN THE MANSAB

	Iranis	*Turanis*	*Afghans*	*Indian Muslims*	*Other Muslims*	*Rajputs*	*Marathas*	*Other Hindus*	*Total*
					1628–36				
Zat	43,900	26,300	7000	11,500	3000	15,500	2500	–	1,09,700
Sawar	63,400	35,150	14,400	17,750	4100	13,150	1550	–	1,49,500
					1637–41				
Zat	15,200	10,500	3700	700	2500	5100	–	100	37,800
Sawar	20,750,	19,050	7000	7600	2800	7900	–	–	65,100
					1642–58				
Zat	88,500	56,300	13,300	25,000	5100	42,800	1000	500	2,32,500
Sawar	95,280	57,000	16,500	30,800	4330	51,600	500	1200	2,57,210

Note: The figures given above have been obtained from the direct references of increments given in individual cases in the annual records of Lahori and Salih.

The submission, therefore, is that additions to sawar rank had their plus as well as minus points. That is why, perhaps, Shahjahan, despite of his moderation had to raise the zat mansab too along with the sawar, and thus tried to maintain some balance between these two. If we look at the total awards in Table 4.1, we will find that the total zat mansab was always more than the total sawar mansab by almost 125 per cent. In the second phase, though the mansab figures decline, this proportion remains stable. The considerable rise of the last phase in both ranks also did not disturb this proportion. By adding to the zat mansab, the nobility could be kept satisfied inasmuch as its personal maintenance was concerned.

So it may be tentatively suggested that although Shahjahan wanted to have larger contingents and therefore gave more promotions in sawar mansabs, he did maintain a certain proportion in between the zat and sawar mansabs throughout his reign.

Before making an assessment of the fortunes of the individual groups of the nobles during these changing political conditions, it will be relevant to say a word about the loss or gain of various ethnic groups with which these individual groups were ultimately associated.

IRANIS

From Table 4.1, it emerges that the share of Iranis in the total award of the mansab remained unsurpassed from the beginning till the end. The foremost reason for the favourable attitude towards this group was its commendable role in the brief succession tussle (see Chapter 3). The Iranis' sincerity, devotion and submission, along with their efficiency both in the battlefield and the administrative offices, have also been pointed out earlier to be the cause of their larger share in mansab figures. In this regard, one should also keep the fact in mind that the Iranis formed the single largest group among the Jahangiri nobles.[22] In view of this fact and their attitude towards the crown, Shahjahan had practically no ground to change the policy of favour to this group.

It may also be pointed out that the Iranis usually held a larger share in sawar mansab, except the last phase where their proportion becomes the same in both zat and sawar mansabs. During the first and second phases, they enjoyed more than 33 per cent of the total sawar mansab. This highlights the point that the sawar mansab was a matter of much concern to the crown and nobles alike. It was raised cautiously, keeping in view the degree of reliability that could be placed on an individual or a group of individuals. Since the Iranis had proved a higher degree of dependability from the days of Akbar, Shahjahan too confirmed his faith in them. That is probably why they held almost 33 per cent of the total sawar mansab under their control. However, their share in the total sawar mansab declined in the third phase.

It is also worth noting that there was hardly any rise in the proportionate share of Iranis in the zat award but a decline in the sawar award, if one compares the figures of the first and last phases. This means that mansabwise, the Iranis were pushed down slightly in the sawar mansab, with no special gain in the zat mansab. Numberwise too, there was no marked difference in their position in the first and last phases.[23] On these grounds, it may be surmised that the 'favour' to the Iranis means that they were being gradually confined to a particular level which they had reached in the opening years of this reign. They could not be thrown out of favour due to their utmost devotion and sincerity. Besides this, it would have been dangerous to violate the traditions of the past, which had marked the Iranis as a leading majority and the most powerful faction at Jahangir's court.[24] This point acquires more validity and strength when we examine the conditions of other groups of the mansab.

TURANIS

From the political developments mentioned in Chapter 3, it emerges that in the first phase the Turanis got lesser opportunities in military expeditions[25] as well as administrative offices.[26] That is probably why they shared a lesser proportion in the total mansab award,[27] as is evident from the figures in Table 4.1. It was less than half the share of the Iranis. But a notable rise in the proportion of the Turanis may be seen in the second phase. In spite of the decline in the total award of mansabs, they improved in both zat and sawar rank and emerged as the second-largest group in the nobility after the Iranis. This favour given to the Turanis in this phase is also evident from the percentage of reduction in their share (shown in Table 4.2). Among the leading racial groups, the smallest curtailment was made from the zat and sawar figures of the Turanis, while the largest curtailment was that of Iranis. This improvement in their condition confirms imperial favour, perhaps due to their excellent performance against the Persians,[28] and perhaps as a calculated attempt to raise them as a group parallel to the Iranis. This point gains further strength when we look at the figures of the last phase, when the difference between the share of the Iranis and the Turanis is reduced further.

It may also be noted that the share of the Turanis in the total sawar mansab exceeds their share in the total zat mansab in the first and second phases. However, in the third phase, it becomes equal. This underlines the rise of yet another group besides the Iranis as a second dependable faction. And this seems to be a favour to this group.

AFGHANS

As seen in Table 4.1 in 1628–36, the Afghans enjoyed almost 9 per cent of the total zat and 10 per cent of the total sawar mansab. These figures suggest the continuation of Jahangir's favourable policy in spite of the rebellion of Khan-e-Jahan.[29] But this rebellion must have alarmed Shahjahan and he would have taken extra precautions to eliminate further possibilities of opposition from this racial group.

In the second phase, when the mansab awards declined drastically due to the above-mentioned reasons, the Afghans in particular had to suffer a lot.

From Table 4.1, it emerges that their share in the total zat falls from 9 per cent (of the preceding phase) to almost 7 per cent. Their decline in the total sawar mansab is still more sharp. From 10 per cent they fall to almost 6.5 per cent of the total award of sawar mansabs. This confirms the doubt that Shahjahan had become suspicious. Therefore, he tried to curtail their power, which rested mainly in the sawar mansab. Hence the greater reduction in their share of sawars.[30]

However, the crown and the Afghan nobility, being interdependent upon each other, tried to improve the condition—Shahjahan by giving them opportunity, and the Afghans by proving their loyalty. As said earlier, in the Balkh-Badakhshan expeditions and later on in Qandhar, they were given adequate representation,[31] and served the crown with all sincerity. The reward for these services may be seen in their rising proportion in the total zat and sawar mansab distributed during this last phase (Table 4.1). This reflects the increasing confidence of the crown in the Afghan nobility. The promotions given to them during this phase (Table 4.3) also indicate their rise. The rise of the Afghans in the last phase highlights the feature of interdependence between the crown and the nobility; simultaneously, it confirms that the rebellion of Khan-e-Jahan Lodhi did not cause any permanent breach between Shahjahan and the Afghans.

INDIAN MUSLIMS

The favourable attitude of Shahjahan towards Indian Muslims is evident from the account in Chapter 3. Their share in mansab awards simply confirms their enviable position. The figures in Table 4.1 suggest a constant rise in their proportion in both zat and sawar ranks. More important is the fact that their share in the sawar mansab was never less than their share in the zat mansab. In 1637–41, which was the period of universal decline, Indian Muslims in fact gained in sawar mansab (Table 4.2). So it may be said that after the Turanis, Indian Muslims were the recipients of special imperial favours.

This favourable attitude towards Indian Muslims was the result of their sincerity and devotion to the Mughal crown at all critical moments. From the battlefield to administrative jobs in almost all capacities, they proved their worth and were marked with special favour.[32] Hence, their rising proportion in mansab awards was the reflection of their services, which confirmed them as confident and reliable servants of the crown.

RAJPUTS

As a keynote of state policy, the Rajputs were always kept in good proportion throughout Shahjahan's reign. Their share in the total mansab grant remains almost the same, in spite of some notable fluctuations in the total mansab figures (Table 4.1).

Decline in the second phase also did not cause any special harm to this group, as other important factions like Iranis and Indian Muslims also had to share the same fate (see Table 4.2). This minimal loss, however, did not affect their noticeable proportionate share in the total mansab figures. In the third phase, their gains, specially in sawar award, are worth noting. This increased their total share in the sawar mansab over their total share in the zat mansab (Table 4.1). It may also be noted that their share in the total promotion figures (pertaining to the three phases as shown in Table 4.3) was always greater than the rest of the nobles (excepting Iranis and Turanis). The gradual rise in their proportion in these promotion figures from the first to the last phase again confirms Shahjahan's faith in this group.

This position of confidence, which the Rajputs enjoyed throughout this period, was mainly due to their excellent military services and due to the goodwill they earned by serving the Mughal crown rising above racial and religious considerations. Their active cooperation and solid support to the state, not only against the Persians,[33] Uzbeks[34] and others,[35] but also against their own racial members[36] who rebelled against the crown, are enough to justify their high proportion in the total mansab figures of various phases of Shahjahan's reign.

MARATHAS

That political developments had their reflection upon the fluctuating figures of the mansab of some ethnic group seems to be more true in the case of Marathas. As is shown earlier, the Deccan wars posed an urgency to accommodate and promote the Marathas in the Mughal nobility. During the first phase, therefore, almost 12 per cent of the total zat and 11 per cent of the total sawar mansab was held by them. The extraordinary favour shown to this group, however, started fading away with the settlement of Deccan affairs. As the political and military utility of this group decreased, their share in the total mansab figures declined accordingly (Table 4.1). The figures of Table 4.2 show these reverses in their share, which cannot be compared with the condition of any other group, not even the Afghans. In the second and the third phases, the share of the Marathas in the total promotion figures also declined rapidly (Table 4.3).

On the basis of these mansab figures, it may be added that the Marathas were never taken as confidants and dependable servants of the crown, because at the very beginning of their rise, their share in the total sawar mansab was lesser than their share in the total zat mansab (Table 4.1). The decline in the second phase confirms this (Table 4.2). The curtailment in their sawar mansab exceeds the deduction in their zat mansab. This attitude of Shahjahan might have some basis in the treacherous role of the Marathas from the very beginning. That is why, perhaps, we cannot compare the Marathas with the Rajputs vis-à-vis the Mughal crown.

On the basis of the above, it may be concluded that the rise or decline in the share of the nobles in total mansab awards was closely linked with the changing political conditions and with their political and military utility for the state. Racial and religious factors, generally, did not occupy a pivotal place in regulating the proportion of the nobles in the total mansab figures. It was basically the quality and period of service which determined the fortunes of mansabdars.

THE ZAMINDARS

Being an essential element of the political and economic structures, zamindars also deserve some attention vis-à-vis the mansab. That they formed a sizeable group within the nobility is evident from Table 2.5. Though drawn from different racial and religious groups, they seem to have acted, generally, as a powerful political faction. The imperial attitude towards this group also depended upon political and military conditions. The basic difference between zamindars and other mansabdars lay in the former's attachment to land. Thus, the mansab was an additional source of political, military and economic strength for the zamindars. Land being their mainstay, they were not wholely dependent upon the crown as the other mansabdars were. And from this peculiarity emerges the basic difference between their attitude towards the crown and vice versa. The fact that most of the rebellions of this period were led by zamindars confirms the basic clash of interests between the crown and this group. The mansab was a device which added to the prestige and resources of the zamindars and simultaneously multiplied the possibilities of their dependence upon the Mughal crown. Therefore, they could be tackled more easily through mansabs. Besides, this, Shahjahan seems to have adopted an attitude towards this group which had far-reaching consequences. Although, technically, the faujdar was responsible for the maintenance of law and order, this job was being assigned to a zamindar outside his own territory. Influential zamindars like Mirza Raja Jai Singh were asked by the emperor to suppress rebellions and to assist a jagirdar in the collection of the revenues. For example, in November 1632, the raja was ordered to crush the rebellion of Kari Singh and Kalliyandas (the local zamindars) in pargana Roshanpur and Naraina which was the jagir of Ratan Singh.[37] When Sardol Kachwaha created problems in the jagir of Yazdani in September 1637, the raja was sent to assist the jagirdar in revenue realization.[38] Similarly, in 1640 the raja was asked to assist the staff of the jagir of Yaminuddaulah Asaf Khan in realizing the revenue.[39] Besides this, there are many other cases where Raja Jai Singh's services were required for revenue realization from khalisa land.[40] Thus, it seems that an attempt was made to treat zamindars more as mansabdars and less as zamindars.

The share of zamindars in the total mansab awards (*a*) suggests their status in the Mughal hierarchy, (*b*) shows the degree of reliability that could be placed in them, and (*c*) gives the proportion they bore with other groups of mansabdars. The fluctuation in their share, on the other hand, highlights the extent of their relevance to changing conditions. Table 4.4 gives a rough idea of their share in the total award.

From the figures given in Table 4.4, it becomes clear that throughout this reign there was but a nominal fluctuation in the share of zamindars

TABLE 4.4: SHARE OF ZAMINDARS IN THE TOTAL MANSAB AWARDS

	Rajputs	*Marathas*	*Indian Muslims*	*Afghans*	*Total*
			1628–36		
Zat	1,12,500,	92,500	3500	2000	2,10,500
Sawar	81,100	72,400	2200	1000	1,56,700
			1637–41		
Zat	75,000	35,000	4000	2000	1,16,000
Sawar	61,700	21,300	2900	1000	86,900
			1642–58		
Zat	1,38,000	29,500	7500	2000	1,77,000
Sawar	1,20,900	16,900	5900	1000	1,44,700

in the total mansab award. It ranged between 17 and 25 per cent in both zat and sawar ranks. This means that political developments at different times did not have much effect upon the basic policy of appeasement and friendliness towards this group.

The second notable thing is that Rajputs formed the only dominant faction of this class. Due to the Deccan wars, when the emperor adopted a favourable attitude towards the Deccanis, a tremendous rise can be seen in the number as well as mansab figures of the Maratha zamindars. However, despite this political exigency, they could not replace the Rajputs.

Equally important is the constant decline in the share of the Maratha zamindars after 1636. This further highlights the difference between the Rajput zamindars and Maratha zamindars vis-à-vis the crown. Perhaps the rise or decline of the latter was not taken seriously as a matter of policy towards the zamindars. They were welcomed in service when the occasion required, and were gradually eliminated when their requirement diminished. On the other hand, the consistency in the favourable attitude towards the Rajputs, in spite even of rebellions from their group, suggests that it was basically around the Rajputs that the policy towards the zamindars was made to revolve.

Shahjahan's favourable policy towards the Rajput zamindars is further confirmed from a constant rise in their share in both zat and sawar mansab from the beginning till the end of his reign. In the first phase, they held more than one-half of the total zat and sawar award given to the zamindars. In the succeeding phase, in spite of a notable decline in the mansab figures, the share of Rajput zamindars in the sawar mansab rose to more than 66 per cent of the total sawar mansab of zamindars. The last phase shows an even more favourable trend, in which their share in the total zat and sawar mansab of zamindars rose to more than 67 per cent. It should also be noted that the Rajput zamindars held a higher proportion in sawar mansab than in zat. This confirms their sound position vis-à-vis the crown; this faith was never shaken even though there was some problem raised by them in every phase.

This favourable attitude was obviously because of the maintenance of the good traditions of the past both by the Rajput zamindars and the Mughal crown. As was shown above in Chapter 3, they always sided in large numbers with the crown, even against a Rajput rebel. Inside as well as outside India, they rendered remarkable service to the Mughal empire.[41] The devotion and sincerity of this group justify the favourable policy of Shahjahan towards the Rajput zamindars.

The figures given earlier also highlight Shahjahan's favourable inclination towards the Indian Muslim zamindars. Although there can be no comparison between them and the Rajputs, the fact remains that from just a marginal position in the first phase, they made notable progress in the second and third phases. Both in zat and sawar mansabs, their share almost doubled what they held in the first phase. But their proportion in the total sawar mansab awarded to zamindars in the last phase was less than the proportion they bore in the total zat mansab. This suggests a higher degree of reliance on Rajput zamindars. Afghan zamindars, however, were not given any notable favour from the first to the third phases.

Another point worth nothing in this regard is that the major portion of the share that the zamindars held in the total awarded mansabs during different phases was occupied exclusively by the khanazads of all sections of zamindars. A trend of constant rise in the proportion of khanazads in both mansabs may be seen. In the last phase, they occupied more than 80 per cent of the total zat and sawar award given to zamindar. The figures are given in Table 4.5.

It is thus clear that khanazads occupied the largest share in the mansab award given to zamindars. Besides this, the share of Rajput zamindars was

TABLE 4.5: SHARE OF KHANAZAD ZAMINDARS IN THE TOTAL MANSAB AWARD OF ZAMINDARS

Total award of zamindars		*Share of khanazads*			
		Rajputs	*Marathas*	*Indian Muslims*	*Total*
			1628–36		
Zat	2,10,500	1,00,000	41,000	1500	1,42,500
Sawar	1,56,700	74,100	30,000	1200	1,05,300
			1637–41		
Zat	1,16,000	64,500	19,000	3000	86,500
Sawar	86,900	55,100	12,000	2500	69,600
			1642–58		
Zat	1,77,000	1,22,500	20,500	6500	1,49,500
Sawar	1,44,700	1,09,100	13,000	5300	1,27,400

the highest among khanazad zamindars, and it kept increasing in each succeeding phase. On the other hand, the proportion of Maratha khanazads gradually declined. But the proportion of Indian Muslim khanazads improved continuously from the first to the last phase. (Afghans do not appear in this category.)

On this basis, it may be said that Shahjahan's policy towards the zamindars was based mainly upon the attitude of various groups within this faction. In the case of those who had given the impression of loyalty and devotion, he reaffirmed his faith and favoured the tried individuals and their descendants, like the Rajputs. However, in the cases of defaulters like the Marathas, he kept trying new people. The nominal share of Afghans remained the privilege of the non-khanazads. The higher proportion of khanazad zamindars in the total award of zamindars is due to the high figures of the Rajputs. In other words, khanazad Rajputs occupied the bulk of the share of zamindars in both zat and sawar mansabs during all the three phases of Shahjahan's period. Their share in the sawar mansab was always greater than their share in the zat mansab, which confirms the higher degree of trust and confidence reposed in Rajput khanazads among the zamindars.

DECCANIS

The share of Deccanis in the total award of mansabs and the fluctuation therein may be seen in Table 4.6.

The figures in Table 4.6 make it clear that it was when the Deccanis could not be ignored for political reasons, they got a good representation in both zat and sawar mansab. In the first phase they enjoyed almost 17 per cent of the total zat and 14 per cent of the total sawar award. Their share in both ranks declined in the succeeding phase, as their political and military utility had come down after the settlement of Deccan affairs. Here, it may

TABLE 4.6: SHARE OF DECCANIS IN THE TOTAL MANSAB AWARDS

	Iranis	*Turanis*	*Afghans*	*Indian Muslims*	*Other Muslims*	*Marathas*	*Other Hindus*	*Total*
				1628–36				
Zat	7000	9000	11,500	10,000	43,000	62,500	1000	1,44,000
Sawar	3000	7000	9500	5500	26,750	47,550	800	1,00,100
				1637–41				
Zat	8000	9000	2500	7000	16,000	20,500	-	63,000
Sawar	5000	7000	1500	4000	10,500	10,200	-	38,200
				1642–58				
Zat	9000	11,500	2500	15,500	25,000	16,000	-	79,500
Sawar	9500	15,000	1500	10,000	16,700	7400	-	60,100

be noted that this decline is mostly because of the heavy curtailment in the share of the Marathas, other Muslims and Afghans. In the last phase too, their share declines in the total zat mansab; however, in sawar mansab they maintained the same proportion which they enjoyed in the second phase (viz., around 7.7 per cent). This was mainly due to the rise of the share of the Iranis, Turanis and Indian Muslims in the total sawar award.

It is thus quite clear that the first phase was the peak period of power of Deccanis in the Mughal nobility. This gives strength to the hypothesis that political developments and diplomatic requirements cast their reflections on the fluctuating figures of the mansab.

FAMILY GROUPS AND THE MANSAB

Coming to family groups, it may be said at the very outset that for constructing the family lineage, I have depended mainly upon *Zakhirat-ul-Khawanin* and *Maasir-ul-Umara*. Sufficient information is available in these works to draws family tables of various ethnic groups of the nobles. With these tables in hand, an attempt has been made to make a rough estimate of the share of different family groups during the three phases of Shahjahan's reign. Only blood relations have been considered as far as the constituents of a family are concerned. This obviously eliminates matrimonial relations. Last, only mansabs of 1000 zat and above have been considered for this rough estimate, because this study is limited to that category only.

IRANIS

It would be justified to begin with the Iranis, because they formed the leading faction of the nobility, numberwise as well as mansabwise.

First, let us have a look at the mansabs held by these groups, calculated according to the above-mentioned method, shown in Table 4.7.

TABLE 4.7: SHARE OF FAMILY GROUPS IN MANSABS: IRANIS

	1628–36	*1637–41*	*1642–58*
		Asaf Khan Yaminuddaulah's family	
Zat	31,000	25,000	35,000
Sawar	36,100	33,400	31,300
		Rustam Khan Safavi's family	
Zat	15,000	13,000	21,500
Sawar	10,400	8450	20,500
		Ali Mardan Khan Amir-ul-Umara's family	
Zat	—	7000	15,000
Sawar	—	10,000	15,900

(contd.)

	1628–36	*1637–41*	*1642–58*
		Islam Khan Mashhadi's family	
Zat	5000	5000	14,000
Sawar	10,000	8000	14,600
		Azam Khan's family	
Zat	7500	7500	12,500
Sawar	6500	6600	10,500
		Khalil Ullah Khan's family	
Zat	6000	5000	14,500
Sawar	3700	4000	10,700
		Iftikhar Khan Turkman's family	
Zat	6500	8000	11,000
Sawar	4800	6750	9500
		Illahwardi Khan's family	
Zat	7000	8000	8500
Sawar	6000	7000	6000
		Mahabat Khan's family	
Zat	14,000	7000	5000
Sawar	24,000	11,000	3000
		Saif Khan Mirza Safi's family	
Zat	6000	6000	5500
Sawar	4600	4600	1450
		Zain Khan Koka's family	
Zat	4500	4000	8000
Sawar	3200	3000	6800
		Khwaja Abul Hasan's family	
Zat	9000	3000	5500
Sawar	8000	2000	2200
		Qasim Khan Namkin's family	
Zat	4000	4000	5500
Sawar	2200	2300	3100
		Baqar Khan Najm-e-Sani's family	
Zat	6000	7000	2500
Sawar	5500	5700	1000
		Lashkar Khan Abul Hasan Mashhadi's family	
Zat	8500	4000	4000
Sawar	7800	3500	1700

(contd.)

	1628–36	*1637–41*	*1642–58*
		Mirza Khan Manochahar's family	
Zat	4000	3000	4000
Sawar	2500	2000	3250
		Asaf Khan Jafar Beg's family	
Zat	4000	1500	2500
Sawar	3100	1500	1500
		Afzal Khan Allami's family	
Zat	7000	9500	4000
Sawar	4100	4600	3000
		Safshikan Mirza Lashkari's family	
Zat	6000	2500	3500
Sawar	3800	2000	2600
		Jansipar Khan Turkman's family	
Zat	6000	1000	–
Sawar	7600	600	–
		Hakim Hammam's family	
Zat	3000	1000	1000
Sawar	500	200	200
		Qazalbash Khan Afshar's family	
Zat	2000	3000	6000
Sawar	1000	3000	6000
		Zulfigar Khan Khanlar's family	
Zat	1500	1500	5000
Sawar	800	800	6800
		Zabardast Khan's family	
Zat	1500	1500	4500
Sawar	1000	1000	2500

Out of these, the family of Asaf Khan seems to have occupied a distinct position. Its collective share in both zat and sawar mansabs was the highest among the Iranis throughout Shahjahan's reign. Other family groups in a majority seem to have improved their position from the first to the last phases.

A tremendous rise in mansab figures may be noted in some cases. This is true for the families of Khalil Ullah Khan, Ali Mardan Khan, Islam Khan, Qazalbash Khan, Zulfiqar Khan, Zabardast Khan, and others. Some families seem to have suffered in the total share, such as those of Mahabat Khan, Khwaja Abul Hasan, Asaf Khan Jafar Beg, Baqar Khan Najm-e-Sani, Lashkar Khan Abul Hasan Mashhadi, Afzal Khan, and others. A third set of those family groups may be seen which were maintained at almost the same levels where they stood at the beginning of the reign. The families of Saif Khan Mirza Safi, Mirza Khan Manochahar, Qasim Khan Namkin and Ilahwardi Khan may be included in this category.

If we try to assess the position of Irani families vis-à-vis their whole racial group, we will find that in the first phase these families occupied more than half of the total zat held by this ethnic group. In the total sawar mansab of the Iranis, their share was much larger, almost 66 per cent. In the succeeding phase, they improved their share among the Iranis further. However, in the last phase, these family groups had to suffer a marginal setback. Yet on the whole they seem to have enjoyed the largest share in the mansab held by the Irani faction as a whole. In other words, the largest proportion of the Iranis as an ethnic group in the total mansab award depended mainly upon the shares of their family groups.

Among the family groups too, they emerged as the strongest faction. In all three phases, they enjoyed more than 33 per cent of the total zat and sawar mansabs held by different family groups. This confirms the stronghold of Irani family groups over all other groups and factions.

These indications get reinforced by the data in Tables 4.8 and 4.9.

TABLE 4.8: POSTION OF IRANIS AMONG ALL FAMILY GROUPS

	Total share of family groups		*Total share of Irani families*
		1628–36	
Zat	4,34,000		1,65,000
Sawar	3,94,600		1,57,200
		1637–41	
Zat	3,25,500		1,38,000
Sawar	3,09,850		1,32,000
		1642–58	
Zat	5,46,500		1,98,500
Sawar	4,81,550		1,64,100

TABLE 4.9: IRANI FAMILY GROUPS VIS-À-VIS THEIR RACIAL GROUP

	Total share of their racial group		*Total share of Irani Families*
		1628–36	
Zat	2,48,000		1,65,000
Sawar	2,08,122		1,57,200
		1637–41	
Zat	1,97,500		1,38,000
Sawar	1,68,900		1,32,000
		1642–58	
Zat	3,00,500		1,98,500
Sawar	2,32,550		1,64,100

TURANIS

The importance of Turani family groups is evident from their share in the mansab, shown familywise in Table 4.10.

From the figures in Table 4.10, it becomes evident that Said Khan's family held the highest share in both zat and sawar mansabs. Furthermore, unlike the Iranis, almost all the Turani families multiplied their strength mansabwise in all three phases. This seems to be the only family group which really gained a lot during the second phase, when all other groups had to lose. It may also be noted that almost half the families enjoyed a higher sawar rank than their zat mansab. So these facts give more strength to the point submitted earlier that a really favourable attitude of the crown can be discerned easily in the case of the Turanis. They were being raised at racial as well as family levels from the second phase onwards.

TABLE 4.10: SHARE OF FAMILY GROUPS IN THE MANSAB: TURANIS'

	1628–36	*1637–41*	*1642–58*
		Abdullah Khan Firoze Jang's family	
Zat	11,500	12,000	18,500
Sawar	8600	9000	18,300
		Said Khan Zafar Jang's family	
Zat	11,500	10,000	19,500
Sawar	12,300	14,400	21,100
		Isa Tarkhan's family	
Zat	5000	6000	9000
Sawar	5000	6500	13,500
		Khan-e-Dauran Nusrat Jang's family	
Zat	5000	6000	11,500
Sawar	10,000	12,000	14,900
		Najabat Khan Mirza Shuja's family	
Zat	3000	4000	7500
Sawar	2000	4000	5200
		Qulij Khan's family	
Zat	4000	6000	8500
Sawar	5000	7500	11,500
		Uzbek Khan Nazar Bahadur Kheshgi's family	
Zat	1000	2000	4500
Sawar	1000	1400	4000
		Khusrau's (son of Nazar Muhammad Khan) family	
Zat	–	–	17,500
Sawar	–	–	6100

TABLE 4.11: POSITION OF TURANIS AMONG ALL FAMILY GROUPS

	Total share of family groups	*Total share of Turani Families*
	1628–36	
Zat	4,34,000	41,000
Sawar	3,94,600	43,900
	1637–41	
Zat	3,25,500	46,000
Sawar	3,09,850	54,800
	1642–58	
Zat	5,46,500	96,500
Sawar	4,81,550	94,600

TABLE 4.12: TURANI FAMILY GROUPS VIS-À-VIS THEIR RACIAL GROUP

	Total share of their racial group	*Total share of Turani families*
	1628–36	
Zat	1,22,000	41,000
Sawar	1,01,100	43,900
	1637–41	
Zat	1,21,000	46,000
Sawar	1,09,700	54,800
	1642–58	
Zat	2,19,000	96,500
Sawar	1,76,100	94,600

However, their strength cannot be compared with that of Iranis, who had always outnumbered them. But an improvement in the position of the Turani family groups may be noted in Tables 4.11 and 4.12.

It emerges from the figures in Tables 4.11 and 4.12 that, starting from a lower point, the Turanis went on improving their position in the second and last phases among family groups.

Equally interesting is the fact that out of the total mansab enjoyed by the Turanis as a racial group, the share of their family groups is almost 33 per cent in zat throughout the reign, and in sawar mansab it is 33 per cent in the first phase and about 50 per cent in the second and third phases. Thus, contrary to the case of Iranis, the share of Turanis as a racial group in the mansab did not depend much upon their family groups.

AFGHANS

Coming to the Afghans, let us first look at the share of their leading family groups in the mansab in Table 4.13.

On the basis of the figures in Table 4.13, it may be said that in the first phase the leading family groups were those of Khan-e-Jahan Lodhi and Darya Khan Rohila. The effects of the former's rebellion and the latter's active support to it may be seen in the second phase. Though, as said above, the Afghans did not suffer much as a racial group, yet Khan-e-Jahan's family had to pay quite heavily for it. In the second and third phases, not a single member of his family could rise up to the level of a hazari. Darya Khan's family was next to that of Khan-e-Jahan's. But mainly due to the sincere efforts of Bahadur Khan, his family again rose to eminence in the last phase and may be regarded as the leading family among the Afghans.

TABLE 4.13: SHARE OF FAMILY GROUPS IN THE MANSAB: AFGHANS'

	1628–36	*1637–41*	*1642–58*
		Rashid Khan Ansari's family	
Zat	4000	5000	9500
Sawar	3600	5000	9500
		Shahbaz Khan Rohila's family	
Zat	5000	2500	2500
Sawar	3400	2000	2000
		Muhammad Khan Niyazi's family	
Zat	4500	4500	5000
Sawar	4000	4000	5000
		Khan-e-Jahan Lodhi's family	
Zat	9000	–	–
Sawar	14,900	–	–
		Darya Khan Rohila's family	
Zat	9000	5000	13,000
Sawar	8700	7700	16,300
		Mubariz Khan Rohila's family	
Zat	3500	4000	5000
Sawar	3500	4000	4600
		Nazr Bahadur Kheshgi's family	
Zat	2000	3500	8500
Sawar	1500	2300	8900
		Sher Khan Taunur's family	
Zat	6500	–	–
Sawar	6000	–	–
		Sher Khan Tarin's family (zamindar)	
Zat	2000	2000	3000
Sawar	1000	1000	1600

Among the Afghans, one may also find some families which improved their mansabs throughout the reign, namely, those of Rashid Khan, Muhammad Khan Niyazi, Mubariz Khan Rohila, Nazr Bahadur Kheshgi and Sher Khan Tarin. On the whole, only two families out of nine had to lose in mansabs; the rest of them increased their shares. This confirms the view that Shahjahan was not hostile towards the Afghans as a racial faction. Even the family of Darya Khan was allowed to rise as a single eminent group among the Afghans in the third phase.

The share of Afghan families in the total mansab enjoyed by different family groups is more or less the same as that of the Afghans, as a racial group, held in the total mansab award of different phases.

The position of Afghan family groups is strong vis-à-vis their own racial group. Their share in the total mansab of the Afghans, as a racial group, is more than half in zat mansab throughout the reign, while in sawar mansab it increases from 50 per cent in the first phase to more than 67 per cent in the subsequent two phases. This means that a family rebellion did not cause any damage to the overall position of the Afghan family groups.

Tables 4.14 and 4.15 substantiate these tentative suggestions.

TABLE 4.14: POSITION OF AFGHANS AMONG ALL FAMILY GROUPS

	Total share of family groups	*Total share of Afghan families*
	1628–36	
Zat	4,34,000	45,500
Sawar	3,94,600	46,600
	1637–41	
Zat	3,25,500	26,500
Sawar	3,09,850	26,000
	1642–58	
Zat	5,46,500	46,500
Sawar	4,81,550	47,900

TABLE 4.15: AFGHAN FAMILY GROUPS VIS-À-VIS THEIR RACIAL GROUP

	Total share of their racial group	*Total share of Afghan families*
	1628–36	
Zat	80,500	45,500
Sawar	70,950	46,600
	1637–41	
Zat	44,000	26,500
Sawar	33,300	26,000
	1642–58	
Zat	75,000	46,500
Sawar	69,000	47,900

INDIAN MUSLIMS

Among Indian Muslims, the family of Syed Khan-e-Jahan Barha occupied a distinguished place. This group started from 5000 zat, 10,000 sawars and finally attained 12,000 zat, 14,500 sawars in the last phase, without any loss. This suggests especial favour shown to this family. The families of Akbar Quli Gakkhar, Syed Bayazid, Ikhlas Khan Shaikh Farid, Murtaza Khan Syed Nizam and Dindar Khan Abdul Wahid were also extended great favour. None of these suffered any setback, but went on gaining ascendancy in the mansab throughout the reign. These observations may be confirmed from Table 4.16.

TABLE 4.16: SHARE OF FAMILY GROUPS IN THE MANSAB: INDIAN MUSLIMS

	1628–36	*1637–41*	*1642–58*
		Akbar Quli Gakkhar's family	
Zat	1500	1500	4000
Sawar	1200	1500	3400
		Hizbar Khan Barha's family	
Zat	5000	5000	3000
Sawar	1800	2000	1800
		Syed Bayazid's family	
Zat	6000	4000	10,000
Sawar	2700	8000	11,300
		Syed Diler Khan Barha's family	
Zat	4000	–	3000
Sawar	3000	–	3000
		Syed Yaqub Bukhari's family	
Zat	2500	–	–
Sawar	1700	–	–
		Ikhlas Khan Shaikh Farid's family	
Zat	5500	5500	9000
Sawar	3300	3300	6300
		Syed Khan-e-Jahan Barha's family	
Zat	5000	5000	12,000
Sawar	10,000	10,000	14,500
		Murtaza Khan Syed Nizam's family	
Zat	3000	3000	4000
Sawar	2000	2000	2700

(contd.)

	1628–36	*1637–41*	*1642–58*
		Mahmud Khan's family	
Zat	3000	–	1000
Sawar	1000	–	1000
		Dindar Khan Abdul Wahid's family	
Zat	–	1000	2000
Sawar	–	650	1650
		Syed Muhammad son of Syed Afzal's family	
Zat	–	–	2000
Sawar	–	–	1100
		Syed Jalal Bukhari s/o Muhammad Bukhari's family	
Zat	–	–	8500
Sawar	–	–	2500

The data in Table 4.16 suggest that most of these groups made notable progress in the third phase. In the second phase, they generally had to remain content with their mansabs of the first phase. It is worth noting here that with the exception of Syed Bayazid's family, no reduction was made in any other case. The families of Akbar Quli and Hizbar Khan seem to have gained 300 and 200 sawars respectively. Even Bayazid's group suffered a loss of 2000 zat, but made a gain of 5300 sawars during this phase. This point becomes more meaningful if we bear in mind that during this period a large number of family groups among the Iranis, Afghans, Rajputs and Marathas had to suffer setbacks in mansabs. Turanis and Indian Muslims virtually seem to have been exempted from this extensive curtailment, and this obviously hints at special treatment extended to them.

The position of Indian Muslims among other family groups and in their own racial group may be explained with the help of Tables 4.17 and 4.18.

TABLE 4.17: POSITION OF INDIAN MUSLIMS AMONG ALL FAMILY GROUPS

	Total share of family groups	*Total share of Indian Muslim families*
	1628–36	
Zat	4,34,000	35,500
Sawar	3,94,600	26,700
	1637–41	
Zat	3,25,500	25,000
Sawar	3,09,850	27,450
	1642–58	
Zat	5,46,500	58,500
Sawar	4,81,550	49,250

TABLE 4.18: INDIAN MUSLIM FAMILY GROUPS' VIS-À-VIS THEIR RACIAL GROUP

	Total share of their racial group	*Total share of Indian Muslim families*
	1628–36	
Zat	68,500	35,500
Sawar	48,700	26,700
	1637–41	
Zat	58,000	25,000
Sawar	51,950	27,450
	1642–58	
Zat	1,14,000	58,500
Sawar	92,450	49,250

It seems that, like the Afghans, Indian Muslim families also enjoyed more or less the same proportion among the family groups, which they, as a racial group, held in the total awarded mansab during the three phases.

These family groups shared more or less half the total share of their racial group in both zat and sawar mansabs in all three phases. This means that the share of Indian Muslims in the total award was not exclusively based upon the share of their family groups, as was the case with Iranis. Individual nobles also enjoyed favour and shared a good proportion of mansabs.

RAJPUTS

Like the Iranis, one may find a large number of family groups among Rajputs which held a relatively greater share of mansabs. The share of these family groups is shown in Table 4.19.

At a glance, one may notice the dominant positions of the families of Rana Karan, Raja Gaj Singh, Bir singh Dev Bundela, Rao Ratan Hara and Raja Jai Singh in the first phase. During the second phase, with the exception of Gaj Singh's family, all these groups had to lose in both zat and sawar mansabs, which highlights extra favour to the house of Jodhpur. The greatest sufferer, however, was the family of Bir Singh Dev Bundela (for well-known reasons). In spite of a great deduction of 14,000 zat and 12,400 sawars, this family still enjoyed a sound position among the above-mentioned losing groups. Obviously an effective check was exercised upon them: they were not totally deprived of favour, but certainly unseated from the prestigious positions they had enjoyed under Jahangir.

Besides these families which enjoyed a big share in mansabs from the beginning of Shahjahan's reign, some groups may be noticed which doubled their share in mansabs by the end of this reign. A striking example of this kind is the family of Raja Gopal Das Gaur. This group, starting from 4500 zat and 3000 sawars, reached 15,000 zat and 18,900 sawars in the last phase, and that too without any loss in the second phase. The families of Kishan

TABLE 4.19: SHARE OF FAMILY GROUPS IN MANSABS: RAJPUTS

	1628–36	*1637–41*	*1642–58*
		Raja Gaj Singh's family	
Zat	13,000	16,500	23,500
Sawar	9300	15,500	21,500
		Rao Sur Bhurtiya's family	
Zat	6000	3000	8000
Sawar	4500	2100	6500
		Raja Jai Singh's family	
Zat	10,500	6000	10,000
Sawar	6500	5700	12,900
		Rao Ratan Hara's family	
Zat	12,000	6000	10,000
Sawar	10,200	5500	9000
		Bir Narain Badgujar's family	
Zat	4000	4000	2000
Sawar	2100	2500	1500
		Kishan Singh Bhadoriya's family	
Zat	1000	1000	3500
Sawar	600	600	2800
		Bir Singh Dev Bundela's family	
Zat	22,000	8000	10,500
Sawar	17,800	5400	9900
		Rai Sal Darbari's family	
Zat	3500	1000	1000
Sawar	2200	500	500
		Pirthiraj Rathor's family	
Zat	2000	2000	3000
Sawar	1000	1700	2500
		Gopal Das Gaur's family	
Zat	4500	6500	15,000
Sawar	3000	5000	18,900
		Raja Basu's family	
Zat	3000	3000	6000
Sawar	500	2000	4500
		Rao Chanda's family	
Zat	3500	1500	5500
Sawar	2500	1000	3200

(contd.)

	1628–36	*1637–41*	*1642–58*
		Rana Karan's family	
Zat	13,000	8000	24,000
Sawar	11,500	7000	15,500
		Rawal Ponja's family	
Zat	1000	1500	2500
Sawar	500	1500	2500
		Ramdas Narauri's family	
Zat	2000	3000	1500
Sawar	1000	1600	1000

Singh Bhadoriya, Raja Basu, Rawal Ponja, etc., may also be included in this category.

With a few exceptions, almost all the Rajput families gained in mansabs in the third phase. The figures rise notably in the cases of Rana Karan, Gopal Das Gaur and Gaj Singh's families. Bir Singh Bundela's family too was raised to the level of the leading groups. Raja Jagat Singh's rebellion during this phase had hardly any effect upon the mansabwise status of Raja Basu's family. On the contrary, during this period, its share in zat and sawar mansabs seems to have doubled.

Among the losers in this entire reign, one can name the families of Bir Singh Dev Bundela, Rai Sal Darbari, Bir Narain Badgujar and Ramdas Narauri. In all these cases, their shares in mansabs gradually declined from the first to the last phase.

Rajput family groups may be regarded as the second-largest faction after the Iranis. In the first phase, in the total share of all the family groups, they held almost 20 per cent of the zat and 17 per cent of the sawar mansabs. In the two subsequent phases, their proportion remained more or less the same.

Their collective mansab figures suggest that among the Rajputs, as a racial group, they occupied a share which was much larger than that of Iranis. So it may be said that the share of Rajputs in the total awarded mansab was basically a family-based award, as was the case with Iranis. The larger share of these families in the sawar mansab, as compared to the zat mansab, suggests that Shahjahan was perhaps trying to keep most of the sawars under the control of some trusted families. This makes more sense if we bear in mind the privileged position of these zamindars, who had strong base in land. The sawar mansab, thus, was a source of additional strength for them. Shahjahan, therefore, extended this favour to this class very cautiously. The families of such confident Rajput mansabdars as Gaj Singh, Jai Singh and Gopal Das Gaur only held larger sawar mansabs, and that too only in the last phase.

TABLE 4.20: POSITIONS OF RAJPUTS AMONG ALL FAMILY GROUPS

	Total share of family groups	*Total share of Rajput families*
	1628–36	
Zat	4,34,000	88,000
Sawar	3,94,600	73,200
	1637–41	
Zat	3,25,500	71,000
Sawar	3,09,850	57,600
	1642–58	
Zat	5,46,500	1,26,000
Sawar	4,81,550	1,12,700

TABLE 4.21: RAJPUTS FAMILY GROUPS VIS-À-VIS THEIR RACIAL GROUP

	Total share of their racial groups	*Total share of Rajput families*
	1628–36	
Zat	1,21,500	88,000
Sawar	86,900	73,200
	1637–41	
Zat	82,500	71,000
Sawar	66,400	57,600
	1642–58	
Zat	1,53,500	1,26,000
Sawar	1,31,500	1,12,700

The positions of Rajputs among all family groups and in their own racial group becomes more clear from Tables 4.20 and 4.21.

MARATHAS

The Marathas as a racial group or as a family group catch our attention specially during the first phase. This is true numberwise as well as mansabwise. The reasons for that have already been mentioned. From the mansab figures of their family groups, the dominance of Jagdev Rai's family becomes evident in the first phase. But it had to suffer a loss of about 17,000 zat and 15,000 sawars, which was the highest among Maratha family groups. The families of Kheluji and Udaji, who proved their loyalty, improved their positions after the deductions of the second phase. The family of Kheluji, specially, gained in sawar mansab in the third phase. The highest sawar mansab of this group among other Maratha families, highlights greater imperial confidence in it.

These points become clear from Table 4.22.

The position of Maratha families among other family groups declines after the first phase more or less in the same proportion as their share, as a racial block, in the total mansab award.

TABLE 4.22: SHARE OF FAMILY GROUPS IN MANSAB: MARATHAS

	1628–36	*1637–41*	*1642–58*
		Jagdev Rao's family	
Zat	25,000	8000	9500
Sawar	18,500	3500	4000
		Kheluji's family	
Zat	13,000	8000	8000
Sawar	11,500	6500	7000
		Udaji's family	
Zat	11,000	3000	3000
Sawar	9000	2000	2000
		Sahuji's family	
Zat	10,000	–	–
Sawar	8000	–	–

In their own racial group, Maratha families occupied more than 50 per cent of the total zat and sawar awards enjoyed by the Marathas as an ethnic group during the first phase. The share of family groups declines in the second phase. In the last phase, however, they again improved in both the ranks and attained more or less the same proportion which they had enjoyed in the first phase.

It is also worth mentioning that these family groups of the Marathas lost 40,000 zat and 35,000 sawars in the second phase. The total loss of the Marathas during this phase was about 61,000 zat and 52,850 sawars. This implies a greater loss of family groups in both ranks. However, the decline in the last phase was mainly shared by the individual mansabdars, as family groups were the gainers.

On the whole, it may be said that family groups were shown more favour and individual Maratha mansabdars could improve their position only during the second phase.

Tables 4.23 and 4.24 show the details which substantiate the above propositions.

To conclude, the whole discussion on the family groups of mansabdars, it may be said that they always held more than 50 per cent of the total awarded mansab. This suggests the superior position of these groups over the individual mansabdars of various ethnic groups. That Shahjahan was more inclined towards them is also evident from the larger proportion they held in the sawar mansab as compared to the zat mansab. The overall deduction during the second phase was about 2,46,500 zat and 1,63,872 sawars. The loss of the family groups, however, was about 1,08,500 zat and 84,750 sawars. Their gain in the third phase was also greater than that of individual mansabdars.

On the whole, it may be said that the bulk of the mansab throughout

TABLE 4.23: POSITION OF MARATHAS AMONG ALL FAMILY GROUPS

	Total share of family groups		*Total share of Maratha families*
		1628–36	
Zat	4,34,000		59,000
Sawar	3,94,600		47,000
		1637–41	
Zat	3,25,500		19,000
Sawar	3,09,850		12,000
		1642–58	
Zat	5,46,500		20,500
Sawar	4,81,550		13,000

TABLE 4.24: MARATHA FAMILY GROUPS POSITION VIS-À-VIS RACIAL GROUP

	Total share of their racial group		*Total share of Maratha families*
		1628–36	
Zat	1,03,500		59,000
Sawar	77,550		47,000
		1637–41	
Zat	42,500		19,000
Sawar	24,700		12,000
		1642–58	
Zat	36,500		20,500
Sawar	20,400		13,000

Shahjahan's reign was occupied by the family groups of the mansabdars. They were favoured from the beginning till the end with larger shares in both the ranks. This implies their greater share in the resources of the state.

PROMOTION IN MANSAB

Being an important aspect of the mansab, promotion was relevant both for the crown and the nobility. The position and status, resources and power of the latter were affected directly by this. On one hand, for the crown this was an effective method to exercise more control over the nobility. On the other hand, this had a direct bearing upon the resources of the state. Promotion played a significant role in deciding the level and status of various ethnic, racial, religious and family groups vis-à-vis the crown as well as within the nobility. The share the various nobles enjoyed in the resources of the state depended largely upon the frequency and quantity of promotions. So this was an important factor which was linked closely with many political, military and economic issues.

Lahori, Waris and Salih have invariably referred to promotions in case of individual mansabdars. In most cases, we have specific information regarding the additions to both zat and sawar mansabs. So there is no dearth of evidence in this regard.

Yet promotion in mansab has not been given the attention it deserves. In his recent writings,[42] M. Athar Ali, however, has made some thought-provoking suggestions. As said earlier, he has drawn the attention of the academic world to the possibilities of a link between promotions and the changing political, military and economic conditions. At another place, he has made some general observations regarding the possible grounds for promotion.[43] It is this illuminating trend which encourages this author to analyse mansab promotions during Shahjahan's period.

In the foregoing pages, it has been explained that enhancement in mansab had a direct link with the changing conditions, and also that more promotions were given in sawar than in zat mansab. The questions yet to be answered are: (*a*) For what specific reasons were promotions granted by Shahjahan? (*b*) Was promotion a meaningful device or a game of mere flattery and manipulation? (*c*) What could be a rough estimate of the promotion figures for various reasons? (*d*) Was promotion a privilege of the established racial, religious or family groups only?

Before attempting these questions, it may be submitted at the very outset that the total promotion figures shown in Table 4.3 cannot be claimed to be complete. This becomes clear from the differences between the mansab figures given by Lahori or Salih in their lists and in their annual records in the cases of many mansabdars. This study, therefore, has to be confined only to those figures which are mentioned as being for promotion, for whatsoever reason, at any place in these works. The increases, not being mentioned in the annual records, cannot help in explaining the nature of promotions. Table 4.3, however, is useful as it contains almost all the recorded cases of promotion mentioned in the annual record (for the mansabdars of 1000 zat and above).

Analysing promotions with direct reference to the political details of the period, one may tentatively suggest four possible grounds of promotion during this period.

PROMOTION FOR MILITARY EXPEDITIONS

The contemporaries, fortunately, are very helpful specially for promotions given for military expeditions. We have adequate details of such additions, mentioned specifically by them. It seems that promotions were granted on the eve, in the midst, as well as immediately after—sometimes even later—expeditions. Such figures, collected from the annual records of Lahori and Salih, are given in Table 4.25.

On the basis of the data in Table 4.25, it may be said that more promotions were given in sawar mansab than in zat mansab for the obvious consideration of the sawars with the expeditions. Less promotions

TABLE 4.25: PROMOTIONS FOR MILITARY EXPEDITIONS

	Iranis	*Turanis*	*Afghans*	*Indian Muslims*	*Other Muslims*	*Rajputs*	*Marathas*	*Total*
				1628–36				
Zat	11,000	6500	4000	7000	2000	10,000	2500	43,000
Sawar	13,850	10,000	10,700	13,300	2200	9800	1050	60,900
				1637–41				
Zat	1000	2500	2800	700	500	3100	-	10,600
Sawar	3800	6000	4800	600	1200	4900	-	21,300
				1642–58				
Zat	19,000	35,100	5500	4500	500	31,300	-	95,900
Sawar	16,950	28,075	9200	11,900	100	36,300	500	1,03,025

were given in the second phase, as the period was comparatively peaceful. Increasing stress upon military activities is directly reflected in a notable rise in promotion figures during the third phase. It is worth noting that the celebrated Iranis gradually lost their ground after the first phase.[44] Turanis and Rajputs emerged as the two leading factions to get more promotions for expeditions. The elimination of the Marathas is also striking after the first phase.

PROMOTIONS FOR APPOINTMENTS

Under the head of 'Promotions for Appointments', one may include all those additions made at the time of appointments to different administrative,

TABLE 4.26: PROMOTIONS FOR APPOINTMENTS

	Iranis	*Turanis*	*Afghans*	*Indian Muslims*	*Other Muslims*	*Rajputs*	*Other Hindus*	*Total*
				1628–36				
Zat	15,700	9000	2000	-	-	-	-	26,700
Sawar	23,850	11,700	2500	1250	-	-	-	39,300
				1637–41				
Zat	7100	4800	500	-	1000	-	100	13,500
Sawar	7500	6750	2000	2700	1400	-	-	20,350
				1642–58				
Zat	28,800	11,400	1600	7100	1800	2500	-	53,200
Sawar	46,080	17,650	1700	5700	1200	3300	200	75,830

military and ecclesiastical offices. Such promotions can be quite safely picked up from the annual records of Lahori and Salih. Table 4.26 gives the details.

The first notable thing in Table 4.26 is the predominance of sawar promotion. This may be justified by the increasing military requirements of various offices such as subedars, faujdars, qiladars, thanadars, etc.[45] Second, Iranis enjoyed the highest share in these promotions. More than half of the total promotions, both in zat and sawar mansabs, were taken by them during all three phases. Equally important is the sharp decline in the proportion of the share of Afghans from the first to the last phase. It is also interesting that from the second phase, some new elements like Other Muslims, Other Hindus and Rajputs (only in the third phase) received promotions for appointments.

PROMOTIONS FOR LONG-STANDING MILITARY, ADMINISTRATIVE OR POLITICAL SERVICES

Under the head of 'Promotions for Long-Standing Military Administrative or Political Services', one may include all those promotions granted for skilful performance in military and administrative offices during or after the tenure was over. Promotions for ambassadorial services, peaceful missions or for any other non-military services, are also grouped in this category. Direct references to such additions are not many. Therefore, the tabulation of such promotions could be possible with direct reference to the available details of the careers of the mansabdars concerned. These details are reproduced in Table 4.27.

Here also, precedence of sawar promotions over zat persists. The supremacy of Iranis over all other factions in all the phases is another significant point. One may also note a decline in the proportion of Turanis and a rise in the share of Afghans and Indian Muslims if the figures of the first phase are to be compared with those of the last one.

PROMOTIONS FOR POLITICAL REASONS

Under 'Promotions for Political Reasons', one can enumerate all promotions given for the consideration of ancestral services, after the death of family heads, or for political reasons and other diplomatic requirements. The details are given in Table 4.28.

From the data in Table 4.28, it emerges that there was no sizeable addition to the figures of the first phase till the end of the reign. This means that promotions for these reasons were not given generously. It was usually to maintain some tradition or under the pressure of some circumstances that such promotions were granted. And for this reason, perhaps, the figures of promotion in zat exceed the promotions in sawar in almost all three phases.

TABLE 4.27: PROMOTIONS FOR LONG-STANDING MILITARY, ADMINISTRATIVE AND POLITICAL SERVICES

	Iranis	*Turanis*	*Afghans*	*Indian Muslims*	*Other Muslims*	*Rajputs*	*Marathas*	*Other Hindus*	*Total*
				1628–36					
Zat	8700	9800	1000	2500	500	–	–	–	22,500
Sawar	17,300	12,400	1200	1600	1400	–	500	–	34,400
				1637–41					
Zat	6100	1000	400	–	1000	1000	–	–	9500
Sawar	8450	5300	200	4000	200	1000	–	–	19,150
				1642–58					
Zat	28,300	6600	6200	12,900	2800	3700	1000	500	62,000
Sawar	25,400	8100	5600	12,600	3030	6400	–	1000	62,130

TABLE 4.28: PROMOTIONS FOR POLITICAL REASONS

	Iranis	*Turanis*	*Indian Muslims*	*Other Muslims*	*Rajputs*	*Total*
			1628–36			
Zat	8500	1000	2000	500	5500	17,500
Sawar	8400	1050	1600	500	3350	14,900
			1637–41			
Zat	1000	2200	–	–	1000	4200
Sawar	1000	1000	300	–	2000	4300
			1642–58			
Zat	12,400	3200	500	–	5300	21,400
Sawar	6850	3175	600	–	5600	16,225

On the basis of the foregoing, the following tentative suggestions may be made with regard to some possible trends in promotions:

(*a*) The exceptionally high figures of promotions for military expeditions and the higher proportion they bear in the total promotion figures (given in Table 4.3) suggest that perhaps this was the strongest ground for promotions in both zat and sawar mansabs.

(*b*) The high and almost stable figures of promotions for appointments and their proportion in the overall promotion figures highlight the possibility of appointment being the second stronger base for enchancement in mansab.

(*c*) The promotion figures for long-standing military, administrative and political services may be regarded as a third strong reason for promotions (in order of preference), because totalwise as well as proportionwise (in the total promotion figures), these figures are higher than the figures of the fourth category (i.e. political reasons).

(*d*) The lowest proportion that the promotion figures for political reasons bear in the total promotion figures suggests that this was comparatively a less important reason for promotions.

(*e*) On the whole, however, it may be said that promotion was a meaningful device to reward the mansabdars for their excellence and competence. There are few examples where this favour was extended for extravagant reasons. One such case is that of Aitqad Khan Bahmanyar.[46] This spoiled son of Asaf Khan, having hardly any job to his credit, was raised from a mansab of 500 zat, 200 sawars to 4000 zat, 1000 sawars.[47] However, since such examples are quite rare, it is unfair to generalize them, and unwise to formulate any opinion regarding promotion on these grounds.

NOTES

1. Abdul Aziz, *The Mansabdari System and the Mughal Army*, Delhi, 1972, p. 171.
2. M. Athar Ali, *The Mughal Nobility under Aurangzeb*, Asia Publishing House, Bombay, 1968, Chapters 2 and 3.

3. S. Nurul Hasan, 'New Light on the Relations of the Early Mughal Rulers with their Nobility', I.H.C., Madras Session, 1944, pp. 389–97.
4. M. Athar Ali, 'Mansab and the Imperial Policy under Shahjahan', I.H.C., Aligarh Session, 1975, pp. 257–66.
5. Ibid., p. 264.
6. Ibid., p. 265.
7. Athar Ali also had this unpleasant experience: op. cit., n. 4, pp. 263–4; Lahori's first list gives a total of 6,78,300 zat and 5,68,050 sawar, while his second list contains a total of 6,94,500 zat and 5,75,050 sawar.
8. Lahori, I, pp. 212–13.
9. Ibid., p. 203.
10. Ibid., pp. 275–6.
11. For the details of this settlement see Lahori, I (b), pp. 167–74 and 210–11.
12. Lahori, II, pp. 136–7 and 193–5.
13. Lahori, I (b), p. 271–4.
14. Lahori, II, pp. 13–14.
15. Ibid., p. 34.
16. Ibid., p. 139.
17. Lahori, I, pp. 113, 117–23, 158–61, 176–7, 180–6, 195 and 202–3.
18. *M.U.*, II, p. 814.
19. Under Jahangir, the income from khalisa came down to Rs. 50 lakh, while the expenditure rose to Rs. 1 crore and 50 lakh: *M.U.*, II, pp. 814–15.
Also see N.A. Siddiqui, *Land Revenue Administration under the Mughals,* Bombay, 1970, pp. 103–4.
20. *M.U.*, II, p. 815. Also N.A. Siddiqui, op. cit., n. 19, pp. 103–4.
21. Lahori, I, pp. 113, 117–23, 158–61, 176–7, 180–86, 195 and 202–3.
22. M. Athar Ali's list of Jahangiri nobles (*Apparatus of Empire*, Delhi, 1985, pp. 41–90) suggests the number of Iranis (1000 zat and above) as 82 out of 271.
23. See Table 2.8. As is shown in Chapter 3, the Iranis were given lesser opportunities to show their mettle on the battlefield. Also see Appendices 3.2, 3.3, 3.4 and 3.5.
24. This is evident from M. Athar Ali's exhaustive list of Jahangir's nobles (op. cit., n. 22, pp. 41–90).
25. See Appendices 3.1 and 3.2.
26. See Chapter 3, Phase I.
27. Such a gap between the share of the Iranis and Turanis also existed during Jahangir's period. They enjoyed almost 23 per cent in the total zat and 21 per cent in the total sawar mansab award. Iranis, on the other hand, had a share of about 29 per cent in the total zat and 35 per cent in the total sawar rank distributed during that period. This rough estimate is based upon Athar Ali, op. cit., n. 22, pp. 41–90.
28. Lahori, II, pp. 33–9, 42–6, 53–4; also Chapter 3, Phase 2.
29. On the basis of Athar Ali's table (op. cit., n. 22, pp. 41–90), it may be said that in spite of the many favours of Jahangir, the Afghans enjoyed almost 6 per cent of the total zat and 5 per cent of the total sawar mansab distributed during his reign.
30. The rise or decline in the share of various ethnic groups in the mansab is shown in Table 4.2.
31. See Appendices 3.4 and 3.5.
32. For their role in political and military affairs, see Chapter 3 and its appendices.
33. For the actual figures of the Rajputs who participated in such expeditions, see Appendix 3.5 of Chapter 3.
34. See Appendix 3.4 of Chapter 3.
35. See Appendix 3.2 of Chapter 3.
36. See Appendix 3.1 of Chapter 3.
37. J.D., no. 28/39 (Shahjahan's Farman to Mirza Raja Jai Singh).
38. Ibid., no. 36/47.
39. Ibid., no. 43/57.

40. Ibid., nos. 34/45, 46/63 and 44/58.
41. For the political and military role of the Rajputs, see Chapter 3 and its appendices.
42. M. Athar Ali, op. cit., n. 4 above, I.H.C., 1975 and *Apparatus of Empire* (Introduction), op. cit., n. 22 above.
43. *Apparatus of Empire* (Introduction), op. cit., n. 22 above.
44. The decline in the representation of Iranis in military expeditions after the first phase is evident from the composition tables of some expeditions given at the end of Chapter 3.
45. While referring to the appointment of Shujat Khan Barha to the subedari of Allahabad, Lahori specifically mentions that the enhancement of 2000 sawars was necessary for administrative reasons as the suba was Zortalab, Lahori, I (b), p. 274.
46. For the details of his life and career see *M.U.*, I, pp. 232–4.
47. For his swift promotions, see Lahori, I (b), p. 242; II, pp. 280, 386 and 431; Salih, III, pp. 71, 141–2, 173 and 453 (L).

CHAPTER 5

Administration and the Nobility

On Mughal administration at central and provincial levels, plenty of material is available, published in the recent past.[1] The efforts made by Ibn-e-Hasan, P. Saran, Noman Ahmed Siddiqi, M. Athar Ali, etc., have not only enriched our knowledge, but have also opened new fields for research and investigation. M. Athar Ali, in particular, introduced a new avenue by enumerating the governors of Shahjahan's reign.[2] This may be applied to other important central and provincial positions as well. On the same lines, in the following pages, an attempt is being made to examine some important administrative posts with direct reference to the nobles.

Besides the fact that the nobility was the creation of the emperor, it was only through these nobles that the execution and implementation of the state's policies could be possible. The organization of mansabdari had a unique capacity of absorbing all government services. Administrative offices, therefore, had to be run by the mansabdars, besides their military obligations determined by the sawar rank. They served at various levels in different administrative capacities during this period.

In this connection, a few questions may be raised which are yet to be answered, such as: What was the term of office for different posts? To what extent did racial and religious considerations have a say in such appointments? Was there any role of family groups in getting specific posts? Can we possibly establish a link between mansab and the post? For a systematic study of such issues, we may pick up a few important posts as samples. This may help in forming a tentative idea on the lines proposed above. We shall first take up some key positions at the centre.

DIWAN-I-KUL

Since the office of Vakil ended with the death of Asaf Khan, the office at the centre to engage our attention first is that of Diwan-i-Kul[3]. Table 5.1, prepared with the help of contemporary evidence, gives the dates of appointment and removal, the mansab and racial group of these office-bearers. As the analysis is based upon these facts, one needs to study the data in Table 5.1 first.

On the basis of the data in Table 5.1, the following may be said.

(*a*) Eight persons were appointed during the whole reign. Diyanat Rai's appointment was an interim arrangement. The first appointment of Rai Raghunath was of the same nature, but for a second time he was a co-sharer of this office with Jafar Khan.[4] Muhammad Amin Khan who worked as his

TABLE 5.1: DIWAN-I-KUL

Name	*Racial/ religious group*	*Mansab*			*Date of*		*Source*
		Previous	*Promotion*	*Present*	*Appoint-ment*	*Relinquish-ment*	
Azam Khan	Irani	5000/5000	–	5000/5000	Mar. 1628	Mar. 1629	Lahori, I, pp. 159, 186 and 257.
Afzal Khan	Irani	4000/2000	1000/500	5000/2500	Mar. 1629	Jan. 1639	Lahori, I, p. 257; II, pp. 132 and 718.
Diyanat Rai	Hindu	1000/150	–	1000/150	Jan. 1639	Nov. 1639	Lahori, II, pp. 92, 132 and 164; *Z.Kh.*, III, p. 81.
Islam Khan	Irani	5000/5000	–	5000/5000	Nov. 1639	July 1645	Lahori, II, pp. 164 and 430; I (b), p. 83.
Sadullah Khan	Ind. M.	4000/1000	1000/500	5000/1500	July 1645	April 1656	Lahori, II, p. 431; Salih, III (L), pp. 216–17; *M.U.*, II, p. 448.
Rai Raghunath	Hindu	1000/200	–	1000/200	Apr. 1656	May 1656	Salih, III (L), pp. 213, 217 and 228.
Muazzam Khan Mir Jumla	Irani	5000/5000	1000/1000	6000/6000	May 1656	Sep. 1657	Ibid., pp. 228 and 262.
Rai Raghunath	Hindu	1000/200	–	1000/200	Sep. 1657	–	Ibid., pp. 213 and 262.
Jafar Khan	Irani	5000/5000	–	5000/5000	Dec. 1657	–	Ibid., pp. 197 and 268.

father's naib is not regarded as a full-fledged Diwan because he was stopped from going to Kachehri after the removal of Muazzam Khan from this office.[5]

(*b*) The fact that six Diwans out of eight were non-khanazads suggests that family considerations had very little to do in these appointments. Afzal Khan and Islam Khan were close companions of Shahjahan in his princehood. Afzal Khan had also proved his loyalty, joining Asaf Khan against Shaharyar. Sadullah Khan was a reputed scholar and was brought to politics by the emperor himself.[6] The established position and sound administrative and military backgrounds of Muazzam Khan were also unquestionable.[7] Jafar Khan too had proved his worth by assisting the emperor, taking the charge of the Diwani after the death of Afzal Khan, and also by rendering good services as Mir Bakhshi and subedar of different provinces.[8] Thus, no person of low potential was elevated to this high office. The appointments of Diyanat Rai and Rai Raghunath, the latter being the co-sharer with Jafar Khan in a permanent capacity, totally eliminate the role of religion as a guiding principle in these appointments.

(*c*) The figures are not helpful in determining the tenure of office of the Diwans, as high fluctuations may be noted. On the whole, it may be said that capable people, retaining the emperor's confidence, were allowed to continue till death, such as Afzal Khan and Sadullah Khan. That is why they held this office for the longest tenures. The removals of Azam Khan and Islam Khan suggest that the emperor always looked for more talented and more suitable persons, and once he was sure of his assessment, people of lower calibre were relieved.

(*d*) In spite of the fact that personal calibre and individual potential were the main guiding factors for appointment to this post, the Iranis, numberwise, superseded others. Out of eight they were five. Yet the fact remains that out of the recorded period of about 30 years, non-Iranis held this office for a long period of more than 12 years. It is also interesting that an Indian Muslim enjoyed the longest term in this office. So the partiality for Iranis need not be over-emphasized.

(*e*) It is also of some interest that about 33 per cent of the persons were given promotion. With the exception of Muazzam Khan, in the cases of Afzal Khan and Sadullah Khan, promotion seems to have been given to raise them to panj hazari. The rest of the Diwans, appointed in independent and permanent capacities, had already reached the level of 5000 zat, hence got no promotion at all. So it may be said that 5000 zat was perhaps treated as a qualifying mansab for this post during this period. This suggests a link between the mansab and the post. The promotion in the mansab of Muazzam Khan may be justified by political considerations and military strategy. Being a Deccani and a new entrant, he was to be shown extra favour.

In continuation of the above, it may be said that although the promotion figures apparently suggest a greater share of the zat, yet if analysed with reference to the previous mansab of the promottee, these figures suggest more rise in the sawar.[9] Last, the Diwans, after leaving office, were normally sent as subedars.[10]

MIR BAKHSHI

Being the head of the military department, and as such the chief representative of the mansabdars, the Mir Bakhshi[11] commanded immense respect and an influential position after the Diwan. The available information about this office is given in Table 5.2.

From Table 5.2, it is clear that 13 mansabdars held this post during this period,[12] and all of them were Iranis. But it is notable that with the exception of Aitqad Khan (son of Asaf Khan), all of them were capable and deserving people. At least 6 of them had gained experience in the office of Bakhshi-e-Doam; the rest of them had distinguished themselves as leading generals and administrators.[13] So the exclusiveness of Iranis in this office cannot be attributed solely as being blind favour to them as a racial group. No doubt the number of khanazads exceeded other mansabdars, but their capability could not be challenged.[14]

About the duration of office, nothing can be said with any certainty due to the evident fluctuations. At the most, it may be said that the longest term of office was five years and a few months, and the shortest nine months. In the cases of Sadiq Khan, Mir Jumla, Salabat Khan, and Asalat Khan, death ended their careers, while Danishmand Khan resigned from service on his own initiative.[15] These facts indicate the risk of specifying an average tenure of these office-bearers. Possibly, these capable Mir Bakhshis would have continued for a longer period, if spared by death!

The mansab figures in Table 5.2, suggest a correspondence between the post and the rank. The lowest recorded mansab is 3000 zat, and the highest 5000.

A glance at the promotions suggests that 9 mansabdars out of 13 were promoted, a much higher rate of promotion as compared to the office of the Diwan. Those already holding 5000 zat were given no promotion in zat mansab, perhaps because it was not thought desirable. The total promotion figure in zat is 4000, while in the case of sawar mansab it is about 4400. The emphasis upon promoting the sawar mansab becomes more clear if the promotion figures are to be compared with the previous mansab figures. Though khanazads enjoyed the maximum of the promotion benefits in both the ranks, their highest gains lay in sawar promotions. It is also worth noting that Asaf Khan's family enjoyed 25 per cent of the total promotion figure in zat and half of this total in the sawar mansab.

MIR-E-SAMAN

The next important administrative position at the centre was that of Mir-e-Saman.[16] During this period, about six persons were appointed to this post.[17] The available details regarding this office are given in Table 5.3.

On the basis of the figures in 5.3, the first thing that one may conclude is of the dominance of Iranis throughout this reign. They were all experienced and tried servants of the crown. Afzal Khan and Mir Jumla had served in this office under Jahangir.[18] Makramat Khan and Aqil Khan were already in this

TABLE 5.2: MIR BAKHSHI

Name	*Racial/ religious group*	*Mansab*			*Date of*		*Source*
		Previous	*Promotion*	*Present*	*Appoint-ment*	*Relinquish-ment*	
Azam Khan	Irani	4500/4000	500/1000	5000/5000	Feb. 1628	Mar. 1628	Lahori, I, pp. 159 and 186.
Sadiq Khan	Irani	4000/4000	–	4000/4000	Mar. 1628	Sep. 1633	Ibid., pp. 181, 186 and 538–9.
Islam Khan	Irani	5000/5000	–	5000/5000	Oct. 1633	Mar. 1635	Ibid., pp. 396 and 542; I (b), p. 83.
Mir Jumla	Irani	4000/1500	1000/500	5000/2000	Apr. 1635	Sep. 1637	Lahori, I (b), pp. 86 and 279.
Mutamad Khan	Irani	4000/1200	–	4000/1200	Sep. 1637	Sep. 1639	Ibid., pp. 242 and 279; II, p. 161.
Salabat Khan	Irani	3000/1000	500 sawars	3000/1500	Sep. 1639	Aug. 1644	Lahori, II, pp. 161 and 380–1.
Asalat Khan	Irani	3000/2500	–	3000/2500	Aug. 1644	Apr. 1647	Lahori, I (b), p. 87; II, pp. 385 and 657.
Jafar Khan	Irani	5000/3500	500 sawars	5000/4000	May 1647	Dec. 1649	Lahori, II, p. 681; Salih, III (B), pp. 104–5.
Khalilullah Khan	Irani	4000/3000	–	4000/3000	Dec. 1649	Feb. 1651	Lahori, II, p. 584; Salih, III (B), pp. 104–5 and 120.
Lahrasp Khan	Irani	3000/3000	1000 zat	4000/3000	Feb. 1651	Dec. 1651	Salih, III (L), pp. 120 and 134.
Aitqad Khan	Irani	3000/300	1000/200	4000/500	Mar. 1652	Nov. 1652	Ibid., pp. 141–2 and 152.
-do-	Irani	4000/500	1000 sawar	4000/1500	Sep. 1653	Mar. 1657	Ibid., pp. 241 and 173, *M.U.*, I, pp. 233–4.
Danishmand Khan	Irani	3000/600	200 sawar	3000/800	Mar. 1657	Nov. 1657	Salih, III (L), pp. 241 and 263–4.
Mohd. Amin Khan	Irani	2500/1000	500/500	3000/1500	Nov. 1657	–	Ibid., p. 264; *M.U.*, III, pp. 613–14.

TABLE 5.3: MIR-E-SAMAN

Name	*Racial/ religious group*	*Mansab*			*Date of*		*Source*
		Previous	*Promotion*	*Present*	*Appointment*	*Relinquishment*	
Afzal Khan	Irani	4000/2000	–	4000/2000	Feb. 1628	Mar. 1629	Lahori, I, pp. 176–7 and 257.
Mir Jumla	Irani	3000/1200	–	3000/1200	Mar. 1629	Apr. 1635	Ibid., pp. 181 and 258; I (b), p. 86.
Makramat Khan Shirazi[1]	Irani	2000/1500	–	2000/1500	Aug. 1638	Sep. 1641	Lahori, I (b), p. 101; II, pp. 103 and 244.
Aqil Khan	Irani	1500/400	500/100	2000/500	Oct. 1641	1643	Lahori, II, pp. 244 and 347.
Sadullah Khan	Ind. M.	1500/300	500/200	2000/500	Nov. 1643	July 1645	Ibid., pp. 347 and 431.
Aqil Khan	Irani	2000/700	–	2000/700	July 1645	Mar. 1646	Ibid., pp. 422, 431 and 491.
Fazil Khan-Alaul Mulk	Irani	1000/100	500/100 500 zat	1500/200 2000/200	Mar. 1646	–	Ibid., pp. 491–2 and 547–8.

Note: [1]It seems that after Mir Jumla's appointment as Mir Bakhshi, Makramat Khan, who was working as Diwan-e-Buyutat, was allowed to work as Mir-e-Saman (Lahori, I, p. 460; I (b), p. 267), even before the formal appointment.

discipline and were promoted from the office of Diwan-i-Buyutat.[19] Sadullah Khan had proved his worth as Arz-e-Mukarrar and Darogha-e-Daulat Khana-e-Khas.[20] Alaul Mulk too was tried as Diwan-e-Tan.[21] Thus, all of them were tried and experienced. That is why most of them were promoted to other offices of dignity after their transfer.[22] That, with the exception of Aqil Khan, all of them were non-khanazads, suggests due recognition of merit and minimizes the role of family considerations in appointments to such important offices.

No decisive comment may be made regarding the term of office of the Mir-e-Saman, because about nine months seem to be the shortest term while the longest is more than ten years. It seems that a suitable candidate was allowed to stay almost permanently (as was the case with Fazil Khan), while others were shifted to other offices according to their calibre and potentialities.

The minimum requirement for this office seems to be 2000 zat. No mansabdar already holding 2000 zat and above was given any promotion. A second promotion of 500 zat was given to Fazil Khan in the same year of his appointment to raise him to that level.[23]

As far as the trend of promotion is concerned, it is evident that the rise in sawar mansab bore a higher proportion than enhancement in zat, if the figures are calculated with reference to the previous mansabs. In total zat, the rise comes to about 38 per cent, while in total sawar mansab it reaches 50 per cent over the pre-promotion mansab figures.

SADR

During this period, three nobles seem to have held the office of Sadarat.[24] Musvi Khan was confirmed in the first regnal year.[25] On his removal in 1642, an Indian Muslim and distinguished scholar, Syed Jalaluddin Bukhari, was appointed and continued in this office till his death.[26] Syed Hidayatullah, whose father Syed Ahmed Qadri had served in this capacity under Jahangir, was the last Sadr of this period.[27]

It is evident that Indian Muslims enjoyed longer tenures as compared to Iranis. The selection of the second Sadr indicates the signficance of knowledge and status in the concerned field as an important consideration in appointments to this office. Regarding the tenure of office, it may be added that there was no specific rule as such. Capable and suitable people were allowed to continue either till death or up to the time they performed their duties satisfactorily. The variation in the mansab of the Sadrs[28] suggests that it was determined keeping in mind the candidate's experience or scholarly attainments and popularity for religious piety. This is clearly borne out from the promotion in mansab and confirmation of Musvi Khan in the opening years, and from the high figures of Shaikh Jalal Bukhari's mansab (i.e. 4000/700). On the other hand, Shaikh Hidayatulah, being no match to his predecessor, was raised only to a mansab of 1500/300 at the time of his appointment. The recorded promotions at the time of appontment as Sadr suggest that the proportion of rise in sawar mansab is greater than this proportion in zat.[29]

From this brief survey of some important posts at the centre, one may draw the following tentative conclusions.

(*a*) Racial, religious and family considerations were not given primacy while selecting nobles for these posts. If the members of one particular race/ family seem to have a preponderance in some office, it should not be linked to racial bias, as in most cases, the selected nobles were fully qualified in every way. The quest for merit led Shahjahan out of his way to introduce some altogether new elements in politics. The rise of Sadullah Khan and of Syed Jalal Bukhari present the best examples of this.

(*b*) Since considerable variations existed in the tenures of office in all these appointments, it may be said that transfers were made not as a rule but as a necessity. If a person was assessed to be more suitable for a different job and a better substitute was available to replace him for a shorter or longer period, then without giving any primacy to the duration, he was shifted to some other position. Afzal Khan replacing Azam Khan and Sadullah Khan assuming the Diwani in place of Islam Khan, give some support to this point. Otherwise capable and befitting persons were allowed to continue for much longer periods, extending till death. It was only death which sealed the careers of Afzal Khan and Sadullah Khan as Diwans; of Sadiq Khan, Mir Jumla, Salabat Khan and Asalat Khan as Mir Bakhshis; and of Syed Jalal Bukhari as Sadr.

(*c*) The figures of promotion at the time of appointment to different offices suggest a link between the post and the mansab. A certain minimum limit of mansab was, perhaps, an important factor in giving promotions on such occasions. Those who had already reached or crossed that minimum level were hardly given any promotion in mansab.

(*d*) A comparison of the proportion of rise in zat and sawar manab highlights the greater emphasis upon raising the latter.

(*e*) Last, it may be said that throughout this regime, Iranis had a stronghold over the important administrative positions at the centre.

Such a study, at provincial level, again will be confined to some important offices, because the aim of this study is not to describe the administrative set-up as such, but simply to highlight the position of the nobility in administrative capacities.

The foremost position at provincial level was occupied by the subedar. In *Badshah Nama* of Lahori, we have enough information regarding the appointments, transfers and promotions of the subedars. Salih supplies such information for the closing years of this regime. Appendix 5.1 contains information about the racial group, mansab, tenure of office, previous post and later assignments of the nobles posted as subedars of some important provinces. The suggestions of M. Athar Ali, in the above-mentioned paper, have been incorporated in this attempt. The information that emerges from Appendix 5.1 not only confirms his deductions, but also, in some ways, adds some other related things such as the selection of subedars from some specific discipline or their promotion to specific posts. Some correspondence between the post and the mansab may also be seen, varying from province to province. An analysis of these subedars with reference to their racial groups may help in making a tentative suggestion regarding some specific areas where some selected racial groups were tried, and the rest either ignored or given less representation. The assessment of the share of khanazads in this whole lot may be another interesting aspect of this attempt. Thus, this study may add some other interesting information to the illuminating analysis of M. Athar Ali.

The first thing to note is that the average term of office of the subedars was always less than three years. Suba-i-Akbarabad is the only exception, being less than two years. However, capable and befitting nobles were allowed exceptionally longer tenures elsewhere. For example, Mutaqid Khan (Orissa), Abdullah Khan Feroze Jang (Bihar), Wazir Khan (Punjab), Husain Beg (Kashmir) and Said Khan (Kabul) continued for more than six years.

Though there seems to be no hard and fast rule regarding the qualifications of the subedars, if we go over the careers of these nobles and systematically note their previous posts, it becomes evident that the subedars were generally picked up from amongst the faujdars, qiladars, bakhshis and from some such important positions at the centre such as Qush Begi, Akhta Begi, Mir-e-Saman, etc. The subedari of the Deccan seems to be the only such prestigious position which was filled by two Diwans of the empire, namely, Azam Khan and Islam Khan.

The correspondence between the mansab and this post can be established with the help of mansab and promotion figures available in contemporary works, but it would be imprudent to generalize about all the subas from one figure. It seems that perhaps geopolitical considerations and military strategy predominated in determining the strength of the mansab of a noble being posted as subedar of a particular suba.

In this regard, one can specifically mention the most vulnerable subas as Qandhar, Kabul and Deccan. There, not a single mansabdar below 4000 zat was appointed as subedar. This highlights the status of these subedaris. Those nobles who had not reached this level were elevated by way of promotions (as is evident from Appendix 5.1). Besides this, if we look at the figures of the sawar mansab, we find that, quite obviously, special consideration was given to the sawar strength of these subedars. It is to be noted that the bulk of them belonged to the first category of mansabdars (in which zat and sawar mansab were equal). Moreover, most of them were given the favour of do-aspa sih-aspa simply to add to their military strength. Thus, the political and military importance of the provinces had a direct reflection upon the mansab of the appointed subedars.

On the other hand, we have provinces as Kashmir, Thatta and Orissa, where conditions were almost stable; there the mansab figures of the appointed subedars are quite low, both in zat and sawar. The majority of these subedars belonged to the second category of mansabdars (where sawar rank was half the zat rank). This means that secure and stable conditions of the provinces did affect the mansabwise status of the subedars. In other words, this led to minimization of the mansab requirement (specially in the sawar), hence, mansabdars of even 1500/500 could be appointed in such subas (like Orissa).

Besides Kabul, Qandhar and the Deccan, there were other provinces where mansabdars of higher zat and sawar ranks were appointed, such as Malwa, Gujrat and Bengal. There, not a single mansabdar of less than 4000 zat was appointed as subedar. The promotions given to Ilahwardi Khan and Sardar Khan (both in Malwa) raised them to 4000 zat. With the exception of Sardar Khan, the sawar mansab of all the subedars of these provinces was 4000 and above, though the number of the recipients of do-aspa sih-aspa favour is less than that in Kabul, Qandhar and the Deccan.

The subas where the mansab of the subedars ranged between 1000 and 7000 in both ranks were Punjab, Multan, Akbarabad, Delhi, Allahabad and Bihar. The number of mansabdars below 3000/3000, however, is very small (i.e. 13/67). It is worth noting that the majority of these subedars either already held equal numbers of zat and sawar, or they were included in this first category of mansabdars by way of promotion. The promotions given to Ilahwardi Khan, Makramat Khan, Jafar Khan and Khalilullah Khan for the subedari of Delhi and the promotions to Aitaqad Khan, Zulfiqar Khan and Qasim Khan for the subedari of Bihar, may be considered necessary to maintain this equilibrium between zat and sawar, perhaps necessary for these subas. Such examples may be produced for the rest of the above-mentioned subas too.[30]

It may also be noted that some selected nobles served in this capacity throughout the regime in all these important subas. Mansabdars as Azam Khan, Mahabat Khan, Islam Khan Mashhadi, Ali Mardan Khan, Said Khan, Qulij Khan, Aitqad Khan, Jafar Khan, Saif Khan, Baqar Khan, Naim-e-Sani, Ilahwardi Khan, etc., covered almost all the important provinces of the empire.

Though it is difficult to discern any definite policy regarding the transfer of subedars, the evidence (of Appendix 5.1) suggests that in most cases they were sent to other subas in the same capacity. It is more true particularly in the cases of the subedars of Kabul, Qandhar, Allahabad, Agra, Bengal and the Deccan. Some faujdaris and qiladaris were so prominent that subedars could be sent to look after them,[31] for example, the faujdaris of Miyan-e-Doab, Kangrah, Jaunpur, Bhakkar, Siwistan, Churagarh and Surat, and the qiladaris of Ahmadnagar, Jaunpur, Rohtas, Junnair and Lahore. This applies to some subedars of Kashmir, Multan, Delhi, Thatta, Malwa, Gujrat, Bihar and Orissa too.

The ethnic composition of the subedars reveals some interesting features. The first notable things is that Iranis enjoyed the largest number of these appointments. Their positions were very strong in the Deccan, Kashmir, Delhi, Thatta, Allahabad, Malwa, Gujrat and Bihar. In some subas as Bengal, Orissa and Awadh, only Iranis held this post. However, in the north-west frontier region and the adjointing subas as Multan and Punjab, their positions seem to be surprisingly weak. Not a single Irani was appointed in Qandhar.

Though numberwise their position was good at Kabul, but their tenure was shorter than others. They enjoyed this office only for about 13 years out of the total recorded period of almost 30 years (see Appendix 5.1).

On the whole, it may be said that Iranis enjoyed exceptional favour and held subedaris in almost all regions and for longer periods, except in the north-west and its contiguous territory. Compared with Jahangir's time, this was definitely a notable change in their condition.[32]

'On the other hand,' observes M. Athar Ali rightly, 'the Turanis under Shahjahan held a much better position.' As our tables suggest, their position was better than under Jahangir, but not better than that of Iranis, as the number of their appointments in different subas is slightly more than 25 per cent of the total number of appointments (see Appendix 5.1). Yet the fact remains that after the Iranis, they were more numerous among the subedars of Shahjahan. In Kabul and Qandhar, they almost monopolized this position. In Multan, Punjab and Thatta too, their position was very strong. But they had hardly any representation at Orissa, Bengal and Awadh. The number of their appointments in Gujrat, Delhi, Kashmir and Deccan also confirms their weak position as compared to Iranis. It is, however, clear that under Shahjahan, Turanis were given better chances to rise in this influential group. Moreover, their stronger hold over the north-west frontier provinces suggests that Shahjahan had placed greater faith in them as compared to Iranis.

Other racial groups as Indian Muslims, Afghans and Rajputs also held this post in different subas. Indian Muslims were appointed in Qandhar, Punjab, Akbarabad and Allahabad. After the death of Sher Khan, only Bahadur Khan Rohila was raised to this position in Multan. Only Raja Jaswant Singh represented the Rajputs in this cadre, and that too in the last phase (1642–58).

It is also worth nothing that khanazads formed a sizeable majority among the subedars. In regions as Kabul, Qandhar, Kashmir and the Punjab, their hold seems to be slightly weak. But in the remaining subas, their positions were very strong.

These observations can be verified from Table 5.4, which is an abridged version of Appendices of this very chapter.

To conclude this discussion on subedars, the following tentative suggestions are being made.

(*a*) There was a certain correspondence between the post and the mansab. The strength of the rank of the nobles highlights the political and military importance of the suba.

(*b*) The tenure of office was always less than three years.

(*c*) In some subas, nobles of some selected races were posted.

(*d*) Iranis still had the largest number in this prestigious group.

(*e*) The majority of the subedars were khanazads. The Iranis excelled over other khanazads, obviously because they outnumbered other racial groups in this office.

(*f*) The promotion figures suggest a clear indication of adding more to the sawar mansab than the zat.

TABLE 5.4: RACIAL AND RELIGIOUS COMPOSITION OF SUBEDARS

Subas	*No. of appointments*	*Iranis*	*Turanis*	*Afghans*	*Indian Muslims*	*Other Muslims*	*Rajputs*
Deccan	10	8	1	1	–	–	–
Orissa	7	7	–	–	–	–	–
Bengal	5	5	–	–	–	–	–
Kabul	10	5	4	–	–	1	–
Qandhar	4	–	3	–	1	–	–
Kashmir	9	7	2	–	–	–	–
Punjab	12	5	3	–	2	2	–
Multan	12	3	8	1	–	–	–
Akbarabad	8	3	2	–	2	–	1
Delhi	13	11	2	–	–	–	–
Thatta	15	8	6	–	1	–	–
Allahabad	10	5	2	–	2	1	–
Awadh	3	3	–	–	–	–	–
Malwa	13	8	3	1	–	–	1
Gujrat	9	7	1	1	–	–	–
Bihar	12	7	4	–	–	1	–
TOTAL	152	92	41	4	8	5	2

FAUJDARS

Almost on the same lines as the foregoing, we may analyse two other important offices, namely, faujdars and qiladars. As in case of subedars, here also sufficient information is available in Lahori, Salih and others regarding the dates of appointment, the promotions given on this occasion, and the transfers of these officials. Valuable data are also to be obtained from biographical works like *Maasir-ul-Umara* and *Zakhirat-ul-Khawanin*. They provide insights to the antecedents of these officials, which help in formulating some plausible suggestions in this regard.

Noman Ahmad Siddiqi has given a brilliant analysis of a faujdar's powers, of the pulls and pressures upon his authority, the typical nature of the relationship that existed between him and other officers, and its ultimate repercussions upon his equation with the central government.[33] The questions left to be answered are almost the same as those raised earlier in the case of subedars. The method of reaching some plausible conclusions in this regard again remains the same. The details of faujdars are given in Appendix 5.2 which is based on the above-mentioned sources and contains the same kind of information as in the case of subedars. But in the cases of faujdars and qiladars, our information is not as comprehensive as in the case of subedars. Some sarkars are not mentioned by the contemporaries, while in the cases of many others, just one or two appointments are mentioned, and there too either the date of appointment or the date of relinquishment of the office is missing.[34] Due to this limited information, this author failed to make a full analysis, and had to concentrate upon only those cases where sufficient details were available. Appendix 5.2, thus, includes only those regions of which sufficient details are provided by the contemporaries.

As it emerges from Appendix 5.2 of faujdars, unlike the cases of subedars, we cannot generalize some period as a general average term of office. Differences may be noted from place to place. For example, the average tenure of the faujdars of Ajmer, Doab, Jaunpur, Siwistan, Bijagarh and Bandar-i-Surat is always less than 3 years. In Qannauj, it is between 4 years and 5 years. At Bangash, Bahraich, Lakhnau-Baiswarah, Kangrah, Mathura, Jammu, Bhakkar, Lakhi-Jangal and Mandsur, the average tenure is less than 2 years. The faujdaris of Tirhut, Patan and Surat show an average term of between 3 years and 4 years. Qannauj and Kalpi are perhaps the two exceptions where the faujdars (who were also the jagirdars), enjoyed the longest term of about 11 years.

This variation in the tenure of office highlights the difference in the political conditions and also the strategic importance of these regions. For example, in Ajmer, up to 1637, the average tenure was less than 2 years, because this is precisely the period when Jujhar Singh Bundela was in rebellion. After his suppression, the condition became more peaceful in Rajputana. So in spite of the minor problems created by Champat Bundela[35] in the post-1637 period, the faujdars were allowed to stay for exceptionally longer periods. Shah Ali remained there in the same capacity for about 11 years.

In regions known for rebellious tendencies like Mathura, Mahaban, Doab, Bangash, Kangrah, Jammu and Siwistan, the faujdars did not enjoy long tenures. The average was generally below three years.

The tenure of faujdars in vulnerable regions like Kabul, Multan and the Punjab was curtailed further, their averages being below two years.

The big faujdaris like Baiswarah, Bahraich, Jaunpur, etc., may also be included in the small category, as the average tenure in these cases was below three years or two years.

Interior and safer areas like Baroda, Surat, Patan (in Gujrat) and Qannauj and Kalpi in suba Agra, may be noted for much longer tenures of office.

So it may be submitted that the tenure of office differed from region to region, as it had a link with the political, economic and strategic signficance of the area.

However, some individuals seem to have enjoyed exceptionally long tenures in different regions. As faujdar of the suburbs of Akbarabad, Agah Khan Khwajasara, for example, continued for about 18 years. In Kalpi and Qannauj, Bahadur Khan Rohila held this position for about 20 and 11 years respectively. Shah Ali held the faujdari of Ajmer for about 11 years. Many more such examples may be cited. The fact remains that such cases of exceptionally long tenures may be traced only in those territories which were the most secure.

The faujdars, as is evident from Appendix 5.2, were picked up from different positions and disciplines. A close scrutiny of the previous positions held by these faujdars, however, reveals that most of them were picked up from the provincial cadre itself, and a very small number was drawn from central offices.[36]

A similar trend may be seen in the transfer of faujdars. Out of 84 cases where later assignments are mentioned, 71 persons were retained in provincial services, and only 13 were sent to serve at the centre: Appendix 5.2

As has been said elsewhere, nothing can be said with certainty as to what the mansabwise criterion of a particular post was. Yet, on the basis of the mansab and promotion figures available at the time of the appointments, one may hypothetically establish a correspondence between the mansab and the post. But since the mansab figure (with or without promotion) differs from region to region, in order to understand this fluctuation, one will have to look into the local conditions as well as the overall political situation because the fluctuation in the mansab of the faujdars, which ultimately determined their status in the Mughal hierarchy, had a direct link with the existing political developments.

As shown earlier, the changing political conditions had a definite reflection upon the mansab figures as a whole, so these conditons played a significant role in the cases of these office-bearers too. The appointments of Umara-i-Uzzam along with those of mansabdars of lower ranks can be satisfactorily explained only by analysing them in the light of the contemporary political situation, along with the due importance of the equation between the emperor and a particular noble at that time. Some examples may be given to establish this point. Take the case of Ajmer, where the mansab figures of the posted faujdars are very high up to 1637, as compared to the post-1637 period: see Appendix 5.2. This vast difference in figures can be explained in terms of the crucial political condition of Rajputana due to the rebellion of Jujhar Singh Bundela. As long as this problem continued, high mansabdars were posted there. But after Jujhar Singh's total suppression, there was hardly any need of such big mansabdars, hence small mansabdars of even 500/500 could safely be appointed. Shah Ali (holding 700/450) was allowed to continue there in this generally safe period, for a long term of about 11 years.

If we look at the faujdars of the suburbs of Akbarabad, not a single noble below 1000/1000 was posted there throughout the reign. Agah Khan Khwajasara, who seems to hold this faujdari for the longest period, was given a promotion of 800 sawars to reach that level. Sadullah Khan, the Diwan and a haft hazari, was also given this responsibility in 1653. Thus it becomes clear that this was an important assignment and only high mansabdars and trusted servants of the crown were posted there. With direct reference to the political developments, however, one can make out some possible reasons for the importance of this region. Obviously, the foremost is that this was the seat of the emperor for the longest period. Second, there was no dearth of rebellious elements. Immediately after the coronation, Marhamat Khan was commanded to crush these rebels with the Ahadis.[37] Above all, Shahjahan's absence from Akbarabad for a total of almost 22 years in his reign on different missions and at different intervals[38] was also a strong factor in this regard. So the administration was always left in strong and reliable hands.

In most other regions of Suba-i-Agra too, the mansabs of the faujdars figure quite high in Appendix 5.2. Special mention may be made of regions like Mathura and Mahaban, Qannauj and Kalpi, Mewat, Koil and Doab. There is hardly any mansabdar below 1000/400 among them, while the highest limit goes up to 4000/4000. The reason for this is not far to seek. There is sufficient evidence to suggest the refractory tendencies in these regions.[39] At the time of Murshid Quli Khan's appointment, while mentioning a promotion of 1300 sawars in his mansab, Lahori specifically points out the indispensability of increasing the strength of the army to govern Mathura and Mahaban.[40]

Military and political strategy is fully reflected from the mansab figures of the faujdars of Kabul. Besides frequent Afghan uprisings,[41] the region was extremely important for the security of the Mughal boundary in the north-west. Therefore, not a single mansabdar below 2000 zat 2000 sawar was posted, at least at Bangash, of which we have sufficient information.

For almost similar political and military reasons, high mansabdars were posted in regions like Kangrah, Jammu and many places in Suba-i-Multan and Thatta.[42] Being provinces contiguous to the north-west frontier region, Multan and Thatta had special significance. Therefore, these faujdaris too were assigned to high mansabdars.

The size of the sarkars also had some link with the mansabs of the faujdars. This may be more true in the cases of sarkar Baiswarah, Bahraich, Gorakhpur and Jaunpur.[43] There is hardly any mansabdar below 1000 zat among them.

Appendix 5.2 also contains some instances where haft hazaris and shash hazaris were also appointed as faujdars, such as Mahabat Khan at Ajmer, Sadullah Khan in the suburbs of Akbarabad, Azam Khan at Mathura and Ilahwardi Khan (a panj hazari) at Jaunpur. The biographical details of the nobles help us in understanding this aspect. In Mahabat Khan's case, it may be stated that this was the time when he was in rebellion against Jahangir and was chasing Prince Khurram.[44] Not having Shahjahan's full confidence, he was given this lower office immediately after the coronation. Azam Khan had incurred royal displeasure by ill-treating the people as subedar of Gujrat, so he was removed from the post[45] and was placed in this lower position. Similarly, Ilahwardi Khan had lost the emperor's confidence due to the controversy of his secret relations with the Shah of Persia and was thrown out of favour during 1652–5,[46] hence this decline in the administrative cadre. However, Sadullah Khan cannot be included with these, because his appointment was an additional job along with the Diwani. When Agah Khan, who had been serving in this capacity for long, failed to manage things properly, the Diwan was given this job temporarily.[47]

Thus, even prestigious mansab holders were given lower posts either in case of royal displeasure, or under the pressure of administrative requirements.

In the light of the above discussion, one may reach the conclusion that a correspondence between the mansab and the post of faujdars may be established only with direct reference to the changing political conditions and military strategy. The fluctuation in the mansabs of faujdars, therefore, can be understood properly with the help of the political details of the period, otherwise there was hardly any rule to determine the mansab of these office-bearers. Generally, in crucial areas or crucial hours, high mansabdars seem to hold this position, while in less vulnerable regions and peaceful environments, lower mansabdars were also appointed in this capacity.

The ethnic composition of the faujdari may be another interesting aspect of this study. On the whole, it seems that out of the total number of appointments (i.e. 172) mentioned in Appendix 5.2, the share of Iranis is the largest. In declining order after them, one can see the Turanis, Indian Muslims and then the Afghans. The presence of Rajputs and Other Hindus, though in negligible number, is also worth noting, because, as compared to the subedari, they seem to occupy better positions in faujdari.

During 1628–36, when Shahjahan was busy in the Deccan, most of the important faujdaris were occupied by Iranis. In regions like Baiswarah, Gorakhpur, Jaunpur, Siwistan, Mathura, Qannauj, Narwar and Bahraich, only Iranis were posted. In succeeding years, they seem to lose this privileged position in almost all regions except Jaunpur. In some places like Jammu, Hisar, Bhakkar, Surat, Junagarh, Tirhut and Bijagarh, not a single Irani was posted throughout the reign.

Though the Turanis stood second, numberwise, yet, like the Iranis, they monopolized some faujdaris like Koil, Jammu, Bhakkar, Surat, Junagarh, Patan and Bijagarh during 1628–36. One may also point out some areas where not a single Turani was appointed throughout this reign, such as Qannauj, Bandari-Surat, Mandsur, the suburbs of Agra, Doab, Lakhi Jangal and Mahaban.

Up to 1636, Afghans were posted in the suburbs of Agra, Kalpi and Mewat. During 1637–41, they were posted in other regions like Jammu and Bijagarh. They were given more opportunities in areas like Qannauj, Bangash, Kangrah, Junagarh, Patan and Mandsur during the last phase (1642–58).

Duirng the first phase, Indian Muslims enjoyed this position in such places like Miyan-i-Doab, Hissar, Lakhi Jangal, Baroda, Tirhut and Mandsur. Ajmer, Sarhind, Siwistan and Bhakkar are areas where they emerged during the second phase. More expansion may be seen in their number in the suburbs of Agra, Mathura, Baiswarah and Shamsabad during the last phase.

Only one Rajput was appointed as faujdar of Ajmer in the first phase. In the second phase too, only one person from this community seems to hold this post at Kangrah. During 1642–58, however, they held this position in the suburbs of Agra in addition to Kangrah.

The position of these racial groups in the whole reign is condensed in Table 5.5, based upon the Appendix 5.2.

On the basis of what is said above, one may reach some tentative conclusions as follows.

(*a*) The numbers of Iranis and Turanis gradually decline in this office

TABLE 5.5: RACIAL AND RELIGIOUS COMPOSITION OF SOME FAUJDARS UNDER SHAHJAHAN

Place	*No. of appointments*	*Iranis*	*Turanis*	*Afghans*	*Indian Muslims*	*Other Muslims*	*Rajputs*	*Other Hindus*	*Unknown*
Ajmer	9	5	1	–	2	–	1	–	–
Akbarabad (suburbs)	11	4	–	1	1	4	1	–	–
Koil	3	1	2	–	–	–	–	–	–
Mathura-Mahaban	5	3	–	–	2	–	–	–	–
Miyan-i-Doab	12	8	–	–	4	–	–	–	–
Qannauj	4	1	–	2	–	–	–	1	–
Kalpi	2	–	–	2	–	–	–	–	–
Narwar	1	1	–	–	–	–	–	–	–
Mewat	3	1	1	1	–	–	–	–	–
Bangash	5	2	2	1	–	–	–	–	–
Bahraich	5	3	1	–	–	–	–	–	1
Gorakhpur	2	1	1	–	–	–	–	–	–
Lakhnau and Baiswarah	7	5	1	–	1	–	–	–	–
Kangrah	9	2	4	1	–	–	2	–	–
Jammu	6	–	4	1	–	1	–	–	–
Shamsabad	1	–	–	–	1	–	–	–	–

Hissar	3	–	2	–	1	–	–	–	–
Sarhind	6	2	1	–	1	–	–	2	–
Jaunpur	9	9	–	–	–	–	–	–	–
Siwistan	10	3	5	–	2	–	–	–	–
Bhakkar	6	–	4	–	2	–	–	–	–
Lakhi Jangal	5	2	–	–	2	–	–	1	–
Multan	2	1	1	–	–	–	–	–	–
Baroda	6	4	1	–	1	–	–	–	–
Surat	6	–	6	–	–	–	–	–	–
Junagarh	3	–	2	1	–	–	–	–	–
Patan	5	2	1	2	–	–	–	–	–
Bandar-i-Surat	10	5	–	–	–	5	–	–	–
Tirhut	5	–	1	–	3	1	–	–	–
Mandsur	8	2	–	1	5	–	–	–	–
Bijagarh	3	–	1	2	–	–	–	–	–
Total	172	67	42	15	28	11	4	4	1

after 1636, while a marked rise may be seen in the number of Indian Muslims. Afghans also seem to have improved their position during the second phase, and maintained almost the same level till the end of the reign. This coincides with Shahjahan's policy of gradually elevating Indian Muslism, strength and mansabwise, as shown earlier. This also confirms his attitude of prestige with compromise towards the Afghans after the rebellion of Khan-e-Jahan. In the last phase, they had earned such confindence that they were posted in disturbed and crucial areas like Kangarh and Bangash.

(*b*) It seems that in post-1636 period, the monopolizing tendency of some racial groups in specific regions was gradually discouraged, like that of Iranis in Mathura, Bahraich, etc., and of Turanis in Jammu, Bhakkar, Junagarh, Patan, etc. Other elements like Indian Muslims and Afghans were also given adequate opportunities to serve in these areas.

(*c*) During the first phase (1628–36) when Khan-e-Jahan rebelled, the Deccan wars were going on and the emperor had to visit the Deccan twice, Iranis held this office in most of the regions of north India. But in disturbed hilly regions like Kangrah and Jammu, Turanis were exclusively in the majority.[48] In the succeeding years too, mostly Turanis and Afghans were posted in such disturbed areas and in other such strategically important regions as Bangash. So it may be said that, generally, Iranis were concentrated in the interior areas while Turanis were mostly posted in more exposed, disturbed and vulnerable regions. Though Mathura and Doab were known for rebellious tendencies, being interior regions, these were usually put under the charge of Iranis and Indian Muslims. The latter were usually not posted in the north-west frontier region.

So it may be said that the racial composition of the faujdari may be analysed according to the requirements of changing political conditions and the characteristics of the different races.

(*d*) The promotion figures given in Appendix 5.2 suggest that promotions were usually made in sawar mansab at the time of appointment of a faujdar, justified by the nature of the job.

QILADARS

Shah Nawaz Khan, while referring to the appointment of Raja Bithaldas Gaur as qiladar of Ranthambore, observes, 'The title of "Raja" was worthless without qiladari. . . .'[49] This highlights the importance of this assignment. Prestigious nobles as Mahabat Khan, Sipahdar Khan, Bithaldas Gaur, Mutaqid Khan, Khalilullah Khan, etc., held this post in different regions and at different times.[50]

This attempt is to probe into some issues as: What was the office tenure of a qiladar? Can a link be established between the mansab and the post? What were the racial and religious backgrounds of these office-bearers? Was there any impact of such factors upon their appointments or removals? From which cadre, generally, were they picked up? What was their next likely post in case of transfer?

The necessary information relating to the first two decades is provided by the official historian Lahori. For the last ten years of the reign, the facts are available in Salih and Waris. However, in some cases *Maasir-ul-Umara* too is of much help. Yet, as compared to that of subedars and faujdars, our information about qiladars is even more limited. This author, therefore, has selected some places regarding which sufficient details are available. This selected evidence is arranged in Appendix 5.3. On this basis, one may make some tentative suggestions which may be regarded as possible answers to the queries raised above.

The appointment of nobles, their mansab with or without promotion and their tenure in a particular region as qiladar, may be reasonably explained with the help of clues like the strategic importance and impregnability of the fort, the dearth or abundance of turbulent elements in that area, and the overall changing political conditions of the period.

The vulnerable position of the north-west frontier regions, namely Kabul and Qandhar, and the important role of these places, which were indispensable to maintain the supply line to those distant forts as Lahore, is quite evident. This had a direct bearing upon the appointments of qiladars. That is why no mansabdars below 1000/500 was ever posted as qiladar of Kabul, Bust, Zamindawar or Qullat. During the Balkh-Badakhshan and Qandhar recovery campaigns, even higher mansabdars were appointed in Kabul. More promotion in sawar (specially in the case of the qiladars of Qandhar), further confirms the hypothesis that strategy and political developments had a direct reflection upon the mansab of the office-bearers. After the Mughal withdrawal from Balkh and the occupation of Qandhar by the Shah, more precautions had to be taken against the Uzbeks, therefore, in the closing years, the fort of Kabul was left under a high mansabdar of 3500/3000.

In other well-known and strong forts like Rohtas and Kangrah in Lahore, Kalinjar in Allahabad, Gwalior in Agra, and Ranthambore in suba Ajmer, usually high mansabdars of 1000 and above were posted. Rohtas[51] for example, was known for its structural strength and was situated in the Ghakkar territory, therefore, the minimum mansab of its qiladars was 2000/1000. Kangrah,[52] though in the Punjab but not very much exposed to the north-west, had qiladars of a minimum mansab of 700/500 and a maximum of 1000/800. Similarly, Kalinjar fort was counted among the strongest forts of Hindustan,[53] but since it existed in the fully secure and interior region of north India, even small mansabdars of 500/200 could be given its charge. But most of the qiladars who had long tenures there held a minimum mansab of 1000/500. Between 1645 and 1647 when Shahjahan was away in the north-west, a higher mansabdar of 1500/1000 was given its charge. Gwalior fort[54] was important not only because of its structural strength, but also because it was used as a prison for noted political prisoners since the olden days. Hence it had to be placed in strong and reliable hands. So Khan-e-Jahan Barha was made its qiladar in 1628 and held its charge for a long period. The significance of the fort of Ranthambore is evident from the fact that as a condition of leading the Qandhar campaign, Shahjahan had demanded this fort from Jahangir to accommodate his family.[55] Being a stronghold in Rajputana and having a convenient exit to the Deccan, this fort was always put under the charge of exceptionally high mansabdars. No one below 3000/2000 was ever posted there. Though for a very brief period, even Mahabat Khan (7000/7000) was given this qiladari. During the second phase of Jujhar Singh's rebellion, this fort was under the charge of Raja Bithaldas Gaur, which highlights the emperor's deep faith in the Rajput nobles. The said raja was eager to get its charge, and was delighted to receive this favour.[56] It also confirms the significance of this fort. In the fort of Dhamoni too, a trusted high mansabdar of 3000/3000 was posted, simply because the fort was captured in 1635 after crushing the rebellion of Jujhar Singh and was a stronghold in Bundelkhand.[57]

A cursory glance at the Deccan forts further confirms the strong link between the mansab figures of the chosen qiladars and the existing local conditions, political atmosphere and military strategy. For example, in the forts of Ahmadnagar, Ḍaulatabad and Junnair, mansabdars of 2000/500 and above were usually posted. In Udgir and Usa too, the mansab of the qiladars was mostly 2000/1000 and above. Thus, compared to the north, the mansabs of the qiladars of the Deccan were generally higher, with few exceptions in the north like Ranthambore, Gawalior and Rohtas, etc.

The mansabs of the qiladars of the three capital cities, namely, Akbarabad, Lahore and Delhi, were usually higher. If one watches Shahjahan's movements from Akbarabad closely, it emerges that during the longer periods of his absence from the capital, such as from August 1638 to January 1643[58] when he was in the north-west to watch the successful surrender of Qandhar and its consolidation, usually very high mansabdars of 4000/3000 were posted. Similarly, when he set out to supervise the Balkh campaign in 1645, only to return in January 1648,[59] three trusted nobles, namely, Baqi Khan, Pirthi Raj Rathor and Girdhar Das Gaur collectively served as qiladars; the first two enjoyed mansabs of 2000/2000 and the last one 1000/800. Between April 1648 and December 1653,[60] the emperor was away to supervise the Qandhar expedition, so Siyadat Khan, a mansabdar of 3000/1500 was assigned this job. After 1653, till his last visit to Akbarabad as emperor in November 1657,[61] Shahjahan did not go very far from the capital, therefore, Girdhardas (enjoying a mansab of 1500/1200) could safely be appointed as a qiladar there. In Shahjahanabad, the mansab of the qiladar was always 3000/1500 and above. In the case of Lahore, however, the mansab figures are comparatively lower, but usually not lower than 1000/400.

If Appendix 5.3 (giving details of the qiladars of these capital cities) is to be compared with Appendix 5.4 (showing Shahjahan's movements to different regions), one would be able to note that these recorded cases of the appointments of qiladars mostly cover those periods when the emperor was away from there. Would it be proper to assume on this basis, that in Akbarabad, Lahore and Shahjahanabad, the qiladars were usually appointed only in the absence of the emperor?

The tenures of qiladars (like their mansabs), differ from place to place due to the local conditons, political atmosphere and military strategy. In the frontier region or the north-west, the terms of qiladars were generally short. The average tenure in Kabul was less than two years while in Zamindawar and Bust, it was less than three years. In the interior and less exposed places as Rohtas, Kangrah, Gwalior, Ranthambore, etc., qiladars enjoyed longer terms. The keepers of some important forts in the Deccan, however, held this position for short terms. The qildars of Ahmadnagar and Daulatabad, for example, enjoyed this position for a maximum period of three years. The tenure of these officials in the three major capital cities was perhaps guided with the longer or shorter tours of the emperor. Except for a brief stay of almost three months, Shahjahan was away from Akbarabad from January 1645 to November 1657 as he was busy in supervising the Balkh campaign and then the Qandhar recovery expeditions. This long period was covered mainly by two qiladars, namely, Baqi Khan and Siyadat Khan. The former shared this position, for some time, with Pirthi Raj and Girdhar Das. Lahore, on the other hand, was visited more frequently by the emperor. From October 1639 to November 1642 and then from November 1645 to February 1652, he went and stayed there almost every year. Therefore, the term of the qiladars does not exceed a few months. It is only after February 1652, when, being disgusted with the Qandhar expeditions, he stopped visiting Lahore, that Yusuf Aqa enjoyed a longer tenure of four years or so. That the emperor's stays and absences from these major centres had some effect upon the tenures of these officials, is equaly true in the case of Shahjahanabad. During the period for which we have the appointments of qiladars, Shahjahan did not move to distant areas. In December 1656, an epidemic occurred in Delhi, so he left for Nurpur leaving Siyadat Khan as qiladar. On his return to the capital in January 1657, he was relieved of his appointment. Thus, it seems that due to the emperor's presence in the vicinity of the capital city and his frequent visits, the qiladars did not enjoy long tenures.

It will not be out of place to talk about the racial composition of the qiladari now. With the help of Appendix 5.3, we can easily point out some areas where specific ethnic groups seemed to enjoy favourable positions vis-à-vis other groups.

Our evidence suggests that the most vulnerable areas of the north-west frontier and the Punjab were usually put under Turani qiladars, as their number exceeds those of all other groups. This highlights Shahjahan's utmost faith in them. The total absence of Iranis in Qandhar and their small number in Kabul and Lahore further confirms their secondary position vis-à-vis the crown, specially in the north-west—and particularly in Qandhar—against the Shah of Persia. This simply implies that, as compared to Iranis, Turanis were trusted more, as far as the defence of this sensitive region was concerned. Iranis, however, formed a majority among the qiladars of the Deccan, where Turanis were few in number.

The Afghan veterans were posted in some important forts of Qandhar, the disturbed hilly region of Kangrah, and had a nominal representation in the Deccan. It is to be noted that they held this position of trust only in the last phase (1642–58) which, as explained above, was the period of recovery for them. In spite of this growing faith in them, not a single Afghan was ever given charge of the forts of the four major cities, viz., Akbarabad, Lahore, Kabul and Shahjahanabad.

Indian Muslims served in this capacity in different parts of the empire from the north-west to the Deccan, but their positions were particularly sound in Lahore, Kangrah, Kalinjar and Gwalior.

The warlike Rajputs were tried in crucial forts of the north-west, though not in large numbers, as well as in strategically important forts of the Deccan like Asir, Gavil and Daulatabad in fairly good numbers. The strong fort of Ranthambore mostly remained in their hands. Even during the rebellion of Jujhar Singh, Bithaldas Gaur held its charge, which shows their utmost reliability vis-à-vis the crown. Requisite faith placed in them is also evident from their overwhelming number among the qiladars of Akbarabad throughout this reign.

The position of these racial groups becomes more clear from Table 5.6, which is an abridgement of the detailed Appendix 5.3.

TABLE 5.6: RACIAL AND RELIGIOUS COMPOSITION OF SOME QILADARS OF SHAHJAHAN'S PERIOD

Name of the fort	*No. of appointments*	*Iranis*	*Turanis*	*Afghans*	*Indian Muslims*	*Other Muslims*	*Rajputs*	*Unknown*
Kabul	9	3	3	–	2	–	1	–
Bust	2	–	1	1	–	–	–	–
Zamindawar	4	–	2	1	1	–	–	–
Qullat	3	–	2	–	–	–	1	–
Akbarabad	8	1	2	–	–	–	5	–
Shahjahanabad	3	3	–	–	–	–	–	–
Lahore	9	1	4	–	2	1	1	–
Rohtas	2	1	1	–	–	–	–	–
Kangrah	5	1	–	1	2	–	–	1
Allahabad	1	–	–	–	–	1	–	–
Kalinjar	5	1	–	–	3	1	–	–
Gwalior	2	–	–	–	2	–	–	–
Ranthambore	4	1	–	–	–	1	2	–
Dhamoni	1	–	1	–	–	–	–	–
Surat	2	1	–	–	1	–	–	–
Ahmadnagar	9	5	1	1	2	–	–	–
Daulatabad	2	1	–	–	–	–	1	–
Junnair	3	2	1	–	–	–	–	–
Gavil	1	–	–	–	–	–	1	–
Chanda	1	–	–	–	1	–	–	–
Asir	3	1	–	–	–	–	2	–
Udgir	3	3	–	–	–	–	–	–
Usa	4	–	2	1	1	–	–	–
TOTAL	86	25	20	5	17	4	14	1

Regarding promotion in the mansab of qiladars at the time of their appointment, it may be said that more promotions were given in sawar than in zat, obviously because of the nature of the job. It is also to be noted that out of the total promotion awards, the maximum figure was shared by qiladars of the Deccan and the nroth-west frontier region. So it may be assumed that the main consideration behind promotions was the military requirement, which was determined by the political condition and military strategy.

At the end, a word may be said about the various disciplines from which qiladars were usually picked up. From Appendix 5.3, it emerges that out of 86 recorded cases of these appointments, only for about 44 cases do we have information regarding their previous posts. It seems that in about 39 cases, qiladars were picked up from amongst those who were already serving in provinces in one capacity or the other. A large number was, however, chosen from amongst faujdars. Usually, nobles serving in the north-west in different offices were also appointed as qiladars in that region.

A rough idea about the transfers may also be made with the help of Appendix 5.3. Out of 36 cases where the later assignments of the qiladars are mentioned, almost 33 persons were retained in provinces in different capacities like faujdars, qiladars, subedars, thanedars, etc.

The following conclusions may be drawn from this discussion on qiladars.

(*a*) The selection of big or small mansabdars dependend mainly upon the nature of the qiladari, which was determined by the local conditions of the place, military strategy of the fort or the overall political developments of the period. Therefore, no uniformity can be seen in the mansab figures of qiladars; variations according to the conditions had always been there.

(*b*) Second, variations in the tenures of the office of qiladars in different regions may be explained in terms of a policy based upon the political conditions and military strategy. The tenure of the qiladars of Akbarabad, Lahore and Shahjahanabad was regulated, perhaps, by the political tours of the emperor.

(*c*) Third, Iranis were not trusted against the Shah of Persia, hence they were not given qiladaris of the Qandhar forts.

(*d*) Turanis, on the other hand, enjoyed greater confidence of the emperor, therefore, in the vulnerable forts of the north-west and the Punjab, they held a very sound position.

(*e*) Last, it may be said that usually qiladars were picked up from amongst nobles serving in the provinces, and they were normally transferred to provincial offices.

NOTES

1. Besides Ibn-e-Hasan, *The Central Structure of the Mughal Empire*, New Delhi, 1970 and P. Saran, *Provincial Government under the Mughals*, Allahabad, 1941; see Chapter 5 on Administration in M. Athar Ali's *Mughal Nobility under Aurangzeb*, Bombay, 1968. Also see N.A. Siddiqui, 'Pulls and Pressures on the Faujdars under the Mughals', I.H.C., Patiala Session, 1967; M. Athar Ali, 'Provincial Governors under Shahjahan', I.H.C., Jabalpur Session, 1970.

2. Athar Ali, 'Provincial Governors under Shahjahan', I.H.C., Jabalpur Session, 1970.
3. For a detailed discussion regarding Vakil and Diwan-i-Kul, see Ibn-e-Hasan, op. cit., n. 1. above, Chapters 4 and 5.
4. From Salih, it is quite clear that on account's papers Rai Rayan's signature, and on parwanas his seal would be affixed below the seal of Jafar Khan (Salih, III (L), p. 268).
5. Salih, III (L), pp. 233–4 and 262.
6. Lahori, II, pp. 219–20; *M.U.*, II, pp. 441–8.
7. *M.U.*, III, pp. 530–55.
8. Lahori, II, pp. 132, 500 and 681; Salih, III (B), pp. 104, 120, etc.; *M.U.*, I, pp. 531–35.
9. The method of reaching this conclusion is that a net rise of 3000/2000 is made over the previous figure of 13,000/8000. This rise in zat is 23 per cent, while in sawar it is 25 per cent.
10. Azam Khan and Islam Khan were both sent as subedars to the Deccan: Lahori, I, p. 257; II, p. 430.
11. For such details as the nature of the work assigned, the status and position of Mir Bakhshi vis-à-vis the crown and in the overall administrative set-up, see Ibn-e-Hasan, op. cit., n. 1 above, Chapter 6.
12. Ibn-e-Hasan, however, has included only nine names in his table. See Ibn-e-Hasan, op. cit., n. 1 above, pp. 230–1.
13. Islam Khan, Mutamad Khan, Salabat Khan, Asalat Khan, Khalilullah Khan and Danishmand Khan had already served as Bakhshi-e-Doam (Lahori, I, p. 291; II, pp. 161, 485 and 491; Salih III (L), pp. 104–5 and 241). Mir Jumla, Jafar Khan, Lahrasp Khan and Muhammad Amin Khan had served in the capacity of Mir-e-Saman, subedar of Punjab, Qur Begi and Diwan respectively (Lahori, I (b), p. 86; II, pp. 344 and 500; Salih, III (L), pp. 233–34 and 262). Amin Khan served in the office of Diwan as his father's naib. Azam Khan was already holding this post and was simply confirmed (*M.U.*, I, pp. 174–80). Sadiq Khan too was an experienced person. He held this office under Jahangir from the ninth to the eighteenth reginal years (*M.U.*, II, pp. 729–31).
14. This can be grasped if one keeps in mind the old Mughal tradition of favouring a few selected families. See Beni Prasad, *History of Jahangir*, pp. 177–80; Irfan Habib, 'Family of Nur Jahan during Jahangir's Regin—a Political Study', *Medieval India—A Miscellany*, Vol. I, Bombay, 1969, pp. 74–95.
15. Lahori, I, pp. 538–9; I (b), p. 279; II, pp. 657 and 380–4; Salih, III (L), pp. 263–4.
16. For the position, powers and other details regarding this office, see Ibn-e-Hasan, op. cit., n. 1 above, Chapter 7.
17. Ibn-e-Hasan's list, however, contains only five names (p. 252). The mansabs of the Mir-e-Samans quoted by him do not tally with the figures given by Lahori. Mir Jumla's mansab is mentioned as 4000/2500. But it is interesting to note that the last mansab attained by this mansabdar was 5000/2000 (Lahori, I (b), pp. 86 and 295). At the time of appointment, his mansab was 3000/1200 (Lahori, I, p. 181) and it was after about one year that he reached 4000/1500 (Lahori, I, p. 320). Fazil Khan Mulla Alaul Mulk got a promotion of 500/100, which raised him to 1500/200 (Lahori, II, pp. 491–2) and not 1500/500 as is mentioned by Ibn-e-Hasan (p. 252). Similarly, when appointed for a second time, Aqil Khan was holding a mansab of 2000/700 (Lahori, II, p. 422) and not 2500/800 (Ibn-e-Hasan). However, the latter was the highest mansab reached by him in this office. But in the case of Sadullah Khan, the mansab given by Ibn-e-Hasan is neither the mansab given at the time of appointment, nor his highest attainment in this office. With a promotion of 500/200, he reached 2000/500 at the time of appointment, and 3500/800 was the highest mansab of the khan in this office (Lahori, II, pp. 347 and 422).
18. Lahori, I, pp. 176–7; *M.U.*, III, pp. 413–18.
19. Lahori, II, pp. 103 and 142.
20. Ibid., pp. 219–20 and 347.

21. Ibid., p. 310.
22. Afzal Khan was made Diwan-i-Kul (Lahori, I, p. 257), Mir Jumla was appointed Mir Bakhshi (Lahori, I (b), p. 85), Makramat Khan took the charge of Suba-e-Delhi (Lahori, II, p. 244), Aqil Khan was assigned the job of Waqa-i-Nawisi of Gujrat (Lahori, II, p. 373), Sadullah Khan was elevated to the high office of Diwan (Lahori, II, p. 431) and Aqil Khan, after his second appointment, was assigned the job of Bakhshi-e-Doam (Lahori, II, p. 491).
23. Lahori, II, pp. 547–8.
24. Lahori, I, p. 181, II, pp. 315–16; Salih, III (L), pp. 2–3. For details regarding this office, its historical background, nature of work, position and status of the sadr, see Ibn-e-Hasan, op. cit., n. 1 above, Chapter 8.
25. Lahori, I, p. 181. Appointed immediately after coronation, Musvi Khan, due to his mistakes, was removed in November 1642 (Lahori, II, pp. 315–16).
26. Lahori, II, pp. 315–16. He died in June 1647 (Lahori, II, p. 682). He enjoyed the highest mansab among the Sadrs, i.e. 6000/2000 (Lahori, II, p. 718).
27. Lahori, II, p. 684; Salih, III (L), pp. 2–3; *M.U.*, II, pp. 456–7.
28. With promotion, Musvi Khan reached 3000/750 (Lahori, I, p. 181); at the time of appointment Jalal Bukhari was given a mansab of 4000/700 (Lahori, II, pp. 315–16) and Hidayatullah was given a mansab of 1500/300 (Salih, III (L), pp. 2–3).
29. Musvi Khan got an increment of 1000/250, i.e. 33 per cent in zat and 50 per cent in sawar. Over the previous mansab of 1000/100 in case of Syed Hidayatullah, an addition of 500 zat and 200 sawars was made, which means 50 per cent addition to the zat and 200 per cent to the sawar.
30. The promotions of Ali Mardan Khan in Punjab, of Yusuf Muhammad Khan Tashqandi and Najabat Khan in Multan, and the promotions in the mansabs of Jansipar Khan and Shujat Khan for the subedari of Allahabad, are some examples of the rise of subedars of these provinces to the first category.
31. The possible reasons other than the importance of these faujdaris, for such demotions, in some cases, have been analysed under 'Faujdars' in Chapter 5.
32. See Irfan Habib, op. cit., n. 14 above, pp. 74–95.
33. N.A. Siddiqi, op. cit., n. 1 above.
34. A long list of places may be given about which Lahori and Salih specially have given insufficient details. Some of them are: Amanabad, Bir, Bhirah, Bari, Bhagalpur, Baglana, Churagarh, Chinpur, Chanda, Chauprah, Fatehpur and Bayana, Hoshangabad, Ilichpur, Iraj, Bhandir, Kuch-Haju, Kallam, Manakpur, Mongher, Mandu, Raprichandwar, Sarangpur, Saronj, Siyalkot, Tondapur, Shahzadpur, Islamabad, Itawah, Jhansi.
35. For Champat Bundela's activities, see Lahori, II, pp. 136–7, 193–5, 221 and 303–4.
36. Out of 172 recorded cases of such appointments, there are about 100 cases where the previous posts of faujdars are mentioned. Out of these, 80 seem to belong to the provincial services and only 20 seem to hold central offices. See Appendix 5.2.
37. Lahori, I, p. 195.
38. See Appendix 5.4.
39. Lahori, I, pp. 195, 196 and 204–5; I (b), pp. 71–2, 76 and 105; *M.U.*, II, p. 24; Salih, III (B), pp. 110–11.
40. Lahori, I (b), p. 105. Murshid Quli Khan was killed by the rebels there in November 1637 (Lahori, II, pp. 7–8).
41. For rebellions in this area, see Lahori, I, pp. 311–14; II, pp. 13–14, 148–49, 154 and 401–2; *M.U.*, II, pp. 430–1, etc. Immediately after the coronation, Nazar Muhammed posed a threat to Kabul (Lahori, I, pp. 212–14).
42. In the case of Kangrah, Lahori clearly says that increasing the strength of the army was indispensable for controlling the situation in such a hilly region (Lahori, I (b), pp. 216–17). For the rebellions of the zamindars of Srinagar, Jammu and Tibbat, see Lahori, I (b), pp. 250–1, 90–3 and 281–6; II, pp. 159–60; Salih, III (L), pp. 126–7, 213 and 215 and B.P. Saxena, *History of Shahjahan of Dihli*, Allahabad, 1958, p. 123.

43. Irfan Habib, *An Atlas of the Mughal Empire*, Delhi, 1982, pp. 29–30, and sheet 8A.
44. *M.U.*, III, pp. 385–409.
45. Lahori, II, p. 290. When Azam Khan could not perform the duty at Mathura, satisfactorily, he was sent to Kashmir and was not given any post (Lahori, II, p. 500).
46. Salih, III (L), pp. 148–9.
47. Ibid., p. 157.
48. Najabat Khan led an expedition against the zamindar of Srinagar in 1635 (Lahori, I (b), pp. 90–3). In 1637, Bhopat (son of Sangram), the zamindar of Jammu, rebelled but was killed by Shah Quli Khan (Lahori, I (b), pp. 250–1).
49. *M.U.*, II, p. 252.
50. Lahori, I, pp. 287 and 399; II, pp. 110 and 244; Salih, III (L), p. 263, etc.
51. *M.U.*, III, pp. 2, 145 and 277–9.
52. *M.U.*, II, pp. 184–90.
53. *M.U.*, III, p. 208.
54. Ibid., p. 54.
55. *M.U.*, II, p. 192. For the description of this fort, see *M.U.*, II, p. 156.
56. Lahori, I, p. 369; *M.U.*, II, p. 252.
57. *M.U.*, II, pp. 217 and 785; Lahori, I (b), pp. 110–11.
58. See Appendix 5.4.
59. Ibid.
60. Ibid.
61. Ibid.

APPENDIX 5.1: SUBEDARS

Name	*Racial group*	*Mansab*			*Tenure of office*	*Previous post*	*Later assignment*	*Sources*
		Previous	*Promotion*	*Present*				
1	2	3	4	5	6	7	8	9
				KABUL				
Lashkar Khan Mashhadi	Irani	3000/ 2000	+ 2000/ 2000	5000/ 4000	Feb. 1628– Nov. 1631	–	SD[1] Delhi	Lahori, I, pp. 120, 125–26, 400 and 440.
Said Khan Zafar Jang	Turani	4000/ 2500	+ 1500/ sawars 1000 × 2h–3h	4000/ 4000 1000 × 2h–3h	Nov. 1631– Feb. 1641	Serving at Kabul	SD Punjab	Ibid., pp. 400–1; II, pp. 222 and 236
Ali Mardan Khan	Irani	7000/ 7000 3000 × 2h–3h	+ 2000 × 2h–3h	7000/ 7000 5000 × 2h–3h	Feb. 1641 –	SD Kashmir	–	Lahori, II, pp. 125 and 222
Qulij Khan	Turani	5000/ 5000 2000 × 2h–3h	+ 2000 sawars 2h–3h	5000/ 5000 4000 × 2h–3h	Sep. 1649 –	SD Punjab	–	Ibid., pp. 35 and 356; Salih, III(B), pp. 100
Murad, Prince[2]	–	–	–	– 1651	Jan. 1650–	SD Deccan	SD Malwa	Salih, III (B), pp. 102, 106 and 125.
Mahabat Khan s/o Mahabat Khan	Irani	4000/ 3000	–	4000/ 3000	Apr. 1651– June 1651	Mir Bakhshi	–	Salih, III (B), pp. 120 and 122.
Said Khan Zafar Jang	Turani	7000/ 7000 5000 × 2h–3h	–	7000/ 7000 5000 × 2h–3h	June. 1651– Jan. 1652	SD Bihar	Died	Lahori, II, p. 636; Salih, III (B), pp. 6, 123 and 134.

(contd.)

1	*2*	*3*	*4*	*5*	*6*	*7*	*8*	*9*
Mahabat Khan s/o Mahabat Khan	Irani	4000/ 3000	+ 1000/ 2000	5000/ 5000	Dec. 1651–1652	Mir Bakhshi	–	Salih, III (L), pp. 120, 134 and 138.
Bahadur Khan (Naib-i-Dara)	Muslim	4000/ 2500	–	4000/ 2500	July 1652–Jan. 1657	SD Gujrat	SD Punjab	Salih, III (L), pp. 63–4, 148, 200–1 and 236.
Rustam Khan Feroze Jang	Turani	6000/ 5000	+ 1000 sawars	6000/ 6000 5000 × 2h–3h	Jan. 1657–1658	–	–	Salih, III (L), p. 236; *M.U.*, II, pp. 275–6.
Mahabat Khan s/o Mahabat Khan	Irani	5000/ 5000	–	5000/ 5000	Mar. 1658	–	–	Salih, III (L), pp. 269 and 451.
				QANDHAR				
Qulij Khan	Turani	4000/ 4000	+ 1000/ 1000 2000 × 2h–3h	5000/ 5000	Mar. 1638–Feb. 1641	SD Multan	SD Multan	Lahori, II, pp. 35, 223–4 and 234.
Safdar Khan	Turani	5000/ 3000	+ 2000 sawars	5000/ 5000	Feb. 1641–Mar. 1644	SD Akbarabad	Died	Lahori, II, pp. 215, 223–4 and 356.
Said Khan Zafar Jang	Turani	6000/ 6000 × 2h–3h	–	6000/ 6000 2h–3h	Mar. 1644–Apr. 1644	SD Punjab	SD Multan	Lahori, II, pp. 47, 356 and 577.
Daulat Khan Khawas Khan	Ind. M.	3000/ 3000	+ 1000/ 1000	4000/ 4000	Aug. 1646–Feb. 1649 July	Darogha-i-Mardum-i-	–	Lahori, II, p. 577; Salih, III (L), p. 77.

KASHMIR

Aitqad Khan Mirza-Shapur	Irani	4000/ 4000	–	4000/ 4000	1628 to Aug. 1632	–	SD Delhi	Lahori, I, pp. 125, 182, 432 and 472.
Khwaja Abul Hasan (Zafar Khan as his naib)	"	6000/ 6000	–	6000/ 6000	Aug. 1632– Mar. 1633	–	Died	Lahori, I, pp. 257, 432 and 473.
Zafar Khan	"	2500/ 1000	+ 500/ 1000	3000/ 2000	Mar. 1633– Nov. 1638	Naib SD Kashmir	–	Lahori, I, p. 474; II, p. 125.
Ali Mardan Khan (Ali Beg as his naib)	"	6000/ 6000	–	6000/ 6000	Nov. 1638– Feb. 1641	–	SD Punjab and Kabul	Lahori, II, pp. 123, 125 and 222.
Shah Quli Khan	Turani	2000/ 2000	+ 1000 zat	3000/ 2000	Feb. 1641– Mar. 1641	FD[1] Bhakkar	Died	Lahori, II, pp. 220–1, 223 and 225.
Tarbiyat Khan	"	2000/ 1200	+ 500/ 300	2500/ 1500	Mar. 1641– Mar. 1642	Qush Begi	Bakhshi	Lahori, II, pp. 183, 225 and 282–3; *M.U.*, I, pp. 488–9.
Zafar Khan	Irani	3000/ 2000	–	3000/ 2000	Mar. 1642 –	–	–	Lahori, I, (b), p. 298; II, pp. 282–3.
Murad, Prince					July 1647– Mar. 1648			Salih, III (L), pp. 2 and 23.
Hussain Beg	Irani	1000/ 400	+ 500/ 1100	1500/ 1500	Mar. 1648– 1655	Akhta Begi	FD Miyan-i-Doab	Lahori, II, p. 492; Salih, III (L), p. 23
Lashkar Khan Yadgar Beg	"	2500/ 1500	+ 500 sawar	2500/ 2000	May 1657 –	Bakhshi II	–	Salih, III (L), pp. 208 and 247.

(contd.)

1	2	3	4	5	6	7	8	9
				PUNJAB				
Asaf Khan 'Yaminuddaulah' (Inayatullah as his naib)	Irani	8000/ 8000 2h–3h	–	8000/ 8000 2h–3h	1628 – May 1632	–	–	Lahori, I, pp. 125 and 425.
Wazir Khan	Indian Muslim	5000/ 5000	+ 1000 × 2h–3h	5000/ 5000 1000 × 2h–3h	May 1632 – Sep. 1639	–	SD Akbara-bad	Lahori, I, p. 425; II, p. 158.
Mutamad Khan	Irani	4000/ 1200	–	4000/ 1200	Sep. 1639–1639–40	Mir Bakhshi	Died	Lahori, I (b), pp. 242 and 279; II, pp. 158 and 168.
Ali Mardan Khan	"	6000/ 6000	1000/ 1000	7000/ 7000	Oct. 1639–Feb. 1641	SDKashmir	SD Kabul	Lahori, II, pp. 163 and 222.
Said Khan Zafar Jang	Turani	6000/ 6000 2h–3h	–	6000/ 6000 2h–3h	Aug. 1641–Mar. 1642	SD Kabul	SD Multan	Lahori, II, pp. 47, 222, 236 and 284–5.
"	"	"	–	"	Nov. 1642–Mar. 1644	SD Multan	SD Qandhar	Lahori, II, pp. 317 and 356.
Qulij Khan	Turani	5000/ 5000 2000 × 2h–3h	–	5000/ 5000 2000 × 2h–3h	Mar. 1644–Aug. 1646	SD Multan	SD Kabul	Lahori, II, pp. 35, 234, 356 and 564; Salih, III (L) and p. 100.
Jafar Khan	Irani	5000/ 3000	–	5000/ 3000	Apr. 1646–May 1647	–	Mir Bakhshi	Lahori, I (b), p. 248; II, pp. 325, 500 and 681.
Syed Salabat Khan (Dara's naib)	Indian Muslim	1500/ 200	–	1500/ 200	Oct. 1650 –	SD Allahabad (Dara's naib)	–	Salih, III (L), p. 115; *M.U.*, II, p. 457.

Muin Khan	Muslim	1000/ 300	–	1000/ 300	July 1656– Jan. 1657	–	–	Lahori, I, p. 230; Salih, III (L), pp. 229 and 236.
Bahadur Khan (Dara's naib)	"	4000/ 2500	–	4000/ 2500	Jan. 1657– Oct. 1657	SD Kabul	SD Bihar	Salih, III (L), pp. 201–1, 236, 263 and 274.
Izzat Khan (Dara's naib)	Irani	2000/ 2000	–	2000/ 2000	Oct. 1657 –	SD Multan	–	Salih, III (L), pp. 212 and 263.
				MULTAN				
Asaf Khan Yaminuddaulah (Amir Khan as his naib)	Irani	8000/ 8000 2h–3h	–	8000/ 8000 2h–3h	1628 to 1631–32	–	–	Lahori, I, pp. 125 and 424.
Najabat Khan	Turani	2500/ 2000	–	2500/ 2000	June 1632 –	FD Multan	FD Kangrah	Lahori, I, pp. 372 and 428; I (b), p. 11
Qulij Khan	"	4000/ 4000	–	4000/ 4000	June 1632– Mar. 1638	SD Allaha-bad	SD Qandhar	Lahori, I, pp. 421, 426 and 428; II, p. 35.
Yusuf Muhammad Khan Tashqandi	"	3000/ 2500	+ 500 sawars	3000/ 3000	Dec. 1638– Aug. 1639	FD Bhakkar	Died	Lahori, II, pp. 128 and 155.
Najabat Khan	"	3000/ 3000	+ 1000/ 1000	4000/ 4000	Aug. 1639– June 1641	FD Kol	–	Lahori, II, pp. 155, and 234.
Qulij Khan	"	5000/ 5000 2000 × 2h–3h	–	5000/ 5000 2000 × 2h–3h	June 1641	SD Qandhar	–	Lahori, II, pp. 35 and 234.
Said Khan Zafar Jang	"	6000/ 6000 2h–3h	–	6000/ 6000 2h–3h	Mar. 1642– Nov. 1642	SD Punjab	SD Punjab	Lahori, II, pp. 47, 236, 284–85 and 317.

(contd.)

1	*2*	*3*	*4*	*5*	*6*	*7*	*8*	*9*
Murad, Prince	Turani	–	–	–	1642–43 to 1646–47			Lahori, II, pp. 307 and 559.
Said Khan Zafar Jang	”	6000/ 6000 2h–3h	–	6000/ 6000 2h–3h	Aug. 1646– Sep. 1647	SD Qandhar	SD Bihar	Lahori, II, pp. 47, 356, and 577; Salih, III (L), p. 6.
Bahadur Khan	Afghan	5000/ 5000	–	5000/ 5000	Sep. 1648– Jul. 1649	–	Died	Lahori, II, p. 554; Salih, III (L), pp. 64–5 and 99.
Aurangzeb, Prince				Jul. 1652	Dec. 1649–			Salih, III (L), pp. 105 and 148.
Muhammad Ali Khan	Turani	2000/ 1000	–	2000/ 1000	1651–2 to 1656	–	SD Bihar	Salih, III (L), pp. 212 and 460 (B).
Izzat Khan	Irani	2000/ 2000 500 x 2h–3h	–	2000/ 2000 500 x 2h–3h	Jan. 1656– Oct. 1657	–	SD Punjab	Salih, III (L), pp. 212, 263 and 458 (B).
Musvi Gilani (Dara's naib)	”	800/ 200	+ 200/ 200	1000/ 400	Oct. 1657 – Multan	Diwan and Bakhshi of	–	Salih, III (L), pp. 147 and 263.
				AKBARABAD				
Islam Khan Mashhadi	Irani	4000/ 2500	+ 500 sawar	4000/ 3000	Dec. 1629– Apr. 1631	Bakshi II	SD Gujrat	Lahori, I, pp. 291 and 369.
Safdar Khan	Turani	3000/ 2000	–	3000/ 2000	Apr. 1631– May 1633	–	–	Lahori, I, pp. 307, 369 and 477–8.
Azam Khan	Irani	5000/ 5000	–	5000/ 5000	Sep. 1635– May 1636	–	SD Gujrat	Lahori, I (b), pp. 105 and 166.

Saif Khan	Irani	4000/ 4000	–	4000/ 4000	Feb. 1638– Jan. 1639	SD Gujrat	SD Bengal	Lahori, I, p. 177; I (b); p. 166; II, pp. 20 and 130.
Safdar Khan	Turani	5000/ 3000	–	5000/ 3000	Jan. 1639– Nov. 1640		SD Qandhar	Lahori, II, pp. 122, 130 and 215.
Wazir Khan	Indian Mulsim	5000/ 5000 1000 × 2h–3h	–	5000/ 5000 1000 × 2h–3h	Nov. 1640– Aug. 1641	SD Punjab	Died	Lahori, II, pp. 158, 215 and 241; I, p. 425.
Jaswant Singh, Raja	Rajput	5000/ 5000 1000 × 2h–3h	–	5000/ 5000 1000 × 2h–3h	Jan. 1645– Apr. 1645	–	–	Lahori, II, pp. 230, 407 and 418.
Ikhlas Khan Sheikh Farid	Ind. M.	2500/ 1500	+ 500 zat	3000/ 1500	Apr. 1645– 1646	–	–	Lahori, II, pp. 418 and 483–4.
				DELHI				
Qulij Khan	Turani	2500/ 2000	–	2500/ 2000	1628 to 1629	–	SD Allahabad	Lahori, I, pp. 118, 126 and 255.
Mahabat Khan	Irani	7000/ 7000 × 2h–3h	–	7000/ 7000 2h–3h	Feb. 1629– Jun. 1632	SD Deccan	SD Deccan	Lahori, I, pp. 117, 255 and 426.
Lashkar Khan Mashhadi	"	5000/ 4000	–	5000/ 4000	Oct. 1632– Mar. 1633	SD Kabul	Retired	Lahori, I, pp. 120, 440 and 472.
Aitqad Khan Mirza-Shapur	"	4000/ 4000	–	4000/ 4000	Mar. 1633 –	SD Kashmir	FD Jaunpur	Lahori, I, pp. 182 and 472; I (b), p. 166.
Baqar Khan Najm-e-Sani	"	4000/ 4000	–	4000/ 4000	1634 – Apr. 1635	SD Gujrat	SD Allahabad	Lahori, I (b), pp. 8, 72, 87 and 274; I, p. 182.
Asalat Khan	"	1500/ 800	+ 1500/ 1700	3000/ 2500	Aprl. 1635– Sep. 1637	Bakhshi of Ahadis	Bakhshi II	Lahori, I (b), pp. 67–8, 87 and 280, II, p. 161.

(contd.)

1	*2*	*3*	*4*	*5*	*6*	*7*	*8*	*9*
Ghairat Khan	Turani	1500/ 800	+ 1000/ 1200	2500/ 2000	Sep. 1637– Sep. 1639	–	QD[1] Lahore	Lahori, I (b), p. 280; II, pp. 158 and 179.
Ilahwardi Khan	Irani	4000/ 4000	+ 1000/ 1000	5000/ 5000	Sep. 1639 –	FD Mathura	–	Lahori, II, p. 158.
Makramat Khan	"	2500/ 2000	+ 500/ 1000	3000/ 3000	Sep. 1641– Dec. 1649	Mir-i-Saman	Died	Lahori, II, pp. 103 and 244; Salih, III (B), p. 104.
Jafar Khan	"	5000/ 4000	+ 1000 sawar 2h–3h	5000/ 5000 1000 × 2h–3h	Dec. 1649– Feb. 1651	Mir Bakhshi	SD Thatta	Salih, III (B), pp. 104 and 120.
Khalilullah Khan	"	4000/ 3000	+ 1000 sawar	4000/ 4000	Feb. 1651 to 1653–4	"	–	Salih, III (B), pp. 104–5 and 120; *M.U.* I., pp. 777–8.
Fazil Khan	"	2000/ 500	+ 500/ 100	2500/ 600	Nov. 1654 –	Mir-i-Saman	–	Salih, III (L), pp. 104 and 191.
Khalilullah Khan	"	5000/ 4000	+ 1000 sawar 1000 × 2h–3h	5000/ 5000 1000 × 2h–3h	Oct. 1657 –	–	–	Salih, III (L), pp. 120 and 263.
				THATTA				
Mirza Isa Tarkhan	Turani	2000+ 1200	2000/ 1300	4000/ 2500	Dec. 1627– Mar. 1628	–	SD Mathura	Lahori, I, pp. 78–9, 181 and 230.
Sher Khwaja Baqi Khan	Irani	4000/ 3500	–	4000/ 3500	Mar. 1628– May 1628	–	Died	Lahori, I, pp. 181 and 200.
Murtaza Khan Mir Hisamuddin Anju	"	4000/ 3000	–	4000/ 3000	May 1628– Oct. 1629	–	Died	Lahori, I, pp. 181, 200 and 287.

Amir Khan s/o Qasim Khan	Irani	2500/ 1500	+ 500/ 500	3000/ 2000	Oct. 1629 –	–	–	Lahori, I, p. 287.
Yusu Muhammad Khan Tashqandi	Turani	2500/ 1200	+ 500/ 800	3000/ 2000	1631–32 to July 1635	–	FD Bhakkar	Lahori, I, pp. 423–4; I (b), p. 101; II, p. 22; *M.U.*, III, p. 965.
Daulat Khan Khawas Khan	Indian Muslim	3000/ 2000	–	3000/ 2000	July 1635– Jun. 1640	–	SD Qandhar	Lahori, I, pp. 474–5; I (b), p. 101; II, pp. 198 and 577.
Ghairat Khan	Turani	2500/ 2000	+ 500 zat	3000/ 2000	Jun. 1640– Mar. 1641	QD Lahore	Died	Lahori, II, pp. 198 and 225.
Shad Khan	"	1500/ 1200	+ 500/ 500	2000/ 1700	Mar. 1641– Jun. 1642	FD Bhakkar	FD Siwistan	Lahori, II, pp. 225 and 302–3.
Amir Khan s/o Qasim Khan	Irani	3000/ 2000	–	3000/ 2000	Jun. 1642– Apr. 1647	FD Siwistan	Died	Lahori, I, p. 287; II, pp. 302–3 and 641.
Mughal Khan s/o Zain Khan	"	2500/ 2000	+ 500 zat	3000/ 2000	Apr. 1647 –	QD Udgir	–	Lahori, II, p. 641.
Aurangzeb, Prince	–	–	–	–	Dec. 1649	–	–	Salih, III, (L), p. 105.
Said Khan, Zafar Jang	Turani	7000/ 7000 5000 × 2h–3h	–	7000/ 7000 5000 × 2h–3h	– Feb. 1651	SD Bihar	SD Kabul	Lahori, II, p. 636; Salih, III (L), 6, 120 and 123.
Zafar Khan	Irani	5000/ 5000	–	5000/ 5000	Feb. 1651 –	SD Delhi	–	Salih, III (L), pp. 104 and 120.
Mughal Khan s/o Zain Khan	"	3000/ 2000	–	3000/ 2000	July 1651 –	–	–	Lahori, II, p. 723; Salih, III (L), p. 126.

(contd.)

1	*2*	*3*	*4*	*5*	*6*	*7*	*8*	*9*
Sardar Khan	Turani	4000/ 3000	–	4000/ 3000	1652–3 to Dec. 1652	FD Churagarh	Died	Lahori, II, p. 721; Salih, III (L), pp. 112 and 152–3; *M.U.*, II, p. 438.
Zafar Khan	Irani	3000/ 1500	+ 500 sawar	3000/ 2000	Dec. 1652 to 1655–6	SD Kashmir	–	Lahori, II, p. 310; Salih, III (L), pp. 141 and 152–3; *M.U.*, II, p. 760.
				ALLAHABAD				
Jansipar Khan	Irani	2500/ 3000	+ 1500/ 1000	4000/ 4000	Mar. 1628– Mar. 1629	–	–	Lahori, I, pp. 126, 185 and 255.
Qulij Khan	Turani	2500/ 1500	+ 500/ 500	3000/ 2000	Mar. 1629– Jun. 1632	SD Delhi	SD Multan	Lahori, I, pp. 255, 426, 126 and 428.
Saif Khan	Irani	4000/ 4000	–	4000/ 4000	Jun. 1632– July 1635	SD Bihar	SD Gujrat	Lahori, I, pp. 177 and 426; I (b), p. 102.
Azam Khan	”	6000/ 6000	–	6000/ 6000	Jul. 1635– May 1636	SD Bengal	SD Gujrat	Lahori, I., p. 343; I (b), pp. 83, 102 and 166.
Baqar Khan Najm-e-Sani	”	4000/ 4000	–	4000/ 4000	1636 to May 1637	SD Delhi	Died	Lahori, I, p. 182, I (b), pp. 87, 274.
Syed Shujat Khan	Indian Muslim	4000/ 2000	+ 2000 sawar	4000/ 4000	Jun. 1637– Aug. 1642	FD Tirhut	–	Lahori, I (b), p. 274; II, p. 307.
Abdullah Khan Feroze Jang	Turani	6000/ 6000	–	6000/ 6000	Aug. 1642– Mar. 1643	SD Bihar	–	Lahori, I, p. 354; II, pp. 136–7, 307 and 332.
Shaista Khan	Irani	5000/ 5000 3000 × 2h–3h	–	5000/ 5000 3000 × 2h–3h	Mar. 1643– Jun. 1645	SD Bihar	SD Malwa	Lahori, II, pp. 21, 332 and 425.

Bahadur Khan (Dara's naib)	Muslim	1000/ 200	–	1000/ 200	Jun. 1645– Jul. 1648	–	SD Gujrat	Lahori, II, pp. 424–5; Salih, III (L), pp. 63–4.
Syed Salabat Khan (Dara's naib)	Indian Muslim	2000/ 400	–	2000/ 400	1651 –	SD Punjab	–	Salih, III (L), pp. 115, 121 and 228; *M.U.*, II, p. 457.
AWADH								
Mirza Khan Manochahar	Irani	3000/ 2000	–	3000/ 2000	– July 1648	FD Kangrah	QD Ahmadnagar	Lahori, I (b), pp. 93 and 298; Salih, III (L), pp. 64 and 125–6.
Aitqad Khan Mirzashapur	"	5000/ 5000	–	5000/ 5000	July 1648– Jan. 1650	SD Bengal	Died	Lahori, II, p. 332; Salih, III (L), pp. 64 and 106
Shahnawaz Khan	"	5000/ 5000 2h–3h	–	5000/ 5000 2h–3h	Dec. 1652 –	SD Malwa	–	Salih, III (L), pp. 102 and 152.
MALWA								
Khan-e-Zaman	Irani	5000/ 5000	–	5000/ 5000	Feb. 1628– May 1628	–	Naib SD Deccan	Lahori, I, pp. 158 and 199.
Khan-e-Jahan Lodhi	Afghan	7000/ 7000 2h–3h	–	7000/ 7000 2h–3h	May 1628– Oct. 1629	SD Deccan	Escaped	Lahori, I, pp. 182, 199 and 275–6.
Mutaqid Khan	Irani	4000/ 2000	–	4000/ 2000	1630–1 to May 1632	FD Ajmer	FD Nawahi-e-Akbarabad	Lahori, I, pp. 79, 362, 372 and 425.
Khan-e-Dauran Nusrat Jang	Turani	4000/ 4000	–	4000/ 4000	May 1632– Nov. 1634	–	SD Paien Ghat (Deccan)	Lahori, I, pp. 396 and 425; I (b), p. 63.

(contd.)

1	2	3	4	5	6	7	8	9
Ilahwardi Khan	Irani	3000/ 2000	+ 1000/ 2000	4000/ 4000	Nov. 1634–1635	Qarawal Begi	SD Khandesh	Lahori, I (b), pp. 5, 63 and 97.
Khan-e-Dauran Nusrat jang	Turani	4000/ 4000	–	4000/ 4000	1635 to Jun. 1644	SD Paien Ghat	SD Deccan	Lahori, I, p. 396; I (b), 97; II, p. 376.
Sardar Khan	"	3000/ 3000	+ 1000 zat	4000/ 3000	July 1644–Jun. 1645	FD Bangash	FD Churágarh	Lahori, II, pp. 223, 378 and 425.
Shaista Khan	Irani	5000/ 5000 4000 × 2h–3h	–	5000/ 5000 4000 × 2h–3h	Jun. 1645–Sep. 1646	SD Allahabad	SD Gujrat	Lahori, II, pp. 377–8, 425 and 583.
Shahnawaz Khan	"	4000/ 4000	+ 1000/ 1000	5000/ 5000	Sep. 1646–July 1648	Nazim of Jaunpur Deccan	Ataliq of Murad in	Lahori, II, p. 583; Salih, III (L), p. 64.
Shaista Khan	"	5000/ 5000 2h–3h	–	5000/ 5000 2h–3h	July 1648–Sep. 1648	SD Gujrat	SD Deccan	Lahori, II, p. 719; Salih, III (L), pp. 63–4 and 102.
Shahnawaz Khan	"	5000/ 5000	–	5000/ 5000	Sep. 1649–Dec. 1652 Deccan	Ataliq of Murad in	SD Awadh	Lahori, II, p. 583; Salih, III (L), pp. 102 and 152.
Murad, Prince					May 1651–Feb. 1654			Salih, III (L), pp. 125 and 180.
Shaista Khan	"	5000/ 5000 2h–3h	–	5000/ 5000 2h–3h	Jan. 1655–Dec. 1657	SD Gujrat	–	Lahori, II, p. 719; Salih, III (L), pp. 180, 199 and 281.
Jaswant Singh	Rajput	6000/ 6000 5000 × 2h–3h	+ 1000/ 1000 5000 × 2h–3h	7000/ 7000	Dec. 1657 –	–	–	Salih, III (L), p. 281.

GUJRAT

Sher Khan Nahar Khan	Afghan	3000/ 2500	+ 2000/ 2500	5000/ 5000	Dec. 1627– Apr. 1631	–	Died	Lahori, I, pp. 76 and 368–9; Mirat, I, pp. 202-3 and 206.
Islam Khan	Irani	4000/ 4000	+ 1000 zat	5000/ 4000	Apr. 1631– Jan. 1633	SD Akbarabad	Mir Bakhshi	Lahori, I, pp. 369, 450–1 and 542; Mirat, I, pp. 207–8.
Baqar Khan Najm-e-Sani	"	4000/ 4000	–	4000/ 4000	Jan. 1633– Mar. 1634	SD Orissa	SD Delhi	Lahori, I, pp. 450–1; I (b), pp. 8 and 72; Mirat, I, pp. 208–9.
Sipahdar Khan	"	5000/ 5000	–	5000/ 5000	Mar. 1634– July 1635	SD Ahmadnagar	QD Junnair	Lahori, I, pp. 182 and 399; I (b), pp. 8 and 102; II, p. 378; Mirat, I, p. 209.
Saif Khan	"	4000/ 4000	–	4000/ 4000	July 1635– May 1636	SD Allahabad	SD Akbarabad	Lahori, I (b), pp. 102 and 166; II, p. 20; Mirat, I, p. 209.
Azam Khan	"	6000/ 6000	–	6000/ 6000	May 1636– Apr. 1642	SD Allahabad	Tiyuldar of Mathura	Lahori, I, p. 343; I (b), pp. 102 and 166; II, pp. 290 and 425; Mirat, I, p. 210.
Mirza Isa Tarkhan	Turani	5000/ 5000 1000 × 2h–3h	+ 1500 sawar × 2h–3h	5000/ 5000 2500 × 2h–3h	Apr. 1642 to 1644–5	FD Surat	FD Surat	Lahori, II, pp. 290, and and 377; M.U., III, pp. 487–8.
Aurangzeb, Prince					Feb. 1645			Lahori, II, p. 411.
Shaista Khan	Irani	5000/ 5000 2h–3h	–	5000/ 5000 2h–3h	July 1652– Feb. 1654	SD Deccan	SD Malwa	Lahori, II, p. 719; Salih, III (L), pp. 102, 148, 180 and 199.

(contd.)

1	2	3	4	5	6	7	8	9
Murad, Prince				Feb. 1654				Salih, III (L), p. 180.
Qasim Khan Mutmad Khan	Irani	5000/ 5000 2h–3h	–	5000/ 5000 2h–3h	Dec. 1657– –	SD Bihar	–	Salih, III (L), pp. 244 and 281.
				BIHAR				
Kahan-e-Alam	Turani	6000/ 5000	–	6000/ 5000	Feb. 1628– Sep. 1628	–	Retired	Lahori, I, pp. 120, 125–6, 228 and 426–7.
Saif Khan	Irani	4000/ 4000	–	4000/ 4000	Sep. 1628– Jun. 1632	SD Gujrat	SD Allahbad	Lahori, I, pp. 77, 177, 228 and 426.
Abdullah Khan Feroze Jang	Turani	6000/ 6000	–	6000/ 6000	Jun. 1632– Feb. 1639	–	–	Lahori, I, pp. 354 and 426; II, pp. 136–7.
Shaista Khan	Irani	5000/ 5000 3000 x 2h–3h	–	5000/ 5000 3000 x 2h–3h	Feb. 1639– Mar. 1643	Naib SD Deccan	SD Allahabad	Lahori, I (b), p. 271; II, pp. 21, 136–7 and 332.
Aitqad Khan Mirza Shapur	"	5000/ 4000	+ 1000 sawar	5000/ 5000	Mar. 1643– Sep. 1646	SD Delhi	SD Bengal	Lahori, I, p. 472; II, pp. 332 and 583.
Azam Khan	"	6000/ 6000	–	6000/ 6000	Oct. 1646 to 1647–8	Tiyuldar of Mathura	FD Jaunpur	Lahori, I, p. 343; II, pp. 425 and 605–6; *M.U.*, I, p. 179.
Said Khan Zafar Jang	Turani	7000/ 7000 5000 x 2h–3h	–	7000/ 7000 5000 x 2h–3h	Sep. 1647– Jun. 1651	SD Multan	SD Kabul	Lahori, II, pp. 577 and 636; Salih, III (L), pp. 6 and 123.
Muhammad Ali Khan (Dara's naib)	"	2000/ 1000	–	2000/ 1000	Jan. 1656 to 1656–7	SD Multan	Died	Salih, III (L), pp. 212 and 460; *M.U.*, III, p. 489.

Jafar Khan	Irani	5000 /5000 2h–3h	–	5000 /5000 2h–3h	May 1656	SD Thatta	Diwan-i-Kul	Salih, III (L), pp. 120, 227 and 268.
Zulfiqar Khan	”	3000/ 2000	+ 1000 sawar	3000/ 3000	May 1656- May 1657	FD Mandsur	–	Lahori, II, p. 334; Salih, III (L), pp. 227 and 244.
Qasim Khan Mutamad Khan	”	4000/ 4000	+ 1000/ 1000	5000/ 5000	May 1657– Nov. 1657	Mir Atish	SD Gujrat	Salih, III (L), pp. 178, 244 and 274.
Bahadur Khan (Dara's naib)	Muslim	4000/ 2500	+ 500 sawar	4000/ 3000	Nov. 1657 –	SD Punjab (Dara's naib)	–	Salih, III (L), pp. 263 and 274.
				BENGAL				
Qasim Khan Juwaini	Irani	5000/ 5000 3000 × 2h–3h	+ 2000 × 2h–3h	5000/ 5000 H × 2h–3h	Aug. 1628– Oct. 1632	–	Died	Lahori, I, pp. 120, 226 and 444.
Azam Khan	”	6000/ 6000	–	6000/ 6000	Oct. 1632– Mar. 1635	SD Deccan	SD Allahabad	Lahori, I, pp. 343, 426 and 444; I (b), pp. 83 and 102.
Islam Khan (Siyadat Khan, his naib)	”	5000/ 5000 4000 × 2h–3h	+ 1000 × 2h–3h	5000/ 5000 H × 2h–3h	Mar. 1635– Jan. 1639	Mir Bakhshi	Diwan-i-Kul	Lahori, I (b), p. 83; II, pp. 164 and 132.
Saif Khan	”	4000/ 4000	–	4000/ 4000	Jan. 1639– Jun. 1640	SD Akbarabad	Died	Lahori, I, p. 177; II, pp. 130 and 198.
Aitqad Khan Mirza Shapur	”	5000/ 5000	–	5000/ 5000	Sep. 1646– Feb. 1648	SD Bihar	SD Awadh	Lahori, II, pp. 332 and 583; Salih, III (L), pp. 19–20 and 64.
Shuja, Prince	–	–	–	–	Feb. 1648– July 1648			Salih, III (L), pp. 19–20 and 64.
Shuja Prince	–	–	–	–	1652			Salih, III (L), p. 148.

(contd.)

1	*2*	*3*	*4*	*5*	*6*	*7*	*8*	*9*
				ORISSA				
Baqar Khan Najm-e-Sani	Irani	4000/ 4000	–	4000/ 4000	1628 to July 1632	(Holding)	SD Gujrat	Lahori, I, pp. 125, 182, 430–1 and 450–1.
Mutaqid Khan	”	4000/ 2500	+ 500 sawar	4000/ 3000	July 1632– Mar. 1640	FD Nawahi-i-Akbarabad	QD Rohtas	Lahori, I, p. 431; II, pp. 183 and 244.
Shahnawaz Khan	”	4000/ 2500	+ 1500 sawar	4000/ 4000	Mar. 1640– Mar. 1642	”	SD Jaunpur	Lahori, I, pp. 476–7; II, pp. 183 and 283.
Muhammad Zaman Tehrani (Shuja's naib)	”	2000/ 2000	–	2000/ 2000	Mar. 1642– Dec. 1645	–	–	Lahori, II, pp. 244, 473 and 283.
Mutaqid Khan	”	4000/ 3000	–	4000/ 3000	Dec. 1645 Jul. 1648	QD Rohtas	FD Jaunpur	Lahori, I, pp. 430–1; II, pp. 244 and 473; Salih, III (L), pp. 64 and 69.
Shuja, Prince	–	–	–	–	July 1648 to 1651–2			Salih, III (L), pp. 64 and 143.
Mir Samsamud-daulah (Shuja's naib)	Irani	1000/ 200	+ 500/ 300	1500/ 500	Oct 1654– Apr. 1655	Diwan of Shuja	Died	Salih, III (L), pp. 22, 192 and 202; *M.U.*, III, p. 384.
Rashid Khan Rahmanyar (Shuja's naib)	”	1500/ 1000	–	1500/ 1000	Apr. 1655 –	–	–	Salih, III, p. 202; *M.U.*, I, pp. 184–5.
				THE DECCAN				
Khan-e-Jahan Lodhi	Afghan	7000/ 7000 2h–3h	–	7000/ 7000 2h–3h	Dec. 1627– May 1628	–	SD Malwa	Lahori, I, pp. 75, 182 and 199.

Mahabat Khan	Irani	7000/ 7000 2h–3h	–	7000/ 7000 2h–3h	May 1628– Feb. 1629	FD Ajmer	SD Delhi	Lahori, I, pp. 82, 117, 199 and 255.
Azam Khan	”	5000/ 5000	–	5000/ 5000	Mar. 1629– Jun. 1632	Diwan-i-kul	SD Bengal	Lahori, I, pp. 159, 257, 426 and 444.
Mahabat Khan	”	7000/ 7000 2h–3h	–	7000/ 7000 2h–3h	Jun. 1632– May 1635	SD Delhi	Died	Lahori, I, pp. 255 and 426; I (b), p. 60
Aurangzeb, Prince					July 1636– Jun. 1644			Lahori, I (b), p. 205; II, p. 376.
Shaista Khan (naib of Aurangzeb)	”	5000/ 5000	+ 2000 × 2h–3h	5000/ 5000 2000 × 2h–3h	May 1637– Feb. 1639	–	SD Bihar	Lahori, I (b), p. 271; II, pp. 136–7.
Khan-e-Dauran, Nusrat Jang	Turani	6000/ 6000	+ 1000/ 1000	7000/ 7000 5000 × 2h–3h	Jun. 1644 to 1644–5	SD Malwa	Died	Lahori, II, pp. 376 and 426–8; *M.U.*, I, pp. 756–7.
Islam Khan	Irani	5000/ 5000 2h–3h	+ 1000/ 1000 2h–3h	6000/ 6000 2h–3h	July 1645– Nov. 1647	Diwan-i-Kul	Died	Lahori, II, pp. 164 and 430; Salih, III (L), p. 9.
Shahnawaz Khan	”	5000/ 5000	–	5000/ 5000	Nov. 1647– Mar. 1648	SD Malwa	Ataliq of Murad, SD Deccan	Lahori, II, p. 583; Salih, III (L), pp. 9 and 23.
Murad, Prince (Shahnawaz Khan, his ataliq)					Mar. 1648– Sep. 1649			Salih, III (L), pp. 23 and 102.

(contd.)

1	*2*	*3*	*4*	*5*	*6*	*7*	*8*	*9*
Shaista Khan	Irani	5000/ 5000 H × 2h–3h	–	5000/ 5000 H × 2h–3h	Sep. 1649– July 1652	SD Malwa	SD Gujrat	Lahori, II, p. 719; Salih, III (L), pp. 102 and 148.
Aurangzeb, Prince					July 1652– 1658			Salih, III (L), p. 148.
Shaista Khan (Aurangzeb's naib)	Irani	6000/ 6000 5000 × 2h–3h	–	6000/ 6000 5000 × 2h–3h	Jan. 1657 –	SD Malwa Holding	–	Salih, III (L), pp. 227 and 233.

Notes: [1] SD: Subedar; FD: Faujdar; QD: Qiladar; Th.D.: Thanadar.
[2] The appointments of the princes are not included in this analysis.

APPENDIX 5.2: FAUJDARS OF SOME IMPORTANT SARKARS AND PARGANAS

Name	*Racial group*	*Faujdar of*	*Mansab*			*Tenure of office*	*Previous post*	*Later assignment*	*Sources*
			Previous	*Promotion*	*Present*				
1	*2*	*3*	*4*	*5*	*6*	*7*	*8*	*9*	*10*
Mahabat Khan	Irani	Ajmer (Suba Ajmer)	7000/ 7000 2h–3h	–	7000/ 7000 2h–3h	Jan. 1628– May 1628	–	SD Deccan	Lahori, I, pp. 82, 117 and 199.
Mutaqid Khan Mirza-Makki	"	"	4000/ 2000	–	4000/ 2000	Apr. 1629– May 1631	–	SD Malwa	Lahori, I, pp. 79, 259, 362 and 372.
Ikhlas Khan Husain Beg	Turani	"	2000/ 1000	–	2000/ 1000	May 1631– Jan. 1633	Diwan-i-Burhanpur	QD Rohtas	Lahori, I, pp. 200, 292, 372 and 451.
Mirza Muzaffar Kirmani	Irani	"	3000/ 1022	–	3000/ 1022	– Apr. 1633	–	–	Lahori, I, pp. 118 and 476.
Raja Bithaldas	Rajput	"	3000/ 2000	–	3000/ 2000	Apr. 1633– Dec. 1637	QD Ranthambore	QD Akbarabad	Lahori, I, pp. 280, 360 and 476; II, pp. 9 and 110.
Shah Ali	Indian Muslim	"	700/ 450	–	700/ 450	Dec. 1637– Apr. 1649	–	–	Lahori, II, pp. 9 and 742; Salih, III (L), p. 93.
Abu Said	Irani	"	2000/ 800	–	2000/ 800	Apr. 1649 to 1652–3	–	–	Salih, III (L), p. 93; *M.U.*, III, p. 515.
Bahadur Kamboh	Indian Muslim	"	500/ 500	–	500/ 500	– May 1657	QD Taragarh	–	Lahori, II, p. 490; Salih, III (L), p. 244.

(contd.)

1	2	3	4	5	6	7	8	9	10
Mir Jafar Astrabadi	Irani	Ajmer (Suba Ajmer)	1000/ 200	–	1000/ 200	May 1657 –	Diwan-i Buyutat	–	Salih, III (L), pp. 218, 244 and 469.
Mutaqid Khan	"	Atraf-i-Akbarabad (Suba Akbarabad)	4000/ 2000	–	4000/ 2000	May 1632– July 1632	SD Malwa	SD Orissa	Lahori, I, pp. 79, 425 and 431.
Makramat Khan Shirazi	"	"	1500/ 600	+ 500/ 400	2000/ 1000	Oct. 1633– Apr. 1635	Diwan-i-Buyutat	Diwan-i-Buyutat	Lahori, I, pp. 542–3; I (b), p. 87.
Agah Khan Khwajasara	Muslim	"	1000/ 1000 400 × 2h–3h	+ 200 × 2h–3h	1000/ 1000 600 × 2h–3h	Jan. 1645– July 1653	FD. Both sides of R. Jamuna (Agra)	FD Atraf-i-Akbarabad	Lahori, II, pp. 407–8; Salih, III (L), p. 157.
Sadullah Khan	Indian Muslim	"	7000/ 7000 2h–3h	–	7000/ 7000 2h–3h	Jan. 1653 –	Diwan-i-Kul (holding)	Diwan-i-Kul	Salih, III (L), pp. 108 and 157.
Agah Khan Khwajasara	Muslim	"	1000/ 1000 600 × 2h–3h	–	1000/ 1000 600 × 2h–3h	Dec. 1656	FD Atraf-i-Akbarabad	–	Salih, III (L), pp. 157 and 234; Lahori, II, pp. 407–8.
Girdhar Das Gaur	Rajput	"	1500/ 1200	–	1500/ 1200	Dec. 1656 –	QD Akbarabad	–	Salih, III (L), pp. 132, 210 and 234.
Ilahwardi Khan	Irani	Akabarabad (this side of R. Jamuna)	3000/ 2000	–	3000/ 2000	July 1632– Apr. 1633	–	Qarawal Begi	Lahori, I, pp. 425, 431 and 477; I (b), p. 5.
Shahnawaz Khan	Irani	"	3000/ 1500	+ 500 sawar	3000/ 2000	Apr. 1633 –	–	Qush Begi	Lahori, I, p. 477; I (b), p. 124.

Agah Khan Khwajasara	Muslim	"	1000/ 200	+ 800 sawar	1000/ 1000	July 1635– Jan. 1645	–	FD Atraf-i-Akbarabad	Lahori, I (b), pp. 101 and 280; II, pp. 20 and 407–8.
Rashid Khan Ansari	Afghan	Akbarabad (other side of R. Jamuna)	3000/ 2000	–	3000/ 2000	July 1632 to 1633	–	–	Lahori, I, pp. 364–5, 431 and 537–8.
Agah Khan Khwajasara	Muslim	"	1000/ 1000	+ 400 sawar × 2h–3h	1000/ 1000 400 × 2h–3h	Mar. 1638– Jan. 1645	FD. This side of R. Jamuna	FD Atraf-i-Akbarabad	Lahori, II, pp. 20, 91, 110 and 407–8.
Najabat Khan	Turani	Koil (Suba Agra)	1500/ 600	+ 500/ 200	2000/ 800	Jan. 1630– May 1631	–	FD Multan	Lahori, I, pp. 292 and 372.
Najabat Khan	"	"	3000/ 2000	–	3000/ 2000	Nov. 1635– Aug. 1639	FD Kangrah	SD Multan	Lahori, I (b), pp. 11, 93 and 121; II, p. 155.
Mirza Nauzar Safavi	Irani	"	1000/ 400	+ 1000/ 1000	2000/ 1400	Aug. 1639– Oct. 1645	–	Qush Begi	Lahori, II, pp. 157 and 470.
Murshid Qulikhan	Irani	Mathura and Mahaban (Suba Agra)	1500/ 1700	+ 500/ 1300	2000/ 2000	Oct. 1635– Nov. 1637	Mir Tuzuk	Died	Lahori, I (b), p. 105; II, pp. 7–8.
Ilahwardi Khan	Irani	"	4000/ 4000	–	4000/ 4000	Dec. 1637– Sep. 1639	FD Lakhnau	SD Delhi	Lahori, I (b), pp. 63 and 278; II, pp. 8 and 158.
Azam Khan	"	"	6000/ 6000	–	6000/ 6000	– July 1645	SD Gujrat	–	Lahori, II, pp. 290 and 425.

(contd.)

1	2	3	4	5	6	7	8	9	10
Makramatkhan Shirazi	Irani	Mathura and Mahaban (Suba Agra)	3000/ 3000 1000 × 2h–3h	+ 1000/ 1000 2h–3h	4000/ 4000 2000 × 2h–3h	July 1645– Dec. 1649	SD Delhi (holding)	Died	Lahori, II, pp. 425–6; Salih, III (L), pp. 103–4.
Abdul Nabi	Indian Muslim	"	1000/ 400	–	1000/ 400	– Apr. 1656	FD Jalesar	FD Shamsabad	Salih, III (L), pp. 157 and 217.
Daud Khan	"	"	2000/ 2000	–	2000/ 2000	July 1656 –	FD of territory between Agra and Delhi	–	Salih, III (L), p. 229; *M.U.*, II, p. 33.
Dindarkhan Syed Bahwah	"	Miyan-i-Doab	2000/ 1200	–	2000/ 1200	Feb. 1628 to 1635–6	–	Died	Lahori, I, pp. 121 and 191; I (b), p. 302.
Syed Lutf Ali Bhakkari	"	"	800/ 400	–	800/ 400	1635– May 1635	–	QD Kangrah	Lahori, I (b), pp. 101 and 314; II, p. 335; *M.U.*, II, p. 460.
Zulfiqar Khan Khanlar	Irani	Miyan-i-Doab	1000/ 600	+ 500/ 200	1500/ 800	May 1635– Mar. 1638	–	Darogha-i-Top Khana	Lahori, I (b), p. 101; II, pp. 37 and 154.
Mirza Hasan Safavi	Irani	Miyan-i-Doab	2000/ 1000	+ 500 zat	2500/ 1000	Mar. 1638– Oct. 1639	–	FD Fathpur	Lahori, II, pp. 91, 164 and 431.
Nuruddaulah	"	"	900/ 300	+ 100/ 100	1000/ 400	Oct. 1639– July 1640	–	–	Lahori, II, pp. 164 and 201.
Zahid Khan	"	"	1000/ 1000	–	1000/ 1000	July 1640– Apr. 1641	–	Qarawal Begi	Lahori, II, pp. 201, 226–8 and 376.
Syed Muhammad s/o Syed Afzal	Indian Muslim	"	1000/ 500	–	1000/ 500	Apr. 1641– Apr. 1642	–	–	Lahori, II, pp. 228 and 293.

Sultan Husain s/o Asalat Khan	Irani	"	900/ 300	–	900/ 300	Feb. 1651 –	Darogha-i-Dagh	–	Lahori, II, p. 738; Salih, III (L), p. 120; *M.U.*, I, p. 252.
Ghazanfar	"	"	1000/ 500	+ 300 sawar	1000/ 800	Aug. 1653– Aug. 1654	Darogha-i-Fil Khana	FD Miyan-i-Doab	Lahori, II, p. 342; Salih, III (L), pp. 173, 188, 234; *M.U.*, II, p. 867.
Husain Beg	"	"	1500/ 1500	–	1500/ 1500	Aug. 1654– Dec. 1656	SD Kashmir	Mir Tuzuk	Salih, III (L), pp. 23, 188, 234 and 263; *M.U.* I, p. 592.
Ghazanfar	"	"	800/ 400	+ 200/ 600	1000/ 1000	Dec. 1656– Dec. 1657	FD Miyan-i-Doab	–	Salih, III (L), pp. 188, 234 and 268.
Syed Bahadur Bhakkari	Indian Muslim	"	700/ 250	+ 300/ 750	1000/ 1000	Dec. 1657 –	Mir Tuzuk	–	Salih, III (L), pp. 115 and 268.
Mirzakhan g/s/o Abdul Rahim Khan-e-Khanan	Irani	Qannauj (Suba Agra)	3000/ 2000	–	3000/ 2000	Feb. 1628– Apr. 1633	–	FD Bahraich	Lahori, I, pp. 121 and 474.
Bahadur Khan Rohila	Afghan	"	4000/ 4000	–	4000/ 4000	Jan. 1637– Mar. 1648	Jagirdar of Kalpi (holding)	SD Multan	Lahori, I, p. 191; I (b), pp. 86–7 and 243; Salih, III (L), pp. 23 and 64–5.
Diler Khan	"	"	900/ 500	+ 100/ 500	1000/ 1000	1648– Mar. 1650	–	–	Salih, III (B), pp. 23 and 110.
Rai Mukand	Hindu	"	800/ 200	–	800/ 200	Mar. 1650 –	Diwan-i-Buyutat	–	SDS, p.178; Lahori, II, p. 741; Salih, III, p. 110.
Bahadur Khan	Afghan	Kalpi (Suba Agra)	4000/ 2000	–	4000/ 2000	Mar. 1628– Mar. 1648	–	SD Multan	Lahori, I, pp. 117 and 191; Salih, III (B), pp. 23 and 65.

(contd.)

1	*2*	*3*	*4*	*5*	*6*	*7*	*8*	*9*	*10*
Diler Khan	Afghan	Kalpi (Suba Agra)	1000/ 1000	–	1000/ 1000	Mar. 1648– Mar. 1650	–	–	Salih, III (B), pp. 23 and 110.
Mukhlis Khan	Irani	Narwar (Suba Agra)	2000/ 2000	–	2000/ 2000	Mar. 1628– Sep. 1628	–	FD Jaunpur	Lahori, I, pp. 181, 191 and 228.
Dilawar Khan Biranj	Afghan	Mewat (Suba Agra)	4000/ 2500	–	4000/ 2500	Feb. 1628 –	–	–	Lahori, I, p. 117; *M.U.*, I, pp. 424–5.
Shah Beg Khan	Turani	"	4000/ 3000	–	4000/ 3000	– 1646–7	SD Berar	–	Lahori, I (b), p. 234; II, 308; Salih, III (B), p. 6, *M.U.*, II, p. 666.
Khalilullah Khan	Irani	"	4000/ 3000	–	4000/ 3000	Sep. 1647 –	Bakhshi-i-Doam (holding)	–	Lahori, II, pp. 385 and 584; Salih, III (B), p. 6.
Sardar Khan	Turani	Two Bangash (Suba Kabul)	3000/ 3000	–	3000/ 3000	Feb. 1641– Apr. 1642	Qur Begi	–	Lahori, I (b), 123; II, pp. 223 and 293.
Saadat Khan	Irani	"	3000/ 2500	–	3000/ 2500	Mar. 1648 to 1649–50	Th.D. Tirmiz	–	Lahori, II, p. 627; Salih, III (B), p. 22; *M.U.*, II p. 462.
Mubarak Khan Niyazi	Afghan	"	2000/ 2000	–	2000/ 2000	1653–4 to 1655–6	QD Orissa	–	Lahori, II, pp. 221 and 726; *M.U.*, II, p. 462; III, p. 513.
Saadat Khan	Irani	"	3000/ 2500	–	3000/ 2500	1655–6 to Aug. 1657	FD Bangash	–	Lahori, II, p. 627; Salih, (L), III, p. 260; *M.U.*, II, p. 462.
Abdullah Khan s/o Said Khan Zafar Jang	Turani	"	2000/ 1500	+ 500 sawar	2000/ 2000	Aug. 1657 –	Th.D. Paien Bangash	–	Lahori, II, p. 174; Salih, II (L), p. 260.

Muhammad Salih n/o Asaf Khan Jafar Beg	Irani	Bahraich (Suba Awadh)	1000/ 800	–	1000/ 800	Mar. 1628 to 1629–30	–	Died	Lahori, I, pp. 184 and 195; I (b), p. 307.
Zulqarnain	–	"	–	–	–	Nov. 1632 (holding) –	–	–	Lahori, I, p. 446.
Mirza Khan Manochahar	Irani	"	3000/ 2000	–	3000/ 2000	Apr. 1633– May 1635	FD Qannauj	FD Kangrah	Lahori, I, pp. 121 and 474; I (b), p. 93.
Mirza Nauzar Safavi	"	"	3000/ 2000	–	3000/ 3000	1649–50 –	Qush Begi	FD Mandu	Salih, III (B), p. 454; *M.U.*, III, p. 556.
Mutaqid Khan s/o Najabat Khan	Turani	Bahraich (Suba Awadh)	1000/ 400	+ 1000/ + 1600 800 × 2h–3h	2000/ 2000 800 × 2h–3h	Mar. 1658 –	Mir Tuzuk	–	Salih, III (L), p. 269; *M.U.*, II, p. 871.
Mukhlis Khan	Irani	Gorakhpur (Suba Awadh)	2500/ 2000	–	2500/ 2000	– May 1634	FD Jaunpur	SD Tilangana	Lahori, I, pp. 228 and 297; I (b), p. 14.
Mahaldar Khan	Turani	"	4000/ 2000	–	4000/ 2000	May 1634 to 1635–6	–	–	Lahori, I (b), pp. 1, 14 and 140.
Lashkar Shikan	Irani	Lakhnau (Suba Awadh)	–	–	–	July 1635	–	–	Lahori, I (b), p. 102.
Ilahwardi Khan	"	Lakhnau and Baiswarah	4000/ 4000	–	4000/ 4000	Feb. 1637– Aug. 1637	SD Khandesh	FD Mathura	Lahori, I (b), pp. 63, 97, 243 and 278; II, p. 8.
Sarandaz Khan	Turani	Lakhnau and Baiswarah	1000/ 800	+ 500/ 400	1500/ 1200	Aug. 1637– Apr. 1641	QD Akbarabad	FD Jammu	Lahori, I (b), pp. 105 and 278; II, p. 228.

(contd.)

1	*2*	*3*	*4*	*5*	*6*	*7*	*8*	*9*	*10*
Syed Murtaza Khan	Indian Muslim	Lakhnau and Baiswarah	3000/ 2000	–	3000/ 2000	– 1650	–	–	Lahori, II, p. 724; *M.U.*, III, p. 584.
Makramat Khan Safavi Murad Kam	Irani	"	2000/ 1200	+ 500 600	2500/ 1800	1650 to Oct. 1651	Qur Begi	FD Jaunpur	Salih, III (L), pp. 1 and 129; *M.U.*, III, p. 584.
Ahmad Beg Khan	"	"	2000/ 1500	+ 500/ 500	2500/ 2000	Oct. 1651– Apr. 1654	FD Multan	–	Lahori, I, p. 372; Salih III (L), pp. 129 and 186.
Iradat Khan Mir Ishaq	Irani	Lakhnau and Baiswarah	2000/ 800	–	2000/ 800	Apr. 1654– Dec. 1655	Arz-i-Waqa-i-Subajat	Same	Salih, III (L), pp. 173, 186 and 210.
Najabat Khan	Turani	Daman-i Koh-i Kangrah (Suba Lahore)	2500/ 2000	+ 500 zat	3000/ 2000	Apr. 1634– May 1635	SD Multan	FD Koil	Lahori, I, p. 428; I (b), pp. 11, 93 and 121.
Mirza Khan Manochahar	Irani	"	3000/ 2000	–	3000/ 2000	May 1635 to 1635–6	FD Bahraich	–	Lahori, I, p. 121; I (b), p. 93; *M.U.*, III, p. 587.
Shah Quli Khan Waqqas Haji	Turani	"	1000/ 800	+ 1000/ 1200	2000/ 2000	Oct. 1636 –	–	FD Jaunpur	Lahori, I (b), pp. 216–17; II, p. 128.
Raj Rup s/o Jagat Singh	Rajput	"	–	–	–	Dec. 1638 –	–	–	Lahori, II, p. 127.
Raja Jagat Singh	"	"	3000/ 2000	–	3000/ 2000	Aug. 1640– Aug. 1641	Th.D. Bangash	QD Qullat	Lahori, I (b), pp. 242 and 298; II, pp. 206 and 236; *M.U.*, II, pp. 240–1.
Khanazad Khan	Turani	"	1500/ 800	+ 200 sawar	1500/ 1000	Aug. 1641– Mar. 1644	Th.D. Ghazni	"	Lahori, II, pp. 173, 236 and 356.
Khanjar Khan	"	"	1000/ 500	–	1000/ 500	Mar. 1645– Nov. 1645	QD Zamindawar	–	Lahori, II, pp. 121–2, 414 and 471.

Murshid Quli Khan-Khurasani	Irani	"	–	–	–	Nov. 1645–Sep. 1646	Daroghai-Fil Khana	Akhta Begi	Lahori, II, pp. 362, 471, 579; *M.U.*, III, p. 493.
Shamsuddin Khan s/o Nazar Bahadur Keshgi	Afghan	Daman-i-Koh-i-Kangrah (Suba Lahore)	1000/800	–	1000/800	1646–7 to 1647–8	FD Mandsor	FD Junagarh	Lahori, II, pp. 162, 232, 579 and 673–5; Mirat, I, p. 231.
Iftikhar Khan Mukhlisullah	Turani	Jammu (Suba Lahore)	2000/1000	+ 1000 sawar	2000/2000	Mar. 1629 to 1631–2	–	Died	Lahori, I, p. 258; I (b), p. 300.
Shah Quli Khan Waqqas-Haji	"	"	2000/2000	–	2000/2000	– Dec. 1638	FD Kangrah	FD Bhakkar	Lahori, I (b), pp. 216–17; II, pp. 128 and 131.
Jalal Kakar s/o Dilawar Khan Kakar	Afghan	"	1500/700	–	1500/700	Dec. 1638–Mar. 1640	–	FD Nasirabad	Lahori, I (b), p. 306; II, pp. 128 and 181; *M.U.*, I, p. 530.
Shukrullah Arab	Muslim	"	–	–	–	– Apr. 1641	Kotwal of Agra	–	Lahori, II, pp. 8 and 228.
Sarandaz Khan	Turani	"	1500/1200	–	1500/1200	Apr. 1641–Aug. 1641	FD Lakhnau	QD Lahore	Lahori, I (b), p. 278; II, pp. 228, 236 and 500.
Khanazad Khan	"	"	1500/1000	–	1500/1000	Aug. 1641–Mar. 1644	FD Kangrah (holding)	QD Qullat	Lahori, II, pp. 236 and 356.
Abdul Nabi	Indian Muslim	Shamsabad (Suba Lahore)	1000/400	–	1000/400	Apr. 1656 –	FD Rapri (holding)	–	Salih, III (L), p. 217.
Dindar Khan, Syed Abdul Wahid	"	Hissar (Suba Delhi)	800/600	–	800/600	Mar. 1628 –	–	QD Kabul	Lahori, I, p. 191; I (b), p. 313; II, p. 156.

(contd.)

1	*2*	*3*	*4*	*5*	*6*	*7*	*8*	*9*	*10*
Tarbiyat Khan Fakhruddin Ahmad	Turani	Hissar (Suba Delhi)	1000/ 700	–	1000/ 700	July 1632– Mar. 1633	FD Sarhind (holding)	Akhta Begi	Lahori, I, pp. 299, 431 and 465–6; I (b), p. 67.
Muhammad Ali Beg	”	”	800/ 400	–	800/ 400	Oct. 1633 –	–	–	Lahori, I, p. 542.
Tarbiyat Khan Fakhruddin Ahmad	”	Sarhind (Suba Delhi)	1000/ 700	–	1000/ 700	July 1632– Mar. 1633	FD Hissar	Akhta Begi	Lahori, I, pp. 299, 431 and 465–6; I (b), p. 67.
Rai Kashidas	Hindu	”	900/ 400	–	900/ 400	– Sep. 1632	–	Diwan-i Lahore	Lahori, I, pp. 432–3; I (b), p. 312.
Diyanat Khan, Hakim Jamala Kashi	Irani	”	1000/ 250	+ 150 sawar	1000/ 400	Sep. 1632 –	Diwan-i-Lahore	Darogha-i-Dagh	Lahori, I, pp. 432–3; II, p. 142.
Muizul Mulk	”	”	1000/ 100	–	1000/ 100	– Oct. 1638	FD Surat	FD Surat	Lahori, I (b), pp. 102 and 312; II, pp. 116–17.
Mir Ali Akbar	Indian Muslim	”	–	–	–	Oct. 1638 –	Karori-i-Sarhind	–	Lahori, I (b), p. 71; II, pp. 116–17.
Rai Todarmal	Hindu	”	1000/ 1000 2h–3h	–	1000/ 1000 2h–3h	Aug. 1640 –	Diwan and Amin of Sarhind (holding)	–	Lahori, II, pp. 319 and 206.
Mukhlis Khan	Irani	Jaunpur (Suba Allahabad)	2000/ 2000	–	2000/ 2000	Sep. 1628 –	FD Narwar	FD Gorakhpur	Lahori, I, pp. 181, 191, and 228; I (b), p. 14.

Aitqad Khan s/o Aitmad-uddaulah	Irani	Jaunpur (Suba Allahabad)	4000/ 4000	–	4000/ 4000	May 1636– May 1642	SD Delhi	SD Bihar	Lahori, I, p. 182; I (b), p. 166; II, pp. 283 and 332.
Shahnawaz Khan	"	"	4000/ 4000	–	4000/ 4000	Mar. 1642– Sep. 1646	SD Orissa	SD Malwa	Lahori, II, pp. 183, 283 and 583.
Mirza Hasan Safavi	"	"	3000/ 2000	–	3000/ 2000	Sep. 1646 to 1647–8	FD Fatehpur Bayana	–	Lahori, II, pp. 431 and 584; *M.U.*, III, p. 478.
Azam Khan	"	"	6000/ 6000	–	6000/ 6000	1647–8 to Jan. 1649	SD Bihar	Died	Lahori, I, p. 343; II, pp. 605–6; Salih, III (L), p. 69; *M.U.*, I, p. 179.
Mutaqid Khan Mirza Makki	"	"	4000/ 4000	–	4000/ 4000	Jan. 1649– Oct. 1651	SD Orissa	Died	Lahori, II, p. 720; Salih, III (L), pp. 64, 69 and 129.
Makramat Khan Murad Kam	"	"	2500/ 1800	+ 500/ 1200	3000/ 3000	Oct. 1651– Feb. 1655	FD Lakhnau	–	Salih, III (L), pp. 129, 200; *M.U.*, I, pp. 212–13; III, p. 584.
Ilahwardi Khan	"	"	5000/ 4000	–	5000/ 4000	Feb. 1655– May 1657	SD Delhi	–	Salih, III (L), pp. 200 and 244; *M.U.*, I, pp. 212–13.
Makramat Khan Murad Kam	"	"	3000/ 3000	–	3000/ 3000	May 1657 –	FD Jaunpur	–	Salih, III (L), pp. 129 and 244.
Ahmad Beg Khan	"	Siwistan (Suba Thatta)	2000/ 1500	–	2000/ 1500	1628 to 1629	–	Deputy SD Multan	Lahori, I, p. 287; I (b), p. 301; *M.U.*, I, pp. 139 and 195.

(contd.)

1	*2*	*3*	*4*	*5*	*6*	*7*	*8*	*9*	*10*
Jan Nisar Khan	Indian Muslim	Siwistan (Suba Thatta)	2500/ 1500	–	2500/ 1500	Mar. 1628– Dec. 1638	FD Lakhi Jangal (holding)	FD Bhakkar	Lahori, I, pp. 476 and 542; II, pp. 35 and 128.
Yakkataz Khan	Turani	"	1500/ 600	+ 900 sawar	1500/ 1500	Dec. 1638– Jun. 1639	–	–	Lahori, II, pp. 128, 150 and 151.
Qazzaq Khan	"	"	1500/ 800	–	1500/ 800	Jun. 1639– Jun. 1641	–	FD Baroda	Lahori, I (b), p. 249; II, pp. 150–1, 234 and 309.
Amir Khan s/o Qasim Khan Namkin	Irani	"	3000/ 2000	–	3000/ 2000	Jun. 1641– Jun. 1642	SD Thatta	SD Thatta	Lahori, I, p. 287; I (b), p. 298; II, 234 and 302–3.
Shujat Khan Shad Khan	Turani	"	2000/ 2000	–	2000/ 2000	Jun. 1642– 1646	SD Thatta	QD Kabul	Lahori, II, pp. 244, 302–3 and 483–4; Salih, III (L), p. 2.
Zabardast Khan	Irani	"	2000/ 1000	–	2000/ 1000	Jan. 1646– Oct. 1649	–	Died	Lahori, II, pp. 405–6, and 480; Salih, III (B), p. 103.
Nurul Hasan	Indian Muslim	"	1000/ 400	–	1000/ 400	Oct. 1649– Sep. 1651	Bakhshi of Ahadis	FD Tirhut	Lahori, II, pp. 501 and 644; Salih, III (L), pp. 103 and 128.
Abul Maali s/o Mirza Wali	Turani	"	1000/ 400	+ 1000/ 1100	2000/ 1500	1652–3 to 1657	–	FD Tirhut	Salih, III (L), p. 242; *M.U.*, III, p. 557.
Muhammad Salih Tarkhan	"	Siwistan (Suba Thatta)	2000/ 1500	+ 500 sawar	2000/ 2000	1657–8 –	FD Junagarh	–	Mirat, I, p. 231; Salih, III (B), p. 458; *M.U.*, III, pp. 560 and 580.

Izzat Khan Khwaja Baba	"	Bhakkar (Suba Multan)	1500/ 1000	+ 500 zat	2000/ 1000	Mar. 1631– Apr. 1633	–	Died	Lahori, I, pp. 365 and 476.
Yusuf Mohd. Khan Tashqandi	"	"	3000/ 2500	–	3000/ 2500	1635 to Dec. 1638	SD Thatta	SD Multan	Lahori, I (b), p. 101; II, pp. 22 and 128; *M.U.*, III, p. 965.
Jan Nissar Khan	Indian Muslim	"	2500/ 1500	+ 500 sawar	2500/ 2000	Dec. 1638– Jan. 1639	FD Siwistan	Died	Lahori, II, pp. 128 and 131.
Shah Quli Khan	Turani	"	2000/ 2000	–	2000/ 2000	Jan. 1639– Jan. 1641	FD Kangrah	SD Kashmir	Lahori, I (b), pp. 216–17 and 301; II, pp. 131, 220–1 and 223.
Shujat Khan Shad Khan	"	"	1000/ 800	+ 500/ 400	1500/ 1200	Jan. 1641– Mar. 1641	Akhta Begi	SD Thatta	Lahori, II, pp. 20–1, 213 and 225.
Syed Chawan	Indian Muslim	"	500/ 240	–	500/ 240	Mar. 1641 –	–	–	Lahori, I (b), p. 322; II, p. 227.
Asad Khan Mamuri	Irani	Lakhi Jangal (Suba Multan)	2500/ 1500	+ 500 zat	3000/ 1500	Nov. 1629– Sep. 1631	Bakhshi II	–	Lahori, I, pp. 288 and 397; *M.U.*, I, pp. 140–4.
Jan Nisar Khan	Indian Muslim	"	2500/ 1200	–	2500/ 1200	Nov. 1631– Apr. 1633	QD Ahmadnagar	FD Siwistan	Lahori, I, pp. 283, 399 and 476; II, p. 35; *M.U.*, I, p. 528.
Sazawar Khan	Irani	"	2500/ 1000	+ 1000 sawar	2500/ 2000	Apr. 1633– Nov. 1634	–	QD Junnair	Lahori, I, p. 476; I (b), p. 64; II, p. 378.
Bakhtiyar Khan Deccani	Indian Muslim	"	2000/ 1000	–	2000/ 1000	Nov. 1634 –	–	FD Tirhut	Lahori, I (b), pp. 64 and 303; II, p. 321.

(contd.)

1	2	3	4	5	6	7	8	9	10
Rai Todarmal	Hindu	Lakhi Jangal (Suba Multan)	–	–	–	July 1641 –	FD Sarhind (holding)	–	Lahori, II, p. 236.
Ahmad Beg Khan	Irani	Multan (Suba Multan)	2000/ 1500	–	2000/ 1500	– May 1631	–	FD Baiswarah	Lahori, I (b), p. 301; I, p. 372; Salih, III (L), p. 129.
Najabat Khan	Turani	"	2000/ 1400	+ 500/ 600	2500/ 2000	May 1631 –	FD Koil	SD Multan	Lahori, I, pp. 292, 372 and 428.
Syed Diler Khan Barha	Indian Muslim	Baroda (Suba Gujrat)	4000/ 2500	+ 500 sawar	4000/ 3000	Dec. 1627– Dec. 1632	–	Died	Lahori, I, pp. 120, 299 and 448; Mirat, I, pp. 203 and 208.
Aitmad Khan Aqa Afzal	Irani	"	1000/ 500	–	1000/ 500	1632–3 to 1636–7	Diwan-i-Gujrat	Diwan-i-Deccan	Lahori, I, p. 185; I (b), p. 207; Mirat, I, pp. 208 and 211.
Mir Shams	"	"	2500/ 2000	+ 500 sawar	2500 2500	Jan. 1637 to 1640–1	QD Surat	FD Patan	Lahori, I (b), p. 242; Mirat, I, pp. 202–3 and 215.
Qazzaq Khan	Turani	"	2000/ 800	+ 1200 sawar	2000/ 2000	Sep. 1642 –	–	–	Lahori, II, p. 309.
Sultanyar (shared the charge with), Asfandyar	Irani	"	600/ 250 { 600/ 600	+ 400/ 750 –	1000/ 1000 { 600/ 600 }	May 1647 –	–	–	Lahori, II, pp. 680 and 745; Mirat, I, p. 222.
Sultanyar	"	"	1000/ 1000	–	1000/ 1000	1653–4 –	–	–	Mirat, I, p. 227.
Begalar Khan	Turani	Surat (Suba Gujrat)	3000/ 2500	–	3000/ 2500	1627–8 to Aug. 1628 (holding)	–	–	Lahori, I, pp. 182 and 221; *M.U.*, I, pp. 401–4.

Jahangir Quli Khan	"	"	3000/ 3000	–	3000/ 3000	Aug. 1628– Feb. 1632	–	Died	Lahori, I, pp. 182, 221 and 409.
Mirza Isa Tarkhan	"	"	4000/ 3000	+ 1000/ 1000 × 2h–3h	5000/ 4000 1000 × 2h–3h	1635 to Apr. 1642	SD Thatta	SD Gujrat	Lahori, I, p. 181; I (b), p. 103; II, p. 290; Mirat, I, pp. 210 and 216; *M.U.*, III, p. 487.
Inayatullah s/o Isa Tarkhan	"	"	1000/ 500	+ 1000/ 1000	2000/ 1500	Apr. 1642 –	–	–	Lahori, II, p. 290; Mirat, I, p. 216.
Isa Tarkhan	"	"	5000/ 5000	–	5000/ 5000	1644–5 to 1650–1	SD Gujrat	–	Mirat, I, p. 225; *M.U.*, III, pp. 487–8.
Muhammad Salih s/o Isa Tarkhan	"	"	1500/ 1000	–	1500/ 1000	1650–1 to 1651–2	Kotwal of Lahore	FD Junagarh	Lahori, II, p. 632; Salih, III (L), p. 122; *M.U.*, III, pp. 488 and 560; Mirat, I, p. 225.
Bahram s/o Jahangir Quli	Turani	Junagarh (Suba Gujrat)	1000/ 500	–	1000/ 500	Feb. 1632 –	–	–	Lahori, I, p. 185; Salih, I (B), p. 464.
Muhammad Salih s/o Isa Tarkhan	"	"	2000/ 1500	–	2000/ 1500	1651–2 to 1654–5	FD Surat	FD Siwistan	Mirat, I, pp. 225 and 231; *M.U.*, III, pp. 438 and 560.
Shamsuddin (shared the charge with), Qutubuddin s/o Nazr Bahadur Kheshgi	Afghan	"	{1500/ 1500 {1500/ 1400	– –	1500/ 1500 {1500/ 1400	1654–5 to 1656–7	FD Kangrah –	– FD Patan	Lahori, II, p. 579; Mirat, I, pp. 231 and 235; *M.U.*, II, pp. 676–7.
Sarfaraz Khan Chughta	Turani	Patan (Suba Gujrat)	4000/ 3000	–	4000/ 3000	Sep. 1631– June 1639	–	Died	Lahori, I, p. 397; I (b), p. 297; II, p. 149; Mirat, I, p. 212.

(contd.)

1	*2*	*3*	*4*	*5*	*6*	*7*	*8*	*9*	*10*
Mir Shams	Irani	Patan (Suba Gujrat)	2500/ 2500	–	2500/ 2500	1644–5 to July 1646	FD Baroda (holding)	FD Bir	Lahori, I (b), p. 242; II, pp. 386 and 511; Mirat, I, pp. 215 and 219.
Mir Shams	"	"	3000/ 3000	–	3000/ 3000	1652–3 to 1654–5	FD Bir	Th.D. Baroda	Lahori, II, p. 511; Mirat, I, pp. 226 and 232; *M.U.*, III, p. 492.
Mujahid Jalori	Afghan	"	800/ 800	–	800/ 800	1654–5 –	–	–	Lahori, II, p. 739; Mirat, I, p. 232.
Qutbuddin s/o Nazr Bahadur Kheshgi	"	"	1500/ 1400	–	1500/ 1400	1656–7 –	–	FD Junagarh	Mirat, I, pp. 231 and 235.
Muizul Mulk	Irani	Bandar-i-Surat (Suba Gujrat)	1000/ 100	–	1000/ 100	– July 1635	–	FD Bandar-i-Surat	Lahori, I (b), pp. 102 and 312; Mirat, I, p. 210.
Hakim Masihuzzaman	"	"	3000/ 500	–	3000/ 500	July 1635– Oct. 1638	–	–	Lahori, I (b), p. 102; II, p. 116; Mirat, I, pp. 209–10 and 212.
Muizul Mulk	"	"	1000/ 100	–	1000/ 100	Oct. 1638– Jun. 1641	FD Bandar-i-Surat	Diwan-i-Gujrat	Lahori, II, pp. 116, 234 and 334; Mirat, I, pp. 212 and 215.
Jam Quli	Muslim	"	–	–	–	Jun. 1641 to 1643–4	–	–	Lahori, II, p. 234; Mirat, I, pp. 215 and 218.
Ali Akbar Safahani	Irani	"	500/ 100	–	500/ 100	Oct. 1641 to 1647–8	–	Died	Lahori, II, pp. 606–7; Mirat, I, p. 223.
Muizul Mulk	"	"	1000/ 100	–	1000/ 100	1647–8 –	Diwan-i-Gujrat	–	Lahori, II, pp. 334 and 738; Mirat, I, p. 223.

Umar Daraz	Muslim	"	–	–	–	1653–4	–	–	Mirat, I, p. 229.
Hafiz Muhammad Nazir	"	"	500/ 100	–	500/ 100	1653–4 to 1656–7	[1]Mutasaddi of Bandar-i Surat	–	Mirat, I, pp. 223, 229 and 234.
Muhammad Amin	"	"	–	–	–	Jan. 1656– Jun. 1656	–	–	Mirat, I, p. 234.
Muhammad Qasim	"	Bandar-i Surat (Suba Gujrat)	–	–	–	Jun. 1656 –	–	–	Mirat, I, p. 234.
Syed Shujat Khan	Indian Muslim	Tirhut (Suba Bihar)	3000/ 2000	–	3000/ 2000	Feb. 1628 –	–	SD Allahabad	Lahori, I (b), p. 274; Salih, I (B), p. 312.
Bakhtiyar Khan Deccani	"	"	2000/ 1000	–	2000/ 1000	Jan. 1643– Jun. 1647	FD Lakhi Jangal	FD Mandsur	Lahori, I (b), pp. 64 and 303; II, pp. 321 and 685; Salih, III (L), p.19.
Nurul Hasan	"	"	1000/ 400	–	1000/ 400	Sept. 1651– Jan. 1655	FD Siwistan	Th.D. Koch	Lahori, II, p. 501; Salih, III (L), pp. 128 and 199.
Sarfraz Khan	Other Muslim	"	4000/ 3000	–	4000/ 3000	– Apr. 1657	–	Died	Salih, I (B), pp. 469–70; III (L), p. 242; Lahori, II, p. 721.
Mir Abul Maali s/o Mirza Wali	Turani	"	2000/ 1400	–	2000/ 1400	Apr. 1657 –	FD Siwistan	–	Salih, III (L), pp. 242 and 459 (B).
Jan Nisar Khan	Indian Muslim	Mandsur (Suba Malwa)	2000/ 1000	–	2000/ 1000	Feb. 1628 –	–	–	Lahori, I, pp. 118–19; Salih, I (B), p. 272.
Shamsuddhin Kheshgi	Afghan	"	1000/ 800	–	1000/ 800	– May 1641	–	FD Kangrah	Lahori, II, pp. 162, 232 and 579.

(contd.)

1	*2*	*3*	*4*	*5*	*6*	*7*	*8*	*9*	*10*
Syed Khadim Barha	Indian Muslim	Mandsur (Suba Malwa)	1000/ 500	–	1000/ 500	May 1641 –	–	–	Lahori, II, p. 232.
Zulfiqar Khan Khanlar	Irani	"	2000/ 800	+ 400 sawar	2000/ 1200	Aug. 1642– May 1643	QD Lahore	SD Bihar	Lahori, II, pp. 223, 306 and 334; Salih, III (L), p. 227.
Jansipar Khan Jamali	"	"	2000/ 1500	–	2000/ 1500	May 1643– Mar. 1645	Bakhshi of mansabdars	–	Lahori, II, pp. 161, 226, 334 and 412.
Janbaz Khan Syed Ahmad	Indian Muslim	"	1000/ 800	+ 500/ 200	1500/ 1000	Mar. 1645– Jan. 1648	QD and FD of Chanda	Died	Lahori, II, pp. 129 and 412; Salih, III (L), p. 19.
Bakhtiyar Khan Deccani	"	"	2000/ 1000	–	2000/ 1000	Jan. 1648 to 1650–1	FD Tirhut	–	Lahori, II, p. 728; Salih, III (L), p. 19; *M.U.*, I, pp. 774–5.
Sher Khan Barha	"	"	2000/ 800	–	2000/ 800	Dec. 1657 –	–	–	Salih, III (L), pp. 268 and 460.
Rahmat Khan Mir Faizullah	Turani	Bijagarh (Suba Tilingana)	1500/ 1500	–	1500/ 1500	Nov. 1636– May 1628 (holding)	–	Died	Lahori, I (b), pp. 134 and 222; II, p. 98.
Rashid Khan Ansari	Afghan	"	4000/ 3000	+ 1000 sawar	4000/ 4000	May 1638 –	SD Burhanpur (holding)	–	Lahori, II, pp. 98–9.
Hadidad Khan	"	"	700/ 500	+ 300/ 500	1000/ 1000	July 1644– Nov. 1648	–	SD Tilingana	SDS, pp. 142–4; Salih, III (L), p. 66.

Note: [1]It seems that 'Mutasaddi' was used as a substitute for 'Faujdar' in this region: Mirat, I, pp. 229–30 and 234.

APPENDIX 5.3: SOME QILADARS OF SHAHJAHAN'S REIGN

Name	*Racial group*	*Qiladar of*	*Mansab*			*Tenure of office*	*Previous post*	*Later assignment*	*Sources*
			Previous	*Promotion*	*Present*				
1	*2*	*3*	*4*	*5*	*6*	*7*	*8*	*9*	*10*
Mughal Khan s/o Zain Khan Koka	Irani	Kabul	1000/ 500	–	1000/ 500	Mar. 1628– Mar. 1630	–	QD of Udgir	Lahori, I, pp. 184–5, 191 and 294; I (b), p.221.
Dindar Khan	Indian Muslim	"	1000/ 650	–	1000/ 650	Aug. 1639– Oct. 1645	FD Hissar	Died	Lahori, I, p. 191; II, pp. 48, 156 and 468.
Syed Asadullah	"	"	700/ 550	+ 300/ 150	1000/ 700	Oct. 1645– Feb. 1646	–	QD Zamindawar	Lahori, II, pp. 468, 485 and 585.
Zulqadr Khan Turkman	Irani	"	2000/ 1800	+ 500/ 200	2500/ 2000	Sep. 1646– 1647	–	–	Lahori, II, pp. 594 and 680.
Lutfullah s/o Said Khan	Turani	"	1500/ 400	+ 300 sawar	1500/ 700	Jan. 1647– Apr. 1647	–	–	Lahori, II, pp. 627 and 641.
Sivaram Gaur	Rajput	"	1500/ 1000	–	1500/ 1000	Apr. 1647– July 1647	QD Asir	QD Mandu	Lahori, I (b), p. 42; II, pp. 388 and 641; Salih, III (L), pp. 2 and 268.
Shad Khan Shujat Khan	Turani	"	2000/ 2000	–	2000/ 2000	July 1647 to 1648–9	FD Siwistan	QD Kabul	Lahori, II, pp. 244 and 302–3; Salih, III (L), pp. 2 and 87; *M.U.*, II, p. 664.
Ibrahim Khan (shared charge with), Abdullah Beq	Irani	"	{1000/ 500 {1000/ 500	– –	1000/ 500 1000/ 500	Jan. 1653 –	–	–	Salih, III (L), p. 157.

(contd.)

1	*2*	*3*	*4*	*5*	*6*	*7*	*8*	*9*	*10*
Shad Khan Shujat Khan	Turani	Kabul	3500/ 3000	–	3500/ 3000	Aug. 1657 –	QD Kabul	–	Salih, III (L), p. 260; *M.U.*, II, p. 664.
Aziullah Khan s/o Yusuf Khan Tukaria	”	Bust (Qandhar)	2500/ 1600	+ 500/ 400	3000/ 2000	Nov. 1638– July 1644	–	Died	Lahori, II, pp. 121 and 379.
Purdil Khan	Afghan	”	2500/ 2200	–	2500/ 2200	July 1644– Jan. 1649	QD Zamindawar	–	Lahori, II, pp. 48 and 379; Salih, III (L), pp. 79–80.
Khanjar Khan n/o Qulij Khan	Turani	Zamind- awar	700/ 350	+ 300/ 150	1000/ 500	Nov. 1638 –	–	FD Kangrah	Lahori, II, pp. 121–2 and 414.
Purdil Khan	Afghan	”	2500/ 2200	–	2500/ 2200	Aug. 1642– July 1644	Th.D. of Qullat	QD of Bust	Lahori, II, pp. 48, 200, 306 and 379.
Khanazad Khan	Turani	” 1000	1500/ sawar	+ 200 1200	1500/	July 1644– 1646–7	QD Qullat	–	Lahori, II, pp. 379, 585 and 641.
Syed Asadullah	Indian Muslim	”	1000/ 700	+ 300 sawar	1000/ 1000	Sep. 1646 to 1648–9	QD Kabul	–	Lahori, II, pp. 468 and 585; Salih, III (L), pp. 80–1.
Raja Jagat Singh	Rajput	Qullat	3000/ 2000	–	3000/ 2000	1642–3 to Mar. 1644	FD Kangrah	–	Lahori, I (b), p. 298; II, pp. 236 and 356; *M.U.*, II, pp. 240–1.
Khanazad Khan	Turani	”	1500/ 1000	–	1500/ 1000	Mar. 1644– July 1644	FD Kangrah	QD Zamindawar	Lahori, II, pp. 236, 356 and 379.
Abdullah s/o Said Khan		”	1000/ 400	+ 400 sawar	1000/ 800	July 1644 –	Th.D. Paien Bangash	–	Lahori, II, pp. 174 and 379.

Sarandaz Khan	Turani	Akbarabad	1000/ 800	–	1000/ 800	Oct. 1635– Aug. 1637	Kotwal of Akbarabad	FD of Lakhnau	Lahori, I, p. 488; I (b), pp. 105 and 278.
Bithaldas Gaur	Rajput	Akbarabad	4000/ 3000	–	4000/ 3000	Aug. 1638– Aug. 1639	FD Ajmer	QD Akbarabad	Lahori, I, p. 476; I (b), pp. 241–2; II, pp. 110, 156 and 241.
Bithaldas Gaur	"	"	4000/ 3000	–	4000/ 3000	Aug. 1641 –	QD Akbarabad	–	Lahori, II, pp. 110 and 241.
Baqi Khan	Turani	"	2000/ 2000	–	2000/ 2000	Jan. 1645– Jun. 1650	Darogha-i-Ghusal Khana	–	Lahori, I (b), p. 301; II, 347 and 407; Salih, III (L), p. 111.
Pirthiraj Rathor*	Rajput	"	2000/ 2000	–	2000/ 2000	Jun. 1646– Jan. 1647	QD Daulatabad	–	Lahori, II, pp. 417, 510 and 628.
Girdhardas Gaur*	"	"	1000/ 700	+ 100 sawar	1000/ 800	Nov. 1646 –	FD Jhansi	–	Lahori, I (b), p. 121; II, p. 610.
Siyadat Khan	Irani	"	3000/ 1000	+ 500 sawar	3000/ 1500	Jun. 1650– Nov. 1655	Bakhshi-II	QD Delhi	Salih, III (L), pp. 111, 210 and 234.
Girdhardas Gaur	Rajput	"	1500/ 1200	–	1500/ 1200	Nov. 1655 Dec. 1656	QD Akbarabad	FD suburbs of Akbarabad	Salih, III (L), pp. 132, 210 and 234.
Siyadat Khan	Irani	Delhi	3000/ 1500	–	3000/ 1500	Dec. 1656– Jan. 1657	"	–	Salih, III (L), pp. 111, 210 and 234–5.
Siyadat Khan	"	"	3000/ 1500	–	3000/ 1500	Feb. 1657 –	–	–	Salih, III (L), pp. 238 and 455.
Khalilullah Khan	"	"	5000/ 5000	–	5000/ 5000	Oct. 1657 –	SD Delhi (holding)	–	Salih, III (L), p. 263.

(contd.)

1	2	3	4	5	6	7	8	9	10
Ghairat Khan	Turani	Lahore	2500/ 2000	–	2500/ 2000	Feb. 1640– Jun. 1640	SD Delhi	SD Thatta	Lahori, I (b), p. 280; II, pp. 158, 179 and 198.
Zulfiqar Khan Khanlar	Irani	"	1500/ 800	–	1500/ 800	July 1640 –	Darogha of Top Khana	FD Mandsur	Lahori, I (b), p. 306; II, pp. 154, 198 and 306
Maheshdas Rathor	Rajput	"	2000/ 2000	–	2000/ 2000	Nov. 1645– Feb. 1646	–	–	Lahori, II, pp. 308, 471 and 484.
Sarandaz Khan	Turani	"	1500/ 1200	–	1500/ 1200	Apr. 1646– May 1646	FD Jammu	Died	Lahori, I (b), p. 278; II, pp. 236, 500 and 506.
Tarbiyat Khan	"	"	1000/ 200	+ 200 sawar	1000/ 400	May 1646– Nov. 1646	Mir Tuzuk	Mir Tuzuk	Lahori, II, pp. 477–8, 506 and 609.
Sher Zaman (shared the charge with) Munawwar s/o Syed Khan-e-Jahan Barha	Indian Muslim	"	{1000/ 250 1000/ 250}	– –	{1000/ 250 1000/ 250}	Mar. 1647 –	–	–	Lahori, II, pp. 474 and 638–9.
"	"	"	{1000/ 250 1000/ 250}	– –	{1000/ 250 1000/ 250}	Mar. 1649 –	–	–	Salih, III (L), p. 72.
Nad Ali	Turani	"	500/ 200	–	500/ 200	Apr. 1651 –	Darogha of Adalat	–	Lahori, II, pp. 336 and 749; Salih, III (L), p. 124.
Yusuf Aqa	Other Muslim	"	700/ 150	+ 300 250	1000/ 400	Feb. 1652– Apr. 1656	–	Darogha of Turk Chelas	Salih, III (L), pp. 136–7 and 218.

Ikhlas Khan Husain Beg	Turani	Rohtas	2000/ 1000	–	2000/ 1000	Jan. 1633 to 1639–40	FD Ajmer	Died	Lahori, I, pp. 292, 372 and 451; II, p. 727.
Mutaqid Khan Mirza Makki	Irani	"	4000/ 4000	–	4000/ 4000	Sep. 1641– Dec. 1645	SD Orissa	SD Orissa	Lahori, I (b), p. 296; II, pp. 183, 244 and 473.
Daulat Khan	Afghan	Kangrah	1000/ 800	–	1000/ 800	– Jan. 1640	–	–	Lahori, I, p. 184; II, p. 175.
Syed Sadr Khan	Indian Muslim	"	700/ 500	–	700/ 500	Jan. 1640 –	–	–	Lahori, I (b), p. 316; II, p. 175.
Syed Lutf Ali Bhakkari	"	"	800/ 400	–	800/ 400	Jan. 1643 to 1652–3	FD Miyan-i-Doab	–	Lahori, I (b), p. 314; II, p. 335.
Syed Khizr	"	"	–	–	–	– July 1657	–	–	Salih, III (L), p. 245.
Safi Khan s/o Islam Khan	Irani	"	1000/ 200	+ 300 sawar	1000/ 500	July 1657 –	–	–	Ibid.
Bahadur Khan Baqi Beg	Other Muslim	Allahabad	1000/ 200	–	1000/ 200	Jun. 1645– Jun. 1650	Naib SD Allahabad (holding)	Naib SD Gujrat	Lahori, II, pp. 424–5; Salih, III (L), p. 112.
Janbaz Khan Syed Ahmad	Indian Muslim	Kalinjar	1000/ 500	–	1000/ 500	Mar. 1629– Jan. 1639	–	QD and FD of Chanda	Lahori, I, pp. 260 and 476; II, p. 129.
Askar Khan Najm-e-Sani	Irani	"	500/ 280	–	500/ 280	Jan. 1639 Dec. 1639	–	–	Lahori, I (b), p. 323; II, pp. 129 and 168.
Naim Beg	Other Muslim	"	500/ 200	–	500/ 200	Dec. 1639 –	–	–	Lahori, I (b), p. 324; II, p. 168.

(contd.)

1	2	3	4	5	6	7	8	9	10
Ikhlas Khan Shaikhul Hidaya	Indian Muslim	Rohtas	1000/ 800	–	1000/ 800	July 1644 –	–	–	Lahori, I (b), p. 307; II, p. 379.
Ikhlas Khan Shaikhul Hidaya	”	”	1500/ 1000	–	1500/ 1000	Mar. 1645– Feb. 1646	–	–	Lahori, II, pp. 344, 411–12, 484 and 488.
Syed Khan-e-Jahan Barha	”	Gwalior	4000/ 3000	–	4000/ 3000	1628 –	–	–	Lahori, I, pp. 117 and 245; *M.U.*, I, pp. 758–9.
Syed Alam b/o Syed Salar Barha	”	”	–	–	–	Dec. 1645 –	–	–	Lahori, II, p. 474.
Mahabt Khan	Irani	Rantham-bore	7000/ 7000 × 2h–3h	–	7000/ 7000 × 2h–3h	– Oct. 1629	SD Delhi (holding)	–	Lahori, I, pp. 117 and 287.
Qiladar Khan	Other Muslim	”	–	–	–	Oct. 1629– Apr. 1631	–	–	Lahori, I, pp. 287 and 369.
Bithaldas Gaur	Rajput	”	3000/ 2000	–	3000/ 2000	Apr. 1631– Dec. 1651	–	FD Ajmer	Lahori, I, pp. 280 and 369; Salih, III (L), pp. 131–2.
Anurodh Gaur	”	”	1500/ 1000	+ 1500/ 2000	3000/ 3000 2h–3h	Dec. 1651 –	–	–	Salih, III (L), pp. 131–2.
Sardar Khan	Turani	Dhamoni	3000/ 2000	+ 1000 sawar	3000/ 3000	Dec. 1635– Mar. 1640	FD Dhamoni (holding)	–	Lahori, I (b), p. 123; II, p. 181.

Mir Shamsuddin	Irani	Surat	2500/ 1500	–	2500/ 1500	Dec. 1627– Jan. 1637	–	FD Baroda	Lahori, I, p. 78; I (b), p. 242; Mirat, I, pp. 202–3.
Syed Ilahdad	Indian Muslim	"	–	–	–	Mar. 1638 –	–	–	Mirat, I, p. 211; Lahori, II, p. 92.
Dayanat Khan Dasht Bayazi	Irani	Ahmadnagar	2500/ 1500	–	2500/ 1500	– Nov. 1630	Bakhshi and Waqa-e-nawis of Deccan	Died	Lahori, I, pp. 205, 258 and 320.
Jan Nisar Khan	Indian Muslim	"	2500/ 1200	–	2500/ 1200	Nov. 1630– Nov. 1631	–	FD of Lakhi Jangal	Lahori, I, pp. 320 and 399; *M.U.*, I, p. 528.
Sipahdar Khan	Irani	"	5000/ 5000	–	5000/ 5000	Nov. 1631– Mar. 1634	–	SD Gujrat	Lahori, I, pp. 182 and 399; I (b), p. 8.
Syed Murtaza Khan	Indian Muslim	"	3000/ 2000	–	3000/ 2000	– Jan. 1640	–	FD Lakhnau	Lahori, I (b), p. 298; II, p. 176, *M.U.*, III, p. 584.
Qazalbash Khan	Irani	"	3000/ 2000	+ 1000 sawar	3000/ 3000	Jan. 1640– Nov. 1648	Th.D. Pathri	Died	Lahori, I (b), p. 249; II, 176; Salih, III (L), p. 66.
Iraj s/o Qazalbash Khan	"	"	500/ 200	+ 1000/ 300	1500/ 500	Nov. 1648 –	–	–	Salih, III (L), p. 66.
Ahmad Khan Niyazi	Afghan	"	2500/ 2000	+ 500/ 1000	3000/ 3000	1649–50 to July 1651	–	Died	*M.U.*, I, p. 187; Salih, III (L), pp. 125–6.
Mirza Khan Manochahar	Irani	"	3000/ 2000	–	3000/ 2000	July 1651– Dec. 1654	SD Awadh	FD Ilichpur	Lahori, II, p. 723; Salih, III (L), pp. 125–6 and 195.
Shah Beg Khan	Turani	"	4000/ 3000	–	4000/ 3000	1654–5 to 1655–6	FD Mewat	–	Lahori, I (b), p. 234; *M.U.*, II, p. 666.
Pirthi Raj Rathor	Rajput	Daulatabad	2000/ 1700	–	2000/ 1700	Jun. 1644– Jun. 1646	–	QD Akbarabad	Lahori, I (b), p. 275; II, pp. 377 and 510.

(contd.)

1	*2*	*3*	*4*	*5*	*6*	*7*	*8*	*9*	*10*
Siyadat Khan	Irani	Daulatabad	2000/ 500	–	2000/ 500	Jun. 1646 to 1649	–	Bakhshi II	Lahori, II, p. 510; Salih, III (L), p. 105; *M.U.*, II, p. 464.
Shah Beg Khan	Turani	Junnair	3000/ 3000	+ 1000 zat	4000/ 3000	Dec. 1636– Sep. 1642	–	SD Berar	Lahori, I (b), p. 234; II, p. 308.
Sipahdar Khan	Irani	"	5000/ 5000	–	5000/ 5000	– July 1644	SD Gujrat	Died	Lahori, I (b), p. 102; II, pp. 320 and 378.
Sazawar Khan	"	"	3000/ 2500	–	3000/ 2500	July 1644 –	FD Lakhi Jangal	FD Tirhut	Lahori, I (b), p. 64; II, pp. 205 and 378; *M.U.*, II, p. 440.
Narsingh Das s/o Dwarka Das	Rajput	Gavil	800/ 800	–	800/ 800	Sep. 1644 –	–	–	Lahori, II, pp. 387 and 739.
Janbaz Khan Syed Ahmad	Indian Muslim	Chanda	1000/ 600	+ 200 sawar	1000/ 800	Jan. 1639– Mar. 1645	QD Kalinjar	FD Mandsur	Lahori, II, pp. 129 and 412.
Siva Ram s/o Balram Gaur	Rajput	Asir	1500/ 1000	–	1500/ 1000	Jun. 1644– Oct. 1644	–	QD Kabul	Lahori, I (b), p. 142; II, pp. 377, 388 and 641.
Gowardhan Rathor	"	"	800/ 400	–	800/ 400	Oct. 1644 –	–	–	Lahori, II, pp. 388 and 740.
Shamsuddin Khan s/o Mukhtar Khan Sabzwari	Irani	"	1000/ 400	–	1000/ 400	1649–50 to 1654–5	Bakhshi of Deccan	Darogha of Topkhana of Deccan	*M.U.*, III, pp. 620–1.
Mughal Khan s/o Zain Khan Koka	"	Udgir	1500/ 1000	+ 500/ 500	2000/ 1500	Oct. 1636– Apr. 1647	QD Kabul	SD Thatta	Lahori, I, p. 191; I (b), p. 221; II, p. 641; *M.U.*, III, p. 490.
Hisamuddin Khan	"	"	1500/ 600	+ 500/ 400	2000/ 1000	1648 to 1657	Bakhshi of Deccan	FD Tilingana	*M.U.*, I, pp. 585–6.

Shamsuddin Khan s/o Mukhtar Khan Sabzwari	Irani	Udgir	1000/ 400	+ 500/ 400	1500/ 800	1656–7– 1657–8	Darogha of Topkhana of Deccan	QD Parinda	Salih, III (L), p. 231; *M.U.*, III, pp. 621–2.
Ihtimam Khan	Indian Muslim	Usa	2000/ 1200	+ 300 sawar	2000/ 1500	Oct. 1636– Aug. 1640	Th.D. Jalnapur	Th.D. Kherla	Lahori, I, p. 397; I (b), pp. 220–1; II, p. 206; *M.U.*, I, pp. 161–2.
Mubarak Khan Niyazi	Afghan	"	2000/ 2000	–	2000/ 2000	Aug. 1640– Jan. 1641	–	FD Bangash	Lahori, I (b), pp. 136 and 138; II, pp. 206 and 221; *M.U.*, III, p. 513.
Uzbek Khan	Turani	"	1000/ 1000	+ 1000/ 1000	2000/ 2000	Jan. 1641– Oct. 1654	–	–	Lahori, II, p. 221; Salih, III (L), p. 192; *M.U.*, I, p. 196.
Khwaja Barkhurdar	"	"	1500/ 1500	+ 500/ 500	2000/ 2000	Oct. 1654 –	–	–	Salih, III (L), p. 192; *M.U.*, I, p. 206.

Note: *Pirthi Raj and Girdhardas shared the qiladari with Baqi Khan (Lahori, II, pp. 510 and 610).

APPENDIX 5.4: SHAHJAHAN'S TOURS DURING HIS WHOLE REIGN

Name of the place left	*Date of leaving*	*Name of the place reached*	*Date of reaching*	*Source*
1	*2*	*3*	*4*	*5*
Agra	Dec. 1629	Burhanpur	Mar. 1630	Lahori, I, pp. 291, 296, 422, 425 and 428; I (b), pp. 3–4, 10, 15, 17, 48–49, 70, 82, 105, 134–5 and 235; II, pp. 20, 23, 110, 123, 141, 147, 156–7, 163, 179, 191, 208, 215, 317, 320, 344, 346, 349, 353–5, 407, 413–14, 419, 467, 470, 500 and 509.
Burhanpur	Apr. 1632	Gwalior	May 1632	
		Agra	Jun. 1632	
Agra	Feb. 1634	Lahore	Apr. 1634	
Lahore	May 1634	Kashmir	Jun. 1634	
Kashmir	Sep. 1634			
Lahore	Jan. 1635	Agra	Mar. 1635	
Agra	Oct. 1635	Burhanpur	Jan. 1636	
		Agra	Jan. 1637	
Agra	Feb. 1638	Agra	Mar. 1638	
Agra	Aug. 1638	Lahore	Nov. 1638	
Lahore	Mar. 1639	Kabul	May 1639	
Kabul	Aug. 1639	Lahore	Oct. 1639	
Lahore	Feb. 1640	Kashmir	Apr. 1640	
Kashmir	Sep. 1640	Lahore	Nov. 1640	
Lahore	Nov. 1642	Agra	Jan. 1643	
Agra	Nov. 1643	Ajmer	Nov. 1643	
Ajmer	Nov. 1643	Agra	Dec. 1643	
Agra	Feb. 1644	Agra	Mar. 1644	
Agra	Jan. 1645	Lahore	Mar. 1645	
Lahore	Apr. 1645	Kashmir	Apr. 1645	
Kashmir	Sep. 1645	Lahore	Nov. 1645	Lahori, II, pp. 594, 609, 638 and 678; Salih, III (L), pp. 5, 19, 24, 57, 67–8, 72, 100, 103, 105, 106, 119, 125–6, 127–8, 135, 142, 149, 152, 174, 176, 191, 196, 234–5, 238, 242–3 and 263–4.
Lahore	Apr. 1646	Kabul	Jun. 1646	
Kabul	Sep. 1646	Lahore	Nov. 1646	
Lahore	Mar. 1647	Kabul	May 1647	
Kabul	Aug. 1647	Agra	Jan. 1648	
Agra	Apr. 1648	Shahjahanabad	Apr. 1648	
Shah-jahanabad	Nov. 1648	Lahore	Dec. 1648	
Lahore	Mar. 1649			
Kabul	Sep. 1649	Lahore	Oct. 1649	
Lahore	Dec. 1649	Shahjahanabad	Jan. 1650	
Shah-jahanabad	Feb. 1651	Kashmir	Jun. 1651	
Kashmir	Aug. 1651	Lahore	Sep. 1651	
Lahore	Feb. 1652	Kabul	Apr. 1652	
Kabul	Aug. 1652	Shahjahanabad	Dec. 1652	
Shah-jahanabad	Nov. 1653	Agra	Dec. 1653	

(contd.)

Name of the place left	*Date of leaving*	*Name of the place reached*	*Date of reaching*	*Source*
1	*2*	*3*	*4*	*5*
Agra	Dec. 1653	Shahjahanabad	Jan. 1654	
Shah-jahanabad	Nov. 1654	Ajmer	Nov. 1654	
Ajmer	Nov. 1654	Shahjahanabad	Dec. 1654	
Shah-jahanabad	Dec. 1656	Nurpur	Dec. 1656	
		Shahjahanabad	Jan. 1657	
Shah-jahanabad	Feb. 1657	Shahjahanabad	May 1657	
Shah-jahanabad	Oct. 1657	Agra	Nov. 1657	

CHAPTER 6

Conclusion

'Shahjahan's reign', in the words of B.P. Saksena, 'presents a paradox. On the one hand there is a remarkable display of grandeur and greatness, on the other signs of decay are but too visible.'[1] Splendour and glory are revealed by the destruction of Ahmadnagar, the submission of Bijapur and Golkonda and the occupation of Qandhar, while the expensive Central Asian project and a couple of futile attempts to regain Qandhar suggest a descent from the higher steps of glory. The gold and jewels overflowing the royal coffers could hardly check the growing darkness which gradually engulfed the whole establishment in the succeeding period. There is ample documentary evidence to suggest that the large-scale expansion of the mansabdari system resulted in insufficiency of revenues available from land. The drastic reforms of 1642 were intended to bridge the gulf between jama figures and the actual hasil. This was done by reducing the contingents to be maintained by the mansabdars and the introduction of the month scale, which in effect meant reduction in the net emoluments of the jagirdar. Added to this was the frequent complaint that jama figures far surpassed the hasil figures from the jagirs. These tendencies were bound to gradually affect the resources and attitudes of both the crown and the nobility. The account the nobility presented in the foregoing pages should be viewed against this background.

Keeping in mind the importance of the changing political and economic conditions, the whole reign of Shahjahan has been divided tentatively into three phases: 1628–36, 1637–41 and 1642–58. The first phase marks the consolidation of power in Shahjahan's reign and its triumph over the rebellions of Jujhar Singh and Khan-e-Jahan Lodhi and the conquest of the Deccan resulting in the absorption of the kingdom of Ahmadnagar. The treaty of 1636 brought a period of comparative peace in the Deccan. For about 20 years, the region remained almost free from the hectic military expeditions of the Mughal forces. But this phase also marks the absorption of the Deccan nobility on one hand, and the settlement of new provinces on the other. During this phase, the foreign element in the Mughal nobility, that is those who migrated to India and those who were born in India but belonged to immigrant families, occupied leading positions, with the Iranis outnumbering the Turanis. The influx of Deccanis in general and the Marathas in particular raised the number of the nobility and also affected the proportions of various ethnic groups within the nobility.

After the treaty of 1636 and the end of hectic military activities in the Deccan, we enter a period of comparative peace. During this phase, a drastic decline in the number of nobles may be seen. This decline mainly affected the Deccanis (including the Marathas), and the Afghans slightly. The remaining groups improved their shares of the first phase. The maximum benefit, however, goes to the Turanis; the Iranis still remained in a leading position. Rajputs and Indian Muslims were among other beneficiaries of this period.

The Balkh and Badakhshan campaigns along with the Qandhar recovery expeditions again built up pressure on military activities. This led to a rise in the number of the nobles for a second time. The need to pacify the older nobility, to reward the old supporters and to integrate the Deccan nobility, resulted in the far-reaching reforms of 1642 in the system of mansabdari in its relationship with jagir. These two noteworthy developments, which ultimately affected the fortunes of the nobles, the attitude of the crown, and the resources and powers of both, thus mark the third phase of Shahjahan's reign. During this period too, the immigrant nobility continued to occupy prominent positions, with Iranis outnumbering the Turanis. The special gains of Indian Muslims and a further loss of Deccanis (including Marathas), are other interesting developments of this phase. There was a slight improvement in the position of Rajputs and a slight decline in the proportion of Afghans.

The khanazads (nobles whose fathers or other relatives had been in imperial service) naturally formed a sizeable number of Shahjahan's nobility. It appears to be a general policy that if the son or a close relative of a high noble served the emperor well, he would reach the same status which his relatives had acquired earlier. It seems, however, that Shahjahan gradually tried to put the brakes on this policy, as is evident from the decline of the mansab figures of some family groups over the years. Otherwise the number of khanazads would have increased so much that no jagir would have been left for anybody else. Nevertheless, their proportion in the total increased from the first to the last phases. Yet the placement of non-khanazads in higher ranks cannot be overlooked.

The absorption of zamindars in the nobility continued under Shahjahan and led to changes in the system. For example, whereas the faujdar was responsible for maintaining law and order, quite often we notice Shahjahan asking influential zamindars to perform the duties which should normally have been performed by the faujdar. In this way, an attempt seems to have been made to treat the zamindars more as mansabdars and less as zamindars. This should have served the purpose of establishing an equilibrium between the non-zamindar mansabdars and the zamindar mansabdars. Perhaps this was the reason why the zamindars remained on Shahjahan's side in large numbers during the rebellion of the younger princes.

It seems that fluctuations in the political and economic conditions had a direct impact upon the fluctuating number of the nobility. In other words, the increasing or decreasing utility of the nobles in changing conditions determined the strength of this group. Under the pressure of economic conditions and taking advantage of the comparatively peaceful political conditions, Shahjahan seems to have tried to control the rising number of nobles (which is confirmed by the decline in the number of the nobles during the second phase). However, the rise in their number during the third phase confirms that the changing conditions were forcing the hands of the emperor.

In order to establish a balance in his nobility, Shahjahan seems to have paid extra attention to the Turanis while not neglecting the Iranis, but gradually confining them to almost the same level which they had reached in the first phase of his reign. The rise of Indian Muslims vis-à-vis Afghans also confirms this. Rajputs, however, were kept in favour in continuation with the traditions of the past. That is why, in spite of many big or small rebellions from this group, there was hardly any change in the crown's attitude, which is evident from the consistency of their proportion in the total number of nobles. However, the Marathas were never treated at par with them. Their rise or decline depended mainly upon their increasing or decreasing utility in changing conditions. This seems to be true in the cases of most of the Deccani nobles.

Shahjahan seems to have adopted a moderate policy of compromise with his nobility. This becomes evident from the continuation of such traditions as the pacification of dissatisfied elements by granting pardon and restoration of mansab and jagir; distribution of the wealth of a deceased noble among his heirs and usually accommodating his descendants in imperial service; and the rareness of avenge full attitude towards the nobles, etc. Therefore, the bulk of the nobles rallied around the Mughal throne through thick and thin and served the crown with all sincerity. Different racial and religious groups—though conscious of their racial or religious identities—normally acted as political factions and hardly ever gave precedence to their racial or religious sentiments over the imperial interest, personal benefits or political considerations. The valuable services of the Rajputs in crushing the rebellions of Jujhar Singh and Jagat Singh, the remarkable support of the Afghans against Khan-e-Jahan Lodhi, and the undivided support of the Turanis during the Central Asian campaigns, suggest that the role of racial or religious factors in the public life of the ruling class was of not much importance. Ethnic differentiation did not affect the functioning of the nobility or its loyalty to the throne during the major part of the reign. The condition that the contingent should not belong to the same ethnic group as the commander, further reduced the chances of ethnic revolts.

This cohesion between the crown and the nobility, as well as among the nobles, rested upon the basic element of mutual interdependence. Therefore, the identity of interests in certain areas was perhaps the basic factor in Shahjahan's compromising attitude and in the nobles' devotion and sincerity towards the crown. The rebellious attitude of the nobility on the other hand exposes the element of mutual contradiction between the crown and the nobility. Since power was the real bone of contention, the possibilities of mutual push and pull could not be eliminated altogether. The minimization or maximization of such possibilities, however, depended upon the prevailing circumstances, policies and plans of the emperor, and also the availability of suitable opportunities to both the crown and the nobles to multiply power.

The linkage between mansab and jagir proved to be an effective weapon in the hands of the crown to control the nobility. At the same time, the absorption of zamindars in the nobility provided an element of stability, which might not otherwise have been there. The dependence of the nobility upon the crown implied by the mansab system was neutralized, to some extent, by sawar rank. The contingents of the mansabdars were the real source of power for them, and these sawars formed the backbone of the empire's military strength. So the award of sawar mansab and promotion or curtailment therein, was a matter of special concern for the crown as well as the nobles.

This study confirms that the rise or decline in mansab figures was mainly the result of changing political and economic conditions. Even though compelled by circumstances to raise the number of mansabdars, Shahjahan seems to have been very circumspect while giving promotions, and quite cautious while sanctioning new awards. Being conscious of the deplorable financial condition he inherited, and being aware of the requirements of the conditions—sometimes created by his own plans—he preferred to give more promotions in sawar than in zat mansab. But this implied more power for the nobles, which was not a wise proposition. That is why, perhaps the bigger portion of the total sawar mansab was put under khanazads, whose loyalty and devotion had been tested for generations. This means that more importance was attached to loyalty than to race or religion.

The old tradition of conferring more favours upon selected nobles and their family members seems to have been continued during this reign as well. The leading family groups held more than half of the total mansab awards. In sawar mansab, their share was even greater than in zat.

Regarding promotion in mansab, it may be said that it was a meaningful device to confirm the crown's hold over the mansabdars, as well as to reward them for their efficiency, thus keeping them satisfied. This study shows that the role of racial or religious bias or manipulations at other levels in the grant of promotions were of hardly any importance. It seems that the strongest ground for the emperor's favour was the quality of performance in military expeditions. Thus, the peak period of promotions was either the eve of some expedition, during the expedition, or at its conclusion. Appointments to various offices, long-standing military, administrative and political services, and political consideration, seem to be other grounds for promotion, in decreasing order of importance.

The role of the nobility in the administration suggests that racial or religious considerations did not normally affect imperial decisions in making appointments to central or provincial offices. It was individual potential and calibre that matterred. Removal from a central office seems to have been for a change for the better, rather than as a time-bound rule. Capable and suitable persons could enjoy a life tenure. There is an obvious correspondence between the mansab and various central offices. The mansabdars chosen were usually promoted to reach the minimum mansab level of the particular post. At provincial level, however, this correspondence between the post and the mansab can be established with direct reference to the prevailing local conditions, overall political developments and the military strategy of the region. The reflection of these developments can be seen in the ebb and flow of the mansab figures of these office-bearers. It is also worth noting that Iranis were not usually posted in the north-west frontier region and its contiguous territory. Almost the same policy was applied to the Afghans. This implies that these groups were not trusted to be assigned the defence of this most crucial area. Turanis, on the other hand, enjoyed this special trust as, mostly, they served there.

Shahjahan's reforms in mansab and jagir provided but a temporary solution to a serious and deep-seated problem. If this step suggests his cognizance of the situation, it simultaneously unveils some old grievances of mansabdars and of the army. With these reforms, a large jagir was required, for the effective maintenance of a small cavalry. A huge and well-equipped army, which was the backbone of the political structure, could then be maintained by multiplying the number of mansabdars. This tendency was bound to increase the quantum of jagir demand. This gave way to an irresistible shortage of paibaqi. The Mughal administration and economy thus got corroded to the extent that it virtually jammed the machine and left the last effective emperor, Aurangzeb, to die in frustration and dismay.

Although the month scale and the system of deductions mitigated the financial burden of mansabdars, the ratio of efficiency to expense was negative. Shahjahan tried to make up for this by retaining the tradition of providing, for the payment of artillery and musketry from khalisa. In all the major campaigns, artillery and musketry paid out of khalisa revenues was allocated to the commander.

It seems that Shahjahan could not successfully find a stable equilibrium between interdependence and contradiction of the nobility and the crown. The presence of the bulk of the nobles who participated in the so-called war of succession in the camp of the rebel princes confirms this. This development might have some link with Shahjahan's policy towards various ethnic groups and his reforms in the mansab system.[2] His deposition and long confinement of about eight years passed almost unnoticed; this underlines Shahjahan's unpopularity among the nobles.

NOTES

1. B.P. Saxena, *History of Shahjahan of Dihli*, Central Book Depot, Allahabad, 1958, p. 296.
2. These issues are discussed in some detail in Chapter 3.

APPENDIX A: LIST OF MANSABDARS OF SHAHJAHAN DURING 1628–36 HOLDING RANKS OF 1000 ZAT AND ABOVE

Sl.No.	*Name and title*	*Initial rank (zar /sawar)*	*Highest rank during the period (zat /sawar)*	*Ethnic group*	*Sub-group: Rajput, Maratha, Afghan, zamindar, etc.*	*Father or other blood relative in service*	*Date of Death (D), Retirement (R), Flight (F), etc.*	*Authorities*
1	*2*	*3*	*4*	*5*	*6*	*7*	*8*	*9*
				MANSABDARS OF 5000 AND ABOVE				
1	Yaminuddaulah Asaf Khan	8000/8000 H × 2h–3h	9000/9000 H × 2h–3h	Irani	–	Father	–	Lahori, I, pp. 113 and 193; I (b), p. 292; *Z.Kh.*, II, pp. 32–46; *M.U.*, I, pp. 151–60.
2	Mahabat Khan Khan-e-Khanan	7000/7000 H × 2h–3h	7000/70000 H × 2h–3h	"	–	"	May 1635 (D)	Lahori, I, p. 117; I (b), pp. 59–60 and 293; *Z.Kh.*, II, pp. 116–173; *M.U.*, III, pp. 385–409.
3	Khan-e-Jahan Lodhi	7000/7000 H × 2h–3h	7000/7000 H × 2h–3h	Indian	Afghan	"	Oct. 1629 (F)	Lahori, I, p. 182; I (b), p. 293; *Z.Kh.*, II, pp. 69–116; *M.U.*, I, pp. 716–32.
4	Mirza Rustam Safavi	6000/ 6000	6000/ 6000	Irani	–	–	1628 (R)	Lahori, I, p. 205; *Z.Kh.*, I, pp. 99–101; *M.U.*, III, pp. 434–41.
5	Khwaja Abul Hasan	5000/ 5000	6000/ 6000	"	–	–	Mar. 1633 (D)	Lahori, I, pp. 182, 257 and 473–4; I (b), p. 293; *M.U.*, I, pp. 737–39.
6	AzamKhan Iradat Khan	5000/ 5000	6000/ 6000	"	–	Uncle	–	Lahori, I pp. 159 and 343; *Z.Kh.*, II p.200; *M.U.*, pp. 174–80.
7	Abdullah Khan Feroze Jang	5000/ 5000	6000/ 6000	Turani	–	Brother	–	Lahori, I, pp. 204 and 354; *Z.Kh.*, II, pp. 173–85; *M.U.*, II, pp. 771 and 777–89.

(contd.)

1	*2*	*3*	*4*	*5*	*6*	*7*	*8*	*9*
8	Khan-e-Alam Mirza-Barkhurdar	6000/ 5000	6000/ 5000	Turani	–	Father	Jun. 1632 (R)	Lahori, I, pp. 120 and 426–7; *Z.Kh.*, II, pp. 201–4; *M.U.*, I, pp. 732–6.
9	Afzal Khan Allami	4000/ 2000	6000/ 4000	Irani	–	–	–	Lahori, I, pp. 176–7; I (b), p. 86; *Z.Kh.*, II, pp. 255–6; *M.U.*, I, pp. 145–51.
10	Islam Khan Mashhadi	4000/ 2000	5000/ 5000 2h–3h	"	–	–	–	Lahori, I, pp. 160–1; I (b), p. 83; *Z.Kh.*, II, pp. 25–7; *M.U.*, I, pp. 162–7
11	Khan-e-Jahan Shaista Khan	5000/ 4000	5000/ 4000	"	–	Father	–	Lahori, I, pp. 180 and 294–6; *Z.Kh.*, II, pp. 188–90; *M.U.*, pp. 690–706.
12	Khan-e-Zaman Mirza Amanullah s/o Mahabat Khan	5000/ 5000	5000/ 5000 4000 × 2h–3h	"	–	"	–	Lahori, I, p. 158; I (b), pp. 62–3; *Z.Kh.*, II, pp. 263–71; *M.U.*, I, pp. 740–8.
13	Lashkar Khan Abul Hasan Mashhadi	5000/ 4000	5000/ 5000	"	–	–	Mar. 1633 (R)	Lahori, I, pp. 120 and 472; I (b), p. 295; *Z.Kh.* I, pp. 207–8; *M.U.*, III, pp. 163–8.
14	Qasim Khan Juwaini	5000/ 5000 2h–3h	5000/ 5000 2h–3h	"	–	Father	1632 (D)	Lahori, I, pp. 120 and 444; I (b), p. 294; *Z.Kh.*, II, p. 252; *M.U.*, III, pp. 78–82.
15	Sipahdar Khan Muhammad Salih	5000/ 5000	5000/ 5000	"	–	Uncle	–	Lahori, I, p. 182; I (b), p. 294; *Z.Kh.*, II, pp. 261–2; *M.U.*, II, pp. 427–9.
16	Khan-e-Dauran Nusrat Jang Khwaja Sabir	3000/ 2000	5000/ 5000 2h–3h	Turani	–	Father	–	Lahori, I, pp. 266–7; I (b), p. 134; *Z.Kh.*, III, pp. 18–25; *M.U.*, I., pp. 749–58.
17	Rustam Khan Muqarrab Khan Deccani	5000/ 5000	5000/ 5000	"	Deccani	–	–	Lahori, I, pp. 378–9 and 384; I (b), p. 294; *Z.Kh.*, III, pp. 91–2; *M.U.*, II, pp. 270–6.

18	Khan-e-Jahan Barha Syed Abul Muzaffar	4000/ 3000	5000/ 5000 2h–3h	Indian	–	–	–	Lahori, I, p. 117; I (b), pp. 83 and 293; *Z.Kh.*, III, pp. 10–12; *M.U.*, I, pp. 758–66.
19	Wazir Khan Hakim Alimuddin	5000/ 3000 1000 × 2h–3h	5000/ 5000	"	–	–	–	Lahori, I, pp. 117 and 425; *Z.Kh.*, III, pp. 15–18; *M.U.*, III, pp. 933–6.
20	Raja Gaj Singh Rathor	5000/ 5000	5000/ 5000	"	Rajput zamindar	Father	–	Lahori, I, p. 158; I (b), p. 294; *Z.Kh.*, II, pp. 300–1; *M.U.*, II, pp. 223–6.
21	Rana Jagat Singh Sisodiya	5000/ 5000	5000/ 5000	"	"	"	–	Lahori, I, p. 161; I (b), p. 294; *M,U.*, II, pp. 200–6.
22	Raja Jujhar Singh Bundela	4000/ 4000	5000/ 5000	"	"	"	1635–6 (D)	Lahori, I, pp. 182 and 294–6; I (b), p. 294; *Z.Kh.*, III, pp. 60–6; *M.U.*, II, pp. 214–15.
23	Rana Karan Sisodiya	5000/ 5000	5000/ 5000	"	"	"	1627–8 (D)	Lahori, I, pp. 80 and 161; *M.U.*, II, pp. 200–6.
24	Rao Ratan Hara	5000/ 5000	5000/ 5000	"	"	"	1631 (D)	Lahori, I, pp. 185–6 and 401; I (b), p. 294; *Z.Kh.*, II, pp. 295–6; *M.U.*, II, pp. 208–11.
25	Bahadurji	5000/ 5000	5000/ 5000	"	Maratha zamindar	"	1635–6 (D)	Lahori, I, p. 400; I (b), p. 295; *M.U.*, I, pp. 520–3.
26	Jadun Rai Kaisth	5000/ 5000	5000/ 5000	"	" Deccani	–	1630–1 (D)	Lahori, I, pp. 182 and 308; *Z.Kh.*, III, p. 141; *M.U.*, I, pp. 520–3.
27	Udaji Ram Deccani	4000/ 4000	5000/ 5000	"	" "	–	1633–4 (D)	Lahori, I, pp. 182, 295–6 and 510; *Z.Kh.*, III, pp. 140–41; *M.U.*, I, pp. 142–5.
28	Kheluji Bhonsle	5000/ 5000	5000/ 5000	"	" "	–	1633 (F)	Lahori, I, pp. 227 and 507–8; *Z.Kh.*, III, pp. 132–3; *M.U.*, III, pp. 520–4.

(contd.)

1	*2*	*3*	*4*	*5*	*6*	*7*	*8*	*9*
29	Maloji b/o Kheluji	5000/ 5000	5000/ 5000	Indian	Maratha zamindar	Brother	–	Lahori, I, p. 293; *Z.Kh.*, III, p. 139; *M.U.*, III, pp. 520–4.
30	Sahuji Bhonsle	5000/ 5000	5000/ 5000	”	” Deccani	–	1632–3 (F)	Lahori, I, pp. 327–8 and 442; *M.U.*, II, pp. 342–58.
31	Yaqut Khan Habshi	5000/ 5000	5000/ 5000	–	”	–	1633 (D)	Lahori, I, pp. 182, 195 and 523; I (b), p. 294; *Z.Kh.*, III, pp. 137–9; *M.U.*, III, pp. 958–63.
32	Aitqad Khan Mirza Shapur	4000/ 4000	5000/ 4000	Irani	–	Father	–	Lahori, I, p. 182; I (b), p. 295; *M.U.*, I, pp. 180–2.
33	Mir Muhammad Mir Jumla	3000/ 1200	5000/ 2000	”	Deccani	–	–	Lahori, I, p. 181; I (b), p. 86; *Z.Kh.*, II, pp. 217–20; *M.U.*, III, pp. 413–18.
34	Mirza Isa Tarkhan	4000/ 2500	5000/ 4000 1000 × 2h–3h	Turani	–	Brother	–	Lahori, I, pp. 78–9; I (b), p. 103; *Z.Kh.*, II, pp. 210–12; *M.U.*, III, pp. 485–8.
35	Said Khan Zafar Jang	2000/ 1100	5000/ 4000 3000 × 2h–3h	”	–	Father	–	Lahori, I, p. 183; I (b), p. 67; *Z.Kh.*, II, p. 361; *M.U.*, II, pp. 429–36.
36	Raja Jai Singh Kachwaha	4000/ 3000	5000/ 4000	Indian	Rajput zamindar	”	–	Lahori, I, p. 120; I (b), p. 86; *Z.Kh.*, III, pp. 117–18; *M.U.*, III, pp. 568–77; I, pp. 173–6.
37	Rahim Khan son-in-law of Ambar Habshi	5000/ 4000	5000/ 4000	–	Deccani	–	1631–2 (D)	Lahori, I, p. 300; I (b), p. 295.
38	Sher Khan Nahar Khan	5000/ 5000	5000/ 5000	Indian	Afghan, Deccani	–	Apr. 1631 (D)	Lahori, I, pp. 78 and 368–9; I (b), p. 294; Mirat, I, p. 203; *Z.Kh.*, II, pp. 345–6; *M.U.*, II, pp. 651–3.

MANSABDARS OF 3000 TO 4500

39	Baqar Khan Najm-e-Sani	4000/ 4000	4000/ 4000	Irani	–	–	–	Lahori, I, p. 182; *Z.Kh.*, II, pp. 254–5; *M.U.*, I, pp. 408–12.
40.	Khwaja Baqi Khan Sher-Khwaja	4000/ 3500	4000/ 3500	"	–	–	1628 (D)	Lahori, I, pp. 181 and 200; I (b), p. 296; *M.U.*, II, pp. 649–50.
41	Alahwardi Khan	2000/ 2000	4000/ 4000	"	–	Brother	–	Lahori, I, pp. 181–2; I (b), p. 63; *Z.Kh.*, II, pp. 205–8; *M.U.*, I, pp. 207–15.
42	Jafar Khan s/o Sadiq Khan	1500 700	4000 3000	"	–	Father	–	Lahori, I, p. 291; I (b), p. 83; *Z.Kh.*, III, pp. 31–2; *M.U.*, II, p. 730; I, pp. 531–5.
43.	Jansipar Khan Turkman	4000/ 4000	4000/ 3000	"	–	–	1628–9 (D)	Lahori, I, p. 185; I (b), p. 296; *M.U.*, I, pp. 516–19.
44	Murtaza Khan Mir Hisammuddin Anju	4000/ 3000	4000/ 3000	"	–	Father	Oct. 1629 (D)	Lahori, I, pp. 181 and 287; I (b), p. 296; *Z.Kh.*, I, pp. 196–7; II, pp. 307–8; *M.U.*, III, pp. 382–4.
45	Musvi Khan, Sadr	3000/ 750	4000/ 750	"	–	Near relative	–	Lahori, I, pp. 181 and 408–9; *Z.Kh.*, II, pp. 220–1; *M.U.*, III, pp. 441–2.
46	Mutaqid Khan Mirza Makki s/o Iftikhar Khan	4000/ 2000	4000/ 3000	"	–	Father	–	Lahori, I, pp. 79 and 430–1; Mirat, I, p. 203; *Z.Kh.*, II, pp. 351–2; III, pp. 45–6; *M.U.*, I, pp. 182–5; III, pp. 482–5.
47.	Sadiq Khan s/o Aqa Tahir	4000/ 4000	4000/ 4000	"	–	"	1633 (D)	Lahori, I, pp. 181 and 538–9; I (b), p. 295; *Z.Kh.*, II, pp. 208–9; *M.U.*, II, pp. 729–31.
48	Saif Khan Mirza Safi	4000/ 4000	4000/ 4000	"	–	Near relatives	–	Lahori, I, p. 177; *Z.Kh.*, II, pp. 238–9; *M.U.*, II, pp. 416–20.

(contd.)

1	2	3	4	5	6	7	8	9
49	Shahnawaz Khan Mirza Badiuzzaman Safavi	3000/ 1500	4000/ 2500	Irani	–	Father	–	Lahori, I, p. 181; I (b), p. 209; *Z.Kh.*, II, pp. 216–17; *M.U.*, II, pp. 670–5.
50	Fidai Khan Hidayatullah	4000/ 3000	4000/ 3000	Turani	–	Brother	–	Lahori, I, pp. 126 and 182; *Z.Kh.*, II, pp. 314–15; *M.U.*, III, pp. 12–18.
51	Mahaldar Khan s/o Mahaldar Khan Charkas	4000/ 2000	4000/ 2000	"	Deccani	–	–	Lahori, I (b), pp. 1 and 297; *Z.Kh.*, III, pp. 134–5; *M.U.*, III, pp. 419–21.
52.	Qulij Khan	2500/ 2000 1000 × 2h–3h	4000/ 4000	"	–	Brother	–	Lahori, I, p. 118; I (b), p. 295; Salih, II, p. 10; *Z.Kh.*, III, pp. 66–7; *M.U.*, III, pp. 92–5.
53	Safdar Khan Khwaja Qasim	2500/ 1200	4000/ 2500	"	–	–	–	Lahori, I, pp. 118 and 408; *Z.Kh.*, III, p. 40; *M.U.*, II, pp. 733–6.
54	Sarfaraz Khan Chaghta	3000/ 500	4000/ 3000	"	–	G. father	–	Lahori, I, p. 183; *M.U.*, II, pp. 421–3.
55	Shah Beg Khan Uzbek	1000/ 400	4000/ 3000	"	–	–	–	Lahori, I, p. 185; I (b), p. 234; *Z.Kh.*, III, pp. 41–2; *M.U.*, II, pp. 665–7.
56.	Syed Diler Khan Barha	4000/ 2500	4000/ 3000	Indian	–	–	1632 (D)	Lahori, I, pp. 120, 299 and 448; I (b), p. 296; *Z.Kh.*, II, pp. 315–16; *M.U.*, II, pp. 412–13.
57	Syed Shujat Khan Barha s/o Syed Jahangir	4000/ 2000	4000/ 2000	"	–	G. father	–	Lahori, I, pp. 439–40; *Z.Kh.*, III, pp. 12–15; *M.U.*, II, pp. 423–6.
58	Babu Khan Biran	4000/ 2500	4000/ 2500	"	Afghan	–	–	Salih, I, p. 267 (B).

59	Bakhtiyar Khan Alawal Khan[1]	–	4000/ 4000	”	”	–	Died	*Z.Kh.*, II, pp. 302–3.
60	Bahadur Khan Rohila	4000/ 2000	4000/ 4000	”	”	Father	–	Lahori, I, p. 117; I (b), pp. 86–7; *Z.Kh.*, III, pp. 48–9; *M.U.*, I, pp. 415–24.
61	Bahlol Mayan	4000/ 3000	4000/ 3000	”	” Deccani	–	Nov. 1629 (F)	Lahori, I, p. 182 and 289; *M.U.*, II, p. 55.
62	Darya Khan Rohila	4000/ 3000	4000/ 4000	”	Afghan	–	Apr. 1630 (F)	Lahori, I, pp. 202–3, 297 and 300; I (b), p. 296; *M.U.*, II, pp. 18–21.
63	Dilawar Khan Biraj	4000/ 2500	4000/ 4000	”	”	–	1631–2 (D)	Lahori, I, pp. 117 and 398; I (b), p. 296; *M.U.*, I, pp. 424–5.
64	Bharat Bundela	3000/ 2500	4000/ 3500	”	Rajput zamindar	G. father	1634 (D)	Lahori, I, pp. 120–1 and 542; I (b), pp. 13–14 and 296; *M.U.*, II, pp. 212–13.
65	Rao Sur Bhurtiya	4000/ 2500	4000/ 3000	”	”	Father	1631 (D)	Lahori, I, pp. 120, 295–6 and 398; I (b), p. 297; *Z.Kh.*, I, p. 215; *M.U.*, II, pp. 211–12.
66	Hamir Rai Deccani	–	4000/ 2500	”	Maratha zamindar (Deccani)	–	1634–5 (D)	Lahori, I (b), p. 297.
67	Jagdev Rai b/o Jadun Rai	4000/ 3000	4000/ 3000	”	Maratha zamindar	Brother	1632–3 (F)	Lahori, I, pp. 308–10; I (b), p. 297; *M.U.*, I, p. 522.
68	Sarfaraz Khan Deccani	4000/ 3000	4000/ 3000	–	Deccani	–	–	Salih, I, pp. 469–70 (B); Lahori, I (b), p. 297; *M.U.*, II, pp. 469–73.

(contd.)

1	*2*	*3*	*4*	*5*	*6*	*7*	*8*	*9*
69	Amir Khan Mir Abul Baga s/o Qasim Khan Namkin	2500/ 1500	3000/ 2000	Irani	–	Father	–	Lahori, I, pp. 183 and 287; *Z.Kh.*, I, pp. 198–200; *M.U.*, I, pp. 172–4; III, pp. 74–82.
70	Asad Khan Mamuri	2500/ 1500	3000/ 1500	"	–	"	Sep. 1631 (D)	Lahori, I, pp. 183, 288 and 397; I (b), p. 299; *Z.Kh.*, II, pp. 275–6 and 304; *M.U.*, I, pp. 140–1.
71	Asalat Khan Mir Abdul Hadi	1000/ 400	3000/ 2500	"	–	Grand father	–	Lahori, I, pp. 319–20 and 432; I (b), p. 87; *Z.Kh.*, III, p. 32; *M.U.*, III, pp. 341–2; I, pp. 167–72.
72	Hakim Masih-uz-Zaman Sadra	3000/ 500	3000/ 500	"	–	Uncle	–	Lahori, I, pp. 159–60; I (b), pp. 102, 299 and 347.
73	Mirza Khan Manochahar	3000/ 2000	3000/ 2000	"	–	Father	–	Lahori, I, p. 121; *Z.Kh.*, II, pp. 318–19; *M.U.*, III, pp. 586–9.
74	Mukhlis Khan	2000/ 2000	3000/ 2000	"	–	–	–	Lahori, I, p. 181; I (B), p. 14; *Z.Kh.*, II, pp. 205–8; *M.U.*, III, pp. 428–31.
75	Mutamad Khan Muhammad Shareef	3000/ 800	3500/ 800	"	–	–	–	Lahori, I, pp. 181 and 432; *Z.Kh.*, II, p. 253; *M.U.*, III, pp. 431–4.
76	Mubariz Khan Rohila	3000/ 3000	3500/ 3500	Indian	Afghan	–	–	Lahori, I, p. 182; I (b), p. 63; *Z.Kh.*, II, pp. 348–9; *M.U.*, III, pp. 442–4.
77	Abdul Rahim s/o Khuda Dost	3500/ 2500	3500/ 2500	–	–	–	–	Lahori, I, p. 205.
78	Shams Khan Deccani	–	3500/ 1250	–	Deccani	–	1630–1 (D)	Lahori, I (b), p. 301.

79	Mirza Muzaffar Kirmani	3000/ 1022	3000/ 1022	Irani	–	–	–	Lahori, I, p. 118.
80	Turkman Khan Mustafa Beg	3000/ 2000	3000/ 2000	"	–	–	1634–5 (D)	Lahori, I, p. 121; I (b), p. 298; *M.U.*, III, pp. 384–5.
81	Zafar Khan s/o Khwaja Abul Hasan	2500/ 1200	3000/ 2000	"	–	Father	–	Lahori, I, pp. 183 and 474; *Z.Kh.*, II, pp. 290–1; *M.U.*, II, pp. 756–63.
82	Begalar Khan s/o Said Khan	3000/ 2500	3000/ 2500	Turani	–	"	1629–30 (D)	Lahori, I, p. 182, I (b), p. 298; *Z.Kh.*, II, pp. 250–2; *M.U.*, I, pp. 401–4.
83	Jahangir Quli Khan	3000/ 3000	3000/ 3000	"	–	"	1632 (D)	Lahori, I, pp. 182 and 409; I (b), p. 297; *Z.Kh.*, II, p. 325; *M.U.*, I, pp. 524–5.
84	Najabat Khan Mirza Shuja	1000/ 400	3000/ 2000	"	–	"	–	Lahori, I, p. 182; I (b), p. 11; *Z.Kh.*, II, pp. 239–42; *M.U.*, III, pp. 821–8.
85	Sardar Khan Shahjahani	3000/ 2000	3000/ 3000	"	–	–	–	Lahori, I, p. 117; I (b), p. 123; *M.U.*, II, pp. 437–8.
86	Shamsher Khan Islam Beg	2000/ 1500	3000/ 2500	"	–	Uncle	1631–2 (D)	Lahori, I, pp. 183, 401 and 417; I (b), p. 298; *M.U.*, I, pp. 404–5.
87	Yusuf Muhammad Khan Tashqandi	2000/ 1000	3000/ 2000	"	–	–	–	Lahori, I, pp. 118–19 and 423–4; *Z.Kh.*, III, pp. 42–3; *M.U.*, III, pp. 963–7.
88	Daulat Khan Maee	2500/ 2000	3000/ 2000	Indian	–	–	–	Lahori, I, pp. 280 and 474–5; *Z.Kh.*, II, p. 378; *M.U.*, II, pp. 24–30.
89	Syed Hizbar Khan Barha	3000/ 1000	3000/ 1000	"	–	–	–	Lahori, I, p. 183; *Z.Kh.*, II, p. 315; *M.U.*, II, pp. 415–16.
90	Kartalab Khan Baswant Rao	2000/ 1000	3000/ 2000	"	Deccani	–	–	Lahori, I, pp. 183 and 307; *Z.Kh.*, III, pp. 142–3; *M.U.*, III, pp. 153–4.

(contd.)

1	*2*	*3*	*4*	*5*	*6*	*7*	*8*	*9*
91	Murtaza Khan Syed Nizam	2500/ 2000	3000/ 2000	Indian	–	Father	–	Lahori, I, pp. 183 and 229; *Z.Kh.* III, pp. 242–3; *M.U.*, III, pp. 479–81.
92	Rashid Khan Ansari	3000/ 1500	3000/ 3000	”	Afghan	–	–	Lahori, I, p. 183; I (b), p. 60; *Z.Kh.*, II, pp. 223–9; *M.U.*, II, pp. 242–50.
93	Shahbaz Khan Rohila Sher Khan	3000/ 500	3000/ 2000	”	”	–	1631 (D)	Lahori, I, pp. 183 and 380–1; I (b), p. 298; *M.U.*, II, pp. 650–1.
94	Amar Singh Rathor	2000/ 1300	3000/ 1500	”	Rajput zamindar	Father	–	Lahori, I, p. 291; I (b), p. 124; *M.U.*, II, pp. 220–3.
95	Anup Singh Badgujar	3000/ 1500	3000/ 1500	”	”	”	–	Lahori, I, p. 121; I (b), p. 309; *Z.Kh.*, II, pp. 364–6; *M.U.*, II, p. 223.
96	Bahar Singh Bundela	2000/ 1200	3000/ 2000	”	”	”	1632–3 (D)	Lahori, I, pp. 121 and 205; I (b), p. 298.
97	Raja Bithaldas Gaur	3000/ 1500	3000/ 2000	”	”	”	–	Lahori, I, pp. 117–18 and 280; *Z.Kh.*, III, p. 92, *M.U.*, II, pp. 250–6.
98	Raja Jagat Singh s/o Raja Basu	3000/ 500	3000/ 500	”	”	”	–	Lahori, I, p. 183; *Z.Kh.*, III, pp. 118–23; *M.U.*, pp. 238–41.
99	Madho Singh s/o Rao Ratan Hara	1000/ 600	3000/ 1600	”	”	”	–	Lahori, I, p. 184; I (b), p. 134; *M.U.*, III, pp. 453–6.
100	Raja Manrup Kachwaha	3000/ 1000	3000/ 1000	”	”	”	1630 (D)	Lahori, I, pp. 118 and 321; I (b), p. 299; *M.U.*, I, pp. 514–16.
101	Pahar Singh Bundela	–	3000/ 2000	”	”	”	–	*S.D.S.*, 33–4; *M.U.*, II, pp. 256–60.

102	Raja Rai Singh Sisodiya	2000/ 1000	3000/ 1500	Indian	Rajput zamindar	Father	–	Lahori, I, p. 195; I (b), p. 142; *M.U.*, II, pp. 297–301.
103	Rao Satarsal Hara	3000/ 2000	3000/ 3000	”	”	G. father	–	Lahori, I, p. 401; I (b), pp. 177 and 294; *Z.Kh.*, III, pp. 133–4; *M.U.*, II, pp. 260–3.
104	Dattaji s/o Bahadurji	2000/ 1000	3000/ 1000	”	Maratha zamindar	Father	–	Lahori, I (b), p. 209; *M.U.*, I, p. 522.
105	Jadun Rai Tilang Rai g/s/o Jadun Rai	3000/ 1500	3000/ 1500	”	”	G. father	–	Lahori, I, p. 310; *M.U.*, I, p. 522.
106	Mankuji Deccani	3000/ 1500	3000/ 1500	”	Maratha (Deccani)	–	–	Lahori, I, p. 306; *S.D.S.*, p. 34.
107	Minaji Yashwant Rai b/o Sahuji	3000/ 1500	3000/ 2000	”	Maratha zamindar	Brother	–	Lahori, I, p. 328; *S.D.S.*, pp. 1–2.
108	Nana Raoji s/o Udaji	3000/ 2000	3000/ 2000	”	”	Father	–	Lahori, I, p. 510; Salih, I, p. 382 (B).
109	Parsoji b/o Maloji	3000/ 1500	3000/ 1500	”	” ”	Brother	–	Lahori, I, p. 256; *Z.Kh.*, III, p. 139; *M.U.*, III, pp. 520–4.
110	Udaji Ram s/o Udaji Ram	3000/ 2000	3000/ 2000	”	”	Father	–	Lahori, I, p. 510; I (b), p. 64; *Z.Kh.*, III, pp. 140–1; *M.U.*, I, p. 144.
111	Darwesh Muhammad	3000/ 2000	3000/ 2000	–	Deccani	–	–	Lahori, I, p. 227.
112	Fakhrul Mulk s/o Yaqut Habshi	3000/ 1500	3000/ 2000	–	–	Father	1632–3 (D)	Lahori, I, pp. 183 and 399; I (b), p. 299.

(contd.)

1	*2*	*3*	*4*	*5*	*6*	*7*	*8*	*9*
113	Habsh Khan Syedi Miftah	–	3000/ 1500	–	Deccani	–	–	Lahori, I (b), pp. 219–21; *Z.Kh.*, III, pp. 112–13; *M.U.*, I, pp. 579–83.
114	Hasan s/o Fakhrul Mulk	2000/ 1500	3000/ 2000	–	–	Father	–	Lahori, I (b), pp. 138, 209 and 299.
115	Syedi Jamal	3000 zat	3000 zat	–	Deccani	–	–	Salih, I, p. 433 (B).
116	Jamshed Khan Deccani	1000/ 1500	3000/ 2000	–	"	–	1630–1 (F)	Lahori, I, pp. 269 and 299; I (b), p. 299.
117	Jauhar Khan Habshi	3000/ 3000	3000/ 3000	–	"	–	–	Lahori, I, p. 368; *Z.Kh.*, III, p. 144.
				MANSABARDS OF 1000 TO 2700				
118	Dayanat Khan, Muhammad Husain-Dasht Bayazi	2000/ 800	2500/ 2500	Irani	–	–	1630	Lahori, I, pp. 119 and 320; I (b), p. 300; *Z.Kh.*, III, p. 124; *M.U.*, II, pp. 22–3.
119	Himmat Khan Alahyar	2500/ 1250	2500/ 1800	"	–	Father	–	Lahori, I, pp. 183 and 447; *Z.Kh.*, II, pp. 351–2; *M.U.*, I, pp. 182–5.
120	Khanjar Khan Turkman (Subhanwardi)	2000/ 1200	2500/ 1700	"	–	–	1629–30 (D)	Lahori, I, p. 183; I (b), p. 300.
121	Murshid Quli Khan Turkman	1000/ 300	2500/ 2500	"	–	–	–	Lahori, I, p. 299; I (b), p. 142; *Z.Kh.*, II, pp. 397–8; *M.U.*, III, pp. 421–8.

122	Safshikan Khan Mirza Lashkari	2500/ 2000	2500/ 2000	Irani	–	Father	–	Lahori, I, p. 183; *Z.Kh.*, II, pp. 305–6; *M.U.*, II, pp. 736–8.
123	Sazawar Khan s/o Lashkar Khan Mashhadi	1000/ 500	2500/ 2000	”	–	”	–	Lahori, I, pp. 121 and 476; *Z.Kh.*, III, pp. 97–8; *M.U.*, II, pp. 438–40.
124	Mir Shams	2500/ 1500	2500/ 2000	”	–	–	–	Lahori, I, p. 78; I (b), p. 4; *Z.Kh.*, II, p. 293; *M.U.*, III, p. 492.
125	Iftikhar Khan Mukhlisullah	2000/ 1000	2500/ 2000	Turani	–	Father	1631–2	Lahori, I, pp. 183 and 299; I (b), p. 300; *Z.Kh.*, II, p. 361; *M.U.*, I, p. 127.
126	Ikhlas Khan Shaikh Farid	1500/ 600	2500/ 1500	Indian	–	”	–	Lahori, I, p. 184; I (b), p. 85; *Z.Kh.*, II, pp. 338–9; *M.U.*, I, pp. 220–2; III, pp. 66–8.
127	Jannisar Khan Kamaluddin Husain	2000/ 1000	2500/ 1500	”	–	–	–	Lahori, I, pp. 118–19 and 542; *Z.Kh.*, III, p. 106; *M.U.*, I, pp. 527–9.
128	Ahmad Khan Niyazi	1500/ 1500	2500/ 2000	”	Afghan	Father	–	Lahori, I, p. 296; I (b), p. 138; *Z.Kh.*, II, pp. 257–60; *M.U.*, I, p. 185–8.
129	Dilawar Khan Deccani	2500/ 1500	2500/ 1500	”	Afghan (Deccani)	–	–	Lahori, I, p. 399.
130	Raja Debi Singh Bundela	2000/ 2000	2500/ 2000	”	Rajput zamindar	Father	–	Lahori, I (b), pp. 13–14, 72 and 300; *Z.Kh.*, II, pp. 370–1; *M.U.*, II, pp. 295–7.
131	Changez s/o Ambar Habshi	2500/ 1000	2500/ 1000	–	Deccani	–	–	Lahori, I, p. 268; Salih, I, p. 331 (B).

(contd.)

1	2	3	4	5	6	7	8	9
132	Khidmatparast Khan Raza Bahadur	2000/ 1200	2500/ 1500	–	–	–	1629 (D)	Lahori, I, pp. 118 and 265; I (b), p. 300; *Z.Kh.*, III, pp. 51–4; *M.U.*, I, pp. 713–16.
133	Nuruddin Quli Safahani	2000/ 700	2000/ 700	Irani	–	–	1632 (D)	Lahori, I, pp. 121 and 418; I (b), p. 304; *Z.Kh.*, II, pp. 371–2; *M.U.*, III, pp. 817–18.
134	Ahmad Beg Khan s/o Aitmad-ud-daulah	2000/ 1500	2000/ 1500	"	–	G. father	–	Lahori, I (b), p. 301; Salih, I, p. 268 (B); *M.U.*, I, pp. 136–9 and 194–5.
135	Ali Quli Darman	2000/ 1200	2000/ 1200	"	–	–	–	Lahori, I, p. 121.
136	Hakimul Mulk Abul Qasim Gilani	150/ 50	2000/ 50	Irani	–	Father	–	Lahori, I, pp. 182 and 227; I (b), pp. 346 and 348.
137	Mirza Hasan Safavi	1500/ 700	2000/ 1000	"	–	"	–	Lahori, I, pp. 184 and 306; *M.U.*, III, pp. 477–9.
138	Sadat Khan Ibrahim Rizvi	1000/ 550	2000/ 1000	"	–	Near relatives	–	Lahori, I, p. 184; I (b), p. 67; *Z.Kh.*, II, pp. 294–5.
139	Iltifat Khan Mirza Murad Safavi	2000/ 700	2000/ 700	"	–	Father	–	Lahori, I, p. 183; *M.U.*, III, p. 583.
140	Khwaja Jahan Khawafi	2000/ 600	2000/ 600	"	–	–	–	Lahori, I, p. 78; *Z.Kh.*, III, pp. 128–9; *M.U.*, I, pp. 748–9.
141	Khalilullah Khan	1500/ 500	2000/ 800	"	–	Brother	–	Lahori, I, p. 535; I (b), pp. 142 and 297; *Z.Kh.*, III, p. 33; *M.U.*, I, pp. 775–82.
142	Mahabat Khan Mirza Lahrasp	2000/ 1000	2000/ 1000	"	–	Father	–	Lahori, I, pp. 118–19; *Z.Kh.*, III, pp. 95–6; *M.U.*, III, pp. 590–5.

143	Makramat Khan Mulla Murshid Shirazi	1000/ 200	2000/ 1500	Irani	–	–	–	Lahori, I, p. 191; I (b), p. 101; *M.U.*, III, pp. 460–2.
144	Muhammad Zaman Tehrani	2000/ 1000	2000/ 1400	"	–	–	–	Lahori, I, pp. 183 and 409; *M.U.*, III, pp. 452–3.
145	Mughal Khan s/o Zain Khan Koka	1000/ 500	2000/ 1500	"	–	Fahter	–	Lahori, I, pp. 184–5; I (b), p. 221; *Z.Kh.*, II, pp. 324–5; *M.U.*, III, pp. 490–2.
146	Mukhtar Khan Sabzwari	2000/ 1200	2000/ 1500	"	–	–	–	Lahori, I, pp. 183 and 265; *M.U.*, III, pp. 409–13.
147	Nurullah Harvi	1500/ 700	2000/ 1200	"	–	–	–	Lahori, I, p. 306; I (b), p. 176.
148	Qazalbash Khan Afshar	2000/ 1000	2000/ 1000	"	Deccani	–	–	Lahori, I, p. 441; *Z.Kh.*, III, pp. 68–9; *M.U.*, III, pp. 85–6.
149	Rizvi Khan Mashhadi	2000/ 1200	2000/ 1200	"	–	–	–	Lahori, I, p. 183; *Z.Kh.*, I, p. 185.
150	Salabat Khan Roshan-zamir	1000/ 200	2000/ 600	"	–	Father	–	Lahori, I, p. 417; I (b), p. 87; *Z.Kh.*, III, pp. 33–4; *M.U.*, II, pp. 731–3.
151	Azizullah Khan s/o Yusuf Khan	2000/ 1000	2000/ 1200	Turani	–	"	–	Lahori, I, p. 183; I (b), p. 83; *M.U.*, II, pp. 789–90.
152	Ibrahim Husain Kashghari	2000/ 1000	2000/ 1000	"	–	–	–	Lahori, I, p. 183.
153	Ikhlas Khan Husain Beg	2000/ 1000	2000/ 1000	"	–	–	–	Lahori, I, p. 292; *M.U.*, I, p. 151.
154	Izzat Khan Baba Khwaja	1000/ 700	2000/ 1000	"	–	Near relatives	1633 (D)	Lahori, I, pp. 184, 365 and 476; I (b), p. 303; *M.U.*, II, pp. 775–6.

(contd.)

1	*2*	*3*	*4*	*5*	*6*	*7*	*8*	*9*
155	Shah Quli Khan Waqqas Haji	1000/ 800	2000/ 2000	Turani	–	–	–	Lahori, I (b), pp. 166 and 216–17; *Z.Kh.*, III, p. 116; *M.U.*, II, pp. 658–60.
156	Mirza Wali s/o Khwaja Hasan Naqshbandi	2000/ 1000	2000/ 1000	"	–	Father	–	Lahori, I, p. 183; *Z.Kh.*, II, p. 256; *M.U.*, III, pp. 456–60.
157	Yaqub Khan Badakhshi	2000/ 1500	2000/ 1500	"	–	–	–	*M.U.*, III, p. 958.
158	Syed Alam Barha b/o Hizbar Khan	1500/ 600	2000/ 800	Indian	–	Brother	–	Lahori, I, pp. 121 and 306; *M.U.*, II, pp. 454–6.
159	Bakhtiyar Khan Deccani	–	2000/ 1000	"	Deccani	–	–	Lahori, I (b), p. 303; *M.U.*, I, pp. 774–5.
160	Syed Bayazid	2000/ 700	2000/ 700	"	–	Father	–	Lahori, I, p. 183; *M.U.*, II, p. 457.
161	Dindar Khan Syed Bahwa	2000/ 1200	2000/ 1200	"	–	Near relatives	1635–6 (D)	Lahori, I, p. 121; I (b), p. 302; *Z.Kh.*, II, p. 304; *M.U.*, II, pp. 23–4.
162	Ihtimam Khan	1000/ 250	2000/ 1500	"	–	–	–	Lahori, I, p. 119; I (b), pp. 136–8; *Z.Kh.*, III, pp. 89–90, *M.U.*, I, pp. 160–2.
163	Ikram Khan Fathpuri	1000/ 500	2000/ 1000	"	–	Father	–	Lahori, I, pp. 184–5 and 299; *Z.Kh.*, III, pp. 274–5.
164	Mahaldar Khan Deccani	2000/ 1000	2000/ 1000	Indian	Deccani	–	–	Lahori, I, p. 183.
165	Mansur s/o Mahmud Khan	2000/ 500	2000/ 500	"	–	Father	–	Lahori, I, p. 442; Salih, I, pp. 505–7 (B).

166	Raja Roz Afzun	500/ 600	2000/ 1000	Indian	Zamindar	–	1635–6 (D)	Lahori, I, p. 182; I (b), pp. 67 and 303; *M.U.*, II, pp. 218–19.
167	Syed Umar b/in-law/o Nizamul Mulk	2000/ 1000	2000/ 1000	"	Deccani	–	–	Lahori, I, p. 399.
168	Babu Khan Karrani	3000/ 1500	2000/ 1500	"	Afghan	–	1630–1 (D)	Lahori, I, p. 121; I (b), p. 302.
169	Mubarak Khan Niyazi	1000/ 700	2000/ 2000	"	"	Uncle	–	Lahori, I, p. 298; I(b), pp. 136–8; *Z.Kh.*, II, p. 261; *M.U.*, III, pp. 512–13.
170	Nazr Bahadur Kheshgi	1500/ 700	2000/ 1500	"	"	–	–	Lahori, I, p. 184; I (b), p. 134; *Z.Kh.*, III, pp. 49–50; *M.U.*, III, pp. 818–21.
171	Sher Khan Tarin	2000/ 1000	2000/ 1000	"	Afghan zamindar	–	–	Lahori, I, pp. 419–21; *Z.Kh.*, III, pp. 102–6; *M.U.*, II, pp. 654–8.
172	Biharidas Kachwaha	1500/ 700	2000/ 1200	"	Rajput zamindar	Father	1631–2 (D)	Lahori, I, pp. 182 and 372; I (b), p. 302; *M.U.*, II, pp. 172–4.
173	Rao Duda g/s/o Rai Chanda	1500/ 1000	2000 1500	"	"	G. father	1633 (D)	Lahori, I, pp. 299 and 521–2; I (b), p. 302; Salih, I, pp. 274–5 (B); *M.U.*, II, pp. 142–8.
174	Jag Raj Bundela	1000/ 1000	2000/ 2000	"	"	Father	1635–6 (D)	Lahori, I, pp. 184 and 339; I (b), pp. 294 and 301; *M.U.*, I, pp. 526–7.
175	Rawal Kalliyan Jaisalmeri	2000/ 1000	2000/ 1000	"	"	–	–	Lahori, I, p. 183.
176	Rao Karan Bhurtiya	2000/ 1500	2000/ 1500	Indian	"	Father	–	Lahori, I, p. 398; *Z.Kh.*, II, pp. 398–9; *M.U.*, II, pp. 287–9.
177	Pirthi Raj Rathor	1500/ 600	2000/ 1600	"	Rajput	–	–	Lahori, I, p. 186; I (b), p. 47; *M.U.*, I, pp. 429–31.

(contd.)

1	2	3	4	5	6	7	8	9
178	Raja Ramdas Narori	1000/ 500	2000/ 1000	"	Rajput zamindar	–	–	Salih, I, p. 269 (B); *M.U.*, II, pp. 226–7.
179	Ani Rai Sanneta	–	2000/ 1000	"	Maratha zamindar (Deccani)	–	–	Lahori, I (b), p. 303.
180	Bithuji s/o Achla	2000/ 1000	2000/ 1000	"	Maratha zamindar	Uncle	–	Lahori, I, p. 310; I (b), p. 295; *M.U.*, I, p. 522.
181	Ganesh Rai	–	2000/ 800	"	Maratha zamindar (Deccani)	–	–	*S.D.S.*, pp. 34–5.
182	Habaji	2000/ 800	2000/ 800	"	Maratha (Deccani)	–	–	Lahori, I, p. 306.
183	Kanbhar Rao	2000/ 1000	2000/ 1000	"	Maratha zamindar (Deccani)	–	–	Lahori, I (b), p. 146; *M.U.*, I, p. 209.
184	Nauji Berbe Rai Sindhiya	2000/ 1000	2000/ 1000	"	"	–	–	Lahori, I, p. 315.
185	Rabi Rai Deccani	2000/ 2000	2000/ 2000	"	"	–	–	Salih, I, p. 393 (B).
186	Rawat Rai Deccani	2000/ 1500	2000/ 1500	Indian	"	–	–	Lahori, I, pp. 288–9.
187	Rustam Rai	–	2000/ 1000	"	"	–	–	*S.D.S.*, p. 34.

188	Samaji s/o Sahuji	2000/ 1000	2000/ 1000	"	Maratha zamindar	Father	–	Lahori, I, p. 328; *M.U.*, II, pp. 342–50.
189	Tanaji Deccani	2000/ 1000	2000/ 1000	"	Maratha (Deccani)	–	–	Lahori, I (b), p. 121.
190	Aqa Haider	2000/ 1000	2000/ 1000	–	Deccani	–	–	Lahori, I, p. 353.
191	Atish Khan Habshi	2000/ 1000	2000/ 1000	–	"	–	–	Lahori, I, p. 183; *Z.Kh.*, III, p. 143; *M.U.*, I, pp. 188–9.
192	Farhan Khan Deccani	2000/ 1000	2000/ 1000	–	"	–	–	Lahori, I, p. 307.
193	Firoze Khan Khwajasara	2000/ 500	2000/ 1000	–	–	–	–	Lahori, I, p. 183; I (b), p. 83; *M.U.*, III, pp. 21–2.
194	Sarvar Khan Habshi	2000/ 1000	2000/ 1000	–	Deccani	–	–	Lahori, I, p. 300; *Z.Kh.*, III, pp. 143–4.
195	Hakim Haziq	1500/ 300	1500/ 300	Irani	–	Father	–	Lahori, I, p. 184; *Z.Kh.*, II, p. 303; *M.U.*, I, pp. 587–90.
196	Mir Abdullah	1000/ 550	1500/ 800	"	–	Near relatives	1634–5 (D)	Lahori, I, pp. 184, 226 and 294–6; *Z.Kh.*, II, pp. 294–5; *M.U.*, III, pp. 314–21.
197	Asad Khan Shuja	1000/ 450	1500/ 1000	"	–	Father	–	Lahori, I, pp. 347 and 451; *M.U.*, III, pp. 292–6.
198	Jansipar Khan Jamali n/o Naqib Khan Qizvini	1000/ 400	1500/ 800	"	–	Uncle	–	Lahori, I, p. 296; I (b), p. 67; *M.U.*, I, p. 530; III, pp. 812–17.
199	Hakim Khushhal	1500/ 200	1500/ 200	"	–	Father	–	Lahori, I, p. 182; *Z.Kh.*, II, p. 303; *M.U.*, I, pp. 563–5.

(contd.)

1	*2*	*3*	*4*	*5*	*6*	*7*	*8*	*9*
200	Multafit Khan	600/ 100	1500/ 500	Irani	–	”	–	Salih, I, p. 281 (B); Lahori, I, pp. 294 and 296; *Z.Kh.*, III, pp. 92–3; *M.U.*, III, pp. 500–3.
201	Sa-adat Khan g/s/o Zain Khan Koka	1500/ 700	1500/ 1200	”	–	G. father	–	Lahori, I, p. 184; I (b), pp. 166–7; *M.U.*, II, pp. 461–3.
202	Sharif Khan Qadimi	1000/ 300	1500/ 1200	”	–	–	–	Lahori, I, pp. 119 and 542; *Apparatus*, p. S-47.
203	Sohrab Khan	1000/ 700	1500/ 800	”	–	Father	–	Lahori, I, pp. 184 and 542–3; *M.U.*, I, pp. 114–15.
204	Yadgar Husain Khan	1500/ 800	1500/ 700	”	–	–	1632–3 (D)	Lahori, I, pp. 184 and 476; I (b), p. 306; *Apparatus*, p. S-172.
205	Zabardast Khan	1000/ 500	1500/ 1000	”	–	–	–	Lahori, I, pp. 119 and 399; *M.U.*, II, p. 372.
206	Zainul Abidin	1500/ 1000	1500/ 1500	”	–	Father	1629–30 (D)	Lahori, I, p. 184; I (b), p. 304; *M.U.*, I, pp. 107–15.
207	Zulfiqar Beg Turkman	1000/ 400	1500/ 600	”	–	–	1631–2 (D)	Lahori, I, pp. 185 and 258; I (b), p. 306; *Apparatus*, p. S-206.
208	Zulfiqar Khan Khanlar	1000/ 600	1500/ 800	”	–	–	–	Lahori, I, p. 432; I (b), p. 101; *M.U.*, II, pp. 85–8.
209	Asfandiyar Khan	1000/ 600	1500/ 1200	Turani	–	Father	–	Lahori, I, pp. 306 and 476; *Z.Kh.*, II, pp. 362–3; *M.U.*, I, p. 568.
210	Khwaja Barkhurdar s/in-law/o Mahabat Khan	1000/ 500	1500/ 800	”	–	Khanazad (near relative)	–	Lahori, I, p. 119; I (b), p. 83; *Z.Kh.*, II, p. 341; *M.U.*, I, pp. 206–7.

211	Ghairat Khan Khwaja Kamgar	1000/ 400	1500/ 600	Turani	–	Khanazad Uncle	–	Lahori, I, pp. 319–20 and 351–2; *Z.Kh.*, III, p. 131; *M.U.*, II, pp. 863–5.
212	Himmat Khan Sharfuddin Husain	1500/ 1000	1500/ 1500	„	–	–	–	Lahori, I, p. 184; I (b), p. 138; *Apparatus*, p. S-170.
213	Iwaz Beg Khan Qaqshal	1000/ 600	1500/ 1000	„	–	–	–	Lahori, I, p. 261; I (b), p. 13; *M.U.*, II, pp. 776–7.
214	Janbaz Khan Khwaja Baba	1000/ 400	1500/ 600	„	–	–	–	Lahori, I, pp. 185 and 299; *Apparatus*, p. S-186.
215	Rahmat Khan Mir Faizullah	1000/ 400	1500/ 1500	„	–	–	–	Lahori, I, p. 297; I (b), p. 134; *M.U.*, II, pp. 219–20.
216	Tarbiyat Khan Fakhruddin Ahmad	1000/ 700	1500/ 1000	„	–	–	–	Lahori, I, p. 299; I (b), p. 67; *Z.Kh.*, III, pp. 43–5; *M.U.*, I, pp. 486–90.
217	Yakkataz Khan	1500/ 400	1500/ 400	„	–	–	–	Lahori, I, p. 119; *Z.Kh.*, III, pp. 89–90.
218	Akbar Quli Gakkhar	1000/ 600	1500/ 1200	Indian	Zamindar	Khanazad (G. father)	–	Lahori, I, pp. 184 and 303; *Z.Kh.*, I, p. 221; *M.U.*, III, pp. 144–8.
219	Qazi Muhammad Said Karhardi	1000/ 100	1500/ 200	„	–	–	1635–6 (D)	Lahori, I, p. 475; I (b), pp. 100, 307 and 344.
220	Syed Yaqub Bukhari	1500/ 1000	1500/ 1000	„	–	Khanazad (Father)	1630–1 (D)	Lahori, I, p. 121; I (b), p. 305; *Z.Kh.*, II, p. 392; *M.U.*, II, pp. 396–9.
221	Jalal Kakar	1500/ 700	1500/ 700	„	Afghan	Father	–	Lahori, I, p. 184; *Z.Kh.*, II, pp. 335–6; *M.U.*, I, pp. 530–1.
222	Jamal Nohani	1500/ 500	1500/ 500	„	„	–	–	Lahori, I, p. 79; *Apparatus*, p. S-10.

(contd.)

1	2	3	4	5	6	7	8	9
223	Purdil Khan	1000/ 400	1500/ 1000	Indian	Afghan	Father	–	Lahori, I, pp. 383–4; I (b), p. 14; *Z.Kh.*, III, p. 131; *M.U.*, I, pp. 424–7.
224	Yasin Khan	1000/ 800	1500/ 1000	"	"	"	1635–6 (D)	Lahori, I, pp. 409 and 430; I (b), p. 305; *M.U.*, II, pp. 651–3.
225	Bhim Rathor	1500/ 700	1500/ 800	"	Rajput	–	–	Lahori, I, p. 186; I (b), p. 138.
226	Chandraman Bundela	1000/ 600	1500/ 700	"	Rajput zamindar	Father	–	Lahori, I, pp. 205 and 372; *Z.Kh.*, II, pp. 363–4.
227	Dwarkadas Kachwaha	1000/ 800	1500/ 1000	"	"	"	1631 (D)	Lahori, I, pp. 121 and 349; I (b), p. 305; *Z.Kh.*, II, pp. 366–7; *M.U.*, II, pp. 172–4.
228	Hardi Ram Kachwaha	1000/ 650	1500/ 1000	"	Rajput	"	1636–7 (D)	Lahori, I, pp. 121 and 306; I (b), p. 305; *Apparatus*, pp. A-608 and S-824.
229	Hathi Singh s/o Rao Duda	1500/ 1000	1500/ 1000	"	Rajput zamindar	"	–	Lahori, I, p. 532; I (b), p. 302; *M.U.*, II, pp. 142–8.
230	Jagmal s/o Kishan Singh Rathor	1500/ 700	1500/ 700	Indian	"	"	1629–30 (D)	Lahori, I, p. 121; I (b), p. 306; *Z.Kh.*, II, pp. 297–300.
231	Karamsi Rathor	1000/ 500	1500/ 800	"	"	"	1630 (D)	Lahori, I, pp. 185, 226 and 304–5; I (b), p. 306; *M.U.*, II, pp. 266–7.
232	Raja Pratap Singh Ujjainia	1500/ 1000	1500/ 1000	"	"	–	–	Lahori, I, p. 221; *M.U.*, II, p. 786.
233	Satarsal Kachwaha	1500/ 1000	1500/ 1000	"	"	Father	1630 (D)	Lahori, I, p. 184; I (b), p. 305; *Z.Kh.*, I, p. 221; *M.U.*, III, pp. 321–2.

234	Siva Ram Gaur n/o Raja Bithaldas	1000/ 500	1500/ 1000	Indian	Rajput zamindar	Uncle	–	Lahori, I, p. 119; I (b), pp. 142 and 296; *M.U.*, II, pp. 263–5.
235	Heluji	–	1500/ 750	"	Maratha (Deccani)	–	–	Salih, I, p. 393 (B).
236	Nirmal Rai	1500/ 700	1500/ 700	"	Maratha zamindar (Deccani)	–	–	*S.D.S.*, pp. 2 and 45.
237	Ranaji	–	1500/ 600	"	Maratha (Deccani)	–	–	*S.D.S.*, p. 34.
238	Aitmad Khan Khwajasara	1500/ 500	1500/ 500	–	–	–	1629–30 (D)	Lahori, I (b), p. 307; *Z.Kh.*, pp. I and 216.
239	Arab Khan	1000/ 600	1500/ 800	–	–	–	–	Lahori, I, p. 545; I (b), pp. 1 and 67; *Z.Kh.*, III, pp. 89–90; *M.U.*, II, pp. 794–5.
240	Khwaja Barkhurdar	–	1500/ 800	–	–	–	–	Lahori, I (b), p. 306.
241	Marhamat Khan Ibrahim Husain	1000/ 500	1500/ 1000	–	–	–	1631 (D)	Lahori, I, pp. 119 and 343; I (b), p. 305.
242	Sarfaraz Khan	–	1500/ 800	–	–	–	–	Lahori, I (b), p. 306.
243	Zabardast Khan	–	1500/ 500	–	–	–	–	Lahori, I (b), p. 305; *Apparatus*, p. S-1642.
244	Aitmad Khan Aqa Afzal	1000/ 500	1000/ 500	Irani	–	–	–	Lahori, I, p. 185; *Z.Kh.*, II, p. 276; *M.U.*, III, pp. 18–21.

(contd.)

1	*2*	*3*	*4*	*5*	*6*	*7*	*8*	*9*
245	Amanat Khan Abdul Haq	900/ 200	1000/ 100	Irani	–	Brother	–	Lahori, I, p. 535; Salih, I, p. 489 (B); *M.U.*, II, p. 790.
246	Diyanat Khan Hakim Jamala Kashi	800/ 200	1000/ 600	"	–	–	–	Lahori, I, p. 191; I (b), p. 121; *Z.Kh.*, III, pp. 36–7; *M.U.*, II, pp. 37–8.
247	Mirza Haider Safavi	1000/ 200	1000/ 200	"	–	Father	1631–2 (D)	Lahori, I, p. 185; I (b), p. 311; *M.U.*, III, p. 555.
248	Husaini b/o Baqar Khan-Najm-e-Sani	1000/ 600	1000/ 800	"	–	Brother	1635–6 (D)	Lahori, I, p. 544; I (b), p. 308; *Z.Kh.*, II, pp. 342–5.
249	Imam Quli	1000/ 400	1000/ 400	"	–	Father	1630 (D)	Lahori, I, pp. 244 and 304–5; I (b), p. 310; *M.U.*, I, p. 519.
250	Karamullah s/o Alimardan Bahadur	1000/ 500	1000/ 500	"	–	"	–	Lahori, I, p. 185; *Z.Kh.*, I, pp. 46–8; *M.U.*, II, pp. 773–5.
251	Mirza Lutfullah s/o Lashkar Khan Mashhadi	1000/ 400	1000/ 800	"	–	"	–	Lahori, I p. 476; I (b), p. 65; *Z.Kh.*, III, pp. 97–9; *M.U.*, III, p. 168.
252	Mir Khan s/o Qasim Khan Namkin	–	1000/ 200	"	–	"	–	Lahori, I (b), pp. 124 and 311; *Z.Kh.*, I, pp. 198–200; *M.U.*, I, pp. 172–4.
253	Mirza Khan s/o Zain Khan Koka	1200/ 500	1000/ 500	Irani	–	Father	1631–2 (D)	Lahori, I, p. 269, I (b), p. 309; *Z.Kh.*, I, pp. 123–4.
254	Muhammad Sharif u/o Baqar Khan Najm-e-Sani	1000/ 700	1000/ 700	"	–	Near relatives	–	Lahori, I, p. 347.

255	Syed Mubarak Qadimi	1000/ 300	1000/ 400	Irani	–	–	1636–7 (D)	Lahori, I, pp. 79 and 302; I (b), p. 311; Mirat, I, p. 203; *Apparatus*, p. S-11.
256	Muizul Mulk Mir Musa	–	1000/ 100	"	–	–	–	Lahori, I (b), p. 312; Mirat, I, p. 210; *Apparatus*, p. S-274.
257	Murtaza Quli b/o Jansipar Khan	1000/ 500	1000/ 600	"	–	Brother	–	Lahori, I, pp. 185 and 315; *M.U.*, I, p. 519.
258	Salih Muhammad s/o Mirza Shahi	1000/ 800	1000/ 800	"	–	Uncle	1629–30	Lahori, I, p. 184; I (b), p. 307; *Z.Kh.*, II, pp. 231–2.
259	Sultan Nazr b/o Saif Khan	1000/ 300	1000/ 300	"	–	Brother	–	Lahori, I (b), p. 102; *Z.Kh.*, II, p. 316; *M.U.*, II, pp. 416–21.
260	Tughril, g/s/o Abdul Rahim Khan-e-Khanan	1000/ 500	1000/ 500	"	–	G. father	–	Lahori, I, pp. 184–5; *Z.Kh.*, I, pp. 31–63.
261	Yahya s/o Saif Khan	1000/ 300	1000/ 300	"	–	Father	–	Lahori, I (b), p. 102; Mirat, I, p. 209; *M.U.*, II, pp. 419–21.
262	Mir Zahiruddin	1000/ 400	1000/ 400	"	–	"	Beginning of the reign (R)	Salih, I, p. 281 (B); *M.U.*, III, pp. 341–2.
263	Mir Abdul Karim	1000/ 200	1000/ 200	Turani	–	–	–	Lahori, I (b), pp. 2–3; *Apparatus*, p. S-777.
264	Abdul Rahman Beg Turnabi	1000/ 500	1000/ 600	Turani	–	–	–	Lahori, I, pp. 230 and 421; *Apparatus*, p. S-1676.
265	Alif Khan Aman Beg s/o Jan Beg	1000/ 1000	1000/ 1000	"	–	Father	–	Lahori, I (b), pp. 216 and 307; *Z.Kh.*, III, pp. 89–90; *M.U.*, I, pp. 191–4.

(contd.)

1	2	3	4	5	6	7	8	9
266	Bahram s/o Jahangir Quli Khan	1000/ 500	1000/ 500	Turani	–	Father	–	Lahori, I, p. 185; *Z.Kh.*, II, p. 325; *M.U.*, I, pp. 524–5.
267	Baqi Khan Qalmaq	700/ 500	1000/ 600	”	–	–	–	Lahori, I (b), p. 2; Salih, I, pp. 619–20 (B); *M.U.*, I, pp. 427–9.
268	Mir Barka Bukhari	1000/ 200	1000/ 200	”	–	–	–	Lahori, I, p. 258; *Apparatus*, p. S-362.
269	Dost Beg s/o Tolak Khan	1000/ 500	1000/ 500	”	–	Father	–	Lahori, I, p. 185; *M.U.*, I, pp. 476–8.
270	Iftikhar Khan Abulbaqa s/o Ahmad Beg Khan	1000/ 600	1000/ 800	”	–	”	–	Lahori, I, p. 446; I (b), p. 11; *Z.Kh.*, II, p. 361; *M.U.*, I, p. 127.
271	Kamil Khan s/o Khan-e-Azam	1000/ 400	1000/ 400	”	–	”	–	Lahori, I, p. 185; *Z.Kh.*, II, pp. 327–8.
272	Latif Khan Naqshbandi	1000/ 400	1000/ 400	”	–	–	–	Lahori, I, p. 185; *Apparatus*, p. S-208.
273	Muhammad Ali Kamrani	1000/ 500	1000/ 500	”	–	–	–	Lahori, I (b), p. 64; *Apparatus*, p. S-994.
274	Qazzaq Khan Baqi Beg Uzbek	1000/ 800	1000/ 800	”	–	Brother	–	Lahori, I (b), p. 134; *Z.Kh.*, II, pp. 346–8; *M.U.*, III, pp. 88–9.
275	Saiful Mulk Kashghari	–	1000/ 400	”	–	–	1632–3 (D)	Lahori, I (b), p. 311; *Apparatus*, p. S-751.
276	Sarandaz Khan Qalmaq	1000/ 400	1000/ 800	”	–	–	–	Lahori, I, pp. 421 and 488; *Z.Kh.*, III, pp. 55–8.

277	Shadi Khan Uzbek	1000/ 400	1000/ 400	Turani	–	–	–	Salih, I, p. 270 (B), *Z.Kh.*, III, pp. 59–60; *M.U.*, II, pp. 661–2.
278	Shujat Khan Shadi Beg s/o Janash Bahadur	1000/ 800	1000/ 800	”	–	Father	–	Lahori, I (b), p. 13; *Z.Kh.*, I, p. 196; *M.U.*, I, pp. 511–12; II, pp. 662–5.
279	Turktaz Khan	1000/ 250	1000/ 400	”	–	–	–	Lahori, I, pp. 119 and 299; *Apparatus*, p. S-50.
280	Uzbek Khan Nazr Bahadur	1000/ 500	1000/ 1000	”	–	–	–	Lahori, I (b), pp. 87, 136 and 138; *S.D.S.*, p. 29; *Z.Kh.*, III, pp. 90–1; *M.U.*, I, pp. 195–8.
281	Abu Muhammad Kamboh	1000/ 800	1000/ 800	Indian	–	–	1632–3 (D)	Lahori, I, p. 315; I (b), p. 308.
282	Syed Alawal Barha	1000/ 600	1000/ 700	”	–	–	1634–5 (D)	Lahori, I, pp. 106 and 399; I (b), p. 308.
283	Syed Ghulam Muhammad Bukhari	1000/ 700	1000 700	”	–	–	1630–1 (D)	Lahori, I, p. 184; I (b), p. 308; *M.U.*, III, pp. 396–9.
284	Ikhlas Khan Shaikh Alahdiya	500/ 300	1000/ 800	”	–	Father	–	Lahori, I (b), p. 177; *Z.Kh.*, II, pp. 351–2; *M.U.*, I, pp. 198–9.
285	Janbaz Khan Syed Ahmad	1000/ 500	1000 600	”	–	–	–	Lahori, I, p. 476; I (b), p. 90.
286	Muzaffar s/o Mahmud Khan	1000/ 500	1000 500	Indian	–	Father	–	Salih, I, pp. 505–7 (B); Lahori, I, p. 442.
287	Parwarish Khan Barha	1000/ 500	1000/ 500	”	–	–	1631 (D)	Lahori, I, pp. 185 and 397; I (b), p. 309.
288	Sadat Khan Bhakkari Deccani	1000/ 500	1000/ 500	”	–	–	–	Salih, I, p. 382 (B); *Z.Kh.*, II, pp. 353–4.

(contd.)

1	2	3	4	5	6	7	8	9
289	Shaikh Sufi Deccani	1000/ 500	1000/ 500	Indian	Deccani	–	–	Salih, I, p. 382 (B); *Apparatus*, p. S-489.
290	Abdul Qadir	1000/ 600	1000/ 600	"	Afghan	–	1636–7 (D)	Lahori, I (b), pp. 70–1 and 309; *M.U.*, II, pp. 246–7.
291	Abdul Rahman Rohila s/o Shahbaz Khan Rohila	1000/ 600	1000/ 600	"	"	Father	–	Lahori, I (b), p. 167; *M.U.*, II, pp. 650–1.
292	Ahdad Khan Mahmand	–	1000/ 500	"	"	–	–	Lahori, I (b), p. 310.
293	Alawal Tarin	1000/ 400	1000/ 600	"	"	–	–	Lahori, I, pp. 119 and 476.
294	Bahadur n/o Khan-e-Jahan Lodhi	1000/ 400	1000/ 400	"	"	Uncle	1630–1 (D)	Lahori, I, p. 276; I (b), p. 311.
295	Daulat Khan Qiyamkhani	1000/ 800	1000/ 800	"	"	–	–	Lahori, I, p. 184.
296	Habib Sur	1000/ 200	1000/ 200	"	"	–	–	Lahori, I, p. 119.
297	Husain s/o Khan-e-Jahan Lodhi	–	1000/ 500	"	Afghan	Father	1629–30 (D)	Lahori, I (b), p. 310.
298	Kakar Khan	1000/ 400	1000/ 400	"	"	–	–	Lahori, I, p. 119; *M.U.*, III, pp. 152–3.

299	Lal Khan	1000/ 700	1000 700	Indian	Afghan	–	1628–9 (D)	Lahori, I, p. 184; I (b), p. 308; *Apparatus*, p. S-187.
300	Nasib Shirani	1000/ 700	1000/ 700	”	”	–	–	Lahori, I, p. 119; *Apparatus*, p. S-34.
301	Pir Khan Mayana	1000/ 600	1000/ 800	”	”	–	1634–5 (D)	Lahori, I, p. 119; I (b), pp. 4 and 308.
302	Shamsher Khan Tarin	1000/ 500	1000/ 500	”	”	–	–	Lahori, I, p. 119; *M.U.*, II, pp. 677–9.
303	Sikandar Rohila	1000/ 800	1000/ 800	”	”	Brother	–	Lahori, I, p. 184; *Z.Kh.*, II, p. 349.
304	Usman Rohila b/o Zakarya	1000/ 300	1000/ 700	”	”	”	–	Lahori, I, p.119; I (b), pp. 141 and 296; *Z.Kh.*, III, p. 116.
305	Sikandar Khan	–	1000/ 450	”	”	–	1631–2 (D)	Lahori, I (b), p. 310; *Apparatus*, p. S-621.
306	Balbhadar Shaikhawat	1000/ 600	1000/ 600	”	Rajput	–	1630 (D)	Lahori, I, pp. 184 and 304–5; I (b), p. 309.
307	Bhagwandas Bundela	1000/ 600	1000/ 600	”	Rajput zamindar	Father	–	Lahori, I, p. 205; *Z.Kh.*, II, pp. 363–4; *M.U.*, II, pp. 197–9.
308	Biharimal Rathor	1000/ 500	1000/ 500	“	”	”	1628–9 (D)	Lahori, I, p. 185; I (b), p. 310; *Z.Kh.*, II, pp. 297–300; *M.U.*, III, pp. 150–2.
309	Bir Narain Badgujar	1000/ 600	1000/ 600	”	”	”	1630–1 (D)	Lahori, I, p. 121; I (b), p. 309; *Z.Kh.*, II, pp. 364–6; *M.U.*, II, pp. 220–3.
310	Raja Girdhar Kachwaha	1000/ 500	1000/ 500	”	”	G. father	1630–1 (D)	Lahori, I, pp. 182 and 304–5; I (b), p. 310.

(contd.)

1	*2*	*3*	*4*	*5*	*6*	*7*	*8*	*9*
311	Hari Singh Rathor	1000/ 600	1000/ 800	Indian	Rajput zamidar	Father	–	Lahori, I, p. 421; I (b), p. 308; *M.U.*, II, p. 268.
312	Jit Singh Rathor	1000/ 500	1000/ 500	”	Rajput	–	1630–1 (D)	Lahori, I, p. 119; I (b), p. 310.
313	Raja Kishan Singh Bhadoriya	–	1000/ 600	”	Rajput zamindar	–	–	Lahori, I (b), p. 309; *M.U.*, II, pp. 228–9.
314	Kishan Singh Hara s/o Rao Ratan Hara	1000/ 600	1000/ 600	”	”	Father	–	Lahori, I, p. 184; I (b), p. 294.
315	Raja Kunwarsen Kishtwari	1000/ 200	1000/ 200	”	”	–	–	Lahori, I, p. 185.
316	Mitr Sen b/o Raja Sujan Singh Tanwar	–	1000/ 500	”	”	–	1632–3 (D)	Lahori, I (b), p. 310.
317	Rawal Ponja	1000/ 500	1000/ 500	”	”	–	–	Lahori, I, pp. 183–4.
318	Rupchand Gawaliari	1000/ 600	1000/ 600	”	”	–	1635–6 (D)	Lahori, I, p. 299; I (b), p. 309.
319	Rawal Samarsi	1000/ 1000	1000/ 1000	”	”	–	–	Lahori, I, p. 184.
320	Raja Sangram	1000/ 600	1000/ 600	”	”	–	–	Lahori, I (b), pp. 137–8.
321	Siyam Singh Sisodiya	1000/ 500	1000/ 500	”	Rajput	–	–	Lahori, I, p. 119.

322	Sri Singh Rathor	1000/800	1000/800	Indian	Rajput	–	–	Lahori, I (b), p. 123.
323	Bhoj Raj Deccani	1000/500	1000/500	”	Maratha (Deccani)	–	–	Lahori, I (b), pp. 220–1; *Apparatus*, p. S-3997.
324	Aitbar Rai	–	1000/400	”	Maratha zamindar (Deccani)	–	–	*S.D.S.*, p. 34; *Apparatus*, p. S-1230.
325	Jasun Rai	1000/500	1000/500	”	”	–	–	*S.D.S.*, pp. 1–2.
326	Ababakr	–	1000/400	–	–	–	1634–5 (D)	Lahori, I (b), p. 311.
327	Agah Khan Khwajasara	–	1000/200	–	–	–	–	Lahori, I (b), p. 257; *Z.Kh.*, III, p. 117.
328	Aitqad Khan Khwaja Qasim	1000/350	1000/500	–	–	–	1631–2 (D)	Lahori, I, pp. 185 and 297; I (b), p. 309.
329	Khanjar Khan	1000/400	1000/400	–	–	–	1630–1 (D)	Lahori, I, p. 119; I (b), p. 311.
330	Khidmat Khan Khwąjasara	1000/500	1000/500	–	–	–	–	Lahori, I, p. 421.
331	Syedi Miran s/o Syedi Jamal	1000 zat	1000 zat	–	–	Father	–	Salih, I, p. 433 (B).
332	Muin Khan	1000/300	1000/300	–	–	–	–	Lahori, I, p. 230.
333	Nobat Khan	1000/400	1000/800	–	–	–	1635–6 (D)	Lahori, I, pp. 119 and 543; I (b), p. 307.

(contd.)

1	*2*	*3*	*4*	*5*	*6*	*7*	*8*	*9*
334	Qal'adar Khan Husaini-chela	1000/ 400	1000/ 400	–	–	–	–	Lahori, I, p. 446; *Z.Kh.*, III, pp. 89–90.
335	Rashid Khan Khwajasara	1000/ 200	1000/ 250	–	–	–	–	Lahori, I, pp. 119 and 441.
336	Sharfa	1000/ 200	1000/ 200	–	–	–	–	Lahori, I, p. 185.
337	Mir Sharif	–	1000/ 200	–	–	–	1631–2 (D)	Lahori, I (b), p. 312.
338	Sharif Khan	–	1000/ 200	–	–	–	1632–3 (D)	Lahori, I (b), p. 311.
339	Wafa Khan Khwajasara	–	1000/ 250	–	–	–	1634–5 (D)	Lahori, I (b), p. 311.
340	Rai Banwaridas	–	1000/ 100	Indian	–	–	1630–1 (D)	Lahori, I (b), p. 312; *Z.Kh.*, II, p. 408.
341	Bhojbal	–	1000/ 800	"	Deccani	–	–	Lahori, I (b), p. 148.
342	Rai Manidas	1000/ 150	1000/ 150	–	–	–	1632–3 (R)	Lahori, I, p. 446; I (b), p. 312.

Note: [1]His mansab is not mentioned by either Lahori or Salih. Farid, who gives his mansab, writes that he passed away in the beginning of this reign: *Z.Kh.*, II, pp. 302–3.

APPENDIX B: LIST OF MANSABDARS OF SHAHJAHAN DURING 1637–41 HOLDING RANKS OF 1000 ZAT AND ABOVE

Sl. No.	*Name and title*	*Highest rank during the period (zat/ sawar)*	*Ethnic group*	*Sub-group: Rajput, Maratha, Afghan, zamindar, etc.*	*Father or other blood relative in service*	*Date of Death (D), Retirement (R), Flight (F), etc.*	*Authorities*
1	*2*	*3*	*4*	*5*	*6*	*7*	*8*
				MANSABDARS OF 5000 AND ABOVE			
1	Yaminuddaulah Asaf Khan	9000/9000 H × 2h–3h	Irani	–	Father	Nov. 1641 (D)	Lahori, I (b), p. 292; II, pp. 257, 259 and 717; *Z.Kh.*, II, pp. 32–46; *M.U.*, I, pp. 151–60.
2	Alimardan Khan Amir-ul-Umara	7000/7000 3000 × 2h–3h	"	–	–	–	Lahori, II, p. 176; *Z.Kh.*, III, pp. 27–9; *M.U.*, II, pp. 795–807.
3	Afzal Khan Allami	7000/4000	"	–	–	Jan. 1639 (D)	Lahori, II, pp. 91, 132 and 718; *Z.Kh.*, II, pp. 255–6; *M.U.*, I, pp. 145–51.
4	Azam Khan Iradat Khan	6000/6000	"	–	Uncle	–	Lahori, I, p. 343; I (b), p. 293; *Z.Kh.*, II, p. 200; *M.U.*, I, pp. 174–80.
5	Abdullah Khan Firoze Jang	6000/6000	Turani	–	Brother	–	Lahori, I, p. 354; I (b), p. 293; *Z.Kh.*, II, pp. 173–85; *M.U.*, II, pp. 771 and 777–89.
6	Khan-e-Dauran Nusrat Jang	6000/6000 2h–3h	"	–	Father	–	Lahori, I (b), pp. 247 and 293; *Z.Kh.*, III, pp. 18–25; *M.U.*, I, pp. 749–58.
7	Said Khan Zafar Jang	6000/6000 2h–3h	"	–	"	–	Lahori, II, p. 47; *Z.Kh.*, II, p. 361; *M.U.*, II, pp. 429–36.

(contd.)

1	*2*	*3*	*4*	*5*	*6*	*7*	*8*
8	Khan-e-Jahan Barha Syed Abul Muzaffar	6000/6000 5000 × 2h–3h	Indian	–	–	–	Lahori, II, p. 235; *Z.Kh.*, III, pp. 10–12; *M.U.*, I, pp. 758–66.
9	Aitqad Khan Mirza Shapur	5000/4000	Irani	–	Father	–	Lahori, I (b), p. 295; *M.U.*, I, pp. 180–2.
10	Alahwardi Khan	5000/5000	"	–	Brother	–	Lahori, II, p. 158; *Z.Kh.*, II, pp. 205–8; *M.U.*, I, pp. 207–15.
11	Islam Khan Mashhadi	5000/5000 3000 × 2h–3h	"	–	–	–	Lahori, I (b), p. 294; *Z.Kh.*, II, pp. 25–7; *M.U.*, I, pp. 162–7.
12	Jafar Khan s/o Sadiq Khan	5000/3000	"	–	Father	–	Lahori, I (b), pp. 248 and 295; II, p. 235; *Z.Kh.*, III, pp. 31–2; *M.U.*, I, pp. 531–5; II, p. 730.
13	Khan-e-Jahan Shaista Khan	5000/5000 3000 × 2h–3h	"	–	"	–	Lahori, II, p. 21; *Z.Kh.*, II, pp. 180–90; *M.U.*, II, pp. 690–706.
14	Khan-e-Zaman Mirza Amanullah	5000/5000 2h–3h	"	–	"	May 1637 (D)	Lahori, I (b), pp. 257 and 294; *Z.Kh.*, II, pp. 263–71; *M.U.*, I, pp. 740–8.
15	Mir Muhammad Amin Mir Jumla	5000/2000	"	Deccani	–	Sep. 1637 (D)	Lahori, I (b), pp. 279 and 295; *Z.Kh.*, II, pp. 217–20; *M.U.*, III, pp. 413–18.
16	Sipahdar Khan Muhammad Salih	5000/5000	"	–	Uncle	–	Lahori, I (b), p. 294; *Z.Kh.*, II, pp. 261–2; *M.U.*, II, pp. 427–9.
17	Mirza Isa Tarkhan	5000/5000 1000 × 2h–3h	Turani	–	Brother	–	Lahori, II, p. 162, *Z.Kh.*, II, pp. 210–12; *M.U.*, III, pp. 485–8.
18	Qulij Khan	5000/5000 2000 × 2h–3h	"	–	"	–	Lahori, II, p. 35; *Z.Kh.*, III, pp. 66–7; *M.U.*, III, pp. 92–5.

19	Safdar Khan Khwaja Qasim	5000/3000	Turani	–	–	–	Lahori, II, p. 122; *Z.Kh.*, III, p. 40; *M.U.*, II, pp. 733–6.
20	Rustam Khan Muqarrab Khan Deccani	5000/5000	”	Deccani	–	–	Lahori, I (b), p. 294; *Z.Kh.*, III, pp. 91–2; *M.U.*, II, p. 270–6.
21	Bahadur Khan Rohila	5000/4000	Indian	Afghan	Father	–	Lahori, II, p. 273; *Z.Kh.*, III, pp. 48–9; *M.U.*, I, pp. 415–24.
22	Wazir Khan Hakim Alimuddin	5000/5000 100×2h–3h	”	–	–	–	Lahori, I (b), p. 294; *Z.Kh.*, III, pp. 15–18; *M.U.*, III, pp. 933–6.
23	Raja Gaj Singh Rathor	5000/5000	”	Rajput zamindar	Father	1639 (D)	Lahori, I (b), p. 294; II, p. 97 and 719; *Z.Kh.*, II, 300–1; *M.U.*, II, pp. 223–6.
24	Rana Jagat Singh Sisodiya	5000/5000	”	”	”	–	Lahori, I (b), p. 294; *M.U.*, II, pp. 200–6.
25	Raja Jai Singh Kachwaha	5000/5000 1000 × 2h–3h	”	”	”	–	Lahori, I (b), p. 294; II, pp. 272–3; *Z.Kh.*, III, pp. 117–18; *M.U.*, I, pp. 173–6; III, 568–77.
26	Raja Jaswant Singh Rathor	5000/5000 1000 × 2h–3h	”	Rajput zamindar	Father	–	Lahori, II, pp. 133 and 230; *M.U.*, III, pp. 599–604.
27	Maloji b/o Kheluji	5000/5000	”	Maratha zamindar	Brother	–	Lahori, I (b), p. 295; *Z.Kh.*, III, p. 139; *M.U.*, III, pp. 520–4.
				MANSABDARS OF 3000 TO 4500			
28	Baqar Khan Najm-e-Sani	4000/4000	Irani	–	–	May 1637 (D)	Lahori, I (b), pp. 274 and 295; *Z.Kh.*, II, pp. 254–5; *M.U.*, I, pp. 408–12.
29	Musvi Khan Sadr	4000/750	”	–	Near relatives	–	Lahori, I (b), p. 297; *Z.Kh.*, II, pp. 220–1; *M.U.*, III, pp. 441–2.

(contd.)

1	*2*	*3*	*4*	*5*	*6*	*7*	*8*
30	Mutamad Khan Muhammad Sharif	4000/1200	Irani	–	–	1639–40 (D)	Lahori, I (b), p. 297; II, p. 721; *Z.Kh.*, II, p. 253; *M.U.*, III, 431–4.
31	Mutaqid Khan Mirza Makki s/o Iftikhar Khan	4000/4000	"	–	Father	–	Lahori, I (b), p. 296; *Z.Kh.*, II, pp. 351–2; III, pp. 45–6; *M.U.*, I, pp. 182–5; III, pp. 482–5.
32	Saif Khan Mirza Safi	4000/4000	"	–	Near relatives	1640 (D)	Lahori, I (b), p. 295; II, pp. 198 and 720; *Z.Kh.*, II, pp. 238–9; *M.U.*, II, pp. 416–20.
33	Shahnawaz Khan Mirza Badiuzzaman Safavi	4000/4000	"	–	Father	–	Lahori, II, p. 183; *Z.Kh.*, II, pp. 216–17; *M.U.*, II, pp. 670–5.
34	Fidai Khan Hidayatullah	4000/3000	Turani	–	Brother	–	Lahori, I (b), p. 296; *Z.Kh.*, II, pp. 314–15; *M.U.*, III, pp. 12–18.
35	Mahaldar Khan s/o Mahaldar Khan Charkas)	4000/2000	"	Deccani	–	–	Lahori, I (b), p. 297; *Z.Kh.*, III, pp. 134–5; *M.U.*, III, pp. 419–21.
36	Najabat Khan Mirza Shuja	4000/4000	"	–	Father	–	Lahori, II, p. 155; *Z.Kh.*, III, pp. 239–42; *M.U.*, III, pp. 821–8.
37	Sarfaraz Khan Chaghta	4000/3000	"	–	G. father	1639 (D)	Lahori, I (b), p. 297; II, pp. 149 and 721; Mirat, I, p. 212; *M.U.*, II, pp. 421–3.
38	Shah Beg Khan Uzbek	4000/3000	"	–	–	–	Lahori, I (b), p. 296; *Z.Kh.*, III, pp. 41–2; *M.U.*, III, pp. 665–7.
39	Mubariz Khan Rohila	4000/4000	Indian	Afghan	–	–	Lahori, II, p. 94; *Z.Kh.*, II, pp. 348–9; *M.U.*, III, pp. 442–4.
40	Rashid Khan Ansari	4000/4000	"	"	–	–	Lahori, II, pp. 98–9; *Z.Kh.*, II, pp. 223–9; *M.U.*, II, pp. 242–50.

41	Syed Shujat Khan Barha s/o Syed Jahangir	4000/4000 2h–3h	Indian	–	G. father	–	Lahori, II, p. 201; *Z.Kh.*, III, pp. 12–15; *M.U.*, II, pp. 423–6.
42	Raja Bithaldas Gaur	4000/3000	”	Rajput zamindar	Father	–	Lahori, I (b), pp. 241–2 and 296; *Z.Kh.*, III, p. 92; *M.U.*, II, pp. 250–6.
43	Sarfaraz Khan Deccani	4000/3000	–	Deccani	–	–	Lahori, I (b), p. 297; *M.U.*, II, pp. 469–73.
44	Asalat Khan Mir Abdul Hadi	3000/2500	Irani	–	G. father	–	Lahori, I (b), p. 297; *Z.Kh.*, III, p. 32; *M.U.*, I, pp. 167–72; III, pp. 341–2.
45	Amir Khan Mir Abul Baqa	3000/2000	”	–	Father	–	Lahori, I (b), p. 298; *Z.Kh.*, I, pp. 198–200; *M.U.*, I, pp. 172–4; III, pp. 74–82.
46	Mirza Hasan Safavi	3000/1500	”	–	”	–	Lahori, II, p. 246; *M.U.*, III, pp. 477–9.
47	Himmat Khan Alahyar	3000/2000	”	–	”	–	Lahori, II, p. 90; *Z.Kh.*, II, pp. 351–2; *M.U.*, I, pp. 182–5.
48.	Makramat Khan Mulla Murshid Shirazi	3000/3000	”	–	–	–	Lahori, II, p. 244; *M.U.*, III, pp. 460–2.
49	Mirza Khan Manochahr	3000/2000	”	–	Father	–	Lahori, I (b), p. 298; *Z.Kh.*, II, pp. 318–19; *M.U.*, III, pp. 586–9.
50	Mukhlis Khan	3000/2000	”	–	–	1637–8 (D)	Lahori, I (b), p. 298; *Z.Kh.*, II, pp. 205–8; *M.U.*, III, pp. 428–31.
51	Nurullah Harvi	3000/2500	”	–	–	Jun. 1639 (D)	Lahori, II, pp. 94, 151 and 723.

(contd.)

1	*2*	*3*	*4*	*5*	*6*	*7*	*8*
52	Qazalbash Khan Afshar	3000/3000	Irani	Deccani	–	–	Lahori, II, p. 176; *Z.Kh.*, III, pp. 68–9; *M.U.*, III, pp. 85–6.
53	Salabat Khan Roshan Zamir	3000/2000	,,	–	Father	–	Lahori, II, p. 228; *Z.Kh.*, III, p. 33–4; *M.U.*, II, pp. 731–3.
54	Sazawar Khan Mashhadi	3000/2500	,,	–	,,	–	Lahori, II, p. 205; *Z.Kh.*, III, pp. 97–8; *M.U.*, II, pp. 438–40.
55	Zafar Khan	3000/2000	,,	–	,,	–	Lahori, II, p. 241; *Z.Kh.*, II, pp. 290–1; *M.U.*, II, pp. 756–63.
56	Azizullah Khan	3000/2500	Turani	–	,,	–	Lahore, II, p. 223; *M.U.*, II, pp. 789–90.
57	Ghairat Khan Khwaja Kamgar	3000/2000	,,	–	Uncle	–	Lahori, II, p. 198; *Z.Kh.*, III, p. 131; *M.U.*, II, pp. 863–5.
58	Sardar Khan Shah-Jahani	3000/3000	,,	–	–	–	Lahori, I (b), p. 297; *M.U.*, II, pp. 437–8.
59	Shah Quli Khan Waqqas Haji	3000/2000	,,	–	–	–	Lahori, II, p. 223; *Z.Kh.*, III, p. 116; *M.U.*, II, pp. 658–60.
60	Yusuf Muhammad Khan Tashqandi	3000/3000 1000×2h–3h	,,	–	–	Aug. 1639 (D)	Lahori, II, p. 150, 155 and 722; *Z.Kh.*, III, pp. 42–3; *M.U.*, III, pp. 963–7.
61	Daulat Khan Maee	3000/2500	Indian	–	–	–	Lahori, II, pp. 227–8; *Z.Kh.*, II, p. 378; *M.U.*, II, pp. 24–30.
62	Syed Hizbar Khan Barha	3000/1000	,,	–	–	1638–9 (D)	Lahori, I (b), p. 299; II, p. 724; *Z.Kh.*, II, p. 315; *M.U.*, II, 415–16.
63	Kartalab Khan Baswant Rao	3000/2000	,,	Deccani	–	–	Lahori, I (b), p. 299; *Z.Kh.*, III, pp. 142–3; *M.U.*, III, pp. 153–4.

64	Murtaza Khan Syed Nizam	3000/2000	Indian	–	Father	–	Lahori, I (b), p. 298; *Z.Kh.*, III, pp. 242–3; *M.U.*, III, pp. 479–81.
65	Amar Singh Rathor	3000/3000	"	Rajput zamindar	"	–	Lahori, II, p. 97; *M.U.*, II, pp. 220–3.
66	Anup Singh Badgujar	3000/1500	"	"	"	1637–8 (D)	Lahori, I (b), p. 299; *Z.Kh.*, II, pp. 364–6; *M.U.*, II, p. 223.
67	Raja Jagat Singh	3000/2000	"	"	"	–	Lahori, I (b), p. 298; *Z.Kh.*, III, pp. 118–23; *M.U.*, II, pp. 238–41.
68	Madho Singh Hara	3000/2500	"	"	"	–	Lahori, II, p. 224; *M.U.*, III, pp. 453–6.
69	Pahar Singh Bundela	3000/2000	"	"	"	–	*S.D.S.*, pp. 33–4; *M.U.*, II, pp. 256–60.
70	Raja Rai Singh Sisodiya	3000/2000	"	"	"	–	Lahori, II, p. 133; *M.U.*, II, pp. 297–301.
71	Rao Satarsal Hara	3000/3000	"	"	G. father	–	Lahori, I (b), p. 297; *Z.Kh.*, III, pp. 133–4; *M.U.*, II, pp. 260–3.
72	Baharji	3000/2500	"	Maratha zamindar	–	1639 (D)	Lahori, II, pp. 108, 141–2 and 733; *M.U.*, I, pp. 412–15.
73	Dattaji s/o Bahadurji	3000/1000	"	"	Father	–	Lahori, I (b), p. 299; *M.U.*, I, pp. 520–3.
74	Jadun Rai, Tilang Rai	3000/1500	"	"	G. father	–	Lahori, I (b), p. 299; *M.U.*, I, pp. 520–3.
75	Mankuji Deccani	3000/1500	"	Maratha (Deccani)	–	–	*S.D.S.*, p. 34; Lahori, I (b), p. 299.

(contd.)

1	2	3	4	5	6	7	8
76	Parsoji b/o Maloji	3000/1500	Indian	Maratha zamindar	Brother	–	Lahori, I (b), p. 299; *Z.Kh.*, III, p. 139; *M.U.*, III, pp. 520–4.
77	Udaji Ram s/o Udaji Ram	3000/2000	"	"	Father	–	Lahori, I (b), p. 299; *Z.Kh.*, III, pp. 140–1; *M.U.*, I, p. 144; *S.D.S.*, p. 35.
78	Firoze Khan Khwajasara	3000/1200	–	–	–	–	Lahori, II, pp. 183–4; *M.U.*, III, pp. 21–2.
79	Habsh Khan Syedi Miftah	3000/1500	–	Deccani	–	–	Lahori, I (b), p. 299; *Z.Kh.*, III, pp. 112–13; *M.U.*, I, pp. 579–83.
80	Hasan s/o Fakhr-ul-Mulk	3000/2000	–	–	Father	–	Lahori, I (b), p. 299.
81	Jauhar Khan Habshi	3000/3000	–	Deccani	–	–	Lahori, I (b), p. 297; *Z.Kh.*, III, p. 144.
				MANSABDARS OF 1000 TO 2700			
82	Iltifat Khan Mirza Murad Safavi	2500/1000	Irani	–	Father	–	Lahori, II, p. 157; *M.U.*, III, p. 583.
83	Murshid Quli Khan Turkman	2500/2500 500 × 2h–3h	"	–	–	1637 (D)	Lahori, I (b), pp. 275 and 300; II, pp. 7–8 and 725; *Z.Kh.*, II, pp. 397–8; *M.U.*, III, pp. 421–8.
84	Safshikan Khan Mirza Lashkari	2500/2000	"	–	Father	–	Lahori, I (b), p. 300; *Z.Kh.*, II, pp. 305–6; *M.U.*, II, pp. 736–8.
85	Mir Shams	2500/2500	"	–	–	–	Lahori, I (b), pp. 242 and 300; *Z.Kh.*, II, p. 293; *M.U.*, III, p. 492.

86	Iwaz Khan Beg Qaqshal	2500/2000	Turani	–	–	–	Lahori, II, p. 48; *M.U.*, II, pp. 776–7.
87	Tarbiyat Khan Fakhruddin Ahmad	2500/1500	"	–	–	–	Lahori, II, p. 225; *Z.Kh.*, III, pp. 43–5; *M.U.*, I, pp. 486–90.
88	Ahmad Khan Niyazi	2500/2000	Indian	Afghan	Father	–	Lahori, I (b), pp. 138 and 300; *Z.Kh.*, II, pp. 257–60; *M.U.*, I, pp. 185–8.
89	Dilawar Khan Deccani	2500/1500	"	Afghan (Deccani)		–	Lahori, I (b), p. 301.
90	Nazr Bahadur Kheshgi	2500/1500	"	Afghan	–	–	Lahori, I (b), p. 301; II, p. 217; *Z.Kh.*, III, pp. 49–50; *M.U.*, III, pp. 818–21.
91	Purdil Khan	2500/2200	"	"	Father	–	Lahori, II, p. 48; *Z.Kh.*, III, p. 131; *M.U.*, I, pp. 424–7.
92	Ikhlas Khan Shaikh Farid	2500/1500	"	–	"	–	Lahori, I (b), p. 301; *Z.Kh.*, II, pp. 338–9; *M.U.*, I, pp. 220–2; III, pp. 66–8.
93	Jannisar Khan Kamaluddin Husain	2500/2000	"	–	–	1639 (D)	Lahori, II, pp. 128, 131 and 725; *Z.Kh.*, III, p. 106; *M.U.*, I, pp. 527–9.
94	Raja Debi Singh Bundela	2500/2000	"	Rajput zamindar	Father	–	Lahori, I (b), p. 300; *Z.Kh.*, II, pp. 370–1; *M.U.*, II, pp. 295–7.
95	Aqil Khan Inayatullah	2000/500	Irani	–	"	–	Lahori, II, p. 244; *Z.Kh.*, III, p. 106; *M.U.*, II, pp. 790–2.
96	Ahmad Beg Khan	2000/1500	"	–	G. father	–	Lahori, I (b), p. 301; *M.U.*, I, pp. 136–9 and 194–5.
97	Fakhir Khan s/o Najm-e-Sani Baqar Khan	2000/1000	"	–	Father	–	*Z.Kh.*, II, pp. 254–5; *M.U.*, III, pp. 26–8.

(contd.)

1	*2*	*3*	*4*	*5*	*6*	*7*	*8*
98	Hakim ul Mulk Abul Qasim Gilani	2000/50	Irani	–	Father	–	Lahori, I (b), pp. 304 and 348.
99	Jansipar Khan Jamali	2000/1500	"	–	Uncle	–	Lahori, II, p. 161; *M.U.*, I, p. 530; III, pp. 812–17.
100	Khalilullah Khan	2000/1500	"	–	Brother	–	Lahori, II, p. 200; *Z.Kh.*, III, p. 33; *M.U.*, I, pp. 775–82.
101	Khwaja Jahan Khawafi	2000/600	"	–	–	–	Lahori, I (b), p. 304; *Z.Kh.*, III, pp. 128–9; *M.U.*, I, pp. 748–9.
102	Mahabat Khan Mirza Lahrasp	2000/1000	"	–	Father	–	Lahori, I (b), p. 303; *Z.Kh.*, III, pp. 95–6; *M.U.*, III, pp. 590–5.
103	Muhammad Zaman Tehrani	2000/2000	"	–	–	–	Lahori, II, p. 244; *M.U.*, III, pp. 452–3.
104	Mughal Khan s/o Zain Khan Koka	2000/1500	"	–	Father	–	Lahori, I (b), pp. 221 and 301; *Z.Kh.*, II, pp. 324–5; *M.U.*, III, pp. 490–2.
105	Mukhtar Khan Sabzwari	2000/1500	"	–	–	1673 (D)	Lahori, I (b), pp. 275 and 302; *M.U.*, III, pp. 409–13.
106	Zulfiqar Khan Khanlar	2000/800	"	–	–	–	Lahori, II, p. 223; *M.U.*, II, pp. 85–8.
107	Mirza Nauzar Safavi	2000/1400	"	–	Father	–	Lahori, II, p. 157; *M.U.*, III, pp. 555–7.
108	Saadat Khan	2000/1500	"	–	G. father	–	Lahori, II, p. 133; *M.U.*, II, pp. 461–3.
109	Abdul Rahim Beg Uzbek	2000/1000	Turani	–	–	–	Lahori, II, p. 182; *M.U.*, II, pp. 793–4.

110	Baqi Khan Qalmaq	2000/2000	Turani	–	–	–	Lahori, I (b), p. 301; *M.U.*, I, pp. 427–9.
111	Ikhlas Khan Husain Beg	2000/1000	"	–	–	1639–40 (D)	Lahori, I (b), p. 303; II, p. 727; *M.U.*, I, p. 151.
112	Janbaz Khan Khwaja Baba	2000/1000	"	–	–	–	Lahori, I (b), p. 303.
113	Qazzaq Khan Baqi Beg Uzbek	2000/800	"	–	Brother	–	Lahori, II, p. 220; *Z.Kh.*, II, pp. 346–8; *M.U.*, III, pp. 88–9.
114	Rahmat Khan Mir Faizullah	2000/1500	"	–	–	1638 (D)	Lahori, II, pp. 98 and 727; *M.U.*, II, pp. 219–20.
115	Uzbek Khan Nazr Bahadur	2000/2000	"	–	–	–	Lahori, II, p. 221; *Z.Kh.*, III, pp. 90–1; *M.U.*, I, pp. 195–8.
116	Mirza Wali	2000/1000	"	–	Father	–	Lahori, I (b), p. 302; *Z.Kh.*, II, p. 256; *M.U.*, III, pp. 456–60.
117	Mubarak Khan Niyazi	2000/2000	Indian	Afghan	Uncle	–	Lahori, I (b), p. 301; *Z.Kh.*, II, p. 261; *M.U.*, III, pp. 512–13.
118	Sher Khan Tarin	2000/1000	"	Afghan zamindar	–	–	Lahori, I (b), p. 303; *Z.Kh.*, III, pp. 102–6; *M.U.*, II, pp. 654–8.
119	Syed Alam Barha	2000/1000	"	–	Brother	–	Lahori, II, p. 199; *M.U.*, II, pp. 454–6.
120	Bakhtiyar Khan Deccani	2000/1000	"	Deccani	–	–	Lahori, I (b), p. 303; *M.U.*, I, pp. 774–5.
121	Ihtiman Khan	2000/1500	"	–	–	–	Lahori, I (b), p. 302; *Z.Kh.*, III, pp. 89–90; *M.U.*, I, pp. 160–2.

(contd.)

1	*2*	*3*	*4*	*5*	*6*	*7*	*8*
122	Ikram Khan Fathpuri	2000/1000	Indian	–	Father	–	Lahori, II, p. 594; *Z.Kh.*, III, pp. 274–5.
123	Sadat Khan Bhakkari Deccani	2000/1500	"	–	–	–	Lahori, I (b), p. 301; *Z.Kh.*, II, pp. 353–4.
124	Syed Umar	2000/1000	"	Deccani	–	–	Lahori, I (b), p. 303.
125	Rao Karan Bhurtiya	2000/1500	"	Rajput zamindar	Father	–	Lahori, I (b), p. 302; *Z.Kh.*, II, pp. 398–9; *M.U.*, II, pp. 287–9.
126	Pirthi Raj Rathor	2000/1700	"	Rajput	–	–	Lahori, I (b), pp. 275 and 301; *M.U.*, I, pp. 429–31.
127	Raja Ramdas Narori	2000/1000	"	Rajput zamindar	–	1640 (D)	Lahori, I (b), p. 303; II, pp. 174 and 728; *M.U.*, II, pp. 226–7.
128	Ani Rai Sanneta	2000/1000	"	Maratha zamindar (Deccani)	–	–	Lahori, I (b), pp. 303.
129	Bithuji s/o Achla	2000/1000	"	Maratha zamindar	Uncle	–	Lahori, I, p. 310; I (b), p. 303; *M.U.*, I, p. 522.
130	Ganesh Rai	2000/800	"	Maratha zamindar (Deccani)	–	–	*S.D.S.*, pp. 34–5.
131	Habaji	2000/800	"	Maratha (Deccani)	–	–	Lahori, I, p. 306; I (b), p. 303.
132	Rawat Rai Deccani	2000/1500	"	Maratha zamindar (Deccani)	–	–	Lahori, I, pp. 288–9; I (b), p. 302.

133	Rustam Rai	2000/1000	Indian	Maratha zamindar (Deccani)	–	–	*S.D.S.*, p. 34.
134	Arab Khan	2000/1500	–	–	–	–	Lahori, I (b), p. 278; *Z.Kh.*, III, pp. 89–90; *M.U.*, II, pp. 794–5.
135	Atish Khan Habshi	2000/1000	–	Deccani	–	–	Lahori, I (b), p. 303; *Z.Kh.*, III, p. 143; *M.U.*, I, pp. 188–9.
136	Farhan Khan Deccani	2000/1000	–	"	–	–	Lahori, I, p. 307.
137	Sarwar Khan Habshi	2000/1000	–	"	–	–	Lahori, I (b), p. 303; *Z.Kh.*, III, pp. 143–44.
138	Aitmad Khan Aqa Afzal	1500/600	Irani	–	–	–	Lahori, II, p. 230; *Z.Kh.*, II, p. 276; *M.U.*, III, pp. 18–21.
139	Muhammad Husain	1500/1500	"	–	–	–	Lahori, II, p. 112; *Apparatus*, p. S-1273.
140	Multafit Khan	1500/600	"	–	Father	–	Lahori, I (b), p. 306; *Z.Kh.*, III, pp. 92–3; *M.U.*, III, pp. 500–3.
141	Sohrab Khan	1500/1200	"	–	"	1640–1 (D)	Lahori, II, p. 730; *M.U.*, I, pp. 114–15.
142	Zabardast Khan	1500/1000	"	–	–	–	Lahori, I, p. 399; I (b), p. 305; *M.U.*, II, p. 372.
143	Zulfiqar Khan Turkman	1500/1200	"	–	Near relatives	–	Lahori, II, p. 228; *Z.Kh.*, II, p. 411.
144	Zulqadr Khan Turkman	1500/1000	"	–	–	–	Lahori, II, p. 200; *M.U.*, II, pp. 84–5.

(contd.)

1	*2*	*3*	*4*	*5*	*6*	*7*	*8*
145	Mir Abdul Karim	1500/1000	Turani	–	–	–	Lahori, II, p. 103.
146	Asfandiyar Khan	1500/1200	”	–	Father	–	Lahori, I (b), p. 304; *Z.Kh.*, II, pp. 362–3; *M.U.*, I, p. 568.
147	Himmat Khan Sharfuddin Husain	1500/1500	”	–	–	1637–8 (D)	Lahori, I (b), p. 304.
148	Iftikhar Khan Abul Baqa s/o Ahmad Beg Khan	1500/1000	”	–	Father	–	Lahori, II, p. 48; *Z.Kh.*, II, p. 361; *M.U.*, I, p. 127.
149	Khanazad Khan	1500/1000	”	–	”	–	Lahori, II, p. 236; *M.U.*, II, pp. 428–37.
150	Sarandaz Khan Qalmaq	1500/1200	”	–	–	–	Lahori, I (b), pp. 278 and 304; *Z.Kh.*, III, pp. 55–8.
151	Yakkataz Khan	1500/1500	”	–	–	–	Lahori, II, p. 128; *Z.Kh.*, III, pp. 89–90.
152	Shujat Khan Shadi Beg	1500/1200	”	–	Father	–	Lahori, II, pp. 220–1; *Z.Kh.*, I, p. 196; *M.U.*, I, pp. 511–12; II, pp. 662–5.
153	Jalal Kakar	1500/1000	Indian	Afghan	”	–	Lahori, II, p. 218; *Z.Kh.*, II, pp. 335–6; *M.U.*, I, pp. 530–1.
154	Jamal Nohani	1500/500	”	”	–	–	Lahori, I, p. 79; I (b), p. 307.
155	Kakar Khan	1500/1000	”	”	–	–	Lahori, I (b), pp. 250 and 305; *M.U.*, III, pp. 152–3.
156	Sikandar Rohila	1500/1000	”	”	Brother	–	Lahori, I (b), p. 305; *Z.Kh.*, II, p. 349.
157	Akbar Quli Gakkhar	1500/1500	”	Zamindar	G. father	–	Lahori, I (b), pp. 242 and 304; *Z.Kh.*, I, p. 221; *M.U.*, III, pp. 144–8.

158	Daulatmand s/o Biharji	1500/1000	Indian	Zamindar	Father	–	Lahori, II, pp. 141–2; *Z.Kh.*, III, p. 144.
159	Bhim Rathor	1500/800	"	Rajput	–	–	Lahori, I (b), p. 306.
160	Chandraman Bundela	1500/800	"	Rajput zamindar	Father	–	Lahori, I (b), p. 306; *Z.Kh.*, II, pp. 363–4.
161	Hari Singh Rathor	1500/900	"	"	"	–	Lahori, II, pp. 101–2; *M.U.*, II, p. 268.
162	Hathi Singh	1500/1000	"	"	"	–	Lahori, I (b), p. 305; *M.U.*, II, pp. 142–8.
163	Rawal Ponja	1500/1500	"	"	–	–	Lahori, I (b), p. 304.
164	Raja Pratap Singh Ujjainia	1500/1000	"	"	–	1637–8 (D)	Lahori, I (b), p. 305; *M.U.*, II, p. 786.
165	Raja Sangram	1500/600	"	"	–	–	Lahori, I (b), pp. 257 and 306.
166	Siva Ram Gaur	1500/1000	"	"	Uncle	–	Lahori, I (b), 305; *M.U.*, II, pp. 263–5.
167	Midni Rai	1500/900	"	Maratha zamindar (Deccani)	–	–	Hyd. 157/8 vide *Apparatus*, p. 172
168	Ranaji	1500/600	"	Maratha (Deccani)	–	–	*S.D.S.*, p. 34.
169	Sharzah Rao Kawa	1500/600	"	Martha zamindar (Deccani)	–	–	*S.D.S.*, p. 88.
170	Khwaja Barkhurdar	1500/800	–	–	–	–	Lahori, I (b), p. 306.

(contd.)

1	*2*	*3*	*4*	*5*	*6*	*7*	*8*
171	Khidmat Khan Khwajasara	1500/500	–	–	–	1640–1 (D)	Lahori, II, p. 731.
172	Sarfaraz Khan	1500/800	–	–	–	–	Lahori, I (b), p. 306.
173	Zabardast Khan	1500/800	–	–	–	–	Lahori, I (b), p. 305.
174	Amanat Khan Abdul Haq b/o Allami Afzal Khan	1000/200	Irani	–	Brother	–	Lahori, II, pp. 133–4, *Z.Kh.*, II, pp. 255–6; *M.U.*, II, p. 790.
175	Diyanat Khan Hakim Jamala Kashi	1000/600	"	–	–	–	Lahori, I (b), p. 308; *Z.Kh.*, III, pp. 36–7; *M.U.*, II, pp. 37–8.
176	Fidai Khan Mir Zarif	1000/200	"	–	–	1641 (D)	Lahori, II, pp. 187, 229 and 737; *M.U.*, III, pp. 10–12.
177	Haqiqat Khan Ishaq Bag Yazdi	1000/250	"	–	–	–	Lahori, II, p. 198; *M.U.*, I, pp. 590–1.
178	Karamullah	1000/500	"	–	Father	–	Lahori, I (b), p. 310; *M.U.*, II, pp. 773–5.
179	Hakim Khushhal	1000/200	"	–	"	–	Lahori, I (b), p. 311; *Z.Kh.*, II, p. 303; *M.U.*, I, pp. 563–5.
180	Mirza Lutfullah	1000/1000	"	–	"	–	Lahori, II, p. 290; *Z.Kh.*, III, pp. 97–9; *M.U.*, III, p. 168.
181	Makramat Khan Mirza Murad Khan Safavi	1000/400	"	–	"	–	Lahori, II, p. 204; *M.U.*, III, pp. 583–8.

182	Marhamat Khan Abdul Rahman s/o Sadiq Khan	1000/400	Irani	–	Father	–	Lahori, II, p. 134; *M.U.*, II, pp. 730–1.
183	Mir Khan	1000/300	”	–	”	–	Lahori, II, p. 7; *Z.Kh.*, I, pp. 198–200; *M.U.*, I, pp. 172–4.
184	Muhammad Sharif	1000/700	”	–	Near relatives	1638–9 (D)	Lahori, I (b), p. 308; II, p. 733.
185	Muizul Mulk Mir Musa	1000/100	”	–	–	–	Lahori, I (b), p. 312.
186	Murtaza Quli	1000/600	”	–	Brother	1637–8 (D)	Lahori, I (b), p. 309; *M.U.*, I, p. 519.
187	Nuruddaulah s/o Mir Hisamuddin Anju	1000/400	”	–	Father	–	Lahori, II, p. 164.
188	Rashid Khan Rahmanyar b/o Ialhyar	1000/750	”	–	Brother	–	Lahori, II, p. 192; *M.U.*, I, pp. 184–5.
189	Mirza Safshikan s/o Mirza Hasan Safavi	1000/400	”	–	Father	–	Lahori, II, pp. 246–7; *M.U.*, III, pp. 477–9.
190	Siyadat Khan Mir b/o Zainuddin Ali Islam Khan Mashhadi	1000/400	”	–	Brother	–	Lahori, II, p. 229; *Z.Kh.*, III, pp. 127–8.
191	Sultan Nazr	1000/300	”	–	”	–	Lahori, I (b), p. 310; *Z.Kh.*, II, p. 316; *M.U.*, II, pp. 416–21.

(contd.)

1	*2*	*3*	*4*	*5*	*6*	*7*	*8*
192	Yahya	1000/300	Irani	–	Father	–	Lahori, I (b), p. 311; *M.U.*, II, pp. 419–21.
193	Zahid Khan s/o Hoori Khanam	1000/1000	"	–	–	–	Lahori, II, pp. 226–7; *Z.Kh.*, III, pp. 125–6; *M.U.*, II, pp. 370–1.
194	Abdul Rahman Beg Turnabi	1000/600	Turani	–	–	1638–9 (D)	Lahori, II, p. 734.
195	Alif Khan Aman Beg	1000/1000	"	–	Father	–	Lahori, I (b), p. 307; *Z.Kh.*, III, pp. 89–90; *M.U.*, I, pp. 191–4.
196	Bahram	1000/500	"	–	"	–	Lahori, I (b), p. 309; *Z.Kh.*, II, p. 325; *M.U.*, I, pp. 524–5.
197	Mir Barka Bukhari	1000/200	"	–	–	–	Lahori, I (b), p. 311.
198	Khwaja Barkhurdar son-in-law of Mahabat Khan	1000/500	"	–	Near relatives	–	Lahori, I (b), p. 309; *Z.Kh.*, II, p. 341; *M.U.*, I, pp. 206–7.
199	Himmat Khan Yusuf Beg Kabuli	1000/5000	"	–	–	–	Lahori, II, p. 148; ***Apparatus***, p. S-1742.
200	Alah Quli Khan Uzbek s/o Yalingtosh	1000/500	"	–	–	–	Lahori, II, p. 230; *M.U.*, I, pp. 189–91.
201	Inayatullah s/o Isa Tarkhan	1000/500	"	–	Father	–	Lahori, II, p. 162; *M.U.*, III, pp. 487–8.
202	Khanjar Khan Mirza Muhammad	1000/500	"	–	Near relatives	–	Lahori, II, pp. 121–2; *M.U.*, III, pp. 94–5.

203	Lutfullah s/o Said Khan	1000/500	Turani	–	Father	–	Lahori, II, p. 279.
204	Latif Khan Naqshbandi	1000/400	”	–	–	–	Lahori, I (b), p. 310.
205	Muhammad Ali Kamrani	1000/500	”	–	–	–	Lahori, I (b), p. 310; *Apparatus*, p. S-1688.
206	Shadi Khan Uzbek	1000/400	”	–	–	–	Salih, I, p. 270 (B); *Z.Kh.*, III, pp. 59–60; *M.U.*, II, pp. 661–2.
207	Turktaz Khan	1000/400	”	–	–	–	Lahori, I (b), p. 310.
208	Urd Sher nephew of Said Khan	1000/600	”	–	Uncle	–	Lahori, II, p. 48.
209	Abdul Rahman Rohila, s/o Shahbaz Khan Rohila	1000/1000	Indian	Afghan	Father	–	Lahori, II, p. 165; *M.U.*, II, pp. 650–1.
210	Ahdad Khan Mahmand	1000/500	”	”	–	–	Lahori, I (b), p. 310.
211	Alawal Tarin	1000/800	”	”	–	–	Lahori, II, p. 48.
212	Daulat Khan Qiyam Khani	1000/800	”	”	–	–	Lahori, I (b), p. 307.
213	Habib Sur	1000/200	”	”	–	–	Lahori, I (b), p. 312.
214	Hadidad Khan b/o Rashid Khan Ansari	1000/1000	”	”	Brother	–	Lahori, II, pp. 98–9; *Z.Kh.*, II, pp. 229–30; *M.U.*, III, pp. 941–3.

(contd.)

1	2	3	4	5	6	7	8
215	Ikhtiyar Khan s/o Mubariz Khan Rohila	1000/600	Indian	Afghan	Father	–	Lahori, II, p. 224.
216	Nasib Shirani	1000/700	"	"	–	–	Lahori, I (b), p. 308.
217	Shamsher Khan Tarin	1000/500	"	"	–	–	Lahori, I (b), p. 310; *M.U.*, II, pp. 677–9.
218	Shamsuddin Khan s/o Nazr Bahadur Kheshgi	1000/800	"	"	Father	–	Lahori, II, p. 162; *M.U.*, II, pp. 676–7.
219	Usman Rohila	1000/700	"	"	Brother	–	Lahori, I (b), p. 308; *Z.Kh.*, III, p. 116.
220	Syed Abdul Wahab	1000/1000	"	–	–	–	Lahori, II, p. 200; *Z.Kh.*, II, p. 339.
221	Adam Khan Tibbati	1000/400	"	Zamindar	–	–	Lahori, II, p. 98.
222	Diler Khan Syed Wali	1000/700	"	–	–	–	Lahori, II, p. 48.
223	Dindar Khan Abdul Wahid s/o Mustafa Khan Bukhari	1000/650	"	–	Father	–	Lahori, II, p. 48; *Z.Kh.*, II, pp. 291–2.
224	Ikhlas Khan Shaikh Alahdiya	1000/800	"	–	"	–	Lahori, I (b), p. 307; *Z.Kh.*, II, pp. 351–2; *M.U.*, I, pp. 198–9.
225	Janbaz Khan Syed Ahmad	1000/800	"	–	–	–	Lahori, II, p. 129

226	Syed Khadim Barha	1000/500	Indian	–	–	–	Lahori, II, p. 232.
227	Syed Muhammad s/o Syed Afzal Barha	1000/500	"	–	–	–	Lahori, II, p. 228.
228	Syed Nurul Ayan s/o Saif Khan Barha	1000/300	"	–	Father	–	Lahori, II, p. 228; *M.U.*, II, pp. 410–11.
229	Allami Sadullah Khan	1000/200	"	–	–	–	Lahori, II, pp. 219–20; *Z.Kh.*, III, pp. 7–9; *M.U.*, II, pp. 441–8.
230	Sher Khan Syed Shahab Barha s/o Syed Ghairat Khan	1000/600	"	–	Father	–	Lahori, II, p. 198; *M.U.*, II, pp. 667–8.
231	Amar Singh Narori g/s/o Ramdas Narori	1000/600	"	Rajput	G. father zamindar	–	Lahori, II, p. 174; *M.U.*, II, p. 227.
232	Anurodh Gaur s/o Bithaldas Gaur	1000/1000	"	"	Father	–	Lahori, II, p. 158; *M.U.*, II, pp. 276–7.
233	Bhagwandas Bundela	1000/600	"	"	"	–	Lahori, I (b), p. 309; *Z.Kh.*, II, pp. 363–4; *M.U.*, II, pp. 197–9.
234	Bhoj Raj s/o Raisal Darbari	1000/500	"	"	"	–	Lahori, II, p. 201; *Z.Kh.*, I, p. 40; II, pp. 366–7.
235	Rai Ganesh Bhadoriya	1000/600	"	"	–	–	*S.D.S.*, p. 29.
236	Gokuldas Sisodiya	1000/600	"	Rajput	–	–	Lahori, II, p. 146.
237	Gopal Singh	1000/700	"	Rajput	Father	–	Lahori, II, p. 48; *M.U.*, I, p. 516.

(contd.)

1	*2*	*3*	*4*	*5*	*6*	*7*	*8*
	s/o Manrupkachwaha				zamindar		
238	Jai Ram s/o Anup Singh Badgujar	1000/1000	Indian	Rajput zamindar	Father	–	Lahori, II, p. 146; *M.U.*, II, pp. 241–2.
239	Raja Kishan Singh Bhadoriya	1000/600	"	"	–	–	Lahori, I (b), p. 309; *M.U.*, II, pp. 228–9.
240	Kunwar Sen Kishtwari	1000/300	"	"	–	–	Lahori, I (b), p. 311.
241	Maheshdas Rathor s/o Dalpat	1000/800	"	"	Father	–	Lahori, II, p. 230; *M.U.*, III, pp. 445–7.
242	Rai Singh Jhala	1000/500	"	Rajput	–	–	Lahori, II, p. 230.
243	Raj Singh Rathor s/o Khewan Rathor	1000/600	"	"	–	–	Lahori, II, p. 156.
244	Ram Singh Rathor s/o Karamsi Rathor	1000/700	"	Rajput zamindar	Father	–	Lahori, II, p. 236; *M.U.*, II, pp. 297–300.
245	Sabal Singh Rathor s/o Raja Suraj Singh	1000/1000	"	"	"	–	Lahori, II, p. 121; *Z.Kh.*, II, pp. 297–300.
246	Rawal Samarsi	1000/1000	"	"	–	–	Lahori, I (b), p. 307.
247	Siyam Singh Sisodiya	1000/500	"	Rajput	–	–	Lahori, I (b), p. 310.
248	Aitbar Rai	1000/400	"	Maratha zamindar (Deccani)	–	–	*S.D.S.*, p. 34.
249	Bhoj Raj	1000/500	"	Maratha	–	–	Lahori, I (b), pp. 220–1.

	Deccani			(Deccani)			
250	Nirmal Rai	1000/600	Indian	Maratha zamindar (Deccani)	–	–	*S.D.S.*, p. 45.
251	Agah Khan Khwajasara	1000/1000	–	–	–	–	Lahori, I (b), pp. 280 and 307; *Z.Kh.*, III, p. 117.
252	Qaladar Khan Husaini Chela	1000/600	–	–	–	1640–1 (D)	Lahori, I (b), p. 308; II, p. 734; *Z.Kh.*, III, pp. 89–90.
253	Yakdil Khan Khwajasara	1000/200	–	–	–	1639 (D)	Lahori, I (b), pp. 250 and 311; II, pp. 168 and 737.
254	Rai Kashidas	1000/250	Indian	–	–	–	Lahori, II, p. 48.
255	Rai Rayan Diyanat Rai	1000/150	"	–	–	–	Lahori, II, p. 92; *Z.Kh.*, III, pp. 81–2.

APPENDIX C: LIST OF MANSABDARS OF SHAHJAHAN DURING 1642–58 HOLDING RANKS OF 1000 ZAT AND ABOVE

Sl. No.	*Name and title*	*Highest rank during the period (zat/sawar)*	*Ethnic group*	*Sub-group: Rajput, Maratha, Afghan, zamindar, etc.*	*Father or other blood relative in service*	*Date of Death (D), Retirement (R), Flight (F), etc.*	*Authorities*
1	*2*	*3*	*4*	*5*	*6*	*7*	*8*
				MANSABDARS OF 5000 AND ABOVE			
1	Alimardan Khan Amir-ul-umara	7000/7000 5000 × 2h–3h	Irani	–	–	May 1657 (D)	Lahori, II, p. 718; Salih, III, pp. 243–5 (B) and 448; *Z.Kh.*, III, pp. 27–9; *M.U.*, II, pp. 795–807.
2	Islam Khan Mashhadi	7000/7000 5000 × 2h–3h	"	–	–	Nov. 1647 (D)	Lahori, II, pp. 679–80 and 718; Salih, III, p. 9 (L); *Z.Kh.*, II, pp. 25–7; *M.U.*, I, pp. 162–7.
3	Khan-e-Dauran Nusrat Jang	7000/7000 5000 × 2h–3h	Turani	–	Father	1645–6 (D)	Lahori, II, pp. 717 and 426–8; *Z.Kh.*, III, pp. 18–25; *M.U.*, I, pp. 749–58.
4	Said Khan Zafar Jang	7000/7000 5000 × 2h–3h	"	–	"	1652 (D)	Lahori, II, pp. 636 and 718; Salih, III, p. 449 (B), pp. 132–3 (L); *Z.Kh.*, II, p. 361; *M.U.*, II, pp. 429–36.
5	Allami Sadullah Khan	7000/7000 5000 × 2h–3h	Indian	–	–	Apr. 1656 (D)	Salih, III, pp. 100, 216–7 (L) and 449 (B); *Z.Kh.*, III, pp. 7–9; *M.U.*, II, p. 441–8.
6	Azam Khan Iradat Khan	6000/6000	Irani	–	Uncle	1649 (D)	Salih, III, pp. 69(L) and 450 (B); *Z.Kh.*, II, p. 200; *M.U.*, I, pp. 174–80.
7	Khan-e-Jahan Shaista Khan	6000/6000 5000 × 2h–3h	"	–	Father	–	Salih, III, pp. 227 (L) and 285 (B); *Z.Kh.*, II, pp. 188–90; *M.U.*, II, pp. 690–706.
8	Muazzam Khan Mir Jumla	6000/6000	"	Deccani	–	–	Salih, III, pp. 228 (L) and 450 (B); *M.U.*, III, pp. 530–55.

9	Abdullah Khan Firoze Jang	6000/6000	Turani	–	Brother	1644 (D)	Lahori, II, pp. 402 and 718; *Z.Kh.*, II, pp. 173–85; *M.U.*, II, 771, 777–89.
10	Khusrau s/o Nazr s/o Nazr Muhammad	6000/5000	”	–	–	–	Salih, III, p. 450 (B); *M.U.*, I, pp. 767–72.
11	Rustam Khan Muqarrab Khan Deccani	6000/6000 5000 × 2h–3h	”	Deccani	–	–	Salih, III, pp. 236 (L) and 449 (B); *Z.Kh.*, III, pp. 91–2; *M.U.*, II, pp. 270–6.
12	Khan-e-Jahan Barha Syed Abul Muzaffar	6000/6000 2h–3h	Indian	–	–	Dec. 1645 (D)	Lahori, II, pp. 272–3, 473–4 and 718; *Z.Kh.*, III, pp. 10–12; *M.U.*, I, pp. 758–66.
13	Syed Jalal Bukhari	6000/2000	”	–	–	1647–8 (D)	Lahori, II, pp. 627 and 718; *Z.Kh.*, III, pp. 29–31; *M.U.*, III, pp. 447–51.
14	Raja Jaswant Singh Rathor	6000/6000 5000 × 2h–3h	”	Rajput zamindar	Father	–	Salih, III, p. 449 (B); *M.U.*, III, pp. 599–604.
15	Aitqad Khan Mirza Shapur	5000/5000	Irani	–	”	1650 (D)	Lahori, II, pp. 332 and 719; Salih, III, pp. 106 (L) and 451 (B); *M.U.*, I, pp. 180–2.
16	Asalat Khan Mir Abdul Hadi	5000/4000	”	–	G. father	Apr. 1647 (D)	Lahori, II, pp. 577, 657 and 720; *Z.Kh.*, III, p. 32; *M.U.*, I, pp. 167–72; III, pp. 341–2.
17	Alahwardi Khan	5000/4000	”	–	Brother	1659 (D)	Salih, III, pp. 200, 323 (L) and 451 (B); *Z.Kh.*, II, pp. 205–8; *M.U.*, I, pp. 207–15.
18	Ja'far Khan	5000/5000 2500 × 2h–3h	”	–	Father	–	Salih, III, p. 451 (B); *Z.Kh.*, III, pp. 31–2; *M.U.*, I, pp. 531–5, II, p. 730.
19	Khalilullah Khan	5000/5000	”	–	Brother	–	Salih, III, p. 451 (B); *Z.Kh.*, III, p. 33; *M.U.*, I, pp. 775–82.

(contd.)

1	*2*	*3*	*4*	*5*	*6*	*7*	*8*
20	Mahabat Khan Mirza Lahrasp	5000/5000	Irani	–	Father	–	Salih, III, p. 451 (B); *Z.Kh.*, III, pp. 95–6; *M.U.*, III, pp. 590–5.
21	Makramat Khan Mullamurshid Shirazi	5000/5000 3000 × 2h–3h	"	–	–	Dec. 1649 (D)	Salih, III, 103–4 (L) and 451 (B); *M.U.*, III, pp. 460–2.
22	Qasim Khan s/o Hashim Khan	5000/5000 2h–3h	"	–	Father	–	Salih, III, pp. 281 (L) and 450 (B); *M.U.*, III, pp. 95–9.
23	Shahnawaz Khan Mirza Badiuzzaman Safavi	5000/5000 3000 × 2h–3h	"	–	"	–	Salih, III, p. 451 (B); *Z.Kh.*, II, pp. 216–17; *M.U.*, II, pp. 670–5.
24	Sipahdar Khan Muhammad Salih	5000/5000	"	–	Uncle	Jul. 1644 (D)	Lahori, II, pp. 378 and 720; *Z.Kh.*, II, pp. 261–2; *M.U.*, II, pp. 427–9.
25	Bahram Sultan s/o Nazr Muhammad	5000 zat	Turani	–	–	–	Salih, III, p. 451 (B); *M.U.*, I, pp. 431–44; II, pp. 802–12.
26	Mirza Isa Tarkhan	5000/5000 2h–3h	"	–	Father	1651 (D)	Lahori, II, pp. 377 and 719; Salih, III, p. 132 (L); *Z.Kh.*, II, pp. 210–12; *M.U.*, III, pp. 485–8.
27	Najabat Khan Mirza Shuja	5000/3000	"	–	"	–	Salih, III, p. 451 (B); *Z.Kh.*, II, pp. 239–42; *M.U.*, III, pp. 821–8.
28	Qulij Khan	5000/5000 4000 × 2h–3h	"	–	Brother	1653–4 (D)	Salih, III, pp. 100, 179 (L) and 451 (B); *Z.Kh.*, III, pp. 66–7; *M.U.*, III, pp. 92–5.
29	Safdar Khan Khwaja Qasim	5000/5000	"	–	–	1645 (D)	Lahori, II, pp. 223–4, 418 and 720; *Z.Kh.*, III, p. 40; *M.U.*, II, p. 733–6.
30	Bahadur Khan Rohila	5000/5000 2h–3h	Indian	Afghan	Father	1649 (D)	Lahori, II, pp. 554 and 719; Salih, III, pp. 99 (L) and 451 (B); *Z.Kh.*, III, pp. 48–9; *M.U.*, I, pp. 415–24.

31	Daulat Khan Maee	5000/5000	Indian	–	–	–	Lahori, II, pp. 679 and 720; *Z.Kh.*, II, p. 378; *M.U.*, II, pp. 24–30.
32	Wazir Khan Hakim Alimuddin	5000/5000 1000 × 2h–3h	”	–	–	Aug. 1641 (D)	Lahori, II, pp. 241 and 719; *Z.Kh.*, III, pp. 15–18; *M.U.*, III, pp. 933–6.
33	Raja Bithaldas Gaur	5000/5000 2500 × 2h–3h	”	Rajput zamindar	Father	1651 (D)	Salih, III, p. 451 (B) and 131–2 (L); *Z.Kh.*, III, p. 92; *M.U.*, II, pp. 250–6.
34	Rana Jagat Singh Sisodiya	5000/5000	”	”	”	1652 (D)	Lahori, II, p. 719; Salih, III, pp. 153 (L) and 451 (B); *M.U.*, II, pp. 200–6.
35	Raja Jai Singh Kachwaha	5000/5000 4000 × 2h–3h	”	”	”	–	Salih, III, p. 451 (B); *Z.Kh.*, III, pp. 117–18; *M.U.*, I, pp. 173–6; III, pp. 568–77.
36	Raja Rai Singh Sisodiya	5000/2000	”	”	”	–	Salih, III, p. 451 (B); *M.U.*, II, pp. 297–301.
37	Rana Raj Singh s/o Rana Jagat Singh Sisodiya	5000/5000	”	”	”	–	Salih, III, pp. 159 (L) and 451 (B); *M.U.*, II, pp. 206–8.
38	Maloji	5000/5000	”	Maratha zamindar	Brother	–	Lahori, II, p. 720; Salih, III, p. 451 (B); *Z.Kh.*, III, p. 139; *M.U.*, III, pp. 520–4.
			MANSABDARS OF 3000 TO 4500				
39	Aitqad Khan Bahmanyar	4000/1000	Irani	–	Father	–	Salih, III, p. 453 (B); *M.U.*, I, pp. 232–4.
40	Musvi Khan Sadr	4000/750	”	–	Near relative	Apr. 1644 (D)	Lahori, II, pp. 372 and 722; *Z.Kh.*, II, pp. 220–1; *M.U.*, III, pp. 441–2.
41	Salabat Khan Roshan Zamir	4000/2000	”	–	Father	Aug. 1644 (D)	Lahori, II, pp. 333, 380–4 and 721; *Z.Kh.*, III, pp. 33–4; *M.U.*, II, pp. 731–3.

(contd.)

1	*2*	*3*	*4*	*5*	*6*	*7*	*8*
42	Taqarrub Khan Hakim Daud	4000/1000	Irani	–	–	–	Salih, III, pp. 183 (L) and 453 (B); *M.U.*, I, pp. 490–3.
43	Abdul Rahman Balkhi, s/o Nazr Muhammad	4000/500	Turani	–	–	–	Salih, III, p. 123 (L); *M.U.*, II, pp. 809–12.
44	Fidai Khan Hidayatullah	4000/3000	"	–	Brother	1646 (D)	Lahori, II, pp. 511 and 721; *Z.Kh.*, II, pp. 314–15; *M.U.*, III, pp. 12–18.
45	Mahaldar Khan Charkas	4000/2000	"	Deccani	–	1641–2 (D)	Lahori, II, p. 721; *Z.Kh.*, III, pp. 134–5; *M.U.*, III, pp. 419–21.
46	Qabad Khan	4000/4000	"	–	–	–	Salih, III, p. 452 (B).
47	Sardar Khan Shahjahani	4000/3000	"	–	–	1652 (D)	Lahori, II, pp. 378 and 721; Salih, III, pp. 152–3 (L); *M.U.*, II, pp. 437–8.
48	Shah Beg Khan Uzbek	4000/3000	"	–	–	–	Lahori, II, p. 721; Salih, III, p. 453 (B); *Z.Kh.*, III, pp. 41–2; *M.U.*, II, pp. 665–7.
49	Khwaja Tayyab Juibari	4000/400	"	–	–	–	Lahori, II, pp. 627 and 722; *M.U.*, II, pp. 750–1.
50	Mubariz Khan Rohila	4000/4000	Indian	Afghan	–	1644 (D)	Lahori, II, pp. 94, 386 and 721; *Z.Kh.*, pp. 348–9; *M.U.*, III, pp. 442–4.
51	Nazr Bahadur Kheshgi	4000/4000	"	"	–	1652 (D)	Salih, III, pp. 100, 137 (L) and 452 (B); *Z.Kh.*, III, 49–50; *M.U.*, III, pp. 818–21.
52	Rashid Khan Ansari	4000/4000	"	"	–	Nov. 1648 (D)	Salih, III, pp. 66 (L) and 452 (B); *Z.Kh.*, II, pp. 223–9; *M.U.*, II, pp. 242–50.

53	Syed Shuja't Khan Barha	4000/4000 2h–3h	Indian	Afghan	G. father	Dec. 1642 (D)	Lahori, II, pp. 319 and 720; *Z.Kh.*, III, pp. 12–15; *M.U.*, II, pp. 423–6.
54	Amar Singh Rathor	4000/3000	"	Rajput zamindar	Father	1644 (D)	Lahori, II, pp. 293–4, 380–3 and 721; *M.U.*, II, pp. 220–3.
55	Pahar Singh Bundela	4000/3000 500 × 2h–3h	"	"	"	1655 (D)	Salih, III, p. 452 (B); *M.U.*, II, pp. 256–60.
56	Rup Singh Rathor g/s/o Raja Kishan Singh	4000/2000	"	"	G. father	–	Salih, III, p. 453 (B); *M.U.*, II, pp. 268–70.
57	Rao Satarsal Hara	4000/4000	"	"	"	1658 (D)	Lahori, II, p. 722; Salih, III, pp. 100, 296 (L) and 452 (B); *Z.Kh.*, III, pp. 133–4; *M.U.*, II, pp. 260–3.
58	Sarfaraz Khan Deccani	4000/3000	–	Deccani	–	–	Lahori, II, p. 721; Salih, III, p. 453 (B); *M.U.*, II, pp. 469–73.
59	Shuja't Khan Shadi Beg	3500/3000	Turani	–	Father	–	*Z.Kh.*, I, p. 196; *M.U.*, II, pp. 662–5.
60	Amir Khan Mir Abul Baqa	3000/2000	Irani	–	"	1647 (D)	Lahori, II, pp. 641 and 723; *Z.Kh.*, I, pp. 198–200; *M.U.*, I, pp. 172–4; III, pp. 74–82.
61	Aqil Khan Inayatullah	3000/1000	"	–	"	1649 (D)	Lahori, II, pp. 679 and 724; Salih, III, pp. 99 (L) and 456 (B); *Z.Kh.*, III, p. 106; *M.U.*, II, pp. 790–2.
62	Danishmand Khan Mulla Shafi Yazdi	3000/600	"	–	–	Nov. 1657	Salih, III, pp. 263–4 (L) and 456 (B); *M.U.*, II, pp. 30–2.
63	Fazil Khan Mulla Alaul Mulk Toni	3000/1000	"	–	–	–	Salih, III, pp. 268 (L) and 456 (B); *M.U.*, III, pp. 524–30.

(contd.)

1	*2*	*3*	*4*	*5*	*6*	*7*	*8*
64	Mirza Hasan Safavi	3000/3000	Irani	–	Father	1649 (D)	Salih, III, pp. 105 (L) and 454 (B); *M.U.*, III, pp. 477–9.
65	Himmat Khan Alahyar	3000/2000	"	–	"	Jan. 1650 (D)	Lahori, II, p. 723; Salih, III, pp. 106 (L) and 454 (B); *Z.Kh.*, II, pp. 351–2; *M.U.*, I, pp. 182–5.
66	Makramat Khan Mirza Murad Khan Safavi	3000/3000	"	–	"	–	Salih, III, p. 129 (L) and 454 (B); *M.U.*, III, pp. 583–8.
67	Miraz Khan Manochahr	3000/3000	"	–	"	–	Salih, III, pp. 195 (L) and 454 (B); *Z.Kh.*, II, pp. 318–19; *M.U.*, III, pp. 586–9.
68	Muhammad Amin Khan s/o Muazzam Khan Mir Jumla	3000/1500	"	–	"	–	Salih, III, pp. 264 (L) and 455 (B); *M.U.*, III, pp. 532 and 613–20.
69	Mughal Khan s/o Zain Khan Koka	3000/2000	"	–	"	–	Lahori, II, pp. 641 and 723; Salih, III, p. 455 (B); *Z.Kh.*, II, pp. 324–5; *M.U.*, III, pp. 490–2.
70	Mirza Nauzar Safavi	3000/3000	"	–	"	1652–3 (D)	Salih, III, p. 454 (B); *M.U.*, III, pp. 555–7.
71	Qazalbash Khan Afshar	3000/3000 500 × 2h–3h	"	Deccani	–	1648 (D)	Lahori, II, pp. 416–17 and 722; Salih, III, pp. 66 (L) and 454 (B); *Z.Kh.*, III, pp. 68–9; *M.U.*, III, pp. 85–6.
72	Sa'adat Khan	3000/3000 800 × 2h–3h	"	–	G. father	–	Salih, III, p. 453 (B); *M.U.*, II, pp. 461–3.
73	Sazawar Khan Mashhadi	3000/12000	"	–	Father	1655–6 (D)	Salih, III, p. 245 (B); *Z.Kh.*, III, pp. 97–8; *M.U.*, II, pp. 438–40.

74	Siyadat Khan b/o Islam Khan Mashhadi	3000/1500	Irani	–	Brother	–	Salih, III, pp. 111 (L) and 455 (B); *Z.Kh.*, III, pp. 127–8.
75	Mirza Sultan Safavi g/s/o Mirza Muzaffar Safavi	3000/1500	”	–	”	–	Salih, III, pp. 233 (L) and 455 (B); *M.U.*, III, pp. 581–3.
76	Zafar Khan	3000/1500	”	–	Father	–	Salih, III, p. 455 (B); *Z.Kh.*, II, pp. 290–1; *M.U.*, II, pp. 756–63.
77	Zulfiqar Khan Khanlar	3000/3000 2h–3h	”	–	–	–	Salih, III, p. 453 (B); *M.U.*, II, pp. 85–8.
78	Zulqadr Khan Turkman	3000/2000 500 × 2h–3h	”	–	–	Mar. 1648	Lahori, II pp. 680 and 723; Salih, III, p. 22 (L); *M.U.*, II, pp. 84–5.
79	Azizullah Khan	3000/2500	Turani	–	Father	1644 (D)	Lahori, II, p. 379 and 722; *M.U.*, II, pp. 789–90.
80	Ghairat Khan Khwaja Kamgar	3000/2000	”	–	Uncle	Mar. 1641 (D)	Lahori, II, pp. 225 and 723; *Z.Kh.*, III, p. 131; *M.U.*, II, pp. 863–5.
81	Iftikhar Khan Khwaja Abul Baqa n/o Abdullah Khan	3000/3000 2h–3h	”	–	”	1657–8 (D)	Salih, III, p. 453 (B); *M.U.*, I, pp. 200–3.
82	Khusrau Beg	3000/150	”	–	–	1641–2 (D)	Lahori, II, p. 275; *Z.Kh.*, III, p. 120; *Apparatus*, p. S-2812.
83	Malik Khan s/o Said Khan	3000/2500	”	–	Father	–	Salih, III, p. 454 (B).
84	Mukhlis Khan Abdullah Beg s/o Mansur Haji Balkhi	3000/2000	”	–	”	–	Salih, III, p. 454 (B); *M.U.*, III, pp. 968–71.

(contd.)

1	*2*	*3*	*4*	*5*	*6*	*7*	*8*
85	Nasiri Khan Syed Mahmud, s/o Khan-e-Dauran Nusrat Jang	3000/2000	Irani	–	Father	–	Salih, III, p. 454 (B); *M.U.*, I, pp. 758 and 782–5.
86	Shah Quli Khan Waqqas Haji	3000/2000	Turani	–	–	1641 (D)	Lahori, II, pp. 225 and 724; *Z.Kh.*, III, p. 116; *M.U.*, II, pp. 658–60.
87	Tahir Khan Tahir Shaikh	3000/1500	"	–	–	–	Salih, III, pp. 180–1(L) and 455 (B); *M.U.*, II, pp. 751–4.
88	Ahmad Khan Niyazi	3000/3000	Indian	Afghan	Father	1651 (D)	Salih, III, pp. 125–6 (L) and 454 (B); *Z.Kh.*, II, pp. 257–60; *M.U.*, I, pp. 185–8.
89	Diler Khan b/o Bahadur Khan Rohila	3000/3000	"	"	Brother	–	Salih, III, p. 276 (L); *M.U.*, II, pp. 42–56.
90	Ghazi s/o Randaulah	3000/2000	"	"	–	–	Salih, III, p. 262 (B); *Apparatus*, p. S-7249.
91	Hayat Khidmatparast	3000/2000	"	"	–	July 1657 (D)	Salih, III, pp. 157, 245 (L) and 455 (B); *M.U.*, I, pp. 583–4.
92	Purdil Khan	3000/3000	"	"	Father	–	Salih, III, p. 454 (B); *Z.Kh.*, III, p. 131; *M.U.*, I, pp. 424–7.
93	Ikhlas Khan Shaikh Farid	3000/2000	"	–	"	–	Salih, III, p. 455 (B); *Z.Kh.*, II, pp. 338–9; *M.U.*, I, pp. 220–2; III, pp. 66–8.
94	Ikhlas Khan Shaikh Alahdiya	3000/2500	"	–	"	–	Salih, III, pp. 178 (L) and 454 (B); *Z.Kh.*, II, pp. 351–2; *M.U.*, I, pp. 198–9.

95	Kartalab Khan Baswant Rao Deccani	3000/2000 2h–3h	Indian	Deccani	–	–	Salih, III, p. 454 (B); *Z.Kh.*, III, pp. 142–3; *M.U.*, III, pp. 153–4.
96	Murtaza Khan Syed Nizam	3000/2000	”	–	Father	1650 (R)	Lahori, II, p. 724; Salih, III, pp. 115 (L) and 454 (B); *Z.Kh.*, III, pp. 242–3; *M.U.*, III, pp. 479–81.
97	Anup Singh s/o Amar Singh	3000/2000	”	Rajput zamindar	–	–	Salih, III, p. 228 (L).
98	Anurodh Gaur	3000/3000 2h–3h	”	”	Father	–	Salih, III, p. 453 (B); *M.U.*, II, pp. 276–7.
99	Bairamdev Sisodiya s/o Suraj Mal Sisodiya	3000/1000	”	”	”	–	Salih, III, pp. 236 (L) and 456 (B); *M.U.*, II, pp. 452–4.
100	Raja Jagat Singh	3000/2000	”	”	”	1646 (D)	Lahori, II, pp. 481 and 724; *Z.Kh.*, III, pp. 118–23; *M.U.*, II, pp. 238–41.
101	Rao Karan Bhurtiya	3000/2000	”	”	”	–	Salih, III, pp. 214–15 (L) and 455 (B); *Z.Kh.*, II, pp. 398–9; *M.U.*, II, pp. 287–9.
102	Madho Singh Hara	3000/3000	”	”	”	1647–8 (D)	Salih, III, p. 454 (B); *M.U.*, III, pp. 453–6.
103	Maheshdas Rathor s/o Dalpat	3000/2500	”	”	”	1647 (D)	Lahori, II, pp. 554, 635 and 723; *M.U.*, III, pp. 445–7.
104	Mukand Singh Hara s/o Madho Singh Hara	3000/2000	”	Rajput zamindar	Father	1657–8 (D)	Salih, III, pp. 283–4 (L) and 455 (B); *M.U.*, III, pp. 509–10.

(contd.)

1	2	3	4	5	6	7	8
105	Raj Rup s/o Raja Jagat Singh	3000/2500	Indian	Rajput zamindar	Father	–	Salih, III, p. 454 (B); *M.U.*, II, pp. 277–81.
106	Ram Singh s/o Raja Jai Singh Kachwaha	3000/2000	”	”	”	–	Salih, III, pp. 213 (L) and 455 (B); *M.U.*, II, pp. 301–3.
107	Ram Singh Rathor	3000/1500	”	”	”	1658 (D)	Salih, III, p. 455 (B); *M.U.*, II, pp. 266–7.
108	Dattaji	3000/1000	”	Maratha zamindar	”	–	Lahori, II, p. 724; Salih, III, p. 456 (B); *M.U.*, I, pp. 520–3.
109	Jadun Rai Tilang Rai	3000/1500	”	”	G. father	–	Lahori, II, p. 724; Salih, III, p. 455 (B); *M.U.*, I, pp. 520–3.
110	Mankuji Deccani	3000/1500	”	Maratha (Deccani)	–	–	Lahori, II, p. 724; Salih, III, p. 455 (B).
111	Parsoji b/o Maloji	3000/2000	”	Maratha zamindar	Brother	–	Lahori, II, p. 724; Salih, III, p. 455 (B); *Z.Kh.*, III, p. 139; *M.U.*, III, pp. 520–4.
112	Rawat Rai Deccani	3000/1500	”	Maratha zamindar (Deccani)	–	–	Lahori, II, p. 724.
113	Udaji Ram s/o Udaji Ram	3000/2000	”	Maratha zamindar	Father	–	Lahori, II, p. 724; Salih, III, p. 450 (B); *S.D.S.*, p. 151; *Z.Kh.*, III, pp. 140–1; *M.U.*, I, p. 144.
114	Bahadur Khan Baqi Beg	3000/2000	–	–	–	–	Salih, III, pp. 442 (L) and 454 (B); *M.U.*, I, pp. 444–7.

115	Firoze Khan Khwajasara	3000/1500	–	–	–	1648–9 (D)	Lahori, II, pp. 398–9 and 724; *M.U.*, III, pp. 21–2; Salih, III, p. 455 (B).
116	Habsh Khan Syedi Miftah	3000/1500	–	Deccani	–	–	Lahori, II, p. 724; *Z.Kh.*, III, pp. 112–13; *M.U.*, I, pp. 579–83.
117	Hamid Khan son-in-law of Malik Ambar	3000/2000	–	"	–	–	Salih, III, p. 455 (B).
118	Hasan s/o Fakhrul Mulk	3000/2000	–	–	Father	–	Salih, III, p. 455 (B).
119	Hasan Khan Deccani	3000/1500 2h–3h	–	Deccani	–	–	Salih, III, p. 455 (B).
				MANSABDARS OF 1000 TO 2700			
120	Abdullah Beg s/o Alimardan Khan	2500/1500	Irani	–	Father	–	Salih, III, p. 243 (L); *M.U.*, II, p. 807; III, p. 155.
121	Ahmad Beg Khan	2500/1500	"	–	G. father	–	Salih, III, p. 456 (B); *M.U.*, I, pp. 136–9 and 194–5.
122	Fakhir Khan	2500/1000	"	–	Father	–	Salih, III, p. 457 (B); *Z.Kh.*, II, pp. 254–5; *M.U.*, III, pp. 26–8.
123	Hisamuddin Khan s/o Nizamuddin Ali	2500/1500	"	–	G. father	–	Salih, III, p. 456 (B); *Z.Kh.*, III, pp. 34–5; *M.U.*, I, pp. 584–7.
124	Ibrahim Khan Ibrahim Beg s/o Alimardan Khan	2500/1000	"	–	Father	–	Salih, III, p. 457 (B); *M.U.*, I, pp. 225–30; II, p. 807.
125	Iltifat Khan Mirza Murad Safavi	2500/1000	"	–	"	1642–3 (R)	Lahori, II, pp. 317 and 725; *M.U.*, III, p. 583.

(contd.)

1	2	3	4	5	6	7	8
126	Lashkar Khan s/o Zabardast Khan	2500/1500	Irani	–	Father	–	Salih, III, p. 456 (B); *M.U.*, III, pp. 168–71.
127	Mirak Shaikh Harvi n/o Qazi Aslam	2500/200	"	–	Uncle	–	Salih, III, p. 457 (B); *M.U.*, III, pp. 89–92 and 518–19.
128	Multafit Khan	2500/1500	"	–	Father	–	Salih, III, p. 456 (B); *Z.Kh.*, III, pp. 92–3; *M.U.*, III, pp. 500–3.
129	Namdar Khan s/o Jafar Khan	2500/1500	"	–	"	–	Salih, III, pp. 218 (L) and 456 (B); *M.U.*, III, pp. 830–3.
130	Nawazish Khan Mirza Abdul Kafi	2500/600	"	–	Brother	–	Salih, III, p. 457 (B); *M.U.*, III, pp. 828–30.
131	Rizvi Khan Mashhadi	2500/500	"	–	–	–	Salih, III, p. 457 (B); *Z.Kh.*, I, p. 185.
132	Safshikan Khan s/o Mirza Lashkari	2500/2000	"	–	Father	1646–7 (D)	Lahori, II, p. 729; *Z.Kh.*, II, pp. 305–6; *M.U.*, II, pp. 736–8.
133	Abdullah Khan s/o Said Khan	2500/2000	Turani	–	Father	–	Salih, III, pp. 268–9 (L); *M.U.*, II, pp. 807–8.
134	Abdul Rahim Beg Uzbek	2500/1000	"	–	–	–	Salih, III, p. 457 (B); *M.U.*, II, pp. 793–4.
135	Alah Quli Khan Uzbek	2500/1500	"	–	–	–	Salih, III, p. 457 (B); *M.U.*, I, pp. 189–91.
136	Iwaz Khan Qaqshal	2500/2000	"	–	–	1641–2 (D)	Lahori, II, p. 725; *M.U.*, II, pp. 776–7.
137	Muhammad Badi s/o Khusrau Sultan	2500/600	"	–	Father	–	Salih, III, p. 457 (B); *M.U.*, I, pp. 770–2; III, pp. 636–7.

138	Qabad Khan Mir Akhur	2500/1000	Turani	–	–	–	Salih, III, pp. 183 (L) and 456 (B); *M.U.*, III, pp. 99–102.
139	Tarbiyat Khan Fakhruddin Ahmad	2500/1500	"	–	–	1643–4 (D)	Lahori, II, p. 725; *Z.Kh.*, III, pp. 43–5; *M.U.*, I, pp. 486–90.
140	Dilawar Khan Deccani	2500/1500	Indian	Afghan (Deccani)	–	–	Lahori, II, p. 725; Salih, III, p. 457 (B).
141	Hadidad Khan	2500/2500	"	Afghan	Brother	1656–7 (D)	Salih, III, p. 456 (B); *Z.Kh.*, II, pp. 229–30; *M.U.*, III, pp. 941–3.
142	Shamsher Khan Tarin	2500/2500	"	"	–	–	Salih, III, pp. 129–30 (L) and 456 (B); *M.U.*, II, pp. 677–9.
143	Syed Hidayatullah s/o Syed Ahmad Qadri	2500/200	"	–	Father	–	Salih, III, pp. 145 (L) and 457 (B); *M.U.*, II, pp. 456–7.
144	Shaikh Miran	2500/200	"	–	–	–	Salih, III, p. 457 (B); *Apparatus*, p. S-7481.
145	Rizvi Khan Syed Ali s/o Syed Jalal Bukhari	2500/500	"	–	Father	–	Salih, III, pp. 201 (L) and 457 (B); *M.U.*, II, pp. 307–9.
146	Sa'adat Khan	2500/800	"	–	–	–	Salih, III, p. 244 (L); *Apparatus*, p. S-8105.
147	Sabal Singh Sisodiya g/s/o Rana Amar Singh	2500/1000	"	Rajput	G. father zamindar	–	Salih, III, p. 457 (b); *M.U.*, II, pp. 468–9.
148	Jauhar Khan Habshi	2500/2000	–	Deccani	–	–	Salih, III, p. 456 (B); *Z.Kh.*, III, p. 144.
149	Sarawar Khan Habshi	2500/1000	–	"	–	1644–5 (D)	Lahori, II, p. 725; *Z.Kh.*, III, pp. 143–4.

(contd.)

1	2	3	4	5	6	7	8
150	Miraz Abu Said g/s/o Aitmaduddaulah	2000/1000	Irani	–	G. father	1652–3 (R)	Salih, III, p. 460 (B); *M.U.*, III, pp. 513–16.
151	Zahid Khan	2000/1500	"	–	–	–	Lahori, II, pp. 399 and 726; *Z.Kh.*, III, pp. 125–6; *M.U.*, II, pp. 370–1.
152	Aitmad Khan Muhammad Ashraf s/o Islam Khan Mashhadi	2000/500	"	–	Father	–	Salih, III, p. 447 (L); *M.U.*, I, pp. 272–4.
153	Asad Khan Muhammad Ibrahim s/o Zulfiqar Khan Qaramanlu	2000/800	"	–	"	–	Salih, III, p. 460 (B); *M.U.*, I, pp. 310–21.
154	Diyanat Khan Hakim Jamala Kashi	2000/700	"	–	–	–	Lahori, II, pp. 417 and 728; *Z.Kh.*, III, pp. 36–7; *M.U.*, II, pp. 37–8.
155	Faizullah Khan s/o Zahid Khan Koka	2000/1000	"	–	Father	–	Salih, III, p. 459 (B); *M.U.*, III, pp. 28–30.
156	Haqiqat Khan Ishaq Beg Yazdi	2000/300	"	–	–	1655 (R)	Lahori, II, pp. 627 and 728; Salih, III, p. 447 (L); *M.U.*, I, pp. 590–1.
157	Iradat Khan Mir Ishaq, s/o Azam Khan	2000/2000	"	–	Father	–	Salih, III, p. 458 (B); *M.U.*, I, pp. 203–6.
158	Iraj Khan s/o Qazalbash Khan Afshar	2000/1500	"	–	"	–	Salih, III, p. 458 (B); *Z.Kh.*, III, pp. 69–70; *M.U.*, I, pp. 268–72; pp. 86–7.

159	Izzat Khan Abdul Razzaq Gilani	2000/2000 500 × 2h–3h	Irani	–	–	–	Salih, III, p. 458 (B); *M.U.*, II, p. 475.
160	Khwaja Jahan Khawafi	2000/600	”	–	–	1643–4 (D)	Lahori, II, p. 728; *Z.Kh.*, III, pp. 128–9; *M.U.*, I, pp. 748–9.
161	Jansipar Khan Jamali	2000/1500	”	–	Uncle	Mar. 1645 (D)	Lahori, II, pp. 412 and 726; *M.U.*, I, p. 530; III, pp. 812–17.
162	Mirza Muhammad s/o Mirza Badi'- Mashhadi	2000/1000	”	–	–	–	*Z.Kh.*, III, pp. 100–1; *M.U.*, I, pp. 222–5.
163	Muhammad Zaman Tehrani	2000/2000	”	–	–	–	Salih, III, p. 458 (B); *M.U.*, III, pp. 452–3.
164	Muftakhir Khan Mir Khalil	2000/1000	”	–	Father	–	Salih, III, p. 172 (L) and 459 (B); *Z.Kh.*, III, pp. 93–5; *M.U.*, I, pp. 785–92.
165	Mu'tamad Khan Muhammad Salih Khawafi	2000/2000	”	–	–	–	Salih, III, p. 460 (B); *M.U.*, III, pp. 510–11.
166	Mirza Safshikan Safavi	2000/1000	”	–	Father	–	Lahori, II, pp. 584 and 727; *M.U.*, III, pp. 477–9.
167	Mir Shams	2000/2000	”	–	–	1657 (D)	Salih, III, pp. 245(L) and 458 (B); *Z.Kh.*, II, p. 293; *M.U.*, III, p. 492.
168	Zabardast Khan	2000/1000	”	–	–	Oct. 1649 (D)	Lahori, II, pp. 405–6 and 727; Salih, III, p. 103 (L); *M.U.*, II, p. 372.
169	Abdul Hadi s/o Safdar Khan	2000/1000	Turani	–	Father	1656 (D)	Salih, III, pp. 229 (L) and 459 (B); *Z.Kh.*, III, p. 40; *M.U.*, I, pp. 772–3.

(contd.)

1	*2*	*3*	*4*	*5*	*6*	*7*	*8*
170	Mirza Abul Ma'ali s/o Mirza Wali	2000/1400	Turani	–	Father	–	Salih, III, p. 459 (B); *Z.Kh.*, p. 256; *M.U.*, III, pp. 456–60 and 557–60.
171	Baqi Khan Qalmaq	2000/2000	"	–	–	1653–4 (D)	Lahori, II, p. 726; Salih, III, p. 458; *M.U.*, I, pp. 427–9.
172	Khwaja Barkhurdar	2000/2000	"	–	Near relatives	–	Salih, III, pp. 192 (L) and 458 (B); *Z.Kh.*, II, p. 341; *M.U.*, I, pp. 206–7.
173	Inayatullah	2000/1500	"	–	Father	–	Salih, III, p. 459 (B); *M.U.*, III, pp. 487–8.
174	Khushhal Beg Kashghari	2000/800	"	–	–	–	Salih, III, p. 460 (B); *M.U.*, I, pp. 773–4.
175	Mansur Haji Balkhi	2000/1000	"	–	–	1647–8 (D)	Lahori, II, pp. 555 and 727; *M.U.*, III, pp. 968–9.
176	Muhammad Ali Khan son-in-law of Qulij Khan	2000/1000	"	–	Near relatives	1656–7 (D)	Salih, III, p. 460 (B); *M.U.*, III, pp. 488–9.
177	Muhammad Salih Tarkhan s/o Isa Tarkhan	2000/2000	"	–	Father	–	Salih, III, p. 458 (B); *M.U.*, III, pp. 560–2.
178	Mubariz Khan Mir Gul Badakhshi	2000/1000	"	–	–	–	Salih, III, p. 230 (L); *M.U.*, III, pp. 595–7.
179	Qabchaq Khan Aman Beg	2000/1000	"	–	–	1648 (left service)	Lahori, II, pp. 680 and 727; *M.U.*, III, pp. 82–5.

180	Qazzaq Khan Beqi Beg	2000/2000	Turani	–	Brother	1650–1 (D)	Lahori, II, pp. 309 and 726; Salih, III, p. 458 (B); *Z.Kh.*, II, pp. 346–8; *M.U.*, III, pp. 88–9.
181	Tarbiyat Khan Shafi'ullah Barlas	2000/1500	”	–	–	–	Salih, III, p. 458 (B); *M.U.*, I, pp. 493–8.
182	Uzbek Khan Nazr Bahadur	2000/2000 500 × 2h–3h	”	–	–	1655–6 (D)	Lahori, II, pp. 417 and 726; *Z.Kh.*, III, pp. 90–1; *M.U.*, I, pp. 195–8.
183	Mirza Wali	2000/1000	”	–	Father	1648–9 (D)	Lahori, II, p. 727; *Z.Kh.*, II, p. 256; *M.U.*, III, pp. 456–60.
184	Jalal Kakar	2000/1500	Indian	Afghan	”	–	Salih, III, p. 459 (B); *Z.Kh.*, II, pp. 335–6; *M.U.*, I, pp. 530–1.
185	Kakar Khan	2000/1000	”	”	–	–	Salih, III, p. 459 (B); *M.U.*, III, pp. 152–3.
186	Mubarak Khan Niyazi	2000/2000	”	”	Uncle	–	Salih, III, p. 458 (B); *Z.Kh.*, II, p. 261; *M.U.*, III, pp. 512–13.
187	Sher Khan Tarin	2000/1000	”	Afghan zamindar	–	1644–5 (D)	Lahori, II, pp. 332 and 728; *Z.Kh.*, III, pp. 102–6; *M.U.*, II, pp. 654–8.
188	Abdul Rahman s/o Rihan Sholapuri	2000/1000	”	Deccani	–	–	Salih, III, p. 259 (L).
189	Bakhtiyar Khan Deccani	2000/1000	”	”	–	–	Lahori, II, p. 728; Salih, III, p. 460 (B); *M.U.*, I, pp. 774–5.
190	Syed Firoze Khan Barha, n/o Syed Khan-e-Jahan	2000/1000	”	–	Uncle	–	Lahori, II, pp. 679 and 727; Salih, III, p. 459 (B); *M.U.*, II, pp. 473–5.

(contd.)

1	2	3	4	5	6	7	8
191	Himmat Khan s/o Syed Shuja'at Khan Barha	2000/1000	Indian	–	Father	–	Salih, III, p. 242 (L); *M.U.*, II, p. 427.
192	Ihtimam Khan	2000/1500	"	–	–	1647–8 (D)	Lahori, II, p. 726; *Z.Kh.*, III, pp. 89–90; *M.U.*, I, pp. 160–2.
193	Ikram Khan Fathpuri	2000/1000	"	–	Father	–	Lahori, II, p. 727; *Z.Kh.*, III, pp. 274–5.
194	Sadat Khan Bhakkari Deccani	2000/1500	"	–	–	–	Lahori, II, 726; Salih, III, p. 458 (B); *Z.Kh.*, II, pp. 353–4.
195	Syed Salabat Khan s/o Syed Bayazid Barha	2000/1500	"	–	Father	–	Salih, III, pp. 199 (L) and 459 (B); *M.U.*, II, pp. 457–9.
196	Sher Khan Syed Shahab Barha	2000/800	"	–	"	–	Salih, III, p. 460 (B); *M.U.*, II, pp. 667–8.
197	Syed Umar	2000/1000	"	Deccani	–	–	Lahori, II, p. 728; Salih, III, p. 459 (B).
198	Amar Singh Chandrawat g/s/o Rao Chanda	2000/1000	"	Rajput zamindar	G. father	–	Salih, III, p. 460 (B); *M.U.*, II, pp. 145–8.
199	Arjun Gaur s/o Raja Bithaldas	2000/1500	"	"	Father	1658 (D)	Salih, III, pp. 283–4 (L) and 458 (B); *M.U.*, II, pp. 254–5.
200	Raja Debi Singh Bundela	2000/2000 500 × 2h–3h	"	"	"	–	Salih, III, p. 457 (B); *Z.Kh.*, II, pp. 370–1; *M.U.*, II, pp. 295–7.
201	Girdhardas Gaur b/o Raja Bithaldas	2000/2000	"	"	Brother	–	Salih, III, pp. 234 (L) and 458 (B); *M.U.*, II, pp. 255–6.

202	Jai Ram Badgujar	2000/1500	Indian	Rajput zamindar	Father	1647–8 (D)	Lahori, II, pp. 608 and 727; *M.U.*, II, pp. 241–2.
203	Pirthi Raj Rathor	2000/2000	"	Rajput	–	1656–7 (D)	Salih, III, p. 458 (B); *M.U.*, I, pp. 429–31.
204	Ratan s/o Maheshdas Rathor	2000/2000	"	Rajput zamindar	Father	1658 (D)	Salih, III, pp. 259 (L) and 458 (B); *M.U.*, III, pp. 446–7.
205	Rao Rup Singh Chandrawat s/o Rao Rup Mukand	2000/1200	"	"	G. father	–	Salih, III, pp. 100 (L) and 459 (B); *M.U.*, II, pp. 142–8.
206	Sabal Singh Rathor	2000/1500	"	"	Father	1647–8	Lahori, II, p. 727; *Z.Kh.*, II, pp. 297–300.
207	Siva Ram Gaur	2000/1500	"	"	Uncle	1658 (D)	Salih, III, pp. 296 (L) and 458; *M.U.*, II, pp. 263–5.
208	Sujan Singh s/o Surajmal Sisodiya	2000/800	"	"	Cousin	1658 (D)	Salih, III, p. 460 (B); *M.U.*, II, pp. 452–3.
209	Sujan Singh s/o Pahar Singh Bundela	2000/2000 500 × 2h–3h	"	"	Father	–	Salih, III, p. 457 (B); *M.U.*, II, pp. 291–3.
210.	Bithuji	2000/1000	"	Maratha zamindar	Uncle	–	Lahori, II, p. 728; Salih, III, p. 460 (B); *M.U.*, I, p. 522.
211	Habaji	2000/800	"	Maratha (Deccani)	–	–	Lahori, II, p. 728; Salih, III, p. 460 (B).
212	Rabi Rai Deccani	2000/1000	"	Maratha zamindar (Deccani)	–	–	Lahori, II, p. 728.

(contd.)

1	*2*	*3*	*4*	*5*	*6*	*7*	*8*
213	Arab Khan	2000/2000 500 × 2h–3h	–	–	–	1653–4 (D)	Lahori, II, pp. 417 and 726; *Z.Kh.*, III, pp. 89–90; *M.U.*, II, pp. 794–5.
214	Atish Khan Habshi	2000/1000	–	Deccani	–	1651–2 (D)	Salih, III, p. 459 (B); *Z.Kh.*, III, p. 143, *M.U.*, I, pp. 188–9.
215	Dilawar Khan Habshi	2000/1500	–	”	–	–	Salih, III, p. 459 (B); *Z.Kh.*, III, pp. 141–2.
216	Farhan Khan Deccani	2000/1000 200 × 2h–3h	–	”	–	–	*S.D.S*, pp. 158–9; Lahori, II, p. 728.
217	Syed Hasan Masaid	2000/1000	–	–	–	–	Salih, III, p. 459 (B).
218	Mahdi Quli Khan	2000/600	–	–	–	–	Salih, III, p. 460(B).
219	Todarmal b/o Biharimal	2000/2000 500 × 2h–3h	Indian	–	Brother	–	Salih, III, p. 457 (B); *Z.Kh.*, II, pp. 408–9; *M.U.*, II, pp. 286–7.
220	Aitmad Khan Aqa-Afzal	1500/600	Irani	–	–	1647–8 (D)	Lahori, II, p. 731; *Z.Kh.*, II, p. 276; *M.U.*, III, pp. 18–21.
221	Bahram s/o Sadiq Khan	1500/300	”	–	Father	–	Salih, III, p. 464 (B); *M.U.*, I, pp. 454–5; II, p. 731.
222	Fidai Khan Muzaffar Hssain s/o Mir Abul Ma'ali Khawafi	1500/800	”	–	Brother	–	Salih, III, p. 244 (L); *M.U.*, I, pp. 247–52.
223	Inayat Khan s/o Zafar Khan	1500/200	”	–	Father	–	Salih, III, p. 464 (B); *M.U.*, II, pp. 762–3.

224	Jafar s/o Alahwardi Khan	1500/800	Indian	–	Father	–	Salih, III, p. 183 (L); *Z.Kh.*, III, p. 129; *M.U.*, I, pp. 229–32.
225	Mir Jafar	1500/500	"	–	–	–	Salih, III, p. 463 (B); *M.U.*, III, pp. 109–15.
226	Mir Lutfullah Shirazi	1500/1000	"	–	–	–	Salih, III, p. 461 (B).
227	Hakim Maumina	1500/200	Irani	–	–	–	Salih, III, p. 464 (B); Lahori, I (b), p. 349.
228	Marhamat Khan Abdul Rahman	1500/400	"	–	Father	1647–8 (D)	Lahori, II, pp. 594 and 732; *M.U.*, II, pp. 730–1.
229	Mir Khan Mir Miron s/o Khalilullah Khan	1500/500	"	–	"	–	Salih, III, p. 463 (B); *M.U.*, I, pp. 277–8.
230	Muhammad Hadi Mir Rafi' (Sadr of Iran)	1500/500	"	–	–	–	Salih, III, p. 463 (B).
231	Muhammad Husain	1500/1500 800 × 2h–3h	"	–	–		Lahori, II, p. 624.
232	Murshid Quli Khan Khurasani	1500/1000	"	–	–	–	Salih, III, p. 462 (B); *M.U.*, III, pp. 493–500.
233	Rahmat Khan Hakim Ziauddin	1500/400	"	–	–	–	Salih, III, p. 463 (B); *M.U.*, II, pp. 283–4.
234	Rashid Khan Rahmanyar	1500/100	"	–	Brother	–	Salih, III, p. 462(B); *M.U.*, I, pp. 184–5.
235	Mir Samsamud-daulah, s/o Murtaza Khan Mir Hisamuddin Anju	1500/500	"	–	Father	–	Salih, III, pp. 192 (L) and 463 (B); *M.U.*, III, pp. 382–4.

(contd.)

1	*2*	*3*	*4*	*5*	*6*	*7*	*8*
236	Mir Shamsuddin s/o Mukhtar Khan Sabzwari	1500/800	Irani	–	Father	–	Salih, III, pp. 231 (L) and 462 (B); *Z.Kh.*, III, p. 82; M.U, III, pp. 620–3.
237	Sultanyar s/o Himmat Khan Alahyar	1500/1500	"	–	"	–	Salih, III, p. 461 (B); *M.U.*, I, pp. 182–5.
238	Yahya	1500/300	"	–	"	–	Salih, III, p. 464 (B); *M.U.*, II, pp. 419–21.
239	Zulfiqar Khan Turkman	1500/1200	"	–	Near relative	–	Lahori, II, p. 228; *Z.Kh.*, II, p. 411.
240	Mir Abdul Karim	1500/200	Turani	–	–	–	Salih, III, p. 464 (B); Lahori, II, p. 732.
241	Abdullah Beg	1500/500	"	–	–	–	Salih, III, p. 101 (L).
242	Abdul Rasul s/o Abdullah Khan Feroze Jang	1500/600	"	–	Father	–	Salih, III, p. 463 (B); M.U, II, pp. 777–89.
243	Khwaja Abdul Wahab Dehbedi	1500/200	"	–	–	–	Lahori, II, p. 609; Salih, III, p. 464.
244	Alif Khan Aman Beg	1500/1500	"	–	Father	1653 (D)	Lahori, II, pp. 417 and 729; Salih, III, p. 461 (B); *Z.Kh.*, III, pp. 89–90; *M.U.*, I, pp. 191–4.
245	Asfandiyar	1500/1500	"	–	"	1643–4 (D)	Lahori, II, pp. 302 and 729; *Z.Kh.*, II, pp. 362–3; *M.U.*, I, p. 568.
246	Dildost s/o Sarfaraz Khan Chaghta	1500/1000	"	–	"	–	Salih, III, p. 462 (B); *M.U.*, II, p. 422.

247	Fathullah s/o Said Khan, Zafar Jang	1500/800	Turani	–	Father	–	Salih, III, p. 462 (B).
248	Hasan Quli Aghar	1500/800	"	–	–	1651–2 (D)	Salih, III, p. 462 (B); *M.U.*, I, pp. 274–5.
249	Iftikhar Khan Abul Baqa s/o Ahmed Beg Khan	1500/1000	"	–	Father	1645–6 (D)	Lahori, II, p. 730; *Z.Kh.*, II, p. 361; *M.U.*, I, p. 127.
250	Khanazad Khan	1500/1200	"	–	"	1647 (D)	Lahori, II, pp. 379, 690–2 and 729; *M.U.*, II, pp. 428–37.
251	Khan-e-Dauran Syed Muhammad s/o Khan-e-Dauran Nusrat Jang	1500/900	"	–	"	–	Salih, III, p. 101 (L); *M.U.*, I, p. 758.
252	Khanjar Khan Mirza Muhammad	1500/1500	"	–	Near relaive	–	Salih, III, p. 461 (B); *M.U.*, III, pp. 94–5.
253	Lutfullah	1500/1000	"	–	Father	1647 (D)	Lahori, II, pp. 627, 690–1 and 730.
254	Muhammad Mohsin s/o Mansur Haji	1500/700	"	–	"	1650 (D)	Salih, III, pp. 101, 106 (L) and 463 (B); *M.U.*, III, pp. 968–9.
255	Haji Muhammad Yar Uzbek	1500/600	"	–	–	–	Salih, III, p. 463 (B).
256	Mu'taqid Khan Muhammad Quli s/o Najabat Khan	1500/500	"	–	Father	–	Salih, III, p. 463 (B); *M.U.*, II, pp. 870–1.

(contd.)

1	*2*	*3*	*4*	*5*	*6*	*7*	*8*
257	Sarandaz Khan Qalmaq	1500/1200	Turani	–	–	1646 (D)	Lahori, II, pp. 506 and 730; *Z.Kh.*, III, pp. 55–8.
258	Shah Muhamma Qutghan	1500/600	"	–	–	–	Salih, III, p. 463 (B); *Apparatus*, p. S-5420.
259	Yakkataz Khan	1500/1500 500 × 2h–3h	"	–	–	1645–6 (D)	Lahori, II, pp. 399 and 729; *Z.Kh.*, III, pp. 89–90.
260	Abdul Rahman s/o Ruknuddin Rohila	1500/1500	Indian	Afghan	Father	–	Lahori, II, p. 411; *Z.Kh.*, II, pp. 310 and 357.
261	Abdul Rahman s/o Shahbaz Khan Rohila	1500/1500	"	"	"	1642–3 (D)	Lahori, II, p. 729; *M.U.*, II, pp. 650–1.
262	Alawal Tarin	1500/800	"	"	–	–	Salih, III, pp. 101 (L) and 462 (B).
263	Asad Khan s/o Rashid Khan Ansari	1500/1000 2h–3h	"	"	Father	Dec. 1654 (D)	Salih, III, pp. 195 (L) and 461 (B); *M.U.*, II, p. 304.
264	Asadullah s/o Nazr Bahadur Kheshgi	1500/1400	"	"	"	–	*M.U.*, III, p. 820.
265	Daulat Khan Qiyam Khani	1500/700	"	"	–	–	Salih, III, p. 463 (B).
266	Ilhamullah s/o Rashid Khan Ansari	1500/1500 500 × 2h–3h	"	"	Father	–	Salih, III, p. 460(B); *M.U.*, II, p. 304; III, p. 943.
267	Jamal Nohani	1500/800	"	"	–	–	Salih, III, pp. 101 (L) and 462 (B).

268	Qutubuddin Khan s/o Nazr Bahadur Kheshgi	1500/1400 600 × 2h–3h	Indian	”	Father	–	Salih, III, p. 461 (B); *M.U.*, III, pp. 102–8.
269	Shamsuddin Khan	1500/1500	”	”	”	–	Salih, III, p. 461 (B); *M.U.*, II, pp. 676–7.
270	Sikandar Rohila	1500/1000	”	Afghan	Brother	1641–2 (D)	Lahori, II, p. 731; *Z.Kh.*, II, p. 349.
271	Syed Abdul Wahab	1500/1500 800 × 2h–3h	”	–	–	1646–7 (D)	Lahori, II, pp. 379 and 729; *Z.Kh.*, II, p. 339.
272	Akbar Quli Gakkhar	1500/1500	”	Zamindar	G. father	1645–6 (D)	Lahori, II, p. 729; *Z.Kh.*, I, p. 221; *M.U.*, III, pp. 144–8.
273	Daulatmand s/o Baharji	1500/1000	”	”	Father	–	Lahori, II, p. 731; Salih, III, p. 462 (B); *Z.Kh.*, III, p. 144.
274	Syed Hasan s/o Syed Diler Khan Barha	1500/1500	”	–	Father	–	Salih, III, pp. 134 (L) and 461 (B); *M.U.*, II, pp. 413–15.
275	Janbaz Khan Syed Ahmad	1500/100	”	–	–	1648 (D)	Lahori, II, pp. 412 and 730; Salih, III, p. 19 (L).
276	Murad Quli s/o Akbar Quli Gakkhar	1500/1000	”	Zamindar	Father	–	Lahori, II, pp. 595 and 730.
277	Syed Shaikhan s/o Syed Diler Khan Barha	1500/1500	”	–	”	–	Waris, p. 263 (a).
278	Wali Mahaldar Khan	1500/800	”	–	–	–	Lahroi, II, p. 731; Salih, III, p. 463 (B).

(contd.)

1	*2*	*3*	*4*	*5*	*6*	*7*	*8*
279	Amar Singh Narori	1500/1000	Indian	Rajput zamindar	G. father	–	Salih, III, p. 462 (B); *M.U.*, II, p. 227.
280	Bhim Rathor	1500/1000	"	Rajput	–	1644–5 (D)	Lahori, II, p. 730.
281	Chandraman Bundela	1500/800	"	Rajput zamindar	Father	–	Lahori, II, p. 731; Salih, III, p. 462 (B); *Z.Kh.*, II, pp. 363–4.
282	Chatar Bhoj Chauhan	1500/1000 500 × 2h–3h	"	"	–	–	Salih, III, p. 461 (B).
283	Gharibdas s/o Rana Karan	1500/700	"	Rajput zamindar	Father	–	Salih, III, pp. 159 (L) and 463 (B); *M.U.*, II, pp. 200–6.
284	Gokuldas Sisodiya	1500/800	"	Rajput	–	–	Lahori, II, pp. 595.
285	Hari Singh Rathor	1500/900	"	Rajput zamindar	Father	1644 (D)	Lahori, II, pp. 373 and 731; *M.U.*, II, p. 268.
286	Hathi Singh	1500/1000	"	"	"	"	Lahori, II, p. 730; *M.U.*, II, pp. 142–8.
287	Madan Singh n/o Raja Kishan Singh Bhadoria	1500/1400	"	"	Uncle	1653 (D)	Salih, III, pp. 173 (L) and 461 (B); *M.U.*, II, p. 229.
288	Rawal Ponja	1500/1500	"	"	–	–	Lahori, II, p. 729; Salih, III, p. 461 (B).
289	Puran Mal Bundela	1500/1500	"	Rajput	–	–	Salih, III, pp. 207 (L) and 461 (B).
290	Rai Singh Rathor s/o Amar Singh Rathor	1500/1000	"	Rajput zamindar	Father	–	Salih, III, p. 461 (B); *M.U.*, II, p. 235.

291	Raja Sangram	1500/600	Indian	Rajput zamindar	–	1641–2 (D)	Lahori, II, p. 731.
292	Siyam Singh s/o Karamsi Rathor	1500/600	"	"	Father	–	Lahori, II, pp. 387 and 731.
293	Ani Rai Sanneta	1500/500	"	Maratha zamindar (Deccani)	–	–	Salih, III, p. 463 (B).
294	Raiba b/o Jadun Rai	1500/500	"	Maratha zamindar	Brother	–	Ibid.
295.	Sharzah Rao Kawa	1500/600	"	Maratha zamindar (Deccan)	–	–	*S.D.S.*, 88; Hyd. 509; *Apparatus*, p. S-3304.
296	Agah Khan Khwajasara	1500/1500 500 × 2h–3h	–	–	–	Dec. 1656 (D)	Salih, III, pp. 234 (L) and 461 (B); *Z.Kh.*, III, p. 117.
297	Firasat Khan Khwajasara	1500/500	–	–	–	–	Salih, III, p. 463 (B).
298	Muhammad Beg	1500/700	–	–	–	–	Salih, III, p. 268 (L).
299	Girdhar Dev	1500/200	"	–	–	–	Salih, III, p. 464 (B).
300	Abdul Wahab Ma'muri	1000/500	Irani	–	Brother	–	Salih, III, p. 467 (B); *Z.Kh.*, II, p. 304; *M.U.*, I, pp. 140–1.
301	Abdul Wahab son-in-law of Lashkar Khan	1000/500	"	–	Near relative	–	Salih, III, p. 467 (B).
302	Abul Qasim s/o Saif Khan	1000/200	"	–	Father	–	Salih, III, p. 469 (B).

(contd.)

1	2	3	4	5	6	7	8
303	Mir Ahmad s/o Sadat Khan Rizvi	1000/600	Irani	–	Father	–	Salih, III, p. 466 (B); *Z.Kh.*, III, pp. 77–8.
304	Mir Ali, s/o Musa-Mazandarani	1000/600	"	–	–	–	Salih, III, p. 466 (B).
305	Amanat Khan Abdul Haq	1000/200	"	–	Brother	–	Lahori, II, p. 737; *Z.Kh.*, II, pp. 255–6; *M.U.*, II, p. 790.
306	Asadullah, s/o Sher Khwaja Khan Baqi	1000/700	"	–	Father	–	Salih, III, p. 465 (B); *M.U.*, II, pp. 649–50.
307	Asfandiyar s/o Himmat Khan Alahyar	1000/1000	"	–	"	–	Salih, III, pp. 197 (L) and 464 (B); *M.U.*, I, pp. 182–5.
308	Danadil g/s/o Abdul Rahim Khan-e-Khanan	1000/250	"	–	G. father	–	Salih, III, p. 469 (B).
309	Ghazanfar s/o Alahwardi Khan	1000/900	"	–	Father	–	Salih, III, p. 465 (B); *Z.Kh.*, III, p. 130.
310	Hasan Ali Khan Bahadur s/o Alahwardi Khan	1000/300	"	–	"	–	Salih, III, p. 469 (B); *M.U.*, I, pp. 593–9.
311	Husain Beg son-in-law of Alimardan Khan	1000/800	"	–	Near relative	–	Salih, III, p. 465 (B); *M.U.*, I, pp. 591–3.
312	Imam Quli Turkman	1000/800	"	–	–	–	Salih, III, p. 465 (B); *Apparatus*, p. S-6336.

313	Ishaq Beg s/o Alimardan Khan	1000/300	Irani	–	Father	–	Salih, III, p. 469 (B); *M.U.*, II, p. 807.
314	Ismail Beg s/o Alimardan Khan	1000/300	"	–	"	–	Salih, III, p. 469 (B); *M.U.*, II, p. 807.
315	Mir J'afar Astrabadi[1]	1000/200	"	–	–	–	Salih, III, p. 469 (B).
316	Karamullah	1000/1000	"	–	Father	–	Lahori, II, pp. 399 and 732; Salih, III, p. 464 (B); *M.U.*, II, pp. 773–5.
317	Hakim Khushhal	1000/200	"	–	"	1641–2 (D)	Lahori, II, p. 737; *Z.Kh.* II, p. 303; *M.U.*, I, pp. 563–5.
318	Mir Mahmud Safahani	1000/200	"	–	–	–	Salih, III, p. 469 (B); *Z.Kh.*, III, pp. 37–8.
319	Mir Khan	1000/500	"	–	Father	Aug. 1644 (D)	Lahori, II, pp. 293–4, 382–3 and 735; *Z.Kh.*, I, pp. 198–200; *M.U.*, I, pp. 172–4.
320	Qazi Muhammad Aslam	1000/100	"	–	–	1651–2 (D)	Lahori, II, pp. 628 and 737; *M.U.*, III, pp. 89–92.
321	Muhammad Murad s/o Salabat Khan Roshan Zamir	1000/100	"	–	Father	–	Salih, III, p. 469 (B); *M.U.*, II, p. 733.
322	Mir Muhammad Sharif s/o Islam Khan	1000/200	"	–	"	–	Salih, III, p. 469 (B); *M.U.*, I, p. 166.
323	Mirza Muhammad Tahir s/o Zafar Khan	1000/500	"	–	"	–	*M.U.*, II, pp. 762–3.
324	Mubarak Ru s/o Saif Khan	1000/200	"	–	"	–	Lahori, II, pp. 422 and 737; Salih, III, p. 469 (B); *Z.Kh.*, III, pp. 238–9; *M.U.*, II, pp. 416–20.

(contd.)

1	*2*	*3*	*4*	*5*	*6*	*7*	*8*
325	Muiz-ul-Mulk Mir Musa	1000/100	Irani	–	–	–	Lahori, II, p. 738; Salih, III, p. 469 (B); Mirat, I, p. 210.
326	Shaikh Musa Gilani	1000/400	"	–	–	–	Salih, III, pp. 263 (L) and 468 (B).
327	Muzaffar s/o Baqar Harvi	1000/1000	"	–	–	–	Salih, III, p. 464 (B).
328	Mirza Najaf Ali s/o Qazalbash Khan Afshar	1000/1000	"	–	Father	1656–7 (D)	Salih, III, p. 464 (B); *Z.Kh.*, III, p. 71; *M.U.*, III, p. 86.
329	Nazir Khan Khwaja Ubaid Asfahani	1000/500	"	–	–	–	Salih, III, pp. 237(L) and 467 (B).
330	Mir Ni'amatullah s/o Mir Zahiruddin	1000/200	"	–	Father	–	Salih, III, pp. 129 (L) and 469 (B); *M.U.*, III, pp. 335–42.
331	Nuruddaulah	1000/400	"	–	"	1647–8 (D)	Lahori, II, p. 736.
332	Mir Qasim Samnani	1000/400	"	–	–	–	Salih, III, p. 468 (B).
333	Qila'dar Khan Shirazi	1000/1000	"	–	–	–	Salih, III, p. 464 (B).
334	Ri'ayat Khan Miram Beg	1000/800	"	–	–	–	Salih, III, p. 465 (B); *Z.Kh.*, III, p. 50.
335	Safi Khan s/o Islam Khan	1000/400	"	–	Father	–	Salih, III, p. 468 (B); *M.U.*, II, pp. 740–2.

336	Safi Quli Siyah Mansur	1000/700	Irani	–	–	–	Lahori, II, pp. 361–2 and 733.
337	Shafi s/o Saif Khan	1000/350	"	–	Father	1647–8 (D)	Lahori, II, pp. 406 and 736; *M.U.*, II, pp. 416–21.
338	Sultan Husain s/o Asalat Khan	1000/5000	"	–	"	–	Salih, III, p. 248 (B); *M.U.*, I, pp. 252–5.
339	Sultan Nazr	1000/400	"	–	Brother	–	Salih, III, p. 468 (B); *Z.Kh.*, II, p. 316; *M.U.*, II, pp. 416–21.
340	Ziauddin Khan Yusuf s/o Amir Khan Mir Abul Baqa	1000/600	"	–	Father	–	Salih, III, p. 466 (B); *M.U.*, I, p. 173.
341	Hakim Fathullah g/s/o Hakim Fathullah	1000/100	"	–	G. father	–	Lahori, II, p. 739; Salih, III, p. 469 (B).
342	Abdullah Beg Sarai	1000/400	Turani	–	–	–	Salih, III, p. 468 (B); *Apparatus*, p. S-4292.
343	Abul Baqa s/o Sharif Khan Hisari	1000/900	"	–	Father	–	Salih, III, p. 465 (B); *Z.Kh.*, III, pp. 87–8.
344	Mughal Khan s/o Shah Rukh Mirza	1000/700	"	–	"	–	Salih, III, p. 465 (B); *Z.Kh.*, I, pp. 21–3; II, p. 324.
345	Abid Khwaja	1000/150	"	–	–	–	Salih, III, pp. 120–1 (L), *M.U.*, III, pp. 120–3 and 837.
346	Bahram	1000/900	"	–	Father	1645–6 (D)	Lahori, II, pp. 406 and 733; *Z.Kh.*, II, p. 325; *M.U.*, I, pp. 524–5.
347	Mir Barka Bukhari	1000/200	"	–	–	1642 (D)	Lahori, II, pp. 311 and 737.

(contd.)

1	*2*	*3*	*4*	*5*	*6*	*7*	*8*
348	Darwesh Beg Qaqshal	1000/500	Turani	–	–	–	Salih, III, p. 467 (B); *Z.Kh.*, III, pp. 75–6.
349	Hashim Beg Kashghari (Muhammad Hashim)	1000/500	”	–	–	–	Lahori, II, p. 605; Salih, III, p. 467 (B).
350	Himmat Khan Yusuf Beg Kabuli	1000/500	”	–	–	1644–5 (D)	Lahori, II, p. 725.
351	Khwaja Inayatullah g/s/o Abdullah Khan Feroze Jang	1000/700	”	–	G. father	–	Salih, III, p. 466 (B); *M.U.*, II, pp. 777–89.
352	Ishaq Beg son-in-law of Yadgar Husain	1000/500	”	–	Near relatives	–	Salih, III, p. 467 (B).
353	Mir Ja'far s/o Mir Haj	1000/700	”	–	Father	–	Salih, III, p. 466 (B).
354	Khalil Beg	1000/800	”	–	–	–	Lahori, II, pp. 406 and 733.
355	Khusrau Beg Turkman	1000/500	”	–	–	–	Lahori, II, pp. 569–70; *Apparatus*, p. S-3609.
356	Latif Khan Naqshbandi	1000/400	”	–	–	1645–6 (D)	Lahori, II, p. 736; *Apparatus*, p. S-3493.
357	Muhammad Ali Kamrani	1000/500	”	–	–	–	Lahori, II, p. 735; Salih, III, p. 467 (B).
358	Muhammad Beg b/o Yadgar Beg Jaulaq	1000/600	”	–	–	–	Salih, III, p. 466 (B); *Apparatus*, p. S-5660.

359	Muhammad Murad Yaldoz	1000/400	Turani	–	–	–	Salih, III, p. 468 (B); *Apparatus*, p. S-4104.
360	Muhammad Sharif Tolakchi s/o Afzal Tolakchi	1000/1000	"	–	Father	–	Salih, III, pp. 172 (L) and 464 (B); *Z.Kh.*, III, pp. 76–7.
361	Nazir Beg Yaldoz Abdullah Khan	1000/600	"	–	–	–	Salih, III, p. 466 (B); *Apparatus*, p. S-4135.
362	Pilang Hamla	1000/600	"	–	–	–	Salih, III, p. 466 (B); *Apparatus*, p. S-4180.
363	Mirza Ruhullah s/o Yusuf Muhammad Khan Tashqandi	1000/400	"	–	Father	–	Salih, III, pp. 197 (L) and 468 (B); *M.U.*, III, pp. 966–7.
364	Sarbaland Khan, Khwaja Rahmatullah Dehbedi	1000/500	"	–	–	–	Salih, III, pp. 237 (L) and 467 (B); *M.U.*, II, pp. 477–8.
365	Shadi Khan Uzbek	1000/400	"	–	–	1648–9 (left service)	Salih, I, p. 270 (L); III, p. 73; *Z.Kh.*, III, pp. 59–60; *M.U.*, II, pp. 661–2.
366	Turktaz Khan	1000/400	"	–	–	1647–8 (D)	Lahori, II, p. 736.
367	Urd Sher	1000/600	"	–	Uncle	1644–5 (D)	Lahori, II, p. 734.
368	Yadgar Beg Arlat	1000/500	Turani	–	–	–	Salih, III, p. 467 (B); *Apparatus*, p. S-7651.
369	Adam Khan Panni	1000/500	Indian	Afghan	–	–	Salih, III, p. 467 (B); *Apparatus*, p. S-6888.

(contd.)

1	2	3	4	5	6	7	8
370	Ahdad Khan Mehmand	1000/500	Indian	Afghan	–	–	Salih, III, p. 467 (B); Lahori, II, p. 735.
371	Aman Beg s/o Bahadur Khan Rohila	1000/400	”	”	Father	–	Salih, III, p. 468 (B).
372	Daulat Khan b/o Sher Khan Tarin	1000/600	”	”	Brother	–	Salih, III, pp. 144 (L) and 466 (B).
373	Dilawar Khan s/o Bahadur Khan Rohila	1000/500	”	”	Father	–	Salih, III, pp., 99 and 142 (L); *M.U.*, I, p. 424.
374	Fath Khan u/o Usman Khan Rohila	1000/900	”	”	Uncle	–	*S.D.S.*, pp. 195–7; *Z.Kh.*, III, pp. 116–17; *M.U.*, III, pp. 22–6.
375	Ikhtiyar Khan Rohila	1000/600	”	”	Father	1641–2 (D)	Lahori, II, pp. 224 and 734.
376	Isa, u/o Usman Khan Rohila	1000/800	”	”	Uncle	–	Salih, III, p. 465 (B).
377	Muhabbat Ghilzai	1000/600	”	”	–	1641–2 (D)	Lahori, II, p. 735.
378	Nasib Shirani	1000/700	”	”	–	1645–6 (D)	Lahori, II, p. 74.
379	Usman Khan Rohila	1000/800	”	”	, Brother	–	Lahori, II, p. 733; Salih, III, p. 465 (B); *Z.Kh.*, III, p. 116.

380	Syed Abdul Muqtadir g/s/o Murtaza Khan Syed Nizam	1000/700	Indian	–	G. father	–	Salih, III, p. 466 (B); *M.U.*, III, pp. 479–81.
381	Abdul Nabi	1000/500	"	–		–	Salih, III, p. 467 (B); *M.U.*, II, p. 448.
382	Adam Khan Tibbati	1000/500	"	Zamindar	–	Sep. 1656 (D)	Salih, III, pp. 126, 229–30 (L) and 468 (B).
383	Syed Ahmad b/o Syed Muhammad	1000/500	"	–	Brother	–	Salih, III, p. 467 (B).
384	Syed 'Alam Barha	1000/400	"	–	"	–	Salih, III, p. 468 (B); *M.U.*, II, pp. 454–6.
385	Syed Asadullah b/o Syed Dindar Khan Bukhari	1000/1000	"	–	"	–	Lahori, II, pp. 585 and 732; Salih, III, p. 464 (B).
386	Syed Bahadur Bhakkari s/o Syed Luft Ali	1000/500	"	–	Father	–	Salih, III, p. 467 (B); *M.U.*, II, pp. 460–1.
387	Diler Khan Syed Wali	1000/700	"	–	–	Jan. 1641 (D)	Lahori, II, pp. 222 and 733.
388	Dindar Khan Abdul Wahid Bukhari	1000/650	"	–	Father	1645 (D)	Lahori, II, pp. 468 and 734; *Z.Kh.*, II, pp. 291–2.
389	Syed Hasan s/o Syed Khan-e-Jahan Barha	1000/500	"	–	"	–	Salih, III, p. 466 (B).
390	Ghairat Khan Shaikh Daud	1000/500	"	–	–	–	Salih, III, p. 467 (B).

(contd.)

1	2	3	4	5	6	7	8
391	Jabbar Quli Gakkhar u/o Kamal Gakkhar	1000/900	Indian	Zamindar	Uncle	–	Salih, III, pp. 101 (L) and 465 (B); *Z.Kh.*, I, p. 221; *M.U.*, III, pp. 144–8.
392	Syed Mansur Khan s/o Syed Khan-e-Jahan Barha	1000/400	"	–	Father	–	Salih, III, pp. 230–1 (L) and 468 (B); *M.U.*, II, pp. 449–52.
393	Syed Maqbul Alam s/o Syed Alam Barha	1000/400	"	–	"	–	Lahroi, II, pp. 554 and 736; Salih, III, p. 468 (B); *M.U.*, II, pp. 454–6.
394	Syed Muhammad	1000/600	"	–	–	–	Lahori, II, pp. 554 and 734.
395	Shaikh Mua'zzam s/o Islam Khan Fathpuri	1000/800	"	–	Father	1658 (D)	*M.U.*, I, p. 120.
396	Syed Munawwar s/o Syed Khan-e-Jahan Barha	1000/400	"	–	"	–	Salih, III, p. 468 (B); *M.U.*, II, pp. 465–8.
397	Syed Khadim Barha	1000/500	"	–	–	1646–7 (D)	Lahori, II, pp. 232 and 735.
398	Muzaffar s/o Mahmud Khan	1000/1000	"	–	Father	–	Sálih, I, pp. 505–7 (B); III, p. 464 (B).
399	Syed Najabat Khan s/o Syed Shujat Khan Barha	1000/500	"	–	"	–	Salih, III, pp. 236 (L) and 467 (B); *M.U.*, II, p. 427.
400	Syed Nurul Ayan Ayan	1000/300	"	–	"	–	Salih, III, p. 469 (B); *M.U.*, II, pp. 10–11.

401	Nurul Hasan	1000/400	Indian	–	–	–	Lahori, II, pp. 501 and 736; Salih, III, p. 468 (B).
402	Syed Qutub Bukhari	1000/1000 2h–3h	”	–	–	–	Salih, III, p. 464 (B).
403	Salabat Khan Deccani	1000/500 100 × 2h–3h	”	Deccani	–	–	*S.D.S.*, p. 208; ***Apparatus***, pp. S-6525 and 6596.
404	Syed Salar Barha b/o Syed 'Alam	1000/1000	”	–	Brother	–	Salih, III, p. 464 (B).
405	Shadman Pakhliwala s/o Sultan Husain	1000/900	”	Zamindar	Father	Sep. 1656 (D)	Lahori, II, p. 577; Salih, III, pp. 230 (L) and 465 (B); *M.U.*, I, pp. 565–6.
406	Syed Sher Zaman s/o Syed Khan-e-Jahan Barha	1000/200	”	–	”	–	Salih, III, p. 469 (B); *M.U.*, II, p. 465.
407	Bhagwandas Bundela	1000/600	”	Rajput zamindar	”	1640–1 (D)	Lahori, II, p. 734; *Z.Kh.*, II, pp. 363–4; *M.U.*, II, pp. 197–9.
408	Bhim, s/o Raja Bithaldas Gaur	1000/400	”	”	”	–	Salih, III, pp. 132 (L) and 468 (B).
409	Bhoj Raj	1000/500	”	”	”	–	Lahori, II, p. 201; *Z.Kh.*, I, p. 40; II, pp. 366–7.
410	Chatar Sen n/o Siyam Singh Sisodiya	1000/500	”	”	Uncle	–	Salih, III, p. 466 (B).
411	Fath, s/o Karna	1000/800	”	Rajput	–	–	Salih, III, p. 465 (B); ***Apparatus***, p. S-7621.
412	Girdhardas s/o Rawal Ponja	1000/1000	”	Rajput zamindar	Father	–	Salih, III, p. 242 (L).

(contd.)

1	*2*	*3*	*4*	*5*	*6*	*7*	*8*
413	Gopal Singh Kachwaha	1000/1000	Indian	Rajput zamindar	Father	–	Lahori, II, pp. 385 and 732; Salih, III, p. 464 (B); *M.U.*, I, p. 516.
414	Gordhan Rathor	1000/500	”	Rajput	–	–	Salih, III, p. 467 (B).
415	Jagat Singh Rathor s/o Pirthi Raj Rathor	1000/500	”	”	Father	–	Salih, III, p. 466 (B).
416	Jagram Kachwaha	1000/700	”	”	–	–	Salih, III, p. 465 (B).
417	Kirat Singh s/o Raja Jai Singh Kachwaha	1000/900	”	Rajput zamindar	Father	–	Salih, III, p. 465 (B); *M.U.*, III, pp. 156–8.
418	Raja Kishan Singh Bhadoria	1000/600	”	”	–	1643 (D)	Lahori, II, pp. 348 and 735; *M.U.*, II, pp. 228–9.
419	Raja Kishan Singh Gaur	1000/500	”	”	–	–	Salhi, III, pp. 142 (L) and 467 (B).
420	Kanwar Sen Kishtwari	1000/400	”	”	–	1648 (D)	Lahori, II, pp. 468 and 736; Salih, III, p. 66 (L).
421	Maha Singh s/o Raja Madan Singh Bhadoria	1000/800	”	”	Father	–	Salih, III, pp. 173 (L) and 465 (B); *M.U.*, II, pp. 229–30.
422	Maheshdas Rathor (servant of Raja Gaj Singh)	1000/500	”	Rajput	–	–	Lahori, II, p. 474; Salih, III, p. 467 (B).
423	Raja Pirthi Chand	1000/400	”	Rajput zamindar	–	–	Lahori, II, pp. 273–4 and 736.

424	Pratap s/o Balbhadar Cheru	1000/1000	Indian	Rajput zamindar	–	–	Lahori, II, pp. 360–1 and 733; Salih, III, p. 462 (B).
425	Rai Singh Jala	1000/700	”	Rajput	–	–	Salih, III, p. 466 (B).
426	Raj Singh Rathor	1000/600	”	”	–	1641–2 (D)	Lahori, II, p. 734.
427	Rawal Sabal Singh son-in-law of Rawal Manohar Jaisalmeri	1000/700	”	Rajput zamindar	Near relatives	–	Salih, III, p. 466 (B).
428	Rawal Samarsi	1000/1000	”	”	–	–	Lahori, II, p. 732; Salih, III, p. 464 (B).
429	Sangram	1000/1000 600 × 2h–3h	”	”	–	–	*S.D.S.*, p. 138.
430	Sujan Singh s/o Mohkam Singh	1000/500	”	Rajput	–	–	Salih, III, p. 467 (B).
431	Tillok Chand s/o Rai Manohar Kachwaha	1000/500	”	Rajput zamindar	Father	–	Lahori, II, pp. 595 and 735.
432	Udai Bhan s/o Ram Singh	1000/500	”	Rajput	–	–	Salih, III, p. 467 (B).
433	Bhoj Raj Deccani	1000/500	”	Maratha (Deccani)	–	–	Lahori, II, p. 735; Salih, III, p. 468 (B).
434	Khande Rai	1000/300	”	Maratha zamindar (Deccani)	–	–	*S.D.S.*, p. 151.
435	Renuji	1000/700	”	Maratha (Deccani).	–	–	*S.D.S.*, p. 138.

(contd.)

1	2	3	4	5	6	7	8
436	Abid Khwajasara	1000/200	Indian	–	–	–	Salih, III, p. 469 (B).
437	Dayanat Khan	1000/400	–	–	–	–	Salih, III, p. 468 (B).
438	Husain Ali s/o Qasim Khan	1000/400	–	–	–	–	Salih, III, p. 244 (L).
439	Khan Beg	1000/700	–	–	–	–	Salih, III, p. 122 (L).
440	Muhammad Murad	1000/100	–	–	–	1647–8 (D)	Salih, III, p. 469 (B); Lahori, II, p. 648.
441	Ya'qub Dilawar	1000/600	–	–	–	–	Salih, III, p. 466 (B).
442	Yusuf Aqa	1000/500	–	–	–	–	Salih, III, p. 467 (B).
443	Syed Yusuf s/o Malik Ambar	1000/500	–	Deccani	–	–	Salih, III, p. 467 (B).
444	Bihari Mal	1000/100	"	–	–	–	Salih, III, p. 469 (B); *Z.Kh.*, II, pp. 408–9.
445	Rai Kashidas	1000/250	"	–	–	–	Lahori, II, pp. 48 and 736.
446	Rai Mukand Narnoli	1000/200	"	–	–	–	Salih, III, p. 469 (B); *Z.Kh.*, II, pp. 401–3; *M.U.*, II, p. 237.
447	Rai Rayan Diyanat Rai	1000/150	"	–	–	–	Lahori, II, p. 737; *Z.Kh.*, III, pp. 81–2.
448	Rai Rayan Raghunath	1000/400	"	–	–	–	Salih, III, p. 468 (B); *M.U.*, II, p. 282

Note: [1]Perhaps his account is not given in *M.U.* and *Z.Kh.* yet it is clear that belonging to Astrabad, which is in Iran, he was an Irani (*M.U.*, Vol. III, pp. 244 and 350).

Bibliography

CHRONICLES

Allami, Abul Fazl, *Ain-i-Akbari*, Vol. I, H. Blochmann (tr.), 1927; Vols. II and III, H.S. Jarrett (tr.), Calcutta, 1948–9.

——— *Akbar Nama*, H.M. Beveridge (tr.), Vols. I, II and III, Delhi, 1972.

Babar, *Babar Nama*, A.S. Beveridge (tr.), Vols. I and II, Delhi, 1970.

Badauni, Mulla Abdul Qadir, *Muntakhab-ut-Tawareekh*, Ranking (ed. and tr.) Vol. I, Delhi, 1973; W.H. Lowe (tr.), Vol. II, Delhi, 1973; Wolseley Haig (tr.), Vol. III, Delhi, 1973.

Bhandari, Sujan Rai, *Khulasat-ut-Tawareekh,* Zafar Hasan (ed.), Delhi, 1918.

Biyat, Bayazid, *Tazkira-i-Humayun Wa Akbar*, M. Hidayat Husain (ed.), Calcutta, 1941.

Brahman, Chandra Bhan, *Guldasta*, MS Sir Sulaiman Collection, Maulana Azad Library, Aligarh.

Jahangir, *Tuzuk-i-Jahangiri*, Syed Ahmed Khan (ed.), Ghazipur and Aligarh, 1863–4.

Kazim, Mohd., *Alamgir Nama*, Calcutta, 1865–73.

Khafi Khan, Muhammad Hashim, *Muntakhab-al-Lubab*, Anees Jahan Syed (tr.), *Aurangzeb in Muntakhab-al-Lubab*, Bombay, 1977.

Khan, Ali Mohd., *Mirat-i-Ahmadi*, Syed Nawab Ali (ed.), Baroda, 1928.

Lahori, Abdul Hamid, *Badshah Nama*, Vols. I and II, Maulvi Kabiruddin and Maulvi Abdul Rahim (eds.), Calcutta, 1867–8.

Nagar, Isar Das, *Futuhat-i-Alamgiri*, Tasneem Ahmad (ed. and tr.), Delhi, 1978.

Razi, Aqil Khan, *Waqiat-i-Alamgiri*, Zafar Hasan (ed.), Aligarh, 1946.

Sadiq, Mohd., *Tareekh-i-Shahjahani*, Rotograph, Department of History, Aligarh Muslim University, Aligarh.

Salih, Kambo Mohd., *Amal-i-Salih*, Vols. I, II and III, G. Yazdani (ed.), Calcutta, 1923–30 and Lahore edition, 1958–60.

Sen, Bhim, *Nuskha-i-Dilkusha,* J.N. Sarkar (tr.), Bombay, 1972.

Waris, Mohd., *Badshah Nama*, Transcript, Department of History, Aligarh Muslim University, Aligarh.

ARCHIVAL MATERIAL, DOCUMENTS, COLLECTION OF LETTERS, ADMINISTRATIVE LITERATURE

Ahkam-e-Alamgiri, Sir J.N. Sarkar (ed.), Calcutta, 1912.

Aurangzeb, *Kalimat-i-Taiyabat*, letters collected by Inayatullah Kashmiri, S.M. Azizuddin Husain (ed. and tr.), Delhi (n.d.).

Barha, Khan-e-Jahan Syed Muzaffar Khan, *Arzdasht-ha-i-Muzaffar*, Rotograph, Department of History, Aligarh Muslim University, Aligarh.

Dastur-ul-Amal-i-Shahjahani, MS Sir Sulaiman Collection, 675/53, Maulana Azad Library, Aligarh.

Hyderabad Documents: A huge collection is preserved in the Andhra Pradesh Archives. This includes a variety of documents such as *Yaddasht*, *Chahra*, *Parwana*, *Dagh-o-Tasiha*, etc. These are basically first-rate source material of the economic history of the Deccan. This rich repository of documents is invaluable for the study of the administrative system, political history from the seventeenth century, agrarian relations, prices and trade of our period.

Imperial Farmans (1577–1805 AD), K.M.L. Jhaveri (ed.), Bombay, 1928.

Insha-i-Zubdat-ul-Araiz, MS in the personal library of Professor Syed Nurul Hasan. Letters written by Prince Aurangzeb to Shahjahan relating to the Qandhar Campaign of 1652.

Jaipur Documents: Transcript in the personal liberary of Professor Syed Nurul Hasan. This valuable collection contains *Akhbarat*, *Farmans* and *Nishans* from the days of Jahangir to Farrukh Siyar.

Khulasat-us-Siyaq, MS Sir Sulaiman Collection, 410/143, Maulana Azad Library, Aligarh.

Malikzada, *Nigar Nama-i-Munshi*, Lucknow, 1882.

Mughal Archives, Mohd. Ziauddin-Ahmad Shakeb (ed.), State Archives, Andhra Pradesh, Hyderabad, 1977.

Munshi Thakur Lal Kaisth, *Dastur-al-Amal-i-Shahjahani*, Rotograph, Department of History, Aligarh Muslim University, Aligarh.

Ruqqat-i-Alamgiri, Syed Najib Ashraf Nadvi (ed.), Azamgarh, 1930. Letters written by Prince Aurangzeb to Shahjahan, Jahan Ara Begum, Dara Shukoh, Shah Shuja, Murad Bakhsh and other princes and nobles.

Selected Documents of Aurangzeb's Reign, Yusuf Husain (ed.), Hyderabad, 1959.

Selected Documents of Shahjahan's Reign, Yusuf Husain (ed.), Hyderabad, 1950.

Selected Waqai of Deccan (1660–71), Yusuf Husain (ed.), Hyderabad, 1953.

Yusuf Mirak, *Mazhar-i-Shahjahani*, AD 1634, Vol. II, Pir Hisamuddin Rashidi (ed.), Karachi, 1961.

DICTIONARIES

'Bahar', Munshi Tek Chand, *Bahar-i-Ajam,* Lucknow, 1916.

Mukhlis, Anand Ram, *Mirat-al-Istilah,* MS Anjuman-Taraqqi Urdu Library, Aligarh.

BIOGRAPHIES AND TAZKIRAS

Bhakkari, Shaikh Farid, *Zakhirat-ul-Khawanin*, Vols. I, II and III, Syed Moinul-Haq (ed.), Karachi, 1961, 1970 and 1974.

Khan, Shah Nawaz, *Maasir-ul-Umara*, Vols. I, II and III, Molvi Abdur Rahim (ed.), Bibliotheca Indica, 1888.

Ram, Kewal, *Tazkirat-ul-Umara*, S.M. Aziz-uddin Husain (tr.), Delhi, 1985.

Singh, Surat, *Tazkira-i-Pir Hassu Taili*, written in AH 1057, MS Department of History, Aligarh Muslim University, Aligarh.

EUROPEAN TRAVELLERS' ACCOUNTS

Bernier, Francois, *Travels in the Mughal Empire, 1656–68,* A. Constable (tr.), V.A. Smith (ed.), Delhi, 1989.

De Laet, *Description of India and Fragment of India History,* J.S. Hoyland (tr.) and annotated by S.N. Banerjee, *The Empire of the Great Mogol,* Bombay, 1928.

Manucci, Niccolao, *Storia Do Mogor, 1653–1708,* William Irvine (tr.), Calcutta, 1965–6.

Mundy, Peter, *Travel's*, Vol. II: *Travel's in Asia, 1630–34,* R.C. Temple (ed.), 2nd series, London, 1914.

Pelsaert, *Jahangir's India*, Geyl and Moreland (trs.), Cambridge, 1925.

MODERN WORKS (SELECT)

Ahmad, Syed, *Umara-i-Hunud* (Urdu, n.d.).

Athar Ali, M., *The Apparatus of Empire,* Delhi, 1985.

———, *The Mughal Nobility under Aurangzeb,* Bombay, 1968.

Aziz, Abdul, *The Mansabdari System and the Mughal Army,* Delhi, 1972.

Blake, Stephen P., *Shahjahanabad: The Sovereign City in Mughal India,* Cambridge, 1990.

Chandra, Satish, *Medieval India,* Delhi, 1982.

———, *The Parties and Politics at the Mughal Court (1707–40),* Aligarh, 1959.

Crooke, W., *The Tribes and Castes of the North-Western Provinces and Oudh,* Calcutta, 1896.

Fuhrar, A., *The Monumental Antiquities and Inscriptions in the North-Western Provinces and Oudh,* Allahabad, 1891.

Fukazawa, Hiroshi, *The Medieval Deccan: Peasants, Social System and States, Sixteenth to Eighteenth Centuries,* Delhi, 1991.

Habib, Irfan, *Agrarian System of Mughal India,* Bombay, 1963.

———, *An Atlas of the Mughal Empire*, Delhi, 1982.

Habib, Irfan (ed.), *Madhya Kalin Bharat* (Hindi), Delhi, 1981.

Hambly, Gavin, *Cities of Mughal India: Delhi, Agra and Fatehpur Sikri,* New York, 1968.

Husain, Afzal, *The Nobility under Akbar and Jahangir*, Delhi, 1999.

Ibn-e-Hasan, *The Central Structure of the Mughal Empire*, Delhi, 1970.

Joshi, Rita, *The Afghan Nobility and the Mughals (1526–1707)*, Delhi, 1985.

Khan, Ahsan Raza, *Chieftains of the Mughal Empire during the Reign of Akbar*, Delhi, 1977.

Khosla, Ram Prasad, *Mughal Kingship and Nobility*, Delhi, 1976 (rpt.).

Koft, Dirk H.A., *Naukar, Rajput and Sepoy—The Ethnohistory of Military Labour Market in Hindustan, 1450–1850,* Cambridge, 1990.

Levy, *Social Structure of Islam*, Cambridge, 1957.

Moreland, W.H., *Aqrarian System of Moslem India*, Cambridge, 1929.

———, *From Akbar to Aurangzeb*, London, 1923.

———, *India at the Death of Akbar*, London, 1920.

Pearson, M.N., *Portuguese in India*, Cambridge, 1987.

Ranawat, Manohar Singh, *Shahjahan Ke Hindu Mansabdar*, Jodhpur, 1973.

Richard, John F. (ed.), *Kingship and Authority in South Asia*, Madison, 1978.

Richard, John F., *The Mughal Empire*, Delhi, 1993.

Rizvi, Syed Athar Abbas, *Religious and Intellectual History of the Muslim in Akbar's Reign*, Delhi, 1975.

Saran, Parmatma, *The Provincial Government of the Mughals* (*1626–1658*), Allahabad, 1941.

Sarkar, Jadu Nath, *History of Aurganzeb*, 5 vols., Calcutta, 1912, 1916 and 1930.

———, *Mughal Administration*, Calcutta, 1952.

Saxena, Banarsi Prasad, *History of Shahjahan of Dihli,* Allahabad, 1958.

Sen, S.N., *The Military System of the Marathas*, Bombay, 1958.

Sharma, Sri Ram, *The Religious Policy of the Mughal Emperors*, Delhi, 1988.

Shyamaldas, Kavi Raj, 'Vir Vinod', (Hindi), Vols. 1–4, Department of History, Aligarh Muslim University, Aligarh.

Siddiqi, Noman Ahmad, *Land Revenue Administration under the Mughals*, Bombay, 1970.

Streusand, Douglas, *The Formation of the Mughal Empire*, Delhi, 1989.

Tod, James, *Annals and Antiquities of Rajasthan,* popular edn., Vols. I and II, London, 1914.

Tripathi, Ram Prasad, *Rise and Fall of the Mughal Empire,* Allahabad, 1959.

———, *Some Aspects of Muslim Administration*, Allahabad, 1936.

Wilson, H.H., *A Glossary of Judicial and Revenue Terms, and C., of British India*, London, 1875.

PERIODICAL LITERATURE (SELECT LIST OF ARTICLES)

Alvi, Rafi Ahmad, 'New Light on Mughal Cavalry', I.H.C., Varanasi Session, 1969, pp. 272–81.

Askari, S. Hasan, 'Bihar in the time of Shahjahan', I.H.C., Madras Session, 1944, pp. 348–59.

Athar Ali, M., 'Mansab and Imperial Policy under Shahjahan', I.H.C., Aligarh Session, 1975, pp. 257–66.

———, 'Provincial Governors under Shahjahan', I.H.C., Jabalpur Session, 1970, pp. 288–93.

———, 'The Objectives behind the Mughal Expedition to Balkh and Badakhshan', I.H.C., Patiala Session, 1967.

———, 'The Religious Issue in the War of Succession 1658–59', *Medieval India Quarterly,* Vol. V, Aligarh, 1963.

Chandra, Satish, 'The Deccan Policy of the Mughals—A Reappraisal', *I.H.R.*, Vol. IV, No. 2 and Vol. V.

Habib, Irfan, 'The Family of Nur Jahan during Jahangir's Reign—a Political Study', *Medieval India—A Miscellany,* Vol. I, Bombay, 1969.

———, 'The Mansab System, 1596–1637', I.H.C., Patiala Session, 1967.

Hasan, Syed Nurul, 'Aspects of Zamindari System in Deccan (1695–1707)', I.H.C., Srinagar Session, 1969.

———, 'New Light on the Relations of the Early Mughal Rulers with their Nobility', I.H.C., Madras Session, 1944, pp. 389–97.

———, 'Position of the Zamindars in the Mughal Empire', I.H.C., Ranchi Session, 1964.

———, 'The Problem of Nationalities in Medieval India', I.H.C., Madras Session, 1944, pp. 370–6.

———, 'The Theory of Nur Jahan Jumla—an Examination', I.H.C., Trivandrum Session, 1958.

Husain, Afzal, 'Marriage among the Mughal Nobles as an Index of Status and Aristocratic Integration', I.H.C., Muzaffarpur Session, 1972, pp. 304–12.

Husain, Iqbal, 'Family of Darya Khan Rohila', I.H.C., Jabalpur Session, 1970.

Khan, Iqtidar Alam, 'The Nobility under Akbar and the Development of his Religious Policy, 1560–80', *J.R.A.S.*, London, 1968.

Khan, Muhammad Afzal, 'Position of Aitmad-ud-Daula's Family during the Reign of Shahjahan', I.H.C., Hyderabad, 1978.

Qaisar, Ahsan Jan, 'Distribution of the Revenue Resources among the Mughal Nobility', I.H.C., Allahabad Session, 1965, pp. 237–43.

Siddiqi, Noman Ahmad, 'Implications of the Month-Scale in the Mansabdari System', I.H.C., Delhi Session, 1961, pp. 157–62.

———, 'Pulls and Pressures on the Faujdars under the Mughals', I.H.C., Patiala Session, 1967, pp. 243–55.

———, 'The Faujdars and the Faujdari under the Mughals', M.I.Q., Vol. 4, 1961.

Index

administrative offices/posts
  Diwan-i-Kul 116-18
  Faujdars 127-34
  Mir Bakhshi 119
  Mir-e-Saman 119-22
  Qiladars 134-9
  Sadr 122-3
  Subedar 123-7
Afghan, Karimdad 27
Afghans family group, share in mansabs 98-100
Afghans mansabdars 31-3, 51-3, 61-2, 86-7, 194
Ahmad, Syed 43
Aitmaduddaulah 27
Akbar 13-14, 24-5, 27-30, 32-3, 43-4, 46, 81, 85
Ali, M. Athar 13, 15, 18, 35-6, 46, 64, 76-8, 83, 116, 123, 126
Ali, Shah 128-9
Amber, Malik 37
Ansari, Rashid Khan 57
Aurang, Nazar Beg 51
Aurangzeb 13, 35-6, 46, 61, 80-1
Aziz, Abdul 15, 18, 76

Babar 32
Badakhshan 61
Badgujar, Bir Narain 105
Badshah Namas 16, 18
Bahadurji Rai 45
Bahmanyar, Aitqad Khan 113
Banarsi Prasad 49, 52
Barha, Khan-e-Jahan 51, 54
Barha, Syed Alam 53
Barha, Syed Alawal 54
Barha, Syed Diler Khan 54
Barha, Syed Hizbir Khan 53
Barha, Syed Khan-e-Jahan 45
Barha, Syed Mansur Khan 45
Baswant Rai 45
Bayazid, Syed 101-2
Beg, Asaf Khan Jafar 95
Beg, Hakim 27
Beg, Husain 124
Beg, Khalil 57
Bernier, Francois 46
Bhadoriya, Kishan Singh 104
Bhakkari, Farid 18, 27, 46
Bhonsle, Sahu 55
Bihari Mal 37
Biranj, Dilawar Khan 51, 53
Bithuji Rai 45
Bukhari, Shaikh Jalal 122-3
Bukhari, Syed Jalaluddin 122
Bulaqi 49
Bundela, Bir Singh Dev 103, 105
Bundela, Champat 80, 128
Bundela, Jujhar Singh 21, 26-7, 44, 49, 51, 54, 62, 80, 83, 128-9, 136, 138, 190, 192

Chahar-Chaman 16
Chandra Bhan 16
Crown attitude towards
  ethnic group mansabdars 48-65
    Afghans 51-3, 61-2
    Indian Muslims 53-4, 58, 62
    Iranis 49-50, 61
    Marathas 54-5, 63
    Rajputs 34, 54, 58, 62-3
    Turanis 50-1, 56-8, 61
  nobility 43-65, 192-3
  property of deceased mansabdars 45-7

Dara Shikoh 46, 56, 59, 61, 77, 80
Darbari, Rai Sal 105
Das, Rai Kasi 37
Deccanis mansabdars 34-5, 54, 58, 92-3, 191

Family group share in mansabs
  Afghans 98-100
  Indian Muslims 101-3
  Iranis 93-6
  Marathas 106-8
  Rajputs 103-6

Turanis 97-8
Farid, Ikhlas Khan Shaikh 101
Feroze Jang, Abdullah Khan 51, 124

Gaj Singh 103, 105
Gakkhar, Akbar Quli 101
Gaur, Bithaldas 46, 134, 136, 138
Gaur, Girdhar Das 136-7
Gaur, Gopal Das 103, 105
Gujrati, Diyanat Rai 37
Gujrati, Mulla Abdul Latif 54

Habashi, Atish Khan 59
Habib, Irfan 15, 76
Habshi, Yaqut Khan 37
Hara, Rao Ratan 103
Hasan, Khwaja Abul 49-50, 95
Hasan, S. Nurul 14, 76
Hidayat Ullah, Fidai Khan 50
Hidayatulah, Shaikh 122
History of Shahjahan of Delhi 13
Humanyun 14, 25, 33, 43-4

Ibn-e-Hasan 15, 116
immigrant nobility 27-8
Indian Muslims
Family group share in mansabs 101-3
mansabdars 30-1, 53-4, 58, 87, 191-2
Iranis
family group share in mansabs 93-6
mansabdars 29-30, 50-1, 56-8, 61, 85-6
military and administrative capability 49-50

Jadun Rai 44-5, 55
Jafar, Syed 53
Jagat Singh 44, 62, 83, 105, 192
Jagdev Rai 45, 55, 106
Jahangir 29, 32, 35, 44, 46, 50, 59, 80-1, 86, 103, 126, 130, 136
Jai Singh 89, 103, 105
Jaswant Singh 126
Joshi, Rita 57

Kakar, Rahim Khan 51
Kamgar, Ghairat Khan Khwaja 57
Kari Singh 89
Khan, Abdullah 54
Khan, Afzal 45, 49, 95, 118-19, 123
Khan, Agah 130
Khan, Aitqad 50, 119, 125
Khan, Ali Mardan 46, 56-7, 80, 93, 95, 125
Khan, Amanat 45
Khan, Aqil 119, 122
Khan, Asaf 45-6, 49, 51, 53, 93, 95, 113, 116, 118-19
Khan, Asalat 49-50, 62, 119, 123
Khan, Azam 49-50, 123-5, 130
Khan, Bahadur 47, 51-3
Khan, Baqar 50, 95, 125
Khan, Baqi 136-7
Khan, Danishmand 119
Khan, Darya 100
Khan, Daulat Khan Khawas 58
Khan, Dilawar 53
Khan, Dorab 34
Khan, Fazil 122
Khan, Hizbar 102
Khan, Ibrahim 46
Khan, Ihtimam 54
Khan, Ilahdad 51
Khan, Ilahwardi 49, 96, 125, 130
Khan, Iltifat 49
Khan, Iqtidar Alam 27, 30
Khan, Islam 50, 95, 118, 123-4
Khan, Jafar 116, 118, 125
Khan, Jahagir Quli 50
Khan, Jan Nisar 54, 58
Khan, Jansipar 57
Khan, Khalilullah 49, 95, 125, 134
Khan, Lashkar 50
Khan, Lutfullah 45
Khan, Mahabat 47, 49-52, 54, 95, 125, 130, 134, 136
Khan, Makramat 119, 125, 129
Khan, Mubariz 53
Khan, Muhammad Amin 116
Khan, Multafit 49
Khan, Murshid Quli 130
Khan, Murtaza 54
Khan, Musvi 62, 122
Khan, Mutamid 49, 124, 134
Khan, Muzzam 118
Khan, Purdil 53
Khan, Qasim 50, 96, 125
Khan, Qazalbash 95
Khan, Qulij 51, 57, 125
Khan, Rahim 37
Khan, Rashid 53, 100
Khan, Rustam 93, 95
Khan, Sadiq 16, 119
Khan, Sadullah 27, 43, 62, 118, 122-3, 129-30
Khan, Safdar 50-1, 57

Khan, Said 56, 125
Khan, Saif 45, 50, 52, 96, 125
Khan, Salabat 45, 119, 123
Khan, Sardar 51, 125
Khan, Shah Nawaz 18, 27, 45-7, 49, 81, 134
Khan, Shahbaz 53
Khan, Sher 53, 57, 126
Khan, Sher Khan Nahar 52
Khan, Sikandar 52
Khan, Sipahdar 49, 134
Khan, Siyadat 136-7
Khan, Syed Shujat 54, 58
Khan, Taklu 34
Khan, Tarbiyat 43, 57
Khan, Wazir 47, 54, 58, 124
Khan, Yaminuddaulah Asaf 49-51, 89
Khan, Zabardast 95
Khan, Zafar 49, 80
Khan, Zulfiqar 95, 125
Khanazads, among mansabdars 24-5, 89-92, 191
Khan-e-Zaman 49, 52
Kheloji 45, 55
Kheshgi, Nazar Bahadur 52-3, 62, 100
Kheshgi, Shamsuddin 53
Khulasat-ut-Tawareekh 16
Khurram, Prince 130
Khusro 49
Khwajasara, Agah Khan 128-9

Lahori, Abdul Hamid 14, 18-21, 27, 34-5, 46, 49, 53, 78, 81, 109, 111, 127, 130, 135
Lodhi, Khan-e-Jahan 21, 26, 32, 49, 51-4, 80, 83, 87, 99, 190, 192

Maasir-ul-Umara 16, 18, 93, 127, 135
Mahmand, Ahdad 53
Mahmand, Ahdad-Khan 26
Mahmand, Muhammad Khan 51
Mai, Daulat Khan 53-4
Malika Banu 45
Manochahar, Mirza Khan 96
Mansab awards, share of
  Afghans among 86-7
  Deccanis among 92-3
  family group and 93-108
  Indian Muslims among 87
  Iranis among 85-6
  Khanazad zamindars among 91-2
  Marathas 88-9
  promotions in 108-13, 193
    for appointments 110-11
    for longstanding military, administrative or political services 111
    for military expeditions 109-10
    for political reasons 111-13
  Rajputs among 87-8
  Turanis among 86
  Zamindars 89-92
mansabdari system
  nobility and 76-113
  reforms in 21, 191, 194
  see also mansabdars
mansabdars
  action against 43-4
  Afghans 31-3, 51-3, 61-2, 86-7, 194
  by family groups 93-108
  composition of 24-38
  Deccanis 34-5, 54, 58, 92-3, 191
  evidence relating to escheat 47-8
  grades 22
  immigrants among 27-8
  in lists of Lahori and Salih 19
  in Shahjahan's reign 20-38, 45-65, 191-3
  Indian Mulims among 30-1, 53-4, 58, 87, 191-2
  Iranis among 29-30, 50-1, 85-6
  Khanazads among 24-5, 191
  kings attitude towards property of deceased 45-7
  Marathas 35-6, 54-5, 88-9, 192
  other Hindus among 37-8, 55
  other Muslims among 36-7
  promotions 23, 108-13, 193
  racial and religious groups 25-7
  Rajputs among 33-4, 54, 87-8, 192
  see also Mansab awards
  strength during 1628-58 19-22
  Turanis among 28-9, 49-50, 56-8, 66, 86, 191-2
  zamindars among 25-6, 89-92, 191
Manucci, Niccolao 30, 46
Marathas
  family group share in mansab 106-8
  mansabdars 35-6, 54-5, 88-9, 192
Mashhadi, Islam Khan 46, 48, 125
Mashhadi, Lashkar Khan Abul Hasan 95
Mir Jumla 119, 123
Miyana, Bahlol Khan 52
Miyana, Pir Khan 26, 53
Mohammad, Nazr 80
Moreland, W.H. 15
Mughal Nobility under Aurangzeb 13

Mumtaz-Uz-Zamani 48
Munawwar, Syed 45
Murad, Muhammad 45, 61

Naim-e-Sani 125
Narauri, Ramdas 105
Niyazi, Ahmad Khan 26, 53
Niyazi, Mubarak Khan 53
Niyazi, Muhammad Khan 100
Nizam, Murtaza Khan Syed 101
nobility,
  additions in during 1628 to 1652 20
  administration and 116-39, 193
  composition of 24-38
  contemporary account 18
  crown and 43-65, 192-3
  immigrant nobility 27-8
  in lists of Lahori and Salih 19
  mansab system and 76-113
  strength of 18-24
Nohani, Jamal Khan 62
Nur Jahan 49
Nusrat Jang, Khan-e-Dauran 46, 51, 57

Ponja, Rawal 104

Qadri, Syed Ahmed 122
Qaramanlu, Zulfiqar Khan 57

Raghunath, Rai 37, 116, 118
Raj Rup 44
Raja Basu 104
Rajputs
  family group share in mansabs 103-6
  mansabdars 33-4, 54, 87-8, 192
Rana Karan 103, 105
Rao Ratan 54
Ratan Singh 89
Rathor, Amar Singh 45
Rathor, Pirthi Raj 136-7
Rohila, Abdul Rehman 53
Rohila, Bahadur Khan 26, 53, 61-2, 126, 128
Rohila, Darya Khan 24, 47, 53, 99
Rohila, Mubariz Khan 53, 100
Rohila, Zakaria 44

Safavi, Mirza Rustam 46-7
Safavi, Shah Tahmasp 34
Said, Qazi Muhammad 54
Saksena, B.P. 13, 190
Salih, Kambo Mohd., 14, 18-22, 27, 46, 53, 78, 109, 111, 127, 135
Saran, P. 15, 116
Sarkar, Jadu Nath 55
Sarti, Baqar Khan Najme 43
Shah, Adil 51, 56
Shah, Nizam 44, 55
Shah, Qutab 56
Shahjahan
  Central Asian expeditions 59-63, 192
  policy towards nobility 44-5, 47-65, 191-3
    Afghans 51-3, 61-2
    Indian Muslim 53-4, 58, 62
    Iranis 49-50, 61
    Marathas 54-5, 63
    Rajputs 34, 54, 58, 62-3, 90
    Turanis 50-1, 56-8, 61
Sheikhzadas, *see* Indian Muslim mansabdars
Shuja, Prince 54
Siddiqi, Noman Ahmad 15, 116, 127
Suja, Prince 51
Sujan Rai 16
Sur, Habib Khan 26

Tareekh-i-Shahjahani 16
Tarin, Alawal 62
Tarin, Ali Khan 51
Tarin, Shamsher Khan 62
Tarin, Sher Khan 34, 53, 100
Tilang Rai 45
Todar Mal 37
Turani
  family group among mansabs 97-8
  mansabdars 50-1, 56-8, 61
  military and administrative capability 50-1

Ujjainia, Pratap 86

Wahab, Syed Abdul 54
Wahid, Dindar Khan Abdul 101
Waris, Mohd. 14, 18, 27, 109, 135

Yazdi, Inayatullah 50
Yulam Bahadur 51
Yusuf Aqa 137

Zafar Jang, Said Khan 57
Zakhirat-ul-Khawanin 16, 18, 93, 127
Zaman, Syed Sher 45
zamindars, among mansabdars 25-6